Beyond the Bandstand

MUSIC IN AMERICAN LIFE

The Music in American Life series documents and celebrates the dynamic and multifaceted relationship between music and American culture. From its first publication in 1972 through its half-century mark and beyond, the series has embraced a wide variety of methodologies, from biography and memoir to history and musical analysis, and spans the full range of musical forms, from classical through all types of vernacular music. The series showcases the wealth of musical practice and expression that characterizes American music, as well as the rich diversity of its stylistic, regional, racial, ethnic, and gendered contexts. Characterized by a firm grounding in material culture, whether archival or ethnographic, and by work that honors the musical activities of ordinary people and their communities, Music in American Life continually redefines and expands the very definition of what constitutes music in American culture, whose voices are heard, and how music and musical practices are understood and valued.

For a list of books in the series, please see our website at www.press.uillinois.edu.

Beyond the Bandstand

Paul Whiteman in American Musical Culture

Edited by
W. ANTHONY SHEPPARD

UNIVERSITY OF ILLINOIS PRESS
Urbana, Chicago, and Springfield

1 2 3 4 5 C P 5 4 3 2 1
∞ This book is printed on acid-free paper.

Publication of this book is supported by the General Fund of the American Musicological Society.

Library of Congress Cataloging-in-Publication Data
Names: Sheppard, William Anthony, 1969– editor.
Title: Beyond the bandstand : Paul Whiteman in American musical culture / edited by W. Anthony Sheppard.
Description: Urbana : University of Illinois Press, 2024. | Series: Music in American life | Includes bibliographical references and index.
Identifiers: LCCN 2024017537 (print) | LCCN 2024017538 (ebook) | ISBN 9780252046100 (hardcover) | ISBN 9780252088209 (paperback) | ISBN 9780252047329 (ebook)
Subjects: LCSH: Whiteman, Paul, 1890–1967—Criticism and interpretation. | Music and race—United States—History—20th century. | Jazz—Social aspects—United States—History—20th century. | Jazz—History and criticism.
Classification: LCC ML422.W4 B49 2024 (print) | LCC ML422.W4 (ebook) | DDC 781.65092—dc23/eng/20240423
LC record available at https://lccn.loc.gov/2024017537
LC ebook record available at https://lccn.loc.gov/2024017538

Contents

A Note on the Paul Whiteman Collection at Williams College

LISA CONATHAN, HEAD OF SPECIAL COLLECTIONS

The Special Collections Department of the Williams College Libraries, Williamstown, Massachusetts, provides a home to the Paul Whiteman Collection, a remarkable set of materials that documents a constellation of topics in twentieth-century American popular music. While centered on the phenomenal figure of Paul Whiteman and his transformative impacts on American pop culture, the commodification of celebrity, and the business of music, the massive collection also documents a larger swath of American popular music history. Over a thousand boxes occupy six hundred linear feet of shelf space to house music, photographs, scrapbooks, and business records. The collection also includes an extensive set of recordings, Whiteman's personal memorabilia, and other unique musical artifacts associated with his ensembles. The wide array of formats included in the collection encourages the study of objects, audio, and visual depictions alongside printed resources. The objects include musical instruments, such as the diminutive piano played by Bing Crosby's Rhythm Boys and Mike Pingatore's banjo, and an astonishingly wide range of memorabilia that reflects Whiteman's influence on pop culture and relationship to marketing.

The majority of the collection comprises sheet music, both as printed and circulated in the early decades of the twentieth century, and the parts and scores, many handwritten, used by the Paul Whiteman Orchestra in their wildly popular performances. Highlights include works by George Gershwin (*Rhapsody in Blue* and *An American in Paris*) and Ferde Grofé (*Grand Canyon Suite*), but there are also many lesser-known pieces that provide opportunities for today's scholars and performers to offer new insights on and interpretations of American music from the 1920s to the 1950s.

In 1935 Williams College was an unlikely destination for such a voluminous and prominent collection associated with a superstar known for his flashy and prolific public performances rather than as a figure potentially inspiring academic study. A fortuitous yet murky set of circumstances, however, led Whiteman to donate the material over several years beginning in 1935, with the remainder arriving as a bequest upon his death in 1967. Biographer Don Rayno cites two of Whiteman's employees who had relationships with Williams College, as recounted by the early curator and faculty member Irwin Shainman. Whiteman's attorney David Pollack visited the college in the mid-1930s and was charmed enough by the campus to send his son Peter to Williams. Likely motivated by his camaraderie with the Williams College president, Pollack may have connected Whiteman, with his massive collection of music, and President Tyler Dennett, with his commitment to a progressive, modern liberal arts education. Shainman also recounted that Estella Karn, Whiteman's publicity agent, had previously worked for Dennett.[1] Regardless of who the intermediary was, the prospect came at an opportune time. Dennett firmly believed that the college had to modernize, especially to evolve away from the provincial "old-boy network" of the early decades of the twentieth century. The prospect of a gift that promised to modernize an aspect of the curriculum and draw significant attention to a small, rural college must have been compelling, though Dennett was concerned about whether Williams should "give dignity to Mr. Whiteman in return for a gift of some considerable value," presumably by lending the prestige of an elite institution of higher education.[2] The college trustees reviewed and accepted the gift after debating the role of music in the liberal arts curriculum as distinguished from a performance-based education in a conservatory.[3] A contemporary editorial in the student newspaper praised the increased prominence given to music in the curriculum while acknowledging the discomfort that some may have felt by the association with contemporary pop culture. "There is no need at all for Williams to be embarrassed," the editorial assures, as "jazz represents the greatest departure from the charted paths" of otherwise "imitative" American music.[4]

In the 1930s Williams did not have a program of study in contemporary music, with only a single course on music history and appreciation offered in the Department of Performing Arts. Whiteman's goal in accumulating and donating the material was to found a museum of American music "from the earliest Colonial music up to the introduction of electrical instruments of today," an endeavor that would "make Williams College a center for the study of modern American music."[5] Whiteman's plan to establish an American music museum at the college was never realized.

Early curators and custodians of the collection expressed frequent concern for the facilities at Williams and their ability to care for the collection.[6] Whiteman promoted the planned museum with fundraisers, including two concerts. The first was held in Williams College's Chapin Hall in May 1936, attracting a crowd of Williams alumni as well as locals. The second was held at New York's Hippodrome in December 1936. Today, the collection is housed in Williams's Sawyer Library and the library's shelving facility, providing controlled and secure storage for the material.

Since the Whiteman collection first came to Williams in the 1930s, subsequent acquisitions now serve to contextualize and complement the material. The papers of Whiteman scholar Rayno and curator Carl Johnson add to the volume of records and research material. The collection of retired Williams lecturer in jazz Andrew W. Jaffe supports research on the later twentieth century. The acquisition of the personal library and record collection of Sterling A. Brown (Williams class of 1922) adds a corpus of music collected by a central figure of African American literary arts, which highlights and contextualizes the stark whiteness of Whiteman's pop culture. All of these collections are available to the public for research in the library's Special Collections. Having been recently processed to contemporary archival standards, the collection now features a comprehensive online finding aid. The Special Collections Department welcomes inquiries about the collection, and we hope that future researchers will draw on the collection to continue the work of the contributors to this volume.

Notes

1. Rayno, *Paul Whiteman*, 2:126.
2. Tyler Dennett to Board of Trustees, memo, July 12, 1935, Williams College Archives, Williamstown, Massachusetts.
3. "Paul Whiteman Treasures."
4. "More Emphasis on Music," 2.
5. Paul Whiteman to Tyler Dennett, October 10, 1935, Williams College Archives.
6. For further details on the early curatorial management of the collection, see Shainman, "Notes."

Beyond the Bandstand

INTRODUCTION

Naming and Placing Whiteman

W. ANTHONY SHEPPARD

For over a century, critics, fans, and scholars have focused more intently on labeling Paul Whiteman (1890–1967) than on determining his full impact on American music and popular culture, on naming him rather than placing him within a broad historical context. He was by far the most commercially successful bandleader in the 1920s and was one of the most famous celebrities in the United States and abroad. His name and image seem to turn up everywhere in popular culture from the 1920s to the 1950s, from Broadway to Hollywood, radio to television, concert halls to dance clubs. The "potato head"-shaped cartoon rendition of his face was once nearly as iconic as line drawings of Mickey Mouse and, like Mickey, his image appeared in numerous animated films. Whiteman's most consistent and controversial moniker was "the King of Jazz," but he was also referred to in his lifetime and beyond as the "Dean of Modern American Music," the "greatest name in modern American music," and—with warm reference to his patriarchal role as a pop music career-launcher—simply as "Pops."[1]

Whiteman's assortment of nicknames indicates both the broad stylistic range of his music making and the difficulty faced in assigning him a satisfactory title or appropriate category that would cover his multifaceted career. Attempting to name or label Whiteman has always produced divergent results. In 1936 Whiteman held a benefit concert in Chapin Hall at Williams College, Williamstown, Massachusetts, to raise funds for his proposed museum of American music to be established on the campus. Coverage in the student newspaper attests to the more general effort in the media at the time to designate Whiteman appropriately. In a highly positive review, a student reporter claims that the performance "showed, in its skillful presentation of popular music in nearly all of its possible forms, the right of Paul Whiteman to his title, 'The King of Jazz.'"[2] Here, Whiteman is clearly viewed as a producer of a more polished form of popular music and as encompassing the full range of American popular styles. A separate article from the same 1936 issue discusses Whiteman's educational plans to establish a program of study at the college for commercial music making, broadcasting, and recording that would run alongside training in the artistic aspects of music. (This plan was never adopted by the college's liberal arts faculty nor was Whiteman's American music museum ever established.) This second student reporter refers to Whiteman with the more academic appellation Dean of American Music.[3] In attempting to name Whiteman, these two students inadvertently point to the inherent tensions in his career-long attempt to straddle, reconcile, or even merge the realms of popular and concert hall music.

Perhaps the most appropriate title for Whiteman would be Monarch of the Middlebrow.[4] Scholarly attitudes toward American middlebrow culture of the mid-twentieth century have evolved in recent decades. Rather than automatically disdaining middlebrow music as a form of crassly commercial artistic compromise, scholars have gradually come to investigate this music on its own terms and to detail, rather than quickly dismiss, its historical significance.[5] Whiteman's entire career may be viewed as an attempt to promote "cultural uplift" as he pursued a personal mission to establish an American musical middlebrow, a cultural register that he clearly understood to be white. He began his musical career as an orchestral violist performing European classical music with the Denver and San Francisco Symphony Orchestras. His imposing father, the aptly named Wilberforce, had trained in Europe and led the music program for the Denver school system. He largely disapproved of his son's career in popular music and was critical of Paul's ample physique, early marriage, and personal habits.[6] Don Rayno begins his monumental two-volume biography of Whiteman with the story of a day in March 1914 when Whiteman, aged twenty-four and still living with his parents, overheard his father say to Paul's mother that Paul was a "lazy fellow" and should move out.[7] It hardly requires extensive psychoanalytical analysis to suggest that the younger Whiteman's efforts to make "a lady of jazz" in the 1920s and thereby reach a predominantly white audience, to legitimate his brand of symphonic jazz, and, more generally, to reconcile European-based classical and American popular musical styles stemmed in part from a desire to satisfy his stern father.[8]

In his 1948 book *Records for the Millions*, Whiteman admonishes jazz fans to collect at least some classical recordings and vice versa: "Start early to fight against any bias that you may sense in yourself."[9] He points back to John Philip Sousa as a precedent for his own attempts to popularize classical music, and the book includes lists of recordings in multiple stylistic categories that Whiteman recommends for his readers. A close investigation of Whiteman's career reveals that he never really walked away from European classical music. For instance, his band's second recording session on August 19, 1920, included not only "The Japanese Sandman" and "Whispering," which he made hit numbers, but also a medley featuring Amilcare Ponchielli's "Dance of the Hours." This was a dance band conductor who stated in a book titled *Jazz* that his favorite opera was Wagner's *Parsifal*.[10] In his later years, he continued to conduct pops-style concerts of light classical works. Though he distanced himself from the term at several points, his ensembles "jazzed the classics" early on.[11] Alongside his efforts to raise the social status of jazz and orchestral dance music in the 1920s and beyond, we could say that Whiteman was also keenly interested in making a flapper or a bobby-soxer out of classical music while maintaining, of course, its presumed whiteness. He commissioned and premiered concert works that, often, incorporated some popular syncopated stylistic elements and jazz timbres from a wide range of composers, including John Alden Carpenter, Aaron Copland, Duke Ellington, George Gershwin, Ferde Grofé, Roy Harris, Richard Rodgers, Lee Sowerby, William Grant Still, Igor Stravinsky, and Victor Young.[12] Whiteman was, and is still, most closely associated with Gershwin, and for over forty years Whiteman never tired of referring to his 1924 commission and premiere of Gershwin's *Rhapsody in Blue*, the single piece that consistently served as Whiteman's theme music on the radio and television and that he conducted an astonishing number of times over the decades in concerts across the country and in Europe.[13] Whiteman, appearing onscreen as himself, even reenacted both the moment when he had commissioned Gershwin and the premiere of the piece in the 1945 Gershwin biopic *Rhapsody in Blue*.

A comprehensive investigation of Whiteman's career suggests that he occupied a position similar in American music history to that of Sousa, James Reese Europe, and Leonard Bernstein in attempting to bridge classical and popular music and to promote American music on a global scale with nationalist ambitions in mind.[14] As Carol J. Oja has put it, Whiteman was arguably "one of the most important figures in the United States in challenging the barriers between high and low art, playing a parallel role to that of Gunther Schuller or Wynton Marsalis later in the twentieth century, and his work set in place models for the populist nationalism to which so many American composers turned during the mid-1930s."[15] Furthermore, the tensions and even anxiety he experienced in attempting to negotiate between "high" and "low" cultural registers calls to mind the music making and biographies of a wide range of American figures, including Charles Ives, Will Marion Cook, Duke Ellington, Bernstein, Keith Jarrett, and Marsalis. As with each of these musicians, Whiteman's place in any one musical category has been subject to intense critical scrutiny.

Whiteman's coronation in the media as the King of Jazz clearly benefitted his career at the expense of contemporaneous Black jazz musicians, but it proved detrimental to subsequent critical assessments of his place in American music history. Rayno has traced the first reference to Whiteman as King of Jazz to a 1919 article in a Pasadena, California, newspaper.[16] However, Rayno finds that the title was launched nationally by Whiteman's publicist

FIGURE 0.1 Whiteman's wry take on his King of Jazz crown. Publicity still courtesy of Williams College Special Collections.

Estella Kahn following Whiteman's landmark 1924 Experiment in Modern Music concert.[17] Though Rayno and others have argued that Whiteman has been unfairly criticized for his moniker—given that he neither crowned himself nor, apparently, liked the title as seems comically evident in figure 0.1—he did little to discourage its use in the press, nor did he suggest that it might better fit a Black jazz musician, and the 1930 Whiteman-centered cinematic musical revue *King of Jazz* further ensured its ubiquity.[18] Rayno rightly asserts that it is a mistake to evaluate Whiteman's career "strictly from the perspective of jazz," given that he led a variety of ensemble types playing music that included syncopated dances, Broadway numbers, European classical works, and newly commissioned jazz-inspired symphonic pieces. However, it appears that the question of whether to include Whiteman in jazz history at all persists.[19] Crucial to these debates is whether we choose to assess Whiteman's recordings with our current definitions of "jazz" in mind or whether we attempt to decipher how this term was applied during the central decades of his career.

Even during his lifetime, critics began to debate whether Whiteman's music qualified as "jazz," and this debate clearly intensified in the 1970s. For example, in the journal *Popular Music & Society* in 1972, five years after Whiteman's death, Russell B. Nye argues that Whiteman's contributions should be viewed in terms of the stylistic expectations of American popular culture in the 1920s, rather than in relation to later definitions of jazz. Nye points both to Whiteman's immense commercial success and to the range of music and venues he performed in with his band.[20] This positive assessment of Whiteman's career was met by a sharp rebuttal from Jon H. Rieger and Brian Rublein, who assert that Whiteman had no significant impact on the history of jazz and had proven detrimental to the genre by displacing Black musicians and whitewashing jazz style.[21] Though they crucially drew attention to Whiteman's undeniable white privilege, they also unfortunately engaged in ad hominem assault by referring to Whiteman as "a roly-poly type" and as "a fat cat," and they too easily dismissed his music as "slickly orchestrated stuff."[22] Some prominent Black musicians and critics also disparaged Whiteman's impact on jazz history. For example, in 1972 Max Roach observed:

> It is of course a crowning irony that Paul Whiteman became named as "the King of Jazz." And, during the same period, the foremost black musician was labelled, "the Duke"—Duke Ellington. It is sufficient to point out here that Duke Ellington has continued into the 1970's as a vital force in black music, and that his Twenties and Thirties compositions are still alive—*Caravan, Black, Brown and Beige, Mood Indigo*—and still played. Whereas, there's not a single Paul Whiteman tune or arrangement still alive.[23]

The question of Whiteman's status as a jazz musician clearly remained unresolved into the early 1980s when William H. Youngren prominently called for critics to give "Whiteman his due" in the *Atlantic Monthly*. Youngren emphasizes approvingly, without taking into account the evident racial segregation, that Whiteman had sought out "real" jazz musicians from 1925 to 1927 to expand his range into "hot jazz" but acknowledges that many of Whiteman's bands' arrangements in the 1930s had become "slick and flashy."[24] In a sense the debate was apparently eventually laid to rest as jazz historians in the late twentieth and early twenty-first centuries, by and large, ignored Whiteman in their textbooks and in the classroom.[25] A thorough survey of jazz-history books published during that period reveals that Whiteman is almost always mentioned briefly—primarily in relation to Bix Beiderbecke or with reference to Whiteman's 1924 Experiment in Modern Music concert at Aeolian Hall—but he is rarely discussed at any length.[26] In the past decade, scholars have tended to follow John Howland's solution in employing the term "symphonic jazz" to classify Whiteman's core output and impact on jazz history.[27]

Whiteman himself grappled with his relationship to jazz throughout much of his career, occasionally in print. His most extended and intriguing discussion of these issues appears in his 1926 coauthored autobiography, *Jazz*.[28] He famously acknowledges jazz's Black origins in the book's opening sentence: "Jazz came to America three hundred years ago in chains." However, the second paragraph opens: "For that matter, the negroes themselves knew no more of jazz than their masters."[29] Near the end of the book, with shocking matter-of-factness, Whiteman points to music's utility with the following example: "Music has been used by Southern planters of all time to speed up work among the negroes."[30] At various points in the book, in statements to the press, and in actions taken and those not taken throughout his career, Whiteman toggled back and forth in his views on the genre's racial association and on the position of Black musicians in modern American music. He states that "the chief contribution of the white American to jazz so far has been his recognition of it as legitimate music," and he disavows having played any part in inventing jazz: "All I did was to orchestrate jazz."[31] Whiteman even offers anecdotes and statements that inadvertently support critical claims that his music was not jazz at all and that "hot jazz" players such as, most famously, Beiderbecke must have felt constrained playing under him. For instance, he relates that a clarinetist and saxophonist from New Orleans named Gus Miller refused to learn how to read notation while playing in Whiteman's band because he felt by doing so he would lose his jazz abilities. Miller eventually quit, explaining that he could not play Whiteman's "pretty" style and that Whiteman's band could not play blues.[32]

In a primitivist vein, Whiteman refers in this book to jazz as both "barbarous and sophisticated" and states that "jazz, as an intoxicant, is a tremendous influence for good in the world," claiming that jazz has provided Americans with an energy, primarily through its rhythm, that the machine age otherwise deprived them of. (He appears to have white citizens in mind when he employs the term "American.") On multiple pages, particularly in chapter 7, he defends jazz against the virulent antijazz social, moral, medical, and aesthetic criticism of the day, without referencing racism in antijazz bias. Though the book is clearly framed as a celebration of jazz, at multiple points he reaffirms the highbrow/lowbrow dichotomy to its detriment, even suggesting that jazz should ultimately help Americans to hear and appreciate classical music and pointing out that jazz employs melodies from European composers. He ends *Jazz* by noting the positive recognition the genre received from numerous white classical musicians and composers, as though such endorsements proved jazz's worth, and by claiming that after he devotes his working life to jazz, he plans to retire to a ranch and "spend my declining years among the classics."[33] Though he titled this autobiographical book *Jazz*, the King of Jazz clearly remained, even at the height of his popularity, his father's son to some extent.

Whiteman's relationship to jazz proves most problematic when considered within the systemic racism of the United States that shaped his entire career. Whiteman's prominence resulted in the economic and critical displacement of Black musicians. He was one of multiple white male musical "kings" accorded creative credit by the media in the twentieth century at the expense of Black musicians: King of Ragtime—Irving Berlin, instead of Scott Joplin; King of Jazz—Whiteman, instead of Louis Armstrong; King of Swing—Benny Goodman, instead of Duke Ellington; King of Rock 'n' Roll—Elvis Presley, instead of Chuck Berry—though they finally got it right with the King of Pop, Michael Jackson.[34] This displacement of Black musicians frequently took bizarre forms. For example, the 1941 Bing Crosby vehicle *Birth of the Blues* begins with the following text appearing on the screen: "Dedicated to the musical pioneers of Memphis and New Orleans who favored the 'hot' over the 'sweet'—those early jazz men who took American music out of the rut and put it 'in the groove.'" This text certainly could be read as a direct repudiation of everything Whiteman represented in the history of jazz and as something of a low blow given that Whiteman had "discovered" Crosby. However, rather than celebrating Black musicians active at the turn of the century, the heroic early-jazz man of this fictional film turns out to be a white clarinetist character played by Crosby. Furthermore, the entire film climaxes somewhat abruptly at the end with brief interpolated shots of what the blues ultimately gave to American music—a panoply of mostly white musical heroes (though Ellington and Armstrong are included) that culminates with a sweeping pan to Whiteman emphatically conducting a dance band. Thus, despite its opening dedication, this film concludes by claiming Whiteman as an apotheosis of the blues.[35]

In teaching American music history over the past quarter century, I largely ignored Whiteman, beyond making the obvious joking reference to his name ("White-man, what's in a name?") and citing his career as a prime example of white cooption of Black music and displacement of Black musicians.[36] I was not alone in leaving Whiteman out. However, in this book, in nearly every chapter, we move well beyond his name by confronting, rather than avoiding, the racial implications of Whiteman's career. To ignore Whiteman's centrality to American music in the 1920s and 1930s or to gloss over the ways in which racial assumptions and racist policies enabled his career would result in ahistorical scholarship. Rather than ignoring Whiteman in our teaching and scholarship, Michael Tanksley, for example, has called on jazz educators and scholars to emphasize how racial ideologies contributed to Whiteman's impact on American music. Tanksley has surveyed jazz-history books and general-reference works and has uncovered a penchant for colorblind language in the typically brief discussions of Whiteman, with, for example, published references to Whiteman's "mainstream audience appeal" failing to note the whiteness of that "mainstream." As Tanksley concludes, avoiding discussion of structural racism in our music histories "leads to the dissemination of colorblind historical narratives and perpetuates structural racism within American music institutions."[37] We believe that investigating Whiteman's full impact on American popular culture is crucial at this cultural moment, though we are fully cognizant of the inherent dangers. As Christi Jay Wells concludes in chapter 2 of the current volume: "Writing about Whiteman can be a vexing task for many reasons, but one among them is certainly the concern that, given his symbolic prominence as an iconic cultural appropriator in jazz and popular music discourse, offering a nuanced treatment of the complexities of his career and reception or, indeed, paying him any close attention at all may reinforce the very structures of privilege and oppression that created the conditions of possibility for his prominence in the first place."

Nearly every chapter in this volume makes some reference to Whiteman's controversial promotional title. However, we aim to go further by investigating Whiteman's place in the development of middlebrow aesthetics, in the history of jazz style and reception, in the rise of celebrity culture, in the sordid intersections between Jim Crow policies and American popular culture, in the evolving norms of the music industry and its legal regulation, in the impact of American popular music in Europe, and in the centrality of music for the new media of radio, sound film, and television. In doing so, we note the astonishing range of his musical activities as a classical violist, dance band leader and violinist, World War I navy bandleader, sometime composer and arranger, orchestral conductor, radio disc jockey, ABC vice president, industry advocate, music publisher and book author, television host, and astonishingly successful talent scout—not to mention all of the cameo and benefit appearances arising from his celebrity status. We follow Whiteman from small clubs to glamorous dance halls, from Broadway revues to Hollywood, from radio and recording studios to television screens across the country, and from Denver to San Francisco, New York to London, Fort Worth to Philadelphia.[38] The sheer breadth of his career led Whiteman to work with a wide range of musicians, from Al Jolson to Bill Haley. Whiteman was certainly one of the most well-connected American musical figures in the twentieth century, and he was particularly proud of the number of soloists, composers, and arrangers he had discovered and promoted.

Previous scholarship on Whiteman has focused primarily on his 1924 Aeolian Hall concert and association with Gershwin, on how his "sweet" symphonic style dominated the jazz market, on analyzing his hit recordings, and on the star musicians who played in his band, such as Beiderbecke, Crosby, Mildred Bailey, Jimmy Dorsey, Tommy Dorsey, Johnny Mercer, Frankie Trumbauer, and Jack Teagarden. Rayno's detailed biography of Whiteman is likely never to be superseded, given Rayno's extensive archival research and his extraordinarily informative Whiteman chronology and annotated discography. It has served as a crucial resource throughout this book. *Beyond the Bandstand: Paul Whiteman in American Musical Culture* is the first collected volume on this major figure, and it offers an array of new critical and historical perspectives. Our focus is not on naming or renaming Whiteman, nor do we seek to rehabilitate or condemn his career. Whiteman was dethroned long ago in jazz historiography but has yet to be placed more appropriately in American music history. Though details of Whiteman's life and recording career have informed our work throughout, his biography is not our primary focus, nor do we reexamine his hit records given that these are topics that have been the focus of earlier scholarship. From 1920 to 1950 Whiteman was a central figure in American popular culture, one who shaped the development of the recording industry, the media, social dance, copyright law, and the dissemination of popular music on radio, television, and film. We aim to offer a broad understanding of Whiteman's multifaceted career and thereby reveal both connections across the popular culture industry and the centrality of race in American music history.

Throughout this book we explore Whiteman's impact on American music and popular culture as we place him within a broader context and in relation to diverse topics. The eight chapters have been arranged loosely in pairs. The first two focus on ways in which race impacted Whiteman's reception in the press. Stephanie Doktor explores how Whiteman's body shaped his public image. At a time in American culture when fatness accrued moral stigma, Whiteman's weight was both problematic and essential to his persona as the King of Jazz. The press was simply obsessed with Whiteman's body. Throughout his life Whiteman was self-conscious about his size, but he harnessed this anxiety as a source of self-deprecating humor that played well with audiences. Doktor reveals the ways in which racism intersected with images of the ideal masculine body and how Whiteman's size placed him too close to Black musical bodies, during a period in which fatness was increasingly associated with Blackness, while his size also suggested he had neutralized jazz's erotic dangers. Contemporaneous antijazz campaigns denounced the music as racially and sexually threatening to the white social order. Numerous jazz bands donned formal wear and displayed a masculine physical image in part to counter such criticism. Whiteman, however, did not match the slim-and-fit ideal, and his body inspired numerous caricatures, cartoons, and comic publicity. Doktor traces the reception of Whiteman's corporeality, noting that despite his size, he, nevertheless, dominated the popular music scene.

Building on their earlier scholarship on Whiteman's reception in the Black press, Christi Jay Wells focuses in chapter 2 on the prominent Chicago-based Black journalist, arranger, and bandleader Dave Peyton. In "The Musical Bunch," a weekly column published in the *Chicago Defender* from 1925 to 1929, Peyton focused on the Black musical scene and on jazz more broadly. As a musician, Peyton brought an insider's knowledge to his critical assessments of Whiteman and other musicians. Wells carefully considers the tension in Peyton's writings between an admiration for Whiteman's musicianship and stylistic achievements and a more fundamental effort to acknowledge Black precursors, particularly James Reese Europe. Peyton was also keen to proclaim the potential of Black musicians to create successful symphonic jazz on their own. He called out Gershwin's *Rhapsody in Blue*—the piece most closely associated with Whiteman—as an example of derivative music that he hoped Black musicians would soon surpass in symphonic compositions. As Wells reveals, Peyton's admiration for Whiteman coexisted alongside his pointed critique of persistent structural racism in the music industry.

Chapters 3 and 4 detail the distinctive sound and aesthetics crafted largely by Whiteman's arrangers. In his 1926 book *Jazz*, Whiteman proclaims, "The secret of the success of modern dance music is in its arrangement."[39] John Howland traces the roots and dissemination across musical media and genres of a Modern American Music aesthetic that Whiteman and his arrangers played a major role in defining. Howland tracks this style across the 1920s to the 1940s as it flourished on the radio, on Broadway stages, and in Hollywood soundtracks. This aesthetic aimed to glamorize popular music, particularly in its Modern Metropolitan Music format, which signaled the utmost in sophisticated urbanity, commonly (but not exclusively) coded as white, most clearly in representations of New York City. Howland analyzes multiple adaptations of Louis Alter's 1928 *Manhattan Serenade,* including Whiteman's 1940 recording. This historical study includes discussion of the Modern American Music piano-solo publication series of Robbins Music, a firm that Whiteman was closely associated with.

In his chapter, Ryan Raul Bañagale focuses specifically on arrangements of Orientalist numbers prepared for Whiteman's ensembles, particularly in the 1920s. Orientalist representation runs throughout Whiteman's career, from his very first recording session on August 8, 1920, which focused on test runs of the band playing "The Japanese Sandman," to multiple episodes of his 1949–52 *Goodyear Revue* television show. Whiteman's first East Coast performances were held at Atlantic City's Ambassador Hotel in the Japanese Tea Room each afternoon and in the Pompeian Grill each night. Furthermore, Bañagale argues that Orientalism was featured in Whiteman's 1924 Experiment in Modern Music concert, both in Victor Herbert's *Suite of Serenades* and in Ferde Grofé's orchestration of Gershwin's *Rhapsody in Blue.* He identifies some 120 Orientalist arrangements in Whiteman's library held at Williams College but focuses on those numbers that involve East Asian representation. He also notes that Orientalist musical effects are detailed in Arthur Lange's influential 1926 manual *Arranging for the Modern Dance Orchestra* and offers focused discussion of arrangements used by Whiteman for "Cho-Cho-San," "Orientale," and "Japanese Sandman" during this period. As Bañagale astutely observes, even when Orientalist lyrics were not sung in instrumental arrangements performed and recorded by Whiteman, they were likely present in the audience members' minds as several of these songs had great popular success.

To a large extent, the experience of and reaction to Whiteman's music making was determined by the venue. Chapters 5 and 6 consider the settings of Whiteman's performances in the 1920s, both domestically and abroad, and how these venues shaped the reception of Whiteman and indicated his aesthetic goals in positioning his music along the high/low cultural continuum. Sarah Caissie Provost compares two landmark performances in American music history: Whiteman's 1924 concert at Aeolian Hall and Benny Goodman's 1938 Carnegie Hall performance. In both cases, performing in these celebrated high-art venues served to legitimate Whiteman's and Goodman's music. Provost focuses in detail on their concert programs, examining racial implications, in particular, and considers Whiteman's other Experiment in Modern Music concerts as well. By carefully noting differences in their programming she is able to reveal Whiteman's and Goodman's attitudes toward jazz and its history, as well as their larger artistic goals for its future. Provost notes that though both bandleaders commissioned classical composers, Goodman kept separate his pursuits in jazz and European classical music and viewed jazz as already worthy of such high-art settings, whereas Whiteman aimed to create a more classical, symphonized form of jazz targeting white audiences. Whiteman and Goodman were both instrumental in the transition of jazz from serving as dance music to being received as a form of concert music.

Catherine Tackley also investigates the role of venue in aesthetic evaluations of Whiteman's ensemble, focusing specifically on Whiteman's 1923 and 1926 performance tours to the United Kingdom where he appeared in both cabarets and major concert halls. Whiteman's performances in the United Kingdom fueled controversies concerning American bands displacing native talent, and he was met by opposition from the Musicians' Union, though his white privilege helped pave the way during his visit. Tackley reveals the significant impact of Whiteman's brand of "symphonised syncopation" on the development of British popular music, including the role of Whiteman's recordings on early British jazz musicians with the major bandleader Jack Hylton as a primary example. Whiteman's subsequent performances in Germany, the Netherlands, and Paris in 1926 created an opening for Hylton, the Savoy Orpheans, and other British jazz musicians on the continent. Tackley notes that these European tours burnished Whiteman's image back in the States and that his 1923 UK concerts may even be viewed as direct precursors to his programming strategy for the 1924 Aeolian Hall concert, as he attempted to demonstrate an evolution from "noisy jazz" to his own refined style.

Our final chapters point to the full range of Whiteman's musical activities by exploring lesser-known aspects of his career, specifically his role in the evolution of US copyright law and his significant contributions to the new medium of music television. Drawing on her legal expertise, Katherine M. Leo offers a detailed historical account and analysis of the landmark 1940 *RCA v. Whiteman* case and its impact on radio broadcasting. Leo explains how the Copyright Act of 1909 had ambiguous implications for the new medium of commercial radio emerging in the 1920s. Throughout his career Whiteman was active off the podium in shaping the music industry and in advocating for the rights of musicians. As Leo suggests, it is not surprising that Whiteman would be involved in a landmark federal copyright case given his celebrity status and leading position in both music recording and radio broadcasting.

Leo's study sheds light on Whiteman's recording contracts and his views on the differences between performing live in a radio broadcast versus having a recording of one's performance broadcast over the radio. It is clear that despite his involvement in litigation and advocacy, performing live with his ensemble remained Whiteman's primary focus. Whiteman lost the case with the court ruling that once someone purchases a record, they are free to use it as their property, including to broadcast it via radio. Thus, Whiteman was involved in a federal case that directly shaped how Americans would experience recorded music for decades to come. Indeed, Whiteman became a DJ himself playing records on his multiple radio programs.

In the book's concluding chapter, I investigate Whiteman's extensive late-career activities in music television. Whiteman held the position of vice president and music director at ABC and hosted four musical shows: *TV Teen Club* (1949–54), *The Paul Whiteman Goodyear Revue* (1949–52), *On the Boardwalk with Paul Whiteman* (1954), and *America's Greatest Bands* (summer 1955). These shows encompassed American popular music styles from ragtime and Tin Pan Alley to jump blues and the advent of rock 'n' roll. *TV Teen Club*, an amateur-competition variety show, featured numerous future stars of American popular music, and it shaped subsequent music television, most directly with *American Bandstand*. *Goodyear Revue* primarily featured adult performers in a deluxe presentation of middlebrow musical culture, one that persisted in such programs as *The Lawrence Welk Show*. Nationally broadcast in the early civil rights era, these two Whiteman shows were shaped by racial politics. *TV Teen Club* was remarkably integrated, and its filming, scripts, and promotional materials indicate that integration was a conscious goal. In contrast, *Goodyear Revue* was rigorously segregated, avoiding Black performers almost entirely. With these television shows, Whiteman furthered his mixed legacy with regards to acknowledging the contributions of Black musicians to modern American music.

• • •

The origins of this book trace back to November 2017 when Lisa Conathan, head of special collections at Williams College, and I first discussed how to bring more scholarly attention to the Whiteman Collection and how best to celebrate the impending completion of this major archival collection's cataloging. I noted at the time that 2020 would mark the hundredth anniversary of Whiteman's first recordings, specifically the astonishingly successful release of "Whispering" and "The Japanese Sandman" by the Victor Talking Machine Company in 1920. Plans to hold a symposium on Whiteman were repeatedly postponed due to the pandemic, but the Paul Whiteman in American Music symposium eventually took place on campus in August 2022, and most of the chapters in this volume originated as papers delivered at that event. Several of the chapters in this volume are based directly on research carried out in this unique archival collection, and it is our hope that other scholars will be spurred to investigate this resource. The publication of *Beyond the Bandstand: Paul Whiteman in American Musical Culture* coincides with the hundredth anniversary of the other most prominent landmark event in his career, the 1924 Experiment in Modern Music concert that featured the premiere of Gershwin's *Rhapsody in Blue* at New York City's Aeolian Hall.

I thank Conathan for helping to launch this project and for approving the symposium's funding through the Sawyer Library Special Collections at Williams College. Amy Wood in the Department of Music provided essential support for the symposium on the financial side, and Maia Sheppard proved indispensable in helping me run the symposium itself. Many thanks to Laurie Matheson, director, University of Illinois Press, for her keen interest in this book and to project manager Megan Donnan and freelance copyeditor Mary Lou Kowaleski. My colleagues and I are particularly grateful to the anonymous readers, who offered insightful suggestions on the first draft. Finally, I thank the contributors for their patience, perseverance, and incisive chapters, which, together, offer all readers interested in the history of American music and popular culture multiple new and provocative insights on the career of Paul Whiteman.

Notes

1. From the mid-1930s onward there was a shift away from referring to Whiteman as the King of Jazz and instead to employ some form of the appellation Dean of Modern American Music. For instance, in a February 16, 1936, radio broadcast of *Paul Whiteman's Musical Varieties* (a recording of which is held at the Paley Center for Media Archive, New York City), he was announced as the Dean of Modern American Music. By the late 1940s Whiteman was typically referred to as "the greatest name in modern American music," which is how each episode of his television program *The Goodyear Revue* began.

2. Hector, "Whiteman Concert Draws."

3. W. B. Norton, "Course in Commercial Music." In his 1926 book with Mary Margaret McBride, *Jazz*, Whiteman also argues that universities should establish chairs for jazz studies, 279–80. A 1936 article in the Williams student newspaper from the week prior to Whiteman's Chapin Hall concert reports that a suggestion to feature Whiteman's band on the college's Thompson Concert Series had been rejected in 1933 as not being suitable to a series devoted to and named the Art of Music. See "1933 Thompson Concert Committee," 1, 7.

4. On Whiteman's aim to establish jazz as a middlebrow music and his claims to have domesticated the genre, see Dunkel, "W. C. Handy, Abbe Niles," 125–26.

Without using the term "middlebrow," Gilbert Seldes had discussed Whiteman's music along these lines in 1924 as is noted in Evans, *Writing Jazz*, 96, 117.

5. On the term "middlebrow" as applied to music, see, for example, Howland, "Between the Muses and the Masses"; Chowrimootoo, *Middlebrow Modernism*, 8–11; and Chowrimootoo and Guthrie, introduction.

6. Whiteman refers to his father as the "best-balanced man I know" but also notes that his father had been "plumb disgusted" when Paul became fat. Whiteman and McBride, *Jazz*, 21.

7. Rayno, *Paul Whiteman*, 1:1. On Whiteman's father's disapproval of jazz and autocratic nature and the hostility between father and son, also see Berrett, *Louis Armstrong & Paul Whiteman*, 1–3, 5–8.

8. As Howland has noted, the phrase "make a lady of jazz" did not originate with Whiteman. See Howland, *Hearing Luxe Pop*, 61.

9. Whiteman, *Records for the Millions*, 67–69.

10. Whiteman and McBride, *Jazz*, 27–28.

11. Whiteman reports that at age sixteen he started "ragging" the classics, and he discusses which types of classics can or should be "jazzed." Whiteman and McBride, *Jazz*, 30, 60–62, 121.

12. Berrett discusses how Whiteman commissioned classical composers in the 1940s. Berrett, *Louis Armstrong & Paul Whiteman*, 143. Also see Rayno, *Paul Whiteman*, 2:254, and Nicholson, *Jazz and Culture*, 193–205. For a more thorough assessment of Whiteman's commissions, see Oja, *Making Music Modern*, 326–29.

13. On Whiteman's association with Gershwin, see Schiff, *Gershwin*, and Oja's chapter 20, "Crossing Over with George Gershwin, Paul Whiteman, and the Modernists," in her *Making Music Modern*. Oja explores how the Gershwin-Whiteman experiment spurred other modernist attempts to bridge the gulf between high and low by harnessing jazz.

14. At multiple points in the book *Jazz*, Whiteman emphasizes his position that America need not look to Europe for music and that jazz is a specifically American music that should be played by Americans born and raised in the United States, ideally whose parents were also US-born. Whiteman and McBride, *Jazz*, 131–33, 237.

15. Oja, *Making Music Modern*, 325.

16. Rayno, *Paul Whiteman*, 1:32–33.

17. Rayno, *Paul Whiteman*, 1:94.

18. For example, see Rayno, *Paul Whiteman*, 1:262n33. Rayno also notes that a photograph of Whiteman being crowned that appears in his book *Jazz* is actually a faked composite image. *Paul Whiteman*, 287n94.

19. Rayno, *Paul Whiteman*, 1:xxiv–xxv. Also see Nicholson, *Jazz and Culture*, 193–208.

20. Nye, "Word about Whiteman," 232–35. In his landmark 1968 book *Early Jazz*, Gunther Schuller offers a brief appreciation of Whiteman in a footnote, 192n21.

21. Rieger and Rublein, "Whiteman," 6–8, 13, 18–19.

22. Rieger and Rublein, "Whiteman," 4, 16.

23. Roach, "What 'Jazz' Means to Me," 3–4. I am grateful to an anonymous reader for suggesting the inclusion of Roach's remarks here. On Ellington's views of Whiteman, see Howland, *Ellington Uptown*, 147–50.

24. Youngren, "Giving Whiteman His Due," 104.

25. As Howland has put it, Whiteman became almost a "taboo subject among jazz proponents." See Howland, *Ellington Uptown*, 144–45.

26. There are, of course, a few exceptions. For instance, Alyn Shipton includes a focus on Whiteman in *A New History of Jazz*, 147–57. Gary Giddins and Scott DeVeaux offer a brief discussion of Whiteman's career and a listening-guide outline of his recording of "Changes," in their textbook *Jazz*, 117–23. The widely viewed 2000 PBS documentary *Jazz: A Film by Ken Burns* accords a fairly celebratory six minutes to Whiteman's role in jazz history in episode 2, "The Gift."

27. See Howland, *Ellington Uptown*, 1–5; "Jazz with Strings," 112–13; and *Hearing Luxe Pop*, 46.

28. On the broader impact of Whiteman's book in shaping perceptions of both jazz and of his own achievements, as well as for an insightful reading of how some Black musicians, such as W. C. Handy, countered Whiteman's prevailing narrative, see Dunkel, "W. C. Handy, Abbe Niles."

29. Whiteman and McBride, *Jazz*, 3–4.

30. Whiteman and McBride, *Jazz*, 295.

31. Whiteman and McBride, *Jazz*, 26, 20. In labeling him a "Pioneer in American Music" in the title of the Whiteman biography, Rayno implicitly suggests Whiteman's precedence in creating symphonic jazz.

32. Whiteman and McBride, *Jazz*, 241–42.

33. Whiteman and McBride, *Jazz*, 9, 149, 153–55, 185–87, 180–84, 296, 298.

34. For an example of how prominent Black musicians were viewed in relation to Whiteman, see Magee, "Before Louis."

35. Whiteman's appearance in this film is also mentioned in Berrett, *Louis Armstrong & Paul Whiteman*, 190–91.

36. This racially motivated pun on his name was made at least as early as 1924. See Seldes, *Seven Lively Arts*, 99.

37. Tanksley offered these observations and remarks in his paper "Jazz Studies, Structural Racism, and Paul Whiteman," delivered at the Paul Whiteman in American Music symposium at Williams College in August 2022. He intends to present this material in a future publication.

38. Our aim in this book is not to be comprehensive, and we thus leave to others any discussion of Whiteman's devotion to car racing, farming, horse breeding, and ranching.

39. Whiteman and McBride, *Jazz*, 217.

1

Black Music, White Bodies, Paul Whiteman's Body

STEPHANIE DOKTOR

Early jazz had a complicated reception, marred most profoundly by the racist logic of Jim Crow segregation. In an era that witnessed the rise of the second Ku Klux Klan, the passing of eugenics legislation, and the persistence of segregated entertainment, the popularity of Black dance music in the 1920s was controversial, especially among white listeners. The Blacksound that came to define an age posed a threat to white control of the burgeoning recording industry.[1] Antijazz fraternities formed, women's clubs boycotted the music, and religious groups protested its circulation.[2] For some, jazz became a scapegoat for all that was wrong with postwar America—the putative consequences of modernization and an increasingly diverse citizenry. For the religious, it was a sonic permutation of the diabolical: "We are in deadly fear of the Jazz Devil, the demon which is consuming the country," reads a 1920 newspaper article.[3] Many white Americans heard its defining features—syncopated rhythms, polyphonic textures, experimental timbres, and scales with variable pitch—through the lens of racial difference, believing jazz to be culturally inferior to Anglo-American music traditions. Some linked syncopation to savagery to assert that the music's rhythmic "nervousness" was degrading the moral fabric of society.

To make jazz less threatening to white middle-class audiences, bandleaders such as Paul Whiteman, Jean Goldkette, and Roger Wolfe Kahn adopted art music's visual and sonic class signifiers. They signaled their proximity to high-class entertainment by using large ensembles with strings, clear forms and textures, straight(er) rhythms, and clear melodic development. "Glorified jazz," as John Howland calls it, wrapped popular tunes in "lavish arrangements that conveyed an aura of contemporary sophistication, glamour, and refinement."[4] Bandleaders also used visual cues to link their musical styles to affluence. Clean-cut, white men wore matching suits and read scores from music stands, playing under the direction of a baton-wielding conductor.[5] Sonically adjacent to classical music, these bands staged scenes from the concert hall. If careers in Black music compromised their relationship to whiteness, complex arranging techniques intervened by way of class. And it worked. These men profited immensely from a new stylistic framing of Black music, and they developed a wide (and a white) listenership for jazz. As a result, white, middle-class men were the primary conduits through which much of the buying public consumed Blacksound.

The visual cues leveraged to sophisticate jazz implicated the body and not just through its garments. Class status was also delineated by a musician's corporeality, which, in the case of these bands was mostly lean and sometimes muscular. By the 1920s physical self-control corresponded to successfully managing one's prosperity.[6] Ideals about white, middle-class masculinity had changed in the 1890s. An abundance of flesh no longer indicated an abundance of riches. Efforts to "improve society" in the Progressive Era ushered in new ideas about what constituted a healthy body, and scientific discourse centered weight in these national conversations. Being "overweight," according to fat-studies scholar Amy Farrell, was "a sign of one's character flaws, even morality."[7] Lean bodies represented the discipline required to reform society and preserve a nation's morality. Social uplift initiatives focused on this type of physique, linking it to middle- and upper-class Americans. But it also linked this body to white masculinity. Historians Rachel Louise Moran and Gail Bederman interpret this ideological shift as a response to radical changes in America's body politic.[8] Women, Black Americans, and Asian and Eastern European immigrants were gaining meager and temporary political and economic advantages. Bederman argues that white middle-class men sought reprieve in physical discipline when faced with these challenges to their authority.[9] In this historical moment, fat represented weakness—a compromise to the integrity of one's racial and gendered power.

Fat also became threatening. Erving Goffman, in his theories of social stigma, argues that "intractable obesity" evoked society's other present-day "problems," which in the early twentieth century included concerns about homosexuality, criminality, mental illness, and communism.[10] A measure of "excess" adipose tissue embodied what were perceived to be America's social controversies. Nothing was more controversial in the 1920s than the nation's "excess" of racial Others. Sabrina Strings and Andrew Curran both make persuasive arguments about the racialization of fat. Just as thin became a sign of "civilized restraint," pseudo-scientists devised racial taxonomies that ranked Black people as the most inferior race *because* of their putative laziness and gluttony.[11] In her extensive history of these stereotypes, Strings relates:

> In the United States, fatness became stigmatized as both black and sinful. . . . Not until after these associations were already in place did the medical establishment begin its concerted effort to combat "excess" fat tissue as a major public health initiative. In this way, the phobia about fatness and the preference for thinness have not, principally or historically, been about health. Instead, they have been one way the body has been used to craft and legitimate race, sex, and class hierarchies.[12]

Strings's argument raises intriguing questions about the causal relationship between the pervasiveness of Black music in the air and the expedient rise of the 1920s "cult of thin." If the "scientific" management of physique offered a salve for racial changes, this chapter asks, How did the cultural dominance of jazz contour the bodies of white men making Black music?

Most successful white jazz musicians adhered to 1920s beauty standards, effectively reinforcing their class status and supplementing the "air of sophistication" they may have sought in visual presentations. However, the decade's most popular jazz bandleader—Paul Whiteman—did not. He was considered "overweight" in a decade when the diet industry first emerged, and his weight was discussed regularly in print media as a problem or used as comedic fodder in an increasingly fatphobic society. Despite or perhaps because of his size, Whiteman had a profound impact on the popularity of jazz. He drove the expansion of the recording industry, which shifted the way Americans experienced entertainment from live to recorded. The violist initially performed in symphony orchestras until he encountered jazz at a nightclub in San Francisco's red-light district. Using racially problematic language, he describes the experience in his 1926 autobiography, *Jazz*:

> [Jazz] screeched and bellowed at me from a trick platform in the middle of a smoke-hazed, beer-fumed room. . . . My whole body began to sit up and take notice. It was like coming out of blackness into bright light. My blues faded when treated by the Georgia Blues that some trombonist was wailing about. My head was dizzy, but my feet seemed to understand that tune. They began to pat wildly. I wanted to whoop. I wanted to dance. I wanted to sing. I did them all. Raucous? Yes. Crude—undoubtedly. Unmusical—sure thing. But rhythmic, catching as the smallpox and spirit-lifting. That was jazz then. I liked it, though it puzzled me. Even then it seemed to me to have vitality, sincerity and truth in it. In spite of its uncouthness, it was trying to say something peculiarly American, just as an uneducated man struggles ungrammatically to express a true and original idea. I wanted to know jazz better and it was immediately clear that I was going to.[13]

Whiteman assembled a dance orchestra and within months found success in San Francisco, Atlantic City, and eventually Manhattan. At the same time, Americans were spending more money on phonograph records than any other form of entertainment. Whiteman's first hit, "Whispering" (1920), sold over two million copies in the first two years.[14] Although his orchestra performed a variety of styles, he was made famous for his jazz. But his jazz was different; it was, according to critics, innovative and free of "noise."[15] Whiteman guided this interpretation by using modifiers such as "jazz classique" and "jazz orchestra" to promote his music. These terms signaled a distinction from Black cultural forms that many white Americans misheard as unmusical and crude, as Whiteman's own description in the above quote indicates. This marketing strategy communicated both a musical and racial difference.[16]

Yet, Whiteman betrayed one expectation of staging "jazz classique"—inhabiting a disciplined, lean body. At the same time, his portly appellation, the King of Jazz, drew on nostalgic conceptions of fat as power. And yet, his fatness desexualized him in ways that seem to have made his white translation of Black culture more acceptable, especially given Black stereotypes about hypersexuality. What follows works through these tensions by analyzing advertisements, news media, and graphic representations of "the king" in caricatures and cartoons. Drawing on fat studies and theories of race, I ask how Whiteman's size facilitated his ability to make and sell Blacksound on an unprecedented scale. The bandleader already negotiated the racial controversy of jazz's rising popularity through sound, but was it possible to do so corporeally? For those committed to protesting jazz, his weight might have symbolized the consequences of playing too closely with representations of Blackness. But what did his body signify for his millions of white fans? I focus on these listeners during the early part of his long and varied career when the reception of jazz was at its most controversial and decidedly racial. I also consider the treatment of other fat entertainers of this time such as Roscoe "Fatty" Arbuckle and Ma Rainey, which serves as a useful point of comparison in order to think through fatphobia's relationship to gender, sexuality, and race in the 1920s. The tendency to dehumanize and desexualize fat bodies during the 1920s "cult of thin," as was the case with Arbuckle, might have worked in Whiteman's favor, as he peddled a style intimately tied to anxieties about interracial sex. However, unlike Rainey, Whiteman's white skin always protected him from total dehumanization. Depictions of Whiteman's physical appearance explicate how the success of Black music imbricated sound and body through race. Presuming that white bandleaders worked as corporeal filters of Black music on behalf of their white listeners, I argue that size mattered. But first, this chapter explores how ideas about race and jazz following World War I enlisted the body as a site for making meaning, specifically as racialized material constituted by class constraints and aspirations, sexual desire, and gender identity.

Jazz(-Age) Bodies

If race and dance music are always already about bodies, then jazz registered those bodies as a *sexual-racial arrangement*. The etymology of the word "jazz" is speculated to have roots in the sex acts and vulgar dancing that took place in seedy dance halls during the early twentieth century. Alan P. Merriam and Fradley H. Garner trace the origins of the term's various connotations in their 1968 essay, "Jazz—the Word."[17] Sex is referenced in definitions beginning in the 1920s. The 1934 *Dictionary of American Slang* even defined jazz as "sexual intercourse; to have it."[18] Jazz was also said to be linked to the word "jasm" and then "gism" or "chism," denoting semen.[19] White men, who reduced Black men and women to sexual objects, published these speculations. Beyond a word, jazz was an important soundtrack for sex workers and working-class youth alike. As Dale Cockrell and Lewis Erenberg have demonstrated, jazz continued to ignite a series of dance crazes that ebbed and flowed since the turn of the century.[20] These choregraphed fads brought working-class youth to dance halls in droves. The potential for cross-racial, erotic interactions drew even more patrons to dance halls, cabarets, and nightclubs. The widespread practice of slumming pushed these desires to the fore, revealing the extent to which sexuality was a racial phenomenon but one that was always shot through with ideas about class privilege.

Nowhere is the centrality of bodies in the popularity of this music more apparent than in the implications of the contemporaneous phrase, "the Jazz Problem"—a 1920s play on the turn-of-the-century debate known as the Negro Problem.[21] The original term encapsulated white concern about Black upward mobility and urban migration—in other words, Black proximity to whites. "The Negro problem" and "the Negro question" appeared during Reconstruction in what Khalil Gibran Muhammad calls a "post-emancipation racial science," but it took on renewed meaning by the 1890s following decades of advancement in Black politics, education, professions, and culture.[22] For white Americans, resolutions to the putative problem centered on controlling itinerant Black populations, hardening racial hierarchies, and theorizing racial difference.[23] But Black social mobility and migration did not just disrupt a racial order; they disrupted a sexual one, too. "If race is always about bodies," writes Richard Dyer, "it is also always about the reproduction of those bodies through heterosexuality."[24] Reproduction dictated racial identity in a "one-drop" social paradigm. Preventing miscegenation was at the core of segregationist policies and practices. It is why eugenicists wrote propaganda about preserving the "Anglo-Saxon race," why politicians passed legislation barring multiracial Americans from passing as white, and why the myth of the Black male rapist permeated US media. Jim Crow ideologies centered on the body in ways that mapped sex onto race.

The 1920s cultural iteration of "the Negro Problem" made clear that the Black music sweeping the nation's radios, stages, and shellac discs posed a problem necessitating a solution. The phrase had what Ronald Radano describes as "a metonymic relation that conflated an insidious music with an enduring social condition."[25] This discursive move unveils the corporeal dimensions of sound because it implies a desire to protect middle-class white bodies against the expressions of (primarily but not exclusively) working-class Black bodies. The word "jazz" became a surrogate for Black Americans, but instead of attempting to control migrating, upwardly mobile Black bodies, this metonymic term sought to censor their sound.

The discursive policing of Black music relied on racist but also corporeal terms. Critics used words such as "disease," "epidemic," "savage," "lascivious," and "mad" to describe its power.[26] They believed it could disable people, both physically and mentally. Anxiety about the music of Others piercing the ears of white men has a long history—from the Sirens of Homer's *Odyssey* to the virgins of Bologna in early modern Italy.[27] In her work on early modern England, Samantha Bassler explicates the gendered binary constructing the relationship among music, "madness," and disability. Often present in such discourse is a "narrative prosthesis" that creates a good/bad dichotomy, where "harmful music, or discord of harmony or meter, exists as a foil for establishing the healthful, curative properties of accepted and normalized musical styles."[28] In the 1920s the narrative prosthesis of jazz's reception featured a racial dichotomy, too—one that conscripted the body. Syncopation, according to historian Russell Johnson, was perceived to be rhythmically "defective" and to cause "epileptic fragments" and "spasmodic motions."[29] In 1926 the Salvation Army in Cincinnati, Ohio, even sued the city to end movie theater construction near a maternity hospital, fearing that the theater would play jazz to accompany silent films.[30] Jazz was also said to worsen neurasthenia—a physical and mental condition indexing the negative effects of modernization on the nervous system. The diagnosis materialized out of concern primarily for the psychological integrity of white, middle-class men, especially after World War I. Direct comparisons between combat noises and jazz abounded. Some scientists even claimed that jazz "produces an atrophied condition on the brain cells" and has "doubled insanity in the United States."[31] Projecting disabilities onto people of color has long been used as a "weapon" to enforce racist actions from slavery to immigration law.[32] Racism and ableism frequently work in tandem, drawing on shared operations of subjugation, as scholars of Black disability studies have persuasively argued. Together, these discourses shaped the reception of jazz. And it was precisely these discourses that Whiteman tried to circumvent in the 1920s and 1930s with his orchestrated approach to Black dance music.

Given that many white Americans believed Black bodies and their attendant cultural sounds were threatening, this chapter considers how white male bodies functioned as a necessary intervention in the success of Black music in Jim Crow America. However, my case study tends to a particular white body perceived to be abnormal. In this way, reception of Whiteman's so-called weight problem resonated with the ableist, anti-Black rhetoric of jazz's reception discussed above. And while fatness is not always understood or experienced as a disability, the former brushes up against the boundaries of the latter.[33] In what follows, I treat them as separate phenomena, focusing primarily on Whiteman's size but never losing sight of the way ableism and fatphobia are sometimes co-constitutive. Bringing fatness into the fray of analyzing the sexual-racial bodies of the Jazz Age, this chapter demonstrates how Whiteman's fatness, in addition to his whiteness, ameliorated discomfort his audiences might have experienced when listening to this sexualized and racialized music dubbed jazz.

Distorting Whiteman

In an industry seeking white interpreters of Black music, Whiteman built an entertainment empire as the King of Jazz.[34] By 1924 Paul Whiteman boasted fifty-two satellite orchestras, with some of these located outside the United States in Paris, Havana, London, and Mexico.[35] After his success with *Rhapsody in Blue,* he embarked on several national and international tours that raked in profits. In 1925 he made $800,000—the equivalent of nearly $14 million today.[36] By the end of the 1920s, he had a weekly radio show, paying him $5,000 for a single, one-hour broadcast.[37] For historian Elijah Wald, Whiteman's unprecedented success transformed jazz's reputation: "What had been considered the sound of low dives and wild youth was now a modern art music and the defining sound of its time."[38]

As one of the best-selling artists of the recording industry, Whiteman became a central figure (and target) in US media and cultural criticism. After debuting George Gershwin's *Rhapsody in Blue* in 1924, Whiteman became a boundary-crossing star, and visual artists began to take him up as a subject. Many of these representations were caricatures, reducing his image to a few exaggerated features. Miguel Covarrubias and William Auerbach were among the first to depict him, in 1924 and 1925, respectively, and they focused their

FIGURE 1.1 *The Paul Whiteman Cycle*, ca. 1924, by Miguel Covarrubias. Photograph of the painting. Courtesy of Alfred Bendiner Memorial Collection, Prints and Photographs Division, Library of Congress. Printed with permission of María Elena Rico Covarrubias.

talents on disfiguring his head. In Covarrubias's painting, his facial features and hairline are small ornamentations on an egregiously large and round head (fig. 1.1). A side portrait features a double chin almost as large as the rest of his face. The Auerbach renderings do the same—tiny facial features and distorted cheeks and chin. A 1927 photo captures the line between grotesque

FIGURE 1.2 Paul Whiteman advertisement, 1927. Paul Whiteman Collection, Williams College Special Collections.

and comic in the field of caricature. Whiteman stands between two disturbingly oversized, puppet heads placed on top of (and visually swallowing) two men (fig. 1.2). Whiteman, in on the joke, holds the men's hands. Exceeding two feet, these papier-mâché heads had small hairlines, noses, and mouths that function just to amplify the remaining flesh. By 1928 the oversized head became a branding strategy; Columbia created what became known as the "potato-head" Whiteman logo and put it on his recordings' multicolor disc labels (fig. 1.3). This same head adorned *Rhapsody in Blue* sheet music covers and the band's kick drum. Other caricatures feature the rest of his body, but as a drawing by *LA Times* staff artist Salvador Baguez demonstrates, his head usually still overshadowed his torso.[39] In this drawing, the head is a large oval with facial features occupying only about one-sixteenth of the vast negative white space. Six jazz musicians, overshadowed by Whiteman's head, play underneath his chin and against a backdrop that is the top half of the bandleader's chest. With a closer look, one can spot two very small ears, folded behind his head's temporal region and blending in with the ornate

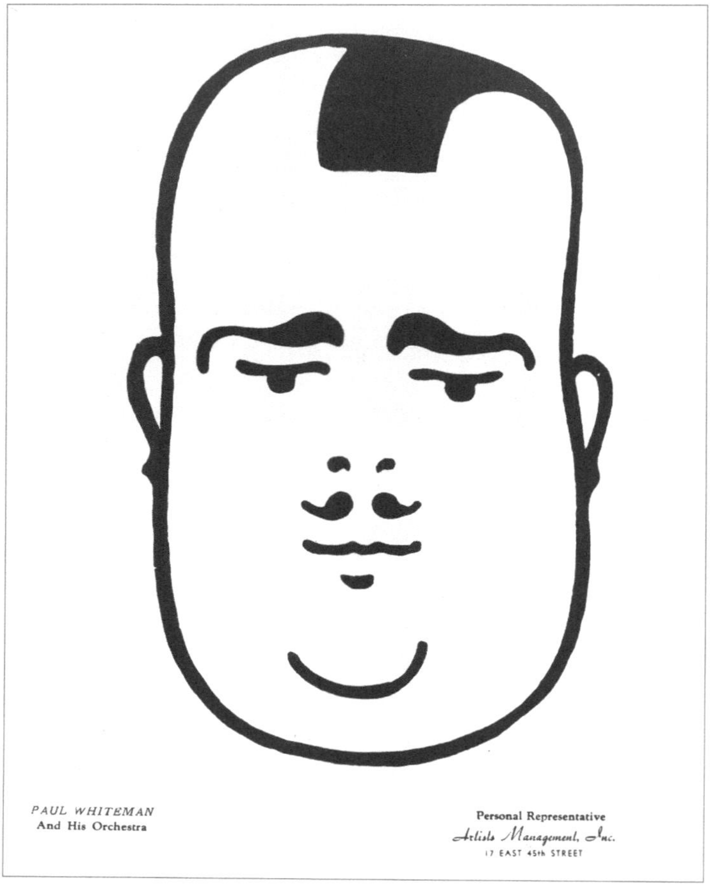

FIGURE 1.3 Potato head, logo, Columbia Records. Paul Whiteman Collection, Williams College Special Collections.

backdrop print. Despite having a body and facial features, he is mostly head in this drawing.[40]

These paintings and drawings deformed Whiteman's body in an attempt to bring together comedy and homage. Caricature's tendency to distort by accentuating difference made it the perfect art form for severing a subject's relationship to their humanity. The same can be said for Blackface minstrelsy. At the turn of the twentieth century, "ethnic caricature" drew on the visual aesthetics of minstrelsy to dehumanize its subjects by "reducing identity to a handful of racial cues" or by exaggerating physical attributes, such as large lips and eyes. Literary theorist Henry Wonham argues that artists rendered Black and Jewish Americans monstrous by making them appear "incapable of emerging fully from a material state." In contrast, realistic drawings reserved autonomy, critical thought, and sentience for depictions of white, middle-class Americans. With roots in physiognomy, ethnic caricature was "among the most abhorrent devices of American chauvinism," according to Wonham.[41] Whiteman's relationship to Black culture amplified the racial resonance of his caricatures. As a white man performing sonic imaginations of Blackness, he, like caricature, extended key components of minstrelsy. His fatness proved central to these representations.

The depictions might have been a response to Whiteman's own star persona. In his marketing gimmickry, the bandleader often performed humorous publicity stunts capitalizing on his size. Dressing up as Santa Claus in Madison Square Garden was but one of the ways Whiteman foregrounded his weight and then leveraged it in playful ways to garner attention. Like other large entertainers, Whiteman may have wanted to control any commentary on his body by using it in his brand, knowing he would be pigeonholed into one character—the funny man. The contemporaneous performances of Oliver Hardy, W. C. Fields, and Arbuckle made weight the raison d'être for their slapstick humor. Hardy was the comedic foil to his thinner counterpart, Stan Laurel; Fields was a malevolent drunk; and Arbuckle, though he played a variety of funny characters, worked with the word "fat" in his name. These fat men were clearly funny but rarely viewed as actors that could play sexual characters convincingly. Comedy stood in for (hetero)masculinity in these roles, as fatness both feminized and desexualized them.[42] In her work on Arbuckle, cultural critic Neda Ulaby argues that fatness was perceived to literally overshadow genitalia.[43] The site of physical gratification for these characters was not located in the groin but in the gut. The desire to eat represented a different type of immoral indulgence. Desexualization enabled Arbuckle to traverse many gender roles, playing a child or a young woman. But his size was the joke; in a fatphobic society, fat people could never be as innocent as a child or objects of desire like a thin woman.

A year after Whiteman recorded his first hit, Arbuckle's sexuality, or lack thereof, became the target of a scandal. In 1921 he was accused of raping silent film actress Virginia Rappe and subsequently rupturing her bladder, which led to her death four days later. Arbuckle was accused of using an object instead of his genitals to sexually assault her, an accusation that further desexualized him. After a third trial, he was declared not guilty, but his career never recovered; he was a pervert in the public eye. Ulaby argues that his indictment was buttressed by a recent announcement about a new film in which he would play a lover: "When the fantasized urge for pleasure and drive for satisfaction coincided with allegations of off-screen perversions, Arbuckle's fat became dangerous and demeaning even to look at." She continues:

> The "scandal" associated with fat eroded support of Arbuckle, reducing his image almost completely to that of a vilified libertine. Society's suspicion that fatness results from a failure to regulate and manage one's body seemed to be articulated in Fatty's on-screen violence, disorders, disasters, and bizarre behaviors and to be confirmed in the news of Arbuckle's commission of "rape" and "murder." Weight connotes unrestrained eating, which here was seen as mirroring a voracious sexual appetite that consumes and destroys the object of desire. Fatness was taken as signifying Arbuckle's uncontrollable desire to consume not only food but starlets as well.

Perhaps the Arbuckle scandal served as a cautionary tale for subsequent fat entertainers, including Whiteman. And yet, there is a difference between the types of entertainment they created. Arbuckle made cheap shorts while Whiteman was performing at Aeolian Hall. Where the former's career could not withstand the scrutiny of what Ulaby describes as the "juridical/reformist/moralistic discourse of censorship (the bourgeois public sphere)," Whiteman was curating his music and persona directly for this sphere.[44] His middlebrow aesthetic rendered his body less abject and less subject to "society's suspicion" about fat people.

Rainey is another 1920s entertainer who leveraged her weight to succeed in a fatphobic industry. As was the case with other women blues singers, such as Bessie Smith, descriptions of Rainey consistently mention her size, and she was broadly billed as "the ugliest woman in show business." Understanding the affective capacity of spectacle, Rainey made sure to take up as much space as possible and to do so in extravagant ways. She became famous because she wore lavish costumes with sequins that accentuated and sexualized her fatness.[45] She sang songs about sex and women "with passionate emotions and appetites."[46] According to Jennifer-Scott Mobley, Rainey's star persona "was among the first to capitalize on white assumptions about unbridled animal sexuality of (fat) black women" and her "willingness to embrace, indeed highlight, the 'otherness' of her appearance as a fat black woman" made her very successful.[47] Contemporaneous with Whiteman's landmark records, she made over one hundred recordings between 1923 and 1928 and held a contract with Paramount Records—an unparalleled feat for a Black musician at this time.[48]

However, where white men such as Arbuckle and Whiteman were effectively desexualized because of their size, Rainey's body was hypersexualized. Like Arbuckle, though, she also encountered legal trouble for her perceived sexual "dysfunction." In 1925 she was arrested for allegedly having an orgy with some of the women with whom she shared a stage.[49] This was not the only time her sexuality was surveilled by the state. She was in trouble with police several other times for publicly expressing her same-sex desire. Rumors about Rainey's lesbianism circulated in the press and made sexuality a central theme in her star persona, whether she wanted it to be or not.[50] Nonetheless, she continued to perform and record erotic songs that detailed her escapades with women, with the 1928 "Prove It on Me Blues" standing as an oft-cited example.

Black women's fat bodies were perceived to be "threatening" in different ways than those of white men. Sabina Strings argues that the growing "preference for thinness" in the early twentieth century emerged from white women's new beauty ideals, set in opposition to Black women's perceived corpulence. In an 1897 *Harper's Bazaar* article, author Edith Bigelow discusses changes in classic beauty for (white) women, arguing that a fat woman "will not be a social success unless she burnt-cork herself, don beads, and then go to that burning clime where women, like pigs, are valued at so much a pound."[51] The racial distinction between white and Black women exceeded beauty standards to include health ones, too. While both Black men and women were perceived to be sexually dangerous—a perception used to justify Jim Crow segregation—race scientists believed Black women were the hosts of deadly venereal diseases. White medical communities blamed the high rates of transmission of syphilis and tuberculosis on Black women (even though both diseases were more common among white people). Strings argues that obesity was just the next "epidemic" blamed on Black women, buttressing beliefs that they inhabited "deadly corporealities" that made them "social dead weight."[52] Historian Tera Hunter writes that "by the end of the nineteenth century, the 'Negro Problem' had become thoroughly medicalized."[53] It did so through growing fears of fat Black women's bodies. The jazz problem, then, was not only related to matters of race but also gender and size underneath the epidermis.

Caricatures of Whiteman drew on both the racialization of his music and his fatness. As Strings makes clear, fears of fat and fears of Blackness were bedfellows, even when "excess" adipose tissue materialized in white bodies. Such a racialization of fat sheds new light on both jazz's reception and the weight of its "King" to navigate racist criticism of Black music. If Whiteman made a "lady out of jazz," according to his own promotional materials, and that woman was white, then she was also thin. As I have argued elsewhere, this slogan tries to capture the racial purity of "jazz classique," filtering out what Whiteman and his audiences perceived to be the "crude" elements of jazz with symphonic scoring and instrumentation.[54] But there is another, even more insidious subtext. (Thin) white women were a protected class in the Jim Crow racial order, and the perceived need to guard their virtue fueled segregation practices in an effort to prohibit interracial sex and protect them from the mythical Black male rapist. By making a lady out of jazz, Whiteman protected white listeners from the potentially deadly effects of Black music piercing their ears. The music's effects were deemed corporeal. By the 1920s weight was a subject of eugenical conversation about increasing concern for the perceived degradation of the Anglo-Saxon race, in particular, white women.[55] Obesity was such a dire threat precisely because it was conflated with Blackness. Whiteman mitigated these concerns with the sophistication and class aspirations of his music but not necessarily with his body. While his fatness might have made him a safer desexualized conduit through which to consume Black music, his body occupied an ambivalent space as caricatures consistently reminded audiences that he was less than other white, middle-class men precisely because his body was so much more.

Animating Whiteman

By the late 1920s and early 1930s, animation became a more prominent way of distorting Whiteman's body, and the legacy of minstrelsy persisted in this new art form. The cartoons drew on race and gender stereotypes, emphasizing intersections between bodies and sound. In the 1933 short *Croon Crazy*, the main character, Cubby Bear, hosts a radio show set to feature Mae West, Al Jolson, and Paul Whiteman—all entertainers famous for their versions of Black culture. Cubby looks like an early version of Mickey Mouse but with more blackface. His large eyes and white mouth starkly contrast the rest of his black body. It is worth noting here that to play Al Jolson, Cubby Bear wipes his face, only to reveal slightly less white framing around his eyes and slightly more black "makeup." The difference between Jolson in blackface and Cubby Bear as himself is hard to distinguish. In this episode his guests cancel at the last minute, but he has no trouble musically impersonating them while donning the masks of each musician. "Sol Rightman" performs first. Cubby Bear blows up a large inflatable tire-shaped tube with hoses connected to a set of jazz band instruments. A clarinet, a trombone, two saxophones, and two tubas hang from the curtain, and a drum set sits off to the side. Cubby Bear stands on top of the tire tube, as if a podium, pulls a baton and mask of Whiteman from its center, slaps the mask on, and starts conducting while tapping his feet to play (send air to) the instruments. The cartoon blurs the boundary of what is real and what is impersonation, bringing the contradictions of the racial imitation at the heart of white American entertainment into sharp relief.[56]

In Disney's 1934 *Music Land*, a short film from the Silly Symphony musical film series, Whiteman appears as an anthropomorphized saxophone. The ten-minute episode depicts star-crossed lovers: the princess (a violin), living in the Land of Symphony, and Whiteman's son the prince (an alto saxophone), living across the Sea of Discord in the Isle of Jazz. Wearing a crown, the King of the Isle sits on a large throne made of drums. His face occupies the oversized bell of the saxophone that is much wider and almost as tall as the instrument's body. The animator made the facial features small, added a double chin, and contorted the bell of the saxophone to make it look like a large belly. While the racial undertones of *Music Land* are bubbling beneath the surface, those of Metro-Goldwyn-Mayer's 1934 *Toyland Broadcast* are the linchpin of this Happy Harmonies short. In addition to caricaturing Bing Crosby and Whiteman, there is a minstrel performance of "Jungle Fever" by the Mills Brothers. Dripping in blackface—which is thrown onto the tops of their heads from above as melting pieces of chocolate that they then lick off around the mouth to create a full minstrel mask—the animated versions of the men sing:

> Dusky maiden, dark-haired siren
> Congo sweetheart
> I'm comin' back to you
> Wild-eyed woman, native dreamgirl
> Jungle fever is in my blood for you.

Smooth, four-part harmonies wash over the racist lyrics matched by equally pernicious imagery of three Black characters with thick-textured, messy hair. They dance behind a fire, which projects their shadows onto the wall, making their "African"-coded features more grotesque in size. As if this was not racist enough, the song gets briefly interrupted by a Black character dancing on top of a large drum in front of a large book, open to an "African jungle" scene. He wears a loincloth, a ring pierces his nose, and he folds his body in impossible ways to play his own behind in the final measure of the drum solo. Whiteman's scene is less egregious but still reinforces the cartoon's indebtedness to minstrelsy. The curtain opens to the King of Jazz drawn as a wobble toy, swaying around uncontrollably, always on the verge of but never falling over (fig. 1.4). He winds up a toybox with four minstrel toys playing in a jazz band featuring piano, saxophone, trumpet, and drums. The toys vibrate robotically as the sticks piercing their plastic torsos move up and down. The military-esque straight rhythms of the Broadway tune "Wedding of the Painted Doll" sound very little like jazz or even like Whiteman.

Perhaps, these cartoons got their inspiration from Whiteman's 1930 feature film *The King of Jazz*, because no other cartoon links minstrelsy, weight, and jazz more clearly than its animated sequence "A Fable in Jazz." The revue-style musical film featured dances, skits, and a performance of *Rhapsody in Blue* on an aggressively large, blue piano with individual keys larger than the men "playing" them. This culminating event in the film is preceded by Jacques Cartier acting out his famous "voodoo dance" on a large drum adorned with wood carvings of African masks. Cartier performed this dance regularly in theater revues. He wore a loin cloth, and his headdress is almost the same height as his own body. He was painted in black lacquer, and his black shadow was projected onto the set screen behind him. The enormity of the set in every scene of the film reminds viewers of Whiteman's size.

FIGURE 1.4 Paul Whiteman character, *Toyland Broadcast*, Happy Harmonies, Metro-Goldwyn-Mayer (1934). Screenshot.

The cartoon sequence early in the film begins with the master of ceremonies Charles Irwin standing before a twenty-foot-high scrapbook opened to the title page, "The King of Jazz." Irwin announces the cartoon sequence:

> Here we have Paul himself. And by the way you may be interested in knowing how he came to be crowned the King of Jazz. Once upon a time, Paul, tiring of life in the great city, had a grand idea. He would go big-game hunting. No sooner said than done. Suiting the action to the camera, we find him a few weeks later in Darkest Africa.[57]

This sequence was one of the first cartoons to feature jazz, according to Daniel Goldmark.[58] The medley, scored by James Dietrich, comprises a variation on a theme from *Rhapsody in Blue*, a snappy version of a spiritual sung by Bing Crosby, and a jazz-inflected arrangement of "Music Hath Charms," replete with syncopation, extended harmonies, and gestures toward improvisation played by jazz musicians Joe Venuti on violin and Eddie Lang on guitar. The cartoon begins with Whiteman hunting in the jungle (fig. 1.5 top), but he quickly becomes the hunted when a large lion comically chases him. The bandleader, running, starts singing the spiritual "My Lord Delivered Daniel" (fig. 1.5, second down). As his hands, oddly positioned and drawn disproportionately large, clap on the strong beats, he starts running sideways. The comical nature of his body coupled with his performance of a spiritual stage a scene right out of a minstrel show. This racial imitation does not help—he is caught. But just before the lion prepares to eat him, Whiteman stands up and plays "Music Hath Charms" on the violin (fig. 1.5 middle). No doubt this song references a line written by English playwright William Congreve: "Music hath charms to soothe the savage breast." It works; the lion dances along. Referencing *The Jazz Singer*, the lion concludes the number in show-tune fashion with his arms stretched out as he says "mammy" à la Al Jolson (fig. 1.5 fourth down). Whiteman is not safe yet. A monkey lobs a coconut at him, striking him on the head. A large bump appears making his head grow larger into the shape of a crown (fig. 1.5 bottom). At the end, his entire face grows disfigured, taking on minstrel-like characteristics. The film cuts back to Irwin, who says, "And that's how Whiteman was crowned king."

The racial/racist symbolism in this cartoon short is far from subtle. Krin Gabbard and Daniel Goldmark argue that the cartoon depicts Whiteman as bringing jazz *to* Africa.[59] Such an interpretation works against much of the discourse about the earliest versions of jazz "coming from Africa." Indeed, in this cartoon, Africa does not represent a continent but rather an imaginary scenescape (and an animated one, no less) standing in for Black culture, animals standing in for Black people. As the master of ceremonies tells us, Whiteman is the King of Jazz because of his explorations in the jungle, his

FIGURE 1.5 Animated sequence from *King of Jazz*, directed by John Murray Anderson, Universal Pictures (1930). *Top to bottom:* Whiteman hunting in "Darkest Africa"; Whiteman singing "My Lord Delivered Daniel"; Whiteman playing "Music Hath Charms"; the lion saying "mammy" and imitating Al Jolson; Whiteman getting crowned King of Jazz.

intimacy with Blackness. As Whiteman himself argues in his autobiography, he had to study jazz closely in its earliest, more "primitive" forms before he was able to refine it. Michael Rogin echoes this notion when he reminds viewers of the cartoon's colonial underpinnings. "The white hunter" comes back with a trophy for America—jazz.[60] And herein lies the connection with minstrelsy and Whiteman's weight. The labor required to "become the King of Jazz" had consequences that misshaped his white body, made palpable by the bump on his head. Put differently, he made a racial sacrifice that deformed his physical integrity. Whiteman's body was perceived to be disfigured not only because of his size but also because of his relationship to Black culture.

Much like the art of caricature, animation is rooted in minstrelsy. Film historian Nicholas Sammond puts this quite eloquently: "Commercial animation in the United States didn't borrow from blackface minstrelsy nor was it simply influenced by it. Rather, American animation is actually in many of its most enduring incarnations an integral part of the ongoing iconographic and performative traditions of blackface. Mickey Mouse isn't *like* a minstrel; he *is* a minstrel." Sammond concedes that this fact might be hard to digest given that minstrelsy is a live-performance tradition. But the same ontological questions at work in those performances also shaped the drawings: "[Blackface] evokes in its tension between surface and interior—between the makeup and the face beneath—a fantastic black persona that is analogous in many ways to cartoon characters who dwell in the flatland on the surface of the page or cel, and again at the liminal boundary of the screen onto which they are projected. Both gain force and substance through their play at the frontiers between ontological realms."[61]

Certainly, Whiteman's association with jazz cornered him into this representational liminality. But the question remains: Did his weight, nevertheless, somehow facilitate the ease with which he succeeded in the jazz marketplace? Perhaps, it is impossible to answer this question given the implicit and subconscious nature of many permutations of fatphobia and anti-Blackness. Regardless, Whiteman tried to lose weight several times, and his weight-loss attempts engaged racialized discourses about fat, as he worked out both his corporeal and his musical miscegenation in the public eye and ear.

"Whiteman's Burden"

Jazz was a "problem" not just because it was popular Black music but because it signaled a shift in who was controlling representations of Blackness. Black music in the twentieth-century marketplace was increasingly performed and recorded by Black Americans.[62] In 1923 Kid Ory and Sidney Bechet recorded, but their opportunities were limited. By 1926, however, Jelly Roll Morton and His Red Hot Peppers signed with Victor Talking Machine Company, and

Louis Armstrong and His Hot Five signed with Okeh Records. By 1928 Armstrong was establishing a national reputation with "Heebie Jeebies" selling forty thousand copies in just a few weeks and the chart-topping "West End Blues" in 1928.[63] Armstrong even had satellite bands like Whiteman did. Duke Ellington, having signed with white publisher Irving Mills, started topping charts with Victor, Okeh, and Columbia Records recordings in 1927 and 1928. Black American jazz became more accessible through radio, too, especially in urban centers, such as Chicago and New York, garnering listeners of all races.[64] At the same time, the Radio Act of 1927, to curb jazz consumption, included a clause that forbade "obscene, indecent or profane" language.[65] Mae West was sentenced to prison for "corrupting the morals of youth." *Buck v. Bell* was passed, making sterilization of the "unfit" legal. And Whiteman started dieting.

In the late 1920s Whiteman weighed close to three hundred pounds. In an era defined by the so-called cult of thin, his body was abnormal. It was often used as a comedic foil in his reception, as we have seen. At times the "joke" was more subtle; writers used words such as "big" that played with the distinction between his musical success and his weight. In a 1930 article about Whiteman's orchestra members, the words "Great BIG Family Man" appear large across the two-page spread, next to his portrait, which is sized about six times larger than those of his band members.[66] In a 1927 advertisement for a gym, however, his weight *was* the joke (fig. 1.6). In this publicity stunt, he "fights" Babe Ruth, whose trainer owned the gym. Whiteman loses after accidentally punching a bystander and then getting clipped by the famous baseball player. After the referee calls it, Whiteman says that Ruth "should have picked on someone his own size."[67] A year later, he embarked on a restrictive soup diet and enlisted media to publicize his progress. At his doctor's suggestion, he stopped eating "peas, beans, potatoes, corn, white bread, sugar, fried meats, beer, ale and wine."[68] This doctor-prescribed diet led him to drink soup for most of the day. He lost eighty-five pounds.

Two years after his soup fast, he was sick in the hospital and exceeded three hundred pounds once again. His soon-to-be wife, actress Margaret Livingston, insisted he lose weight for both his health and her happiness. She put the ceremony off until she was able to "put [her] arms around [him]."[69] She placed him on a very restrictive diet and later published the daily meal plans included in their correspondence in a book called *Whiteman's Burden*, which directly references Rudyard Kipling's jingoistic 1899 poem "The White Man's Burden" (fig. 1.7).[70] The book is a putative love story, with missives featuring hypocoristic addresses like "Dear Pig o' My Heart" and "My darling Weight-Wilter," but the ascetic substance over which they bonded bordered on sadomasochism.[71] Most striking is the dressing he ate almost daily. The "Paul Whiteman Dressing" has a base of nujol oil, which, as archivist Laurel

FIGURE 1.6 Whiteman (*left*) and baseball great Babe Ruth pretending to box (1927), newspaper advertisement. Paul Whiteman Collection, Williams College Special Collections.

Rhame points out, is mineral oil, a laxative.[72] The couple married long before he got down to his "goal weight," but by 1932 he was captured in the press below two hundred pounds (fig. 1.8). Thereafter, his name and image were used to advertise foods promising to keep white bodies lean. A 1932 ad for a performance in St. Louis, Missouri, includes a large-font byline that reads,

WHITEMAN'S BURDEN

by

Margaret Livingston Whiteman

and

Isabel Leighton

New York

The Viking Press

1933

FIGURE 1.7 Frontispiece and title page, *Whiteman's Burden*, by Margaret Livingston Whiteman and Isabel Leighton. Paul Whiteman Collection, Williams College Special Collections.

"I drank all the milk I want" under a photo of Mrs. Whiteman pouring a tall glass of Pevely milk for her husband.[73]

Whiteman's career took off in the 1920s at the same time the diet industry did. Scientific approaches to nutrition centered on counting calories—a reflection of the Progressive Era's fixation on numbers as epistemologically valuable. In 1913 small scales were created for domestic use.[74] In 1918 a book called *Diet and Health with Key to the Calories* sold two million copies.[75] Famous author Henry T. Finck, who was also a music critic, wrote *Girth Control* in 1923 to declare that "the mania to overeat" was "the greatest problem before the human race."[76] At the end of the jazz age, the *New York Times* described America as a "calory-conscious" nation.[77] The calorie had become what food studies scholar Chin Jou describes as "an objective, fail-proof measure of the energy value of food."[78] In other words, fat was something you could and should control.

Discourses about body size disguised virulent ideas about race and US citizenship. After World War I, there was growing concern about white military men who were deemed "unfit," and state programs emerged to "improve the

FIGURE 1.8 "Jazz band leader Paul Whiteman arrives by train, Los Angeles, 1932." *Los Angeles Times*, May 12, 1932.

bodies of future generations."[79] To be thin was to be civilized, to be a good citizen. In his 1926 autobiography, Whiteman talks about all the delicious food he encounters while on tour, but his doctor "[condemned] all indigenous food as fattening."[80] To be thin, then, was also to eat white food. Eugenics fit squarely within these ideas, and the 1920s witnessed its resurgence. University courses, books, and advocacy groups focused on eugenics abounded, and they all coalesced around concern about what white supremacist Madison Grant called "the Passing of the Great Race."[81] Diet plans were certainly more subtle than prohibiting people deemed "feebleminded" from procreating, but their simultaneous emergence is telling. As Black culture flourished so, too, did white supremacy and the promotion of certain body types, materializing in both the rise of the second Ku Klux Klan, which had its highest membership numbers in 1925, and in a new obsession with counting calories.

If what penetrated the ears could not be stopped, what penetrated the mouth could. The vogue for thinness during the Jazz Age is not surprising, then. And yet, the very same people seeking pleasures of the flesh in their listening and dancing habits sought control over other aspects of their body. In her work on flappers, Jou argues that "full emancipation from bodily constraints" was not the intention of these subjects. Instead, those who dieted "swapped restrictions on their carnal appetites for the dietary variety."[82] Perhaps the same can be said for white jazz band leaders. As Whiteman publicly delved into the world of weight loss, he may have found a temporary solution to his controversial position as white leader of the jazz world.

Conclusion

In a 1932 interview following his radical transformation, Whiteman was asked to contemplate if his heavier weight was what initially made him successful. He finds the question preposterous and jokes that he does not have to worry until he is "184 pounds, 15 ounces," since he weighed 185 when he "got [his] first big band on Broadway." However, his business manager and friends believed otherwise. They encouraged him not to diet for fear he would be "unsalable."[83] Though it is difficult to assess if his weight loss affected his reception, it is striking that his extreme dieting occurred when he could be found spending more time hidden behind radio broadcasts and less time on stage. It was also the height of the Great Depression, and much of America felt as though they were being punished for the profligate behavior that defined the previous decade. The recording industry took a big hit; record and record player sales plummeted, and independents went out of business. Artists and repertoire (A&R) men exchanged stylistic adventurousness for economic security, which severely limited opportunities for Black musicians. Much of white society preferred the more conservative sounds of Guy Lombardo, for example. Lush string and vocal arrangements with minimal syncopation required less-stylistic intervention on the part of white band leaders. By the end of the 1930s, Whiteman had gained back the weight he lost.

Whiteman's body took center stage in the reception of his star persona. For antijazzers, his body might have served as a cautionary tale about the disabling effects of Black music on white Americans, reinforcing racist and ableist rhetoric. For his white and middle-class fans, however, he filtered jazz's associations with the working class, with Blackness, and with sex, without distilling it altogether. Perhaps, his fatness was key to his success. Though impossible to prove, the way in which his weight symbolically castrated him could have made his music safer in the same way that his sophisticated arrangements of jazz made Black dance music more palatable for hesitant white listeners. Listening to Whiteman's jazz placed white ears adjacent to but not in direct contact with Blackness of some form. His fatness represented his contiguity to racial impurity, in a way that might have been enticing to listeners who wanted some closeness but not true intimacy with Blackness. The disgust his body induced in fatphobic audiences could have also enhanced the exhilaration one feels when doing something considered socially dangerous. Whiteman's body both shaped his comic, safe, and genial image and suggested a problematic weakness and indulgence. Through his very corporeal presence, Whiteman both made jazz safe for white listeners and suggested the perils of proximity to Blackness. Though the reception of Whiteman's body was largely determined by anti-Black fatphobia, his whiteness always protected him from the potentially deadly consequences of playing jazz while Black in America.

Notes

1. Throughout this chapter, I use the word "Blacksound" to refer to the commodification of Black music and the legacy of Blackface minstrelsy embedded in the recording industry. Theorized by Matthew Morrison, this term tends to the ways in which intellectual property was stolen by white Americans in the nineteenth century to form the foundation of the US entertainment industry. It dispels myths of authenticity about Black music just as it captures the racially dynamic and exploitation-based exchanges that led to the music's commodification. For more on this concept, see Morrison, "Race, Blacksound."

2. Koenig, *Jazz in Print*, 171, 214, 227, 235, 238.

3. Tipton, "Who's Afraid of the Jazz Monsters"; Lemke, *Primitivist Modernism*, 62–64; Ogren, *Jazz Revolution* (1989), 140–61.

4. Howland, *Hearing Luxe Pop*, 76.

5. Middle-class Black dance orchestras used these same visual signifiers to indicate a class distinction in their approach to jazz.

6. See Moran, *Governing Bodies*, 11; Farrell, *Fat Shame*, 27.

7. Farrell, *Fat Shame*, 36.

8. Moran, *Governing Bodies*, 8–9, 10–37; Bederman, *Manliness and Civilization*, 12–20.

9. Bederman, *Manliness and Civilization*, 14–15.
10. Farrell, *Fat Shame*, 7–8, 46–49.
11. Curran, *Anatomy of Blackness*, 157; Strings, *Fearing the Black Body*, 147–67.
12. Strings, *Fearing the Black Body*, 6.
13. Whiteman and McBride, *Jazz*, 32–33.
14. Ogren, *Jazz Revolution* (1989), 89–90; Wald, *How the Beatles Destroyed Rock 'n' Roll*, 85.
15. Howland, "Between the Muses and the Masses," 2; Rayno, *Paul Whiteman*, 1:32–36, 49.
16. I have made a similar argument in "Arranging Whiteness."
17. Merriam and Garner, "Jazz," 384–86.
18. Merriam and Garner, "Jazz," 385.
19. Merriam and Garner, "Jazz," 385–86.
20. Cockrell, *Everybody's Doin' It*; Erenberg, *Steppin' Out*.
21. "Where the Etude Stands on Jazz," 515.
22. Muhammad, *Condemnation of Blackness*, 19.
23. Bruce, *Negro Problem*, 14–24.
24. Dyer, *White*, 25.
25. Radano, *Lying Up a Nation*, 236.
26. "Primitive Savage Animalism," 13.
27. See C. A. Monson, "Putting Bolognese Nun Musicians in Their Place"; B. Gordon, *Monteverdi's Unruly Women*.
28. Bassler, "Madness and Music," 529. The term "narrative prosthesis" was theorized by Mitchell and Snyder, *Narrative Prosthesis*.
29. Johnson, "Disease Is Unrhythmical," 17–18.
30. Johnson, "Disease Is Unrhythmical," 13–14.
31. Johnson, "Disease Is Unrhythmical," 23.
32. See Mollow, "Unvictimizable," 105–6; Dolmage, "Disabled upon Arrival"; Murray, "That 'Weird and Wonderful Posture.'"
33. For foundational discussions on the relationship between fatness and disability, see Cooper, "Can a Fat Woman"; Herndon, "Disparate but Disabled."
34. I have made a similar argument in "Arranging Whiteness."
35. Rayno, *Paul Whiteman*, 1:50; Whiteman, "What Is Jazz Doing," 523.
36. DeLong, *Pops*, 4, 84.
37. Rayno, *Paul Whiteman*, 1:222.
38. Wald, *How the Beatles Destroyed Rock 'n' Roll*, 81.
39. Baguez, "Jazz King."
40. Also see a drawing by bandleader Xavier Cugat, which features a small, barely noticeable violin sandwiched between Whiteman's face and hand and a drawing by caricaturist Vincent Zito, featuring Whiteman's large head in the shape of a violin.
41. Wonham, *Playing the Races*, 33, 30, 109.
42. Gilman, *Fat Boys*, 82, 136–37, 155. Also see Plotz, "*Paul Blart*."
43. Ulaby, "Roscoe Arbuckle," 156.

44. Ulaby, "Roscoe Arbuckle," 160–61.
45. Woldu, "Do These Sequins," 109.
46. Mobley, *Female Bodies*, 101.
47. Mobley, *Female Bodies*, 101.
48. Fürnkranz, "Queer Aesthetics," 46.
49. Lieb, *Mother of the Blues*, 8.
50. Davis, *Blues Legacies*, 40.
51. Bigelow, "Sorrows of the Fat," 278.
52. Strings, "Obese Black Women," 110.
53. Hunter, *To 'Joy My Freedom*, 195.
54. Doktor, "Arranging Whiteness."
55. Strings, *Fearing the Black Body*, 169–86.
56. Although it is beyond the scope of this chapter to provide an exhaustive list of cartoons animating Whiteman, it is worth noting that the *Looney Tunes* episode *Porky at the Crocadero* has similar themes as *Croon Crazy*. Porky dresses up like Whiteman by stuffing a pillow under his shirt and wearing a tuxedo while he conducts *Rhapsody in Blue* and "Avalon." The pillow keeps falling out, so he keeps it in by putting a car jack underneath it. For an extensive analysis of the cartoon, see "Audio Commentaries: Daniel Goldmark on *Porky at the Crocadero*," disc 4, *Looney Tunes Golden Collection, Vol. 5*, dir. by Frank Tashlin (1938; Burbank: Warner Bros. Home Entertainment, 2007).
57. Anderson, *King of Jazz*.
58. Goldmark, *Tunes for 'Toons*, 80.
59. Goldmark, *Tunes for 'Toons*, 40; Gabbard, *Jammin' at the Margins*, 11.
60. Rogin, *Blackface, White Noise*, 139.
61. Sammond, *Birth of an Industry*, 5, 6.
62. I have also pointed out these recording patterns in "Arranging Whiteness."
63. Collier, *Louis Armstrong*, 173.
64. Douglas, *Listening In*, 84–85.
65. Leonard, *Jazz and the White Americans*, 99.
66. Hall, "Great Big Family Man," 32–33, 112–13.
67. "SB 131-Newspaper Clippings, June 1927–February 1928," scrapbooks 1925–56, box 701, Whiteman Collection. Also see "Whiteman and Babe Ruth," photographs, 1915–1967, folder 1, box 640, Whiteman Collection.
68. "Paul Whiteman, Jazz King."
69. M. L. Whiteman and Leighton, *Whiteman's Burden*, 3.
70. Louis Armstrong also wrote a short diet plan with his wife, Lucille Armstrong, in "Lose Weight the 'Satchmo' Way." It, too, included laxatives as a solution. Although many broadsides of the one-sheet plan are held in archival collections, it was also printed in *Ebony* magazine in 1956 around the same time he lost almost one hundred pounds. See Armstrong and Armstrong, "Lose Weight the 'Satchmo' Way."
71. M. L. Whiteman and Leighton, *Whiteman's Burden*, 50, 98.
72. Rhame, "Whiteman's Burden."

73. "Paul Whiteman and His Band, Now at the R.K.O."
74. Stearns, *Fat History*, 20.
75. Jou, "Progressive Era Body Project," 423.
76. Finck, *Girth Control*, xv.
77. "Dietary Discoveries Better Human Health."
78. Jou, "Progressive Era Body Project," 423.
79. Moran, *Governing Bodies*, 3.
80. Whiteman and McBride, *Jazz* (1926), 255.
81. Door, "Assuring America's Place in the Sun," 285; Grant, *Passing of the Great Race*.
82. Jou, "Progressive Era Body Project," 427.
83. "'King of Jazz' Speculates," 7.

2

Paul Whiteman, Cultural Ownership, and Jazz Historiography in Dave Peyton's "The Musical Bunch"

CHRISTI JAY WELLS

> "Our Music." Can we say that any more? In answer I say "no" with quotations on either side of it. The critics, in many instances, have criticized our orchestras and musical shows, saying that they were too much like white orchestras or white shows. What we are up against is the fact that our music, our rhythm, our humor, has been pirated by the other races, and they are doing our stuff which was ours exclusively once.
>
> Then the critics say we are imitating the Nordics when we are only doing our own stuff.
>
> —Dave Peyton, "The Musical Bunch"

These observations, penned by musician and journalist Dave Peyton in 1928 for his weekly *Chicago Defender* column, "The Musical Bunch," outline one of cultural appropriation's most pernicious effects well before that term was broadly applied to the phenomenon. As Peyton outlines the situation, not only were they siphoning work from Black musicians but white musicians' omnipresence as the leading purveyors of musics developed by Black Americans was also fostering an insidious transfer of ownership in the public consciousness whereby Black musicians were painted as interlopers or imitators for performing their own music. Yet, after hearing a 1926 performance of Gershwin's *Rhapsody in Blue* by the Paul Whiteman Orchestra, Peyton entreated his fellow Black musicians thus:

> Those of our group of musicians who find it possible should sacrifice the time to hear this orchestra. There is much to be learned from this group of distinctive musicians. It will do some of our would-be leaders a world of good. They will see in Whiteman an artistic baton man. Every move means something: coloring and painting a score needs more than the waving of the baton. Whiteman has it, and as the creator of the present-day style of syncopation he still remains master.[1]

This effusive praise for Whiteman, crediting him as both "creator" and "master" of the style of tightly organized symphonic jazz Peyton admired, would seem on face to undercut or at least temper his views on race and cultural ownership. Yet, crucial to Peyton's wording here is the word "still" in "he still remains master." In outlining both the achievements of and advantages enjoyed by white orchestras, Peyton situates Whiteman's band as, on the one hand, an orchestra to emulate and, on the other, a group that could readily be surpassed by Black musicians if sufficiently dedicated, driven, and disciplined. His praise for Whiteman and other white bandleaders was both a genuine expression of his own taste and a call to arms for Black musicians to collectively reclaim their birthright as leaders in American popular music, which he was convinced they could do through disciplined practice and dedication to craft.

In a 2018 article for the journal *Jazz & Culture*, I highlight Peyton's complex treatment of Whiteman as part of a broader study of Whiteman's reception in the Black press. There, I argue that Black newspaper writers' diverse, nuanced perspectives on Whiteman and his role in the field of jazz should not undercut or soften later critiques that position him in a lineage of commercially successful white appropriators of Black music but that they should caution us to avoid treating Black voices of the past monolithically, conscripting them to serve a particular narrative at the expense of honoring the range of individual points of view and complex layers of intracommunity discourse.[2] Although his subsequent legacy—steeped, quite understandably, in narratives of white privilege and cultural appropriation—might lead one to assume otherwise (and "one" certainly included myself before I undertook this line of research), during the 1920s and 1930s Whiteman and his music were broadly popular among Black musicians, critics, and fans. Celebrated Black bandleaders, most notably Duke Ellington and Fletcher Henderson, were strong admirers of Whiteman's band and their sound. Whiteman's performances in predominantly Black venues, though sporadic, were well attended and well received. Black critics offered praise in print for the band's significant success and for the quality and professionalism of their musical performances. Whiteman himself, in turn, was often supportive of his Black colleagues and of various fundraising initiatives in Black communities. At the same time, the grossly unequal opportunities afforded Black musicians relative to Whiteman's band and to white musicians, in general, were also relatively frequent topics of conversation in the Black press.

The perspectives of the numerous Black journalists, columnists, musicians, and intellectuals who opined on the Whiteman band in print were informed by a range of rhetorical goals, particular ideologies, and specific industry contexts such that each writer's perspective ought to be considered with attention to this level of specificity. Toward that end, I aim here to dive deeper into Peyton's writings, considering Peyton's discussion of Whiteman within the context of both his own broader career as a pianist, orchestra director, arranger, journalist, and community leader and the full expanse of his four-year run penning "The Musical Bunch." Peyton notably outlines a historical lineage of symphonic jazz music that includes a somewhat inconsistent treatment of the Whiteman orchestra. At times, he credits Paul Whiteman's work as meaningfully innovative but at others suggests Whiteman's output was merely derivative of Black orchestra leaders a decade prior, most notably, James Reese Europe. Rather than seek to reconcile these ostensible contradictions, this chapter places Peyton's sporadic yet significant discussion of Whiteman within his column's broader goals and discursive arcs.

Dave Peyton, Chicago's Music Scene, and the *Chicago Defender*

Dave Peyton was born in 1889, and, like many Black Chicagoans, he was a Southern migrant, having moved north from Louisiana. Both his parents were musicians, and his mother, Anna, was also, per the *Defender*, "a leader in Chicago civic and social life."[3] After balancing his musical career with a position as a postal worker, Peyton began his professional career in 1908 with Poney Moore's Burlesque Show and played piano in Wilbur Sweatman's trio from 1908 to 1912.[4] While working as a professional musician, Peyton also engaged in formal study of harmony and counterpoint, earning—per a writeup in *Musical Enterprise* and republished in the *Defender*—a doctorate from the American College of Music in 1911.[5] As a bandleader, Peyton was a mainstay along "the Stroll," the hub of Black nightlife in Chicago during the 1910s, taking over as bandleader at the Grand Theater in 1912.[6] As leader of the house band at the Grand, Peyton built a strong reputation, and a *Defender* columnist reported in 1913 that "in passing, too much praise cannot be given the members of the orchestra, they are artists each and every one of them, and Dave Peyton as a director is unsurpassed."[7] This columnist praised Peyton's "able leadership" and readily acknowledged that Peyton's orchestra at the Grand was "recognized as the best in the city."[8] These sentiments were echoed two years later by Tony Langston, who reported, "Prof. Dave Peyton, the leader of the Grand Orchestra, is doing a great deal of work for such high-class artists on big time as Belle Oliver and Elizabeth Murray. He is doing constructive work for big orchestras and big time people."[9] Advertising in the *Defender* shows that Peyton had a run at the Sunset Café in late 1921 with his "Clef Club Orchestra," and beginning in 1922, appearances at the Grand begin billing "Dave Peyton's 'Jazz' Boys."[10] Around this time, he was also performing his own arrangements at the Grand to accompany silent films.[11] In 1923 a *Defender* reviewer praised Peyton's seven-piece Grand Theater orchestra both for punching above its weight for its size and for its stylistic range across a spectrum of genres. Of the orchestra, this reviewer observed,

> Dave has demonstrated that a band of symphony size is not absolutely necessary in the delivery of the goods, providing those selected are up to snuff, and as appropriate a name as the one carried would be "A Half Dozen Red Hots." No matter the type of music discoursed, be it the jazziest sort of jazz or the most appealing sort of classic, it is all the same to these boys and the fact that time after time in open competition they have "mopped" against all comers should be sufficient proof that they are away out in front, in a class by themselves.[12]

In approaching what was increasingly referred to as jazz, Peyton's band exhibited the sort of musical versatility—a versatility he notably developed contemporaneously with Whiteman's early career rather than in its wake—for which he would later advocate in his columns.

While working as an orchestra leader, Peyton had a parallel career as a sought-after arranger. Not long after taking up his position at the Grand Theater, Peyton was also running a business on State Street dealing in popular song. A series of 1913 *Defender* advertisements for Dave Peyton's Song Shop bill the establishment as a "Leading Dealer in Popular Music" that also offered the following services: "Orchestrations written, songs taken from voice, acts written and rehearsed."[13] In 1915 he moved from State Street to the Randolph Building in Chicago's Loop District to begin an exclusive arranging contract with the Watterson-Berlin-Snyder Music Company, moving to the firm of Williams and Piron in 1920.[14] He maintained this practice throughout the 1920s, such that the *Defender* would report in 1929, "In Chicago he maintains elaborate offices in the heart of the Loop, where he specializes in arranging for big time stage stars and musical comedy shows."[15] Peyton continued to lead the Grand Theater Orchestra throughout the 1920s, leaving in 1928 for the newly built Regal Theater as the focus of Chicago's South Side nightlife shifted from the Stroll on State Steet to the corner of Forty-Seventh Street and South Parkway, when a number of major theaters opened along that intersection.[16]

Peyton's long residency at the Grand, lasting well into the 1920s, places him as an important figure in the musical life of the Stroll, a strip of State Street on Chicago's south side that came to be the hub of community life in Chicago's "Black Belt" during the 1910s. Roughly coterminous with the flourishing of Peyton's career as a bandleader was a massive influx of new Black migrants to the city, largely within this neighborhood. Peyton's role as a respected orchestra leader likely positioned him as an important and respected voice in the city's Black community and the emergent New Negro movement. As Davarian Baldwin has argued, despite some associations with vice and lower-class entertainment, even those Black Chicagoans with misgivings about State Street's nightlife "had to concede that the music clubs, movie theaters, beauty parlors, and 'sporting dens' on the stroll were some of the most popular and profitable institutions in the community and so ultimately became the structural foundation of Chicago's New Negro intellectual life."[17] This vital connection between Black nightlife and intellectual discourse only grew in the 1920s with jazz as one of its central objects of discussion, for, as Stephanie Doktor points out, "Just as jazz altered conversations about musical representations of blackness, the New Negro Renaissance impacted how people responded to racial inequality, especially through art."[18] Active as a musician throughout the 1920s, Peyton began penning "The Musical Bunch" in 1925. During this time, Peyton was also director of the Tempo Club, an organization of seventy-five Chicago musicians whose purpose and structure look to have been modeled closely on that of the Clef Club under James Reese Europe a decade prior.[19]

Peyton's association with the New Negro ideology of Chicago's Black middle class certainly aligned him with the disposition and mission of the *Chicago Defender*. Launched in 1905, not long before Peyton's professional music career began, the *Chicago Defender* had, by the 1920s, become the most significant and widely circulated Black newspaper nationwide, thanks largely to its founder Robert S. Abbott and, as Lawrence Schenbeck describes it, his "ceaseless personal effort and especially his canny combination of racial advocacy and tabloid techniques."[20] In the 1920s the *Defender* bolstered its coverage of music and popular entertainment as it, in Michelle R. Scott's words, "evolved into a long-lasting national repository of Black entertainment happenings."[21] Peyton's column debuted in September 1925 as a trade column targeted toward the needs and interests of professional musicians. Peyton begins his first column, "In an effort to further the service of this paper to our readers this new column will be devoted to the interest of our professional musicians, endeavoring to give from week to week correct information concerning the gloom-chasing squad."[22] By 1926 he was also serving as the *Defender*'s theatrical editor, and he claimed in 1928 that thirty-thousand musicians read his weekly column.[23] While I have yet to uncover more details surrounding the specific circumstances that led to Peyton's tenure as a *Defender* columnist and editor, his long-standing success, prominence, and reputation as a leader in Black Chicago's music community would have made his an attractive voice to feature on the *Defender*'s pages. As Schenbeck speculates of Peyton's appeal to the paper's founder, "Abbott had undoubtedly discerned in Peyton not only a practical musician and a strong 'race man' but also someone firmly committed to a message of 'uplift': a man could improve himself, obtain and keep gainful employment, *and* be a good example to others."[24] Schenbeck's assessment is quite plausible, especially given that being a "good example to others" included not only current Black residents of Chicago but also those living in the South, as part of the paper's mission under Abbott to encourage Black migration to the city. As Mark K. Dolan explains, featuring the voices of successful Black migrants aided the paper in this mission, "by providing evidence of personal, and thus representative, success—stories of individuals who had 'made it' through hard work, strong character and sound investments."[25] Peyton's column thus held a particular position within the *Defender*'s pages as his aesthetic views broadly supported a racial uplift-driven preference for the aesthetics of classical music in alignment with those of the paper's other music writers, yet his pragmatism as a working musician himself—and one keen to both promote himself and his peers and to guide aspiring musicians toward professional success—would often lead him to a notably more sympathetic position toward popular entertainment in general and jazz music in particular.

Placing "Jazz" in Peyton's Aesthetic System

"What is so great about the Paul Whitman [*sic*], Abe Lyman, Vincent Lopez and many other crack orchestras? It is soft playing, sweet and hot. The barbarous blasting day has gone."[26] This 1927 evocation of Whiteman's band and other "crack orchestras" is fairly typical of Peyton's musical rhetoric, yet the broader aesthetic system underwriting it can be more difficult to pin down. What is clear is that Peyton enjoyed a style of what he called "polite syncopation": orchestrated music performed by classically trained musicians reading from a score. He regarded Whiteman's band as among his favorites performing this "polite syncopation," though he certainly did not credit the style exclusively to Whiteman or to white orchestras, frequently positioning Black bandleaders such as Henderson, Sam Wooding, Erskine Tate, Fess Williams, and Will Marion Cook as equally strong or stronger in his favorite style.[27] Regarding jazz music specifically, Peyton both wrote proudly of jazz's origins in Black cultural practices from the rural South and produced passages such as this one: "Standard music, or what is commonly called 'classics,' is the genuine goods. To jazz music it is what real country butter is to butterine."[28] In his entry on Peyton for *American National Biography*, Barry Kernfeld writes of Peyton's *Defender* columns, "He is considered by some as having been the leading publicist for the city's African-American jazz establishment, aiming to gain acceptance by the white middle class." Earlier in his writeup, however, Kernfeld says of Peyton's writings that he principally "preached his belief in the superiority of European classical music, and he advocated a behavior associated with performers and listeners within that concert tradition."[29] This conflicted framing of Peyton's focus, advocacy goals, and disposition in "The Musical Bunch" in many ways reflects tensions within the column itself. Indeed, depending on the particular week of his column one reads, one might surmise that Peyton was either an enthusiastic fan of jazz or that he detested it. As Dolan has assessed Peyton's views, "In essence, Peyton welcomed jazz, but only jazz that resulted from strict training and the proper cultivation of sound. His discussion of [Louis] Armstrong during these years, however, showed Peyton was beginning to understand the music more on its own terms, suggesting his views were evolving at a slower pace than the music was advancing."[30] Though he makes space for Peyton's own conceptualization, Dolan's assessment of Peyton's work still charts a trajectory from a lesser-to-greater understanding of jazz and, together with his strong focus on Peyton's evolving disposition toward Louis Armstrong, reflects a dichotimization of "true" and "false" jazz both ahistorical to the 1920s and reflective of a rigid racial essentialism to which Peyton himself objected and that, Jeffrey Magee has observed, "diminishes the achievements of black and white musicians alike."[31] Of greater importance than whether Peyton enjoyed or valued jazz personally or, perhaps alternatively, the most critical part of approaching that very question, were the specific ways he defined and applied the term "jazz" across his writings. For, as John Howland has cautioned, the word "jazz" in the 1920s had a far less stable common meaning than it does today, and Peyton's writing on the subject both evinces and offers insight into this very instability.[32]

Peyton's disposition toward jazz in "The Musical Bunch" was forged through a mixture of pragmatic and aesthetic concerns. Indeed, where Catherine Tackley highlights some similar rhetoric among British critics in her contribution to the current volume—Peyton's preference for "polite syncopation" is well aligned with their praise for Whiteman's orchestra as "not the noisy stuff"—a notable difference between them and Peyton is that, as Tackley notes, these writers were largely theater critics rather than music professionals. Peyton, by contrast, was a highly experienced and educated bandleader and arranger—and a longtime advocate for the professional well-being of Chicago's Black musicians—whose writing was fundamentally grounded in that perspective. Broadly, Peyton did not object to jazz, even the sort of ostensibly disorganized "hokum" he may have personally disliked, as one style in which a competent professional musician should be able to play, noting across his columns its tremendous popularity and the need to be at least conversant in it. He worried, however, that focusing exclusively on jazz would lead to bad habits and ultimately limit one's opportunities. There were too many "lax musicians," he lamented, "who have been satisfied to bang away on so-called jazz, and have fallen in a rut that will take much time and study to get out of."[33] He expected that jazz would be a passing trend rather than a lasting genre, and he thus wanted to see Black musicians prepare for the time when jazz would, in his view, inevitably fall out of favor. He cautioned in 1928, "The jazz craze has been a wonderful innovation for the jazz musician, and at this time we cannot tell just how long it is going to last, so the jazz kings should make hay while the sun shines and save their money, and at the same time use their leisure time in studying real music. The tide may turn when we least expect. Better be ready."[34]

From the beginnings of his column in 1925, Peyton was convinced that the polyphonic small-combo music popularized in Chicago by New Orleans transplants such as King Joe Oliver and Armstrong (both of whom he consistently praised as soloists) had already peaked in popularity and was being replaced by music along the lines of the Fletcher Henderson Orchestra's output, which in his view required classical training to perform properly:

> The time is at hand when the musician must be qualified to do all phases of the art, because the modernizing of syncopation by the big arrangers and leaders has thrown a scare into the camp of mediocre musicians. This type has awakened to the fact that fake playing has gone into oblivion, there to remain.
>
> The modern score is so partitioned and the instrumentation so divided as to cause the players to register with one another. The melody goes along smoothly, and all of a sudden comes a "break" for a certain group of the instrumentation, oft-times as difficult as a passage in a symphony suite.[35]

Notably, Peyton places Henderson, whose orchestra he greatly admired, alongside other symphonic jazz musicians both past and present: "The style of jazz the public has gone wild about is that which Paul Whiteman,

Vincent Lopez, the late James Reese Europe, Leroy Smith and Fletcher Henderson's orchestras are putting out—beautiful melodies, garnished with eccentric figurations propelled by strict rhythm."[36] Indeed, Peyton's perception of "the modern score" and his prescriptions for musicians in many ways mirrored those of Whiteman, who claimed that "the modern jazz orchestra is an efficient arrangement. Every player knows exactly what he is to play every minute of the time. Even the smears are indicated in the music. Rehearsals are as thorough and as frequent as in any symphony. The discipline of the orchestra, if it is a good one, must be complete."[37] The spectrum of symphonic jazz for which Peyton advocated aligns not only with Whiteman's perspective but also with Howland's account of the genre as it was understood by a range of white and Black musicians, and Peyton's advocacy affirms Howland's assertions that "proponents of symphonic jazz sought to endow contemporary popular music with an aura of glamour and elevated cultural refinement" and that "symphonic jazz was intimately tied to American preoccupations with class and race."[38]

The "discordant music" to which Peyton refers here would, in a later column, become part of a more elaborate taxonomic model of jazz's ostensible progression toward a form of refined, artistic music. In 1928 he offered a historical taxonomy explaining that jazz grew out of ragtime music, first in the form of "discordant jazz." Peyton attributes this "discordant jazz" to the vocal groups and small instrumental combos of New Orleans, who "would select some tune the gang was familiar with and each person would blend in his or her part, producing counterpoints and fugues unconsciously."[39] Though Peyton expresses a romanticized admiration for this style, he also links it to bad playing habits among contemporary musicians, specifically citing trumpet players' tendency to produce "crude overblown tones."[40] This music, he goes on to claim, developed into "popular jazz," which he describes as primarily a composed or arranged form of music that necessitated notational literacy and classical training to play:

> The style of jazz playing today requires musicianship to handle it. There is no faking, every instrument has its part to perform. The expert arrangers, theorists, as a rule put the notes down on paper in partitioned effect for the sections of the orchestra. The players must be musicians to cut the stuff. Many times you run into grand opera figurations which require technical knowledge of the musicians. The beautiful melodies, garnished with difficult eccentric figures and propelled by artful rhythms, hold grip on the world today, replacing the mushy, discordant jazz music.[41]

His emphasis on the importance of notational literacy must also be seen in the context of long-standing issues of prejudice and constraint as well as the racial uplift–driven practices among his musical contemporaries both prior to and during the 1920s. Henderson was himself a strong advocate for music literacy, prompting a generation of Harlem musicians to learn to sight-read. As Jeffrey Magee explains, the Henderson band's reputation as a strong reading band was politically significant as "the mere sight of a black band reading from parts had a vivid impact on musicians and audiences of the early 1920s."[42] To fully appreciate this powerful symbolic significance, we must turn a decade earlier to the bands of James Reese Europe, whom Peyton admired as both a musician and a leader for race progress. As pianist Eubie Blake, one of the creators of the landmark musical *Shuffle Along*, recalled of his time with Europe's ensemble, Europe was an advocate for music literacy, yet he also pushed his musicians to perform, in David Gilbert's words, a "counterfeit innate musicality" by having his musicians, though highly proficient at sight-reading, memorize their music in order to accommodate the expectations of white patrons.[43] One wonders whether, as a contemporary of Europe's in the 1910s, Peyton himself had experienced a similarly painful negotiation.

Another driving force in Peyton's aesthetic system was his desire to recapture a period in time during the 1900s and 1910s during which, in his view, Black composers, arrangers, and musicians were more readily acknowledged as the originators and best purveyors of popular dance music. As he explains, "During the days when Scott Joplin's Maple Leaf Rag was the sensation of the country our musicians were the envy of the other race because we knew how to interpret what they called at that time 'ragtime.' Today they have dressed it up and call it 'modern jazz,' hiding the simple rag melody with pleasing but difficult symphonic phrases."[44] It may thus be instructive to look briefly at assessments of Peyton's own orchestra during the 1910s. Indeed, *Defender* columnist Carey B. Lewis's 1914 account of the first performance of Peyton's Grand Symphony Orchestra—a large ensemble in the style of James Reese Europe's bands—is illuminating regarding the racial uplift–driven media coverage Peyton himself experienced in the *Defender* as a performer:

> Home talent proved to be artists of the first water and their initial concert has been the initial cause of spreading a wholesome respect for art in the "Windy City." Music lovers packed the house. It was a most appreciative audience. The program varied and suited all classes. To Mr. Peyton is due the credit of gathering together forty or fifty of the best musicians and giving to the public of this city the best musicale in the history of Chicago. The success was not only due to the hospitable audience that listened patiently to the high-class program and artists, but to the fine work done by the orchestra, all of whom are men of ability and training.[45]

Here, Lewis praises Peyton for offering successfully the same type of program Peyton would himself later prescribe for jazz orchestras: dignified concert music, sufficiently varied to appeal to taste across class boundaries and through which the players' display of skill and professionalism reflected well on the Black community, in general.

In one 1929 column, Peyton compares two recordings of "St. Louis Blues," one by the Whiteman orchestra and another by an unnamed Black ensemble.[46] His review, well in line with his broader preference for symphonic "popular jazz" over "discordant jazz," shows a clear preference for the Whiteman rendition: "You can almost see four or five of our musicians blasting away, blowing any old kind of a note and getting all sorts of freakish, weird tones, and in the Whiteman record you appreciate the colorful modulations, the melodic predominance and artistic orchestration."[47] While this assessment is consistent with Peyton's broader admiration for the Whiteman orchestra and its style, his purpose in making this comparison is important, for he is neither claiming the Whiteman orchestra's recording is superior to how top Black ensembles *could* render this piece, nor is he even directly chastising the ensemble whose version he disliked, at least not for a lack of musical skill. Rather, he makes this comparison to reinforce his objection earlier in the column that Black bands and orchestras were often forced by record companies to play only in a style Peyton saw as below their skill level. Peyton wrote of the major record companies:

> They confine us to low jazz and blues. They have an idea that our orchestras cannot play real music for recordings, but they were never so wrong. . . . We are tired of listening to this degraded class of music played by our musicians. We want to hear fine arrangements played in theoretical style. We have the musicians and the proper instrumentations. Then why don't they give us the opportunity?[48]

I have previously quoted Peyton's assessment of these two "St. Louis Blues" recordings at length largely to reinforce his aesthetic admiration for the Whiteman orchestra as one model for Black musicians to emulate.[49] Though this assessment concords with Peyton's rhetoric in other columns, I now feel that my prior framing of this particular quotation did not account sufficiently for this aesthetic critique's broader context and purpose within the specific column in which it appeared. Although Peyton felt that *some* Black ensembles, perhaps, many, should aspire to the level of Whiteman's band, he also felt that a number of Black orchestras were already Whiteman's equal or had surpassed him, though the recording industry continued to limit them to a style Peyton regarded as inferior. In highlighting this inequity and the racialized misperceptions to which it contributed, Peyton anticipates a move in jazz studies in the 1990s and 2000s to decenter recordings as central artifacts where jazz historians, as Jeffrey Magee explains, "challenged the traditional emphasis on sound recordings as the primary source of material for the telling of jazz history, raising thoughtful questions about the recording bias of the jazz canon and about how the 'seductive menace' of records leads historians to construct artifices of musical evolution."[50]

Peyton, Jazz Historiography, and Cultural Ownership

Peyton himself sought throughout his column to correct such "artifices of musical evolution" by underscoring that not only were Black communities in the South the progenitors of the folk musics that formed jazz's roots but also that Black musicians were and long had been the best purveyors of the symphonic jazz music at the time associated with Whiteman and other white orchestra leaders. Peyton's 1928 column on the "origins of jazz," in which he parses the "discordant" from the "popular," also traces a more specific history that draws upon his own two decades of experience as a professional performer in Chicago along the Stroll. Here, Peyton first focuses his attention on composers and arrangers, tracing a line from Scott Joplin to Cook to J. Rosamond Johnson and then to W. C. Handy, James Reese Europe, Clarence Williams, and others.[51] In highlighting these orchestra leaders as the progenitors of symphonic jazz, Peyton offers a counternarrative to Whiteman's claim in his 1926 book *Jazz* that Whiteman himself was the first to orchestrate jazz music, a claim clearly not in keeping with Peyton's own experience as a bandleader and arranger.[52] Though he does not raise this point specifically, Peyton's deep admiration for Europe, who placed a heavy emphasis on notational literacy throughout his leadership of the Clef Club, likely placed him at odds with Whiteman's claim, "Faking was what the early jazz orchestras relied upon. That is, they had no scores, each man working out his part for himself, 'faking' as he went along," a position Peyton may have felt particularly motivated to provide a counternarrative to given the historical pressure discussed above for Black ensembles to conform to this stereotype.[53] Where Mario Dunkel has argued, "By making the history of jazz a teleological history of jazz composing and arranging, Whiteman expropriated the music from improvising, mostly black musicians," Peyton's telling of jazz's history highlights the erasure of jazz composing's and arranging's Black progenitors in Whiteman's narrative.[54]

Even in the section of this column devoted to solo instrumentalists, Peyton identifies a group of pioneers "before Whiteman" who "put syncopation before the public and who deserve as much credit as the composers because without them the works would have gained no publicity."[55] Though at first he lists white musicians exclusively in this category (Ted Lewis, Isham Jones, Paul Biese, Rudy Weidoeft, Paul Specht, and Ben Bernie), Peyton goes on to credit Black clarinetist Wilbur Sweatman for having predated them. Drawing from his own experience as a Chicago musician and, indeed, a member of Sweatman's trio, he goes as far as to credit Sweatman as jazz's true originator, noting of a run of 1905 Chicago performances:

> This writer truly believes Wilbur Sweatman was the creator of jazz music. White musicians would come to this theater from far and near to hear this little freak orchestra. He would moan his tones, shriek them, and all of a sudden in rhythm would rapidly play difficult figures in syncopated mood. This style of playing was adopted by the white musicians and I do not believe any of the authorities on jazz know of this period and of Mr. Sweatman's activities at that time. Nevertheless it is very true and this writer takes the responsibility of handing to Wilbur Sweatman the crown as the creator of real jazz music.[56]

In praising symphonic jazz music, Peyton remarks, "In America the symphonic jazz will live, and it requires real musicians to play it. It is now standard music with the American people, and I am proud to say that our Race are standout factors in its development."[57] Looking even farther back in history to make his point, Peyton explicitly states, referring to the year 1619, that the musical forms and ideas brought to the United States by enslaved Africans "served to form the foundation of present day American music." He further observes, "The Nordics have claimed ragtime, jazz, and the symphony, not wanting to give us credit for anything creative. They would want to see us imitators, but in spite of this condition our music carries its traits and stands out prominently today throughout the civilized world."[58] While Peyton's language here may align literally with the beginning of Whiteman's *Jazz*, which also refers to the year 1619 as the time when, as Whiteman claims in the book's opening sentence, "Jazz came to America three hundred years ago in chains," his purpose is not to credit Black musicians only as jazz's originators but also as the tradition's present day inheritors and those chiefly responsible for its present and future development.[59]

Peyton's historiographic interventions on behalf of jazz's Black pioneers went hand in hand with his explicit discussion of unequal opportunity in the music field. He draws upon both historiographic argument and commentary on contemporary conditions in a 1927 response to "The Colored Brother," a piece by H. L. Mencken in which Mencken was largely dismissive of Black American contributions to the field of music. In response to the credit

Mencken affords Whiteman for his performance of *Rhapsody in Blue*, Peyton positions James Reese Europe as the unsung progenitor of symphonic jazz, directly contesting Mencken's crediting of Whiteman with elevating jazz's stature.

> Now I am going back to the period just after the World war. James Reese Europe and his famous "Hell Fighters" band and orchestra was the first musical organization to give the world the now popular syncopation. If fate had not taken this great musician away at a time when he was just beginning his career, there would be no Lopezes and Whitemans today. Jim Europe, as the musicians called him, was idolized by millionaires, who were his supporters. Jim Europe was the first to conceive the exaggeration of syncopated music and ably demonstrated it with his scores played by the famous "Hell Fighters" band. Mr. Mencken states that Paul Whiteman was the first to make "jazz" a serious matter and on this point this writer is forced to disagree with him.[60]

It's important to underscore the fact that as a musician, Peyton was a contemporary of Europe's. When Peyton launched the thirty-piece Grand Symphony Orchestra in 1914, the *Defender* commented that in founding this ensemble, Peyton would "demonstrate that musicians can do here what James Reese Europe is doing in New York."[61]

Peyton was not only an admirer of James Reese Europe's music but also of his advocacy toward creating opportunities and improving working conditions for Black musicians. In his rebuttal to Mencken, Peyton also writes, "He claims that Race musicians['] opportunities have been precisely equal in the field of music as those of whites. This is very untrue. I know of our composers who have labored in the creation of some musical composition and have finished it, only to find the market closed to them in publication."[62] Indeed, early in his column's run, Peyton began speaking directly to issues of structural racism in the booking process for popular orchestras. While there was significant demand among the general public to hire Black musicians, Peyton claims, "The white musical booking agencies are trying to keep Race musicians out of the lilly-white [*sic*] field."[63] Peyton argues that these white booking agents had traded upon numerous stereotypes associated with Black musicians to erode a broad public interest in Black ensembles during the 1910s and replace it with a state of affairs in the 1920s: "White units, and many of them very mediocre, are getting the bulk of the work, while we have fine combinations on the loafers' bench."[64] Peyton makes clear that he was actively working to address this issue by helping to meet the demand for Black ensembles, and his frequent notes—directed explicitly toward Black musicians—regarding the importance of professionalism as a means of countering stereotypes recall James Reese Europe's work with the Clef Club during the 1910s.[65]

Rhapsody in Blue and Envisioning Jazz's Operatic Future

Trading on both his own experience and James Reese Europe's Clef Club model, Peyton felt that versatility was the key to Black musicians' success and an area where Black musicians distinguished themselves from white musicians owing to the work ethic demanded and greater levels of proficiency required of Black musicians to succeed in a racist system: "Among our Race group of musicians, versatility is the watchword. We have outclassed the Nordic musicians in this respect. I suppose it is because our field is so limited and in order to keep the wolf away from the door we study more in order to hold our jobs."[66] Peyton held that Black musicians were best suited to lead the charge in developing jazz music into a form for larger-scale concert works, such as symphonies and operas, in many ways paralleling Whiteman's own claim, "If jazz does not develop its own theme, its own distinctive language, it will fail to be musically valuable," yet positioning Black musicians as the only ones capable of authentically realizing such a goal.[67] In an article suggesting a turn toward writing jazz operas, which he expected would follow jazz symphonies in elevating the music, Peyton expresses confidence that it would be a Black musician to write one, believing that in this task, white musicians and arrangers would have met the limits of their capability.

> Our white brothers have taken many of our ideas musically and have successfully commercialized them, but this time I am afraid they are up against it. They have written many mechanical, theoretical and melodious jazz numbers, but this "jazz opera" will be written by our Race writers, who alone understand the harmonic and melodic qualities that will give the creation originality.[68]

Although he credited Gershwin's *Rhapsody in Blue* with opening the door to this opportunity, his feelings about the piece itself were lukewarm at best. In 1927 Peyton commented several times on *Rhapsody in Blue* both regarding the piece itself and its association with, and performances by, the Whiteman Orchestra. His first significant discussion of the work came in 1927 in the aforementioned response to Mencken. Here, Peyton responds to Mencken's taking Black musicians to task over Gershwin's *Rhapsody in Blue*, chastising them for, as Peyton paraphrases Mencken's critique, "allowing this musician, who is a white man, to beat us to it, in the writing of this style of music."[69] In response, Peyton effectively takes up Mencken's evocation of *Rhapsody in Blue* to challenge the very notion that Gershwin, or any other white musician, "beat them to it":

> It is true that "Rhapsody in Blue" has merit, beyond a doubt, but in its construction is nothing new, nothing has been created in it. It is only a

> harmoniously flowered theme, with numerous cadences, a book of intense monotony, full of weird shrieks and barbaric expressions.
>
> The basic theme of Geo. Gershwin's "Rhapsody in Blue" is very common among our group of musicians. Every fake piano player has played it for years. He has taken this theme and colored it with theoretical musical phrases, and with the proper exploitation has nationally popularized it.[70]

He further attributes the work's popularity to the simple fact that "Paul Whiteman exploited the piece for Mr. Gershwin with his orchestra."[71]

Peyton would single out this work and Gershwin's approach, more broadly, to encourage Black composers and arrangers to outdo him and for Black musicians to "exploit" their own musical traditions in a manner similar to Whiteman's performances of *Rhapsody in Blue*.

> It would be a fine idea for some of the younger musical theorists to compose an operetta based on the spirituals. It would be an original classic and this writer believes such a creation would startle the country.
>
> Look what Gershwin's "Rhapsody in Blue" did. There is nothing meritorious in the work. It is just a conglomeration of harmonic expressions with an almost hidden thematic basis.[72]

It makes sense that Peyton's turn toward downplaying *Rhapsody in Blue*'s merits as a composition, as well as his encouragement that Black composers and musicians seize the opportunity to produce superior work in its style, would occur in mid- to late 1927 given the renewed commercial interest in the piece sparked by the Whiteman Orchestra's April 1927 recording. This new rendering, benefiting from advancements in recording technology, sold nearly twenty-thousand copies in the second quarter of 1927 alone and prompted multiple new recordings of the work from other orchestras.[73] It is also possible that Peyton, as a savvy industry insider, could have recognized and objected to what Ryan Raul Bañagale identifies as the "racialized marketing techniques" through which a subsequent 1927 release by Victor Irwin (aka Irwin Abrams) was marketed by Columbia Records. As Bañagale argues, their marketing strategy for this recording "caters to the notion that the *Rhapsody* and its symphonic-jazz mode appealed exclusively to white performers and audiences."[74] Whether or not Peyton picked up on and objected to this particular marketing nuance, it seems clear that his broader disposition toward the work's resurgence in popularity aligns with Bañagale's critique, given Peyton's broader efforts to position Black composers and bandleaders as the long-standing best exponents of the type of symphonic renderings of syncopated themes with which Gershwin, Whiteman, and a host of other white musicians and composers found financial success and public acclaim.

Peyton's perception of a trend toward jazz symphonies that could present Black musicians with substantial opportunity was not sparked exclusively by renewed interest in *Rhapsody in Blue*. He was likely also responding to the news that Handy's orchestra had been tapped to perform George Antheil's 1925 *A Jazz Symphony*, following Whiteman's decision not to program the work. Peyton celebrated this development, which, he wrote, "affords the first opportunity Colored musicians have had to interpret an ultra-modern score which contains unheard of harmonies and almost impossible rhythms."[75] He also offers praise for the work and its composer, whom he specifically identifies as white, noting of the piece: "Underlying all is a beauty which could only be produced by the imagination of this creative young genius, George Anthiel [*sic*]."[76] He thus entreats his fellow Black composers and musicians to seize this public interest in jazz-based symphonies:

> Just a hint to our composers: Let's get busy and compose some jazz symphonies. The white brother is running ahead of us. They are taking Jazz themes and expressions and are writing jazz symphonies on them. They are commercializing them. They have awakened the American public to like this new form of music. We are the originators of real syncopation and held the fort until now. Then why should we go to sleep now and let our own music be developed into the symphonic atmosphere when we have theorists in music that are just as capable as anyone in the world.[77]

His call was answered that very year by James P. Johnson's *Yamekraw*, which Peyton praised both for its artistic merits and for its capacity to inspire other Black composers as a work by a prominent Black jazz musician and published by Perry Bradford, a Black songwriter and publisher.[78] Of *Yamekraw*, which Peyton reported Johnson personally sent him an autograph copy of, he said, "Every one of our musicians should have a copy of 'Yamekraw' in the library. . . . Let us show Gershwin that we, the originators of syncopation, can write jazz operas, which will very soon be as popular as the old standard operas."[79] In singling out Gershwin, Peyton picks up on what Howland later argues: that *Yamekraw* was both "a unique African American parallel—and a musical response—to Gershwin's *Rhapsody in Blue*."[80] The following year, Peyton celebrates the premiere of Harry Lawrence Freeman's opera *Voodoo*, noting that it took the composer fourteen years to see it staged, having written the work in 1914.[81] Elsewhere in that same column, Peyton decries the racist stereotypes that blocked Black musicians from opportunity, and he offers solutions to collectively fight them. His words in stressing the urgent necessity of collective action are also instructive regarding his impetus to push for jazz symphonies and operas that would both transgress stereotypes and create opportunities for Black musicians: "The music game is my means of livelihood; it is your means, and we should all band together to protect it."[82]

Conclusion

Though in responding to Mencken, Peyton downplayed the significance of *Rhapsody in Blue* as a composition, when Whiteman performed the piece in Chicago in 1926, as this chapter's introduction discusses, Peyton was effusive in his praise for the bandleader and even for the piece itself. As he wrote of Whiteman's directing, of Gershwin's music, and of Ferde Grofé's arranging: "The barbaric effects that the arranger gets from the instrumentation is unimaginable. The orchestration certainly is a work of genius. The direction of the score by Mr. Whiteman absorbs his very soul. When the number is finished, his face is flushed, every muscle in his huge frame having been exerted by the master conductor in the interpretation of the piece."[83] Indeed, even after accounting for differences in what was regarded as "jazz" between his time and the present, Peyton's writing is riddled with seeming contradictions. Dolan connects Peyton's conflicted and at times contradictory disposition toward jazz music with a broader tension in the *Defender* between what he calls "traditional uplift" and a turn toward "emotive" or "cathartic" uplift.[84] Certainly, this would parallel the broader generational tensions among Black intellectuals in their dispositions toward jazz in the late 1920s, often framed through the discordance between W. E. B. Du Bois's and Langston Hughes's perspectives on Black music and culture, but this tells only part of the story.[85] Equally important considerations are Peyton's audience and his strategic rhetorical goals, as he spoke truth about both the structural racism facing Black musicians and the omnipresence of pernicious racial stereotypes and also about both personal behavior and musical aesthetics. At the same time, he entreated the Black musicians who read his column to be hypervigilant in their professional deportment and their playing to defy these erroneous prejudices.

Regarding white bandleaders, he expressed no personal resentment toward Whiteman, Lopez, Guy Lombardo, Ted Lewis, and other successful white leaders of jazz orchestras. Indeed, Peyton frequently praised their performances and held them up as models of both successful business practices and serious musicianship.[86] While he may have praised some of them for their excellence, even considering them exemplary, he sought to correct any misperception that they had created the style of music they presented or were its greatest performers. In tracing a longer history of arranged, syncopated music, he sought to resist white-centered narratives of jazz's ostensible "development" into an arranged form of orchestral music, including Whiteman's own claim to have been the first jazz orchestrator, by explicitly crediting those Black innovators who were doing this syncopated orchestral work long before the music was called "jazz."

As he makes explicit in his column, "My constructive criticisms are not aimed at any one personally or at any one particular group. They are intended to cover the music field and right the bad conditions that have heretofore existed."[87] In making this claim, Peyton's column resonates with current conversations seeking to shift discussions of racism away from the behavior or beliefs of individuals and toward a focus on dismantling oppression at a structural level.[88] Writing about Whiteman can be a vexing task for many reasons, but one among them is certainly the concern that, given his symbolic prominence as an iconic cultural appropriator in jazz and popular music discourse, offering a nuanced treatment of the complexities of his career and reception or, indeed, paying him any close attention at all may reinforce the very structures of privilege and oppression that created the conditions of possibility for his prominence in the first place. More disconcerting is the possibility that one's discussion of Whiteman could be pulled into the rhetorical gravity of deeply misguided, reactionary "reverse racism" advocacy for ostensibly maligned white jazz musicians. In my 2018 piece, I sought to thread this needle by simply naming these dynamics and my own intentions explicitly.[89] As the value of "intention" inevitably crumbles under the tangible weight of impact, perhaps another—arguably better—path may be found in not only honoring the complexity of Black critical voices of the 1920s but by learning substantively from the models they present. As Peyton's work demonstrates, neither personal nor aesthetic admiration need be understood to blunt the force of structural critique.

Notes

1. Peyton, "Musical Bunch: Things in General," December 4, 1926, 5.

2. Wells, "Ace of His Race."

3. "Dave Peyton on 2 Weeks Trip East."

4. Kernfeld, "Peyton, Dave."

5. Nome, "Dave Peyton." The American College of Music likely refers to an institution founded in 1884, where organist Edward Morris Bowman served as president. Though a correspondence school founded in 1906 in Kansas City, Missouri, by Flora E. McCurdy also bears this name, that school seems to have had fairly limited, rudimentary offerings where an 1875 *New York Times* article regarding plans for the former institution specifies, "The Degree of Doctor of Music will be established and conferred upon students who may be qualified to receive it." The 1884 American College of Music is discussed in "American College of Music" and Hubbard, *American History and Encyclopedia of Music*, 1:90–91. The 1906 correspondence school is discussed in Vogel, "Are You Only an Applauder?" 449, 453–54.

6. Nome, "Dave Peyton."

7. "Musical and Dramatic," . . . April 26, 1913.

8. "Musical and Dramatic," . . . June 14, 1913.

9. Langston, "Theatrical Review."

10. Sunset Café ads ran weekly in the *Chicago Defender* from October from to December 1921. "Jazz Boys."

11. "Feature Picture at the Grand."

12. "Famous Bunch."

13. Advertisements for Dave Peyton's Song Shop, *Chicago Defender*, November 29 and December 6, 1913, 6.

14. "Peyton, the Music Wonder"; "In the Loop."

15. "Dave Peyton on 2 Weeks Trip East."

16. "Chicago Theatrical News."

17. Baldwin, *Chicago's New Negroes*, 30.

18. Doktor, "Jazz Problem," 40.

19. "Tempo Club Show." I say "looks to have been" similar to the Clef Club as there is relatively little coverage of this organization that I have found. Peyton discusses the Tempo Club further in his columns in late 1927 and early 1928, identifying himself still as its president in his January 6, 1928, column and claiming that the group was seeking to establish a fund to support musicians in failing health where the musicians' union fell short. The Tempo Club's size and structure as outlined in the 1924 "Tempo Club Show" story and Peyton's long-standing admiration for James Reese Europe as both a bandleader and an advocate and organizer on behalf of Black musicians lead me to draw this parallel between their two organizations.

20. Schenbeck, "Music, Gender, and 'Uplift,'" 345.

21. Scott, "To Help Enlighten Our People," 59.

22. Peyton, "The Musical Bunch," September 26, 1925, 7.

23. "Big Benefits Planned"; Dave Peyton, "The Musical Bunch: Things in General," September 1, 1928, 6.

24. Schenbeck, "Music, Gender, and 'Uplift,'" 349.

25. Dolan, "Cathartic Uplift," 6.

26. Dave Peyton, "The Musical Bunch: Things in General," May 28, 1927, 6.

27. Wells, "Ace of His Race," 87–88.

28. Peyton, "The Musical Bunch: Standard Music," June 5, 1926, 6.

29. Kernfeld, "Peyton, Dave."

30. Dolan, "Cathartic Uplift," 111–12. Stephanie Doktor echoes this appraisal of Peyton's trajectory toward a greater understanding of and appreciation for jazz in "Jazz Problem," 20.

31. Magee, "Before Louis," 392.

32. Howland, "Between the Muses and the Masses, 2.

33. Peyton, "The Musical Bunch: The Harlem Symphony Orchestra," November 21, 1925, 6.

34. Peyton, "The Musical Bunch: Things in General," June 30, 1928, 6.

35. Peyton, "The Musical Bunch: The Modern Musician," October 24, 1925, 6.

36. Peyton, "The Musical Bunch: The Jazz-Crazed Public," February 27, 1926, 6.

37. Whiteman and McBride, *Jazz*, 211.

38. Howland, *Ellington Uptown*, 2, 3.

39. Peyton, "Musical Bunch: Things in General," March 10, 1928, 6. Dolan also discusses this column, and where he feels Peyton uses the term "discordant jazz" to refer to "the improvisational elements of jazz," to me it seems more likely, considered alongside his other writing, that he is referring more to musical dissonances in polyphonic jazz and to nonstandard timbres he felt evinced poor instrumental technique. Dolan, "Cathartic Uplift," 123–24.

40. Peyton, "Musical Bunch: Things in General," March 10, 1928, 6.

41. Peyton, "Musical Bunch: Things in General," March 10, 1928, 6.

42. Jeffrey Magee, *Uncrowned King of Swing*, 29.

43. Gilbert, "Clef Club Inc.," 440.

44. Peyton, "Musical Bunch: The Modern Musician," October 24, 1925, 6. As Dolan astutely points out, it is unclear in this passage whether the "they" refers to white musicians, contemporary Black jazz musicians, or both. Dolan, "Cathartic Uplift," 125.

45. Lewis, "Symphony Concert."

46. Peyton, "Musical Bunch: Things in General," March 9, 1929, 6.

47. Peyton, "Musical Bunch: Things in General," March 9, 1929, 6.

48. Peyton, "Musical Bunch: Things in General," March 9, 1929, 6. As Chadwick Hansen astutely points out, Peyton also expresses this sentiment in his positive reviews of Fess Williams's sweet recordings. Hansen, "Social Influences on Jazz Style," 500.

49. Wells, "Ace of His Race," 88–89.

50. Magee, *Uncrowned King of Swing*, 8. Magee draws the term "seductive menace" from Jed Rasula's piece "The Media of Memory: The Seductive Menace of Records in Jazz History," in *Jazz among the Discourses*, ed. Krin Gabbard (Durham: Duke University Press, 1995), 134–64.

51. Peyton, "Musical Bunch: The Origin of Jazz," June 16, 1928, 6.

52. Whiteman and McBride, *Jazz*, 20, 39. Peyton reported in his column of May 22, 1926, that he had received a copy of Whiteman's book and that a review would be forthcoming in his next column. However, Whiteman's book is not the direct subject of his May 29 column, nor have I otherwise managed to locate such a review.

53. Whiteman and McBride, *Jazz*, 39.

54. Dunkel, *Stories of Jazz*, 62.

55. Peyton, "Musical Bunch: The Origin of Jazz," June 16, 1928, 6.

56. Peyton, "Musical Bunch: The Origin of Jazz," June 16, 1928, 6. Peyton identifies himself as the pianist in Sweatman's Grand Theatre trio in his column of June 30, 1928.

57. Peyton, "Musical Bunch: The Jazz-Crazed Public," February 27, 1926, 6.

58. Peyton, "Musical Bunch: Things in General," August 11, 1928, 6.

59. Whiteman and McBride, *Jazz*, 1. The Black American poet Alice Dunbar Nelson cited this opening passage of Whiteman's book in her July 3, 1926, column for the *Pittsburgh (PA) Courier*, commending Whiteman for departing from his

white contemporaries in explicitly crediting Black people as jazz's originators. I discuss this in Wells, "Ace of His Race," 90–91.

60. Peyton, "Musical Bunch: Things in General," July 30, 1927, 6.

61. "Musical and Dramatic," *Chicago Defender*, November 14, 1914, 6.

62. Peyton, "Musical Bunch: Things in General," July 30, 1927, 6.

63. Peyton, "Musical Bunch: Great Demand for Race Musicians," October 31, 1925, 6.

64. Peyton, "Musical Bunch: Things in General," December 29, 1928, 6.

65. Europe's efforts are discussed extensively in Gilbert, "Clef Club Inc."

66. Peyton, "Musical Bunch: Things in General," March 24, 1928, 6.

67. Whiteman and McBride, *Jazz*, 117.

68. Peyton, "Musical Bunch: Jazz-Opera," January 16, 1926, 6.

69. Peyton, "Musical Bunch: Things in General," July 30, 1927, 6.

70. Peyton, "Musical Bunch: Things in General," July 30, 1927, 6.

71. Peyton, "Musical Bunch: Things in General," July 30, 1927, 6. It is worth noting here that "exploitation" in the entertainment industry had a broader meaning at this time that was not necessarily pejorative.

72. Peyton, "Musical Bunch: Things in General," October 22, 1927, 6.

73. Bañagale, *Arranging Gershwin*, 49–52.

74. Bañagale, *Arranging Gershwin*, 52. This marketing strategy, as Bañagale details it, involved Columbia's decision to release the work under Abrams's pseudonym Victor Irwin, normally used on recordings for "race label" Okeh records, which Columbia had recently acquired, but under its Harmony imprint.

75. Peyton, "Musical Bunch: Opens Door," April 9, 1927, 6.

76. Peyton, "Musical Bunch: Opens Door," April 9, 1927, 6.

77. Peyton, "Musical Bunch: Things in General," April 30, 1927, 6.

78. Peyton, "Musical Bunch: Things in General," December 10, 1927, 6.

79. Peyton, "Musical Bunch: Things in General," December 10, 1927, 6.

80. Howland, "Jazz Rhapsodies in Black and White," 447. Indeed, Peyton's concerns also proved prescient as Gershwin's 1935 *Porgy and Bess* would, problematically, rise to far more prominence as an operatic representation of Black life in the works of Harry Lawrence Freeman, James P. Johnson, Scott Joplin, Still, and other Black composers.

81. Peyton, "Musical Bunch: Things in General," September 29, 1928, 6.

82. Peyton, "Musical Bunch: Things in General," September 29, 1928, 6.

83. Peyton, "Musical Bunch: Things in General," December 4, 1926, 5.

84. Dolan, "Cathartic Uplift," 40–41, 111–15.

85. Stephanie Doktor frames this as a distinction between Alain Locke and James Weldon Johnson, on the one hand, and Langston Hughes and Zora Neale Hurston, on the other. Doktor, "Jazz Problem," 39.

86. For example, in Peyton, "Musical Bunch," April 7, 1928, 6.

87. Peyton, "Musical Bunch: Things in General," October 20, 1928, 6.

88. Two pieces in popular media that summarize this discourse are Yancey-Bragg, "What Is Systemic Racism?" and King, "What Systemic Racism Means."

89. Wells, "Ace of His Race," 80–82, 97.

3

Paul Whiteman and Modern Metropolitan Music, 1927–40

JOHN HOWLAND

The phrase "Modern American Music" (MAM) was widely tied to the Paul Whiteman organization's promotion of the concert music repertory it commissioned and performed across the 1920s to 1940s, as well as to the stylistically hybrid sound of jazz-leaning, orchestrated popular music with concert-music scoring affectations. In this period, "Modern American Music" also extended in popular press and media to the Whiteman style, or Whitemanesque, jazzy, aspirational popular music idioms and compositions. Both areas overlapped in the MAM piano-solo series of the publishing company Robbins Music, run by the Tin Pan Alley mogul—and frequent Whiteman associate—John J. ("Jack") Robbins. This series began as a central project of Paul Whiteman Publications, a vanity-publishing enterprise that existed for a mere eight months (over summer 1927 to February 1928) as a subsidiary joint venture with Robbins Music. Robbins Music amicably absorbed the catalogue and further built up the MAM series in the decades to come.[1] The series uniformly reflects Whiteman's original aesthetic template, and the post-1928 catalogue includes acquisitions of Whiteman-related compositions. The score series was active circa 1928 to 1950 and had over 240 titles. Popular MAM titles appeared in other Robbins score collections as well, including the Modern American Music for Orchestra (aka the American Concert Series), the Modern American Ballads series (adding song lyrics to themes from MAM works), and band-instrument editions.[2] These Robbins MAM scores, many of which Whiteman commissioned or Whiteman's ensembles performed, are central to this chapter's articulation of Whitemanesque popular music aesthetics in broader American popular culture. In this chapter, "modern American music" refers both to this specific Robbins- and Whiteman-related concert-work repertory (including both solo-piano arrangements and various orchestrations) and this more loosely defined musical idiom. I articulate the latter both broadly as an umbrella concept for Whitemanesque musical entertainment aesthetics and, more specifically, through a study of the stylistic and programmatic topic subset that I call "Modern Metropolitan Music" (MMM). As shall be explored, the specific qualities of this Whitemanesque modern American music ideal—its specific mixed-class modes of presentation, its intentionally hybrid musical idiom, and its markers of mixed high-low entertainment qualities—are woven throughout press and promotional material on Whiteman and illustrated through the ample influence of this sound across American interwar entertainment.

The MAM idiom fundamentally reworked contemporary conventions of popular song, jazz, musical theater, and dance band in arranging, form, harmony, rhythm, and melody to create dressed-to-the-nines, up-to-date, jazzy concert-style works and/or quasi concertos. These *deluxe* arrangements were typically employed as radio, stage, film, or nightclub extended production numbers within a variety-entertainment context. Even Whiteman's celebrated Experiment in Modern Music concert-hall events of the 1920s and 1930s owed much to variety entertainment.[3] MAM works were central to these events as featured concert highlights. These works had programming roles equivalent to elaborate, extended production numbers in variety entertainments (such as stage musicals or vaudeville). Despite being played in a concert-music manner at prestigious classical-music venues like New York's Carnegie Hall, the MAM compositions are, in fact, aspirational, sophisticated popular music arrangements that self-consciously evoke Western concert music. Although this music's orchestral textures and classically evocative stylistic topics commonly (but not exclusively) evoked associations with whiteness, there were other programmatic and textural topics commonly associated with Black popular music and culture that were likewise regularly integrated with such classicistic textures, and there were a number of Black contributors to the MAM idiom.[4] These classicistic and aspirational musical textures derive from popular-idiom practice though and hold a notable formal distance from the aesthetic ideals of the Western concert-music tradition.

The MAM idiom offered an accessible and distinctly *American* modern, popular music urbanity, a kind of showbiz cosmopolitanism for the common folk. There are, of course, racial dimensions here that favor the hegemonic commercial power, influence, and taste-cultures of white America, but the common invocations of jazz-invoked Blackness and programmatic topics in areas of the MAM idiom—by both white and Black composers, performers, bands, and arrangers—underscore this idiom's investment in sustained cultural tensions and represent some degree of modern American diversity. Within the radio entertainment context, this lush arranging mode offered an elevated, enhanced, or "streamlined" (in the Art Deco automotive sense) version of the jazzy modern American dance band or radio orchestra model that Whiteman pioneered. As noted, central to his musical brand are both variety entertainment and elaborate production numbers that dress popular music in a spectacular concert mode. Despite the tuxedoed, baton-wielding, debonaire image of Whiteman's film and radio personality, that same image was greatly tempered for American middle-class consumers by his plainspoken, Western (Coloradan) accent, his welcoming manner, and his self-effacing humor. Despite his outward embrace of the trappings of concert music and the spectacle (and supposedly elevated aura) of its massed ensembles, Whiteman was not an aloof or elitist proselytizer for highbrow culture. Indeed, there is considerable cultural distance between the images of Whiteman and Arturo Toscanini, NBC radio's iconic classical conductor for the masses.[5] Whiteman represented *artful entertainment* in contrast to Toscanini's advocacy of *serious art* for the cultural enrichment and elevation of the masses. The MAM idiom is centrally an expression of such artful entertainment.

In the spread of such "classy" or sophisticated Whitemanesque popular music aesthetics across period entertainment, there are a host of overlaps between Whiteman's direct sphere of activities and a Venn-like network of interrelated circles of peers, associates, and competitors. In tracing a New York–to-Hollywood transmission of the MAM idiom as well as efforts to elevate the idiom above its popular music cultural station, this chapter considers several key media adaptations of songwriter Louis Alter's 1928 *Manhattan Serenade*, an early hit in the Robbins MAM catalogue. As later explained, this publication existed in multiple Robbins arrangements—as a concert-style published score (a piano solo, orchestral and wind-band arrangements, and arrangements for individual instruments), as a popular song published in a Robbins piano-vocal score, and as dance-band and radio-orchestra arrangements. Though he had performed the number in the 1930s, Whiteman did not formally record the *Serenade* until his 1940 concert orchestra release, *Album of Manhattan: Metropolitan Impressions by Louis Alter*. This deluxe Decca album package features five programmatic "metropolitan impression" compositions by Alter over six 78 rpm, twelve-inch discs. The *Serenade* is the featured (and lead) recording. In addition to the original 1928 Robbins piano solo score and this 1940 Whiteman album, further *Serenade* examples considered in this chapter include: the 1928 Nathaniel Shilkret Victor Salon Orchestra premiere recording; a 1929 landmark MGM musical film short, *Manhattan Serenade*, that is underscored by the Shilkret recording; the 1931 Robbins Music stock orchestration by Domenico Savino; a 1931 Whiteman orchestra radio arrangement; and *Serenade* arrangements heard within the 1936 screwball film comedy *My Man Godfrey* (Universal).[6] Through comparative descriptive accounts and critical analyses of select scores and print materials, recordings, and visual media, this chapter aims to illustrate central traits within the associative lexicon and formal conventions of Modern Metropolitan Music.

In sum, this chapter explores how Whiteman's orchestra both participated in and acted as one key model for the cross-entertainment dissemination of these conventions of Whitemanesque symphonic-jazz sound and arranging practices across the orchestras of interwar radio, Broadway musicals, the deluxe movie palaces, and Hollywood film studios of the late 1920s and early 1930s.[7] The Modern American Music idiom involves a panoply of Whiteman-related and often interconnected hybrid arranging and stylistic idioms. As noted, the chapter centrally focuses on the modern metropolitan music stylistic trope. MMM was a central MAM topical subset connected to both the MAM concert works and interwar entertainment. As such, its study here offers a useful means for suggesting important ways in which Whiteman's musical values and stylistic trademarks manifest across media and time. Indeed, cultural memories of the original interwar MAM foundations can be seen as late as the 1972 score to Francis Ford Coppola's *The Godfather* (Paramount), which notably adapts *Manhattan Serenade* several times as one of that film's relatively few nonoriginal musical cues. This familiar example is useful for calling to mind some initial associations of the MMM musical topic. The soundtrack first employs *Manhattan Serenade*, for example, as the bridge cue for a New York–to–Los Angeles flight of the character Tom Hagen, a Corleone family *consigliere* who intends to strong-arm a Hollywood producer. A sweet, swinging version of the cue underscores the glamorous Pan Am–era flight and an aerial pan shot of Hollywood that zooms down to street level on Grauman's Chinese Theatre before the montage shows the New York tenement backlot sets. The *Serenade* returns in a sequence set at a Hollywood mansion that a character describes as the "palace of a king." Despite the highfalutin, new-money trappings, the characters' dialect and dialogue (talk of "two-bit hustlers," etc.) firmly depict them as streetwise New York Italian Americans (or possibly Jewish Americans) with mafioso overtones.

The *Godfather*'s musical soundtrack choice of the *Serenade* aptly enhances the sustained high-low cultural tensions and interwar glitz and pop glamour of these two scenes. The *Serenade* cues stylistically borrow scoring inspiration from both Tommy Dorsey's 1942 swinging, big-band-plus-strings hit of the song version of *Manhattan Serenade*, as well as from the update of this early 1940s swanky jazz-pop sound into what I call the "populuxe" or "luxe pop" sound of the midcentury Great American Songbook tradition. The latter is exemplified in the hi-fi era, 1950s partnership of Frank Sinatra and his arranger Nelson Riddle, both of whom had ties to this 1940s Dorsey orchestra.[8] The 1942 Robbins-published song is based on the concert work's second thematic strain with added lyrics by Harold Adamson. (The theme is shown later in this chapter in the Strain B brass and reeds of example 3.2.) The *Godfather* air-travel cue frames this theme as an evocative, 1950s hi-fi soundtrack of jazzy brushed snare drum, pizzicato bass, and Harmon-muted trumpet lead with brass-unison backing and later adds cocktail-piano filigree and a lush bed of studio strings. Each of the scorings of this material heard in the film illustrates a stylistic growth in luxe pop, a tradition whose origins lie directly in Whitemanesque modern American music of the late 1920s. The *Godfather*'s *Serenade* film cues stylistically share much with the original 1928–31 orchestrations of this work, which I discuss below. Strain B in all of the latter examples includes dance band–style scoring with muted-trumpet lead, jazzy clarinet solos, and sax-section and lush-strings backings, as well as interspersed piano arpeggiations, flute and bass clarinet solos, and so forth. These collective textures, however, are part of a larger theater- or radio-orchestra scoring that alternates three popular song-based thematic strains with various self-consciously, "concert-styled" scoring affectations and interlude passages. Many of the latter are rhapsodic solo-piano textures, but they also include brief passages of non-dance-band orchestral melodrama. The formal routines of these 1928–31 *Serenade* arrangements build drama between these popular music and theatrical (or melodramatic) textures, and they display an overall complexity of form with regard to their varied sections, interludes, tempi shifts, stylistic allusions, and dynamic shadings, as well as virtuosic rubato cadenzas, and other such concert-style stylistic affectations.

With the multiple *Serenade* cues of the *Godfather*, there is a mutual topical reinforcement between the music, particularly, its collective stylistic and orchestration elements, and the lifestyle and "classy" pop-culture and urban-geography images that build these two establishing montages. As this chapter demonstrates, these associations are widely cultivated in American entertainment from the song's 1920s origins through the early 1960s, but their appearance in the 1970s *Godfather* soundtrack illustrates their lasting resonance in collective pop-culture memory. This is the heart of classy American high-low tradition in New York–Hollywood entertainment, and such qualities are central to the cultural associations of the Whitemanesque MMM stylistic trope in both interwar media and the programs, performance, and marketing of the MAM concert-work scores. This chapter aims to articulate both core cultural associations and key musical qualities that were often tied to the MMM substylistic trope and Whitemanesque MAM, in general. The chapter elucidates central facets of this MMM trope through close studies of the aforementioned *Serenade* adaptations that collectively span the era's "spectacular" production-number arranging practices. Within its 1928 to 1940 framing, this chapter sketches Whitemanesque idiomatic transmission from the founding of the MAM score series and the Whiteman orchestra's Publix Paramount movie-prologue shows, to radio shows, and a succession of early sound films involving a Whiteman-related circle of Broadway-to-Hollywood musical migrants. Each offers insights into entertainment uses of Alter's *Manhattan Serenade* and, in turn, suggests how this lineage was likely central to establishing "modern metropolitan" scoring within classical Hollywood film depictions of New York.

Album of Manhattan and "Metropolitan Impressions"

The 1940 Whiteman *Album of Manhattan* will be used as a framing device for this chapter's exploration of Whitemanesque Modern American Music. As the album title implies, all of its tracks are Manhattan themed. Although this topic was an Alter specialty, the MAM catalogue includes a large number of metropolitan-titled works and more that include less-urban titles but graphics and programmatic texts that lean this direction. Metropolitan music is one major subcategory in the MAM series, which also includes touristic Americana themes, aspirational concert-music framing (minuets, caprices, nocturnes, serenades, etc.) tempered with modernistic references, modern gadgetry and machines, and "blue" or jazz referentiality. Each program area can overlap with others. The five central MAM metropolitan themes include programmatic references to

- the smart-set urban or luxury lifestyle,
- the metropolis as "city symphony,"
- the city as theater (including stage and nightclub references),
- the metropolis as cultural melting pot, and
- Black Harlem entertainment.[9]

New York, Los Angeles, and/or Chicago are typically the urban framing. These program themes are centrally reflected in MAM composition titles, such as Vernon Duke's *New York Nocturne* and *Lake Shore Drive*, both 1939 (without Whiteman connections), and Ferde Grofé's 1928 *Metropolis* and 1924 *Broadway at Night* (both for the Whiteman orchestra), among others.

Of course, Whiteman long advocated George Gershwin's metropolitan-music concert works, including the *Rhapsody in Blue* (typically framed by Whiteman with metropolitan references), *135th Street* (an opera), *Second Rhapsody* (based on film music discussed later), and *American in Paris* (different city but modern Americana). However, Whiteman's orchestra variously commissioned, performed, premiered, and recorded many metropolitan

MAM (alongside other MAM) compositions. His 1924–38 Experiment in Modern Music concert series and his concert orchestra tours, recordings, and stage, hotel, and radio engagements of the same period all amply reflect promotions of this metropolitan MAM repertory, with Grofé being Whiteman's most consistent contributor. This music included Grofé's *Broadway at Night* (1924), *Metropolis* (1928), *Tabloid: Four Pictures of a Modern Newspaper* (1934), *Free Air: A Humoresque* [for Bicycle Pump] (aka "Variations Based on Noises from a Garage"), and other works. And like other Whiteman-associated MAM composers, the Robbins series and Grofé's own performance ventures allowed Whiteman to expand his compositions in this area. Such Whiteman-parallel metropolitan MAM compositions included Grofé's *Aviation Suite* (1946), *Cafe Society* (1939), *Hollywood Suite* (1938), *Kodachrome Music* (1939), *Madison Square Garden Suite* (1933), *Symphony in Steel* (1936), *Wheels: A Modern Piano Suite* (1939), and more. As these titles imply, "metropolitan impressions" involve both New York–specific and indirect metropolitan allusions where New York is by default implicitly understood as *the* modern American metropolis. Where Whiteman was not directly involved, the bandleader's earlier support, nonetheless, enabled these later parallel, non-Whiteman compositions. The recipients of such Whiteman MAM advocacy include Peter de Rose (*Deep Purple*, 1935), Dana Suesse (*Valses*, 1933), Matt Malneck and Frank Signorelli (*Park Avenue Fantasy*, 1934), Johnny Green (*Night Club*, 1933), and Duke Ellington (*Blue Bell[e]s of Harlem*, 1938), among others. Some of these individuals developed competing "modern American" radio orchestras (e.g., Grofé and Green). And then there were some composers like Alter whose music both paralleled and intersected with the Whiteman orchestra over a longer period of time. This is the history behind Alter's music on the Whiteman *Album of Manhattan*.

Manhattan Serenade is critically useful as an archetype of Whitemanesque Modern Metropolitan Music. While more-detailed musical discussion will be pursued in the later individual media studies, it is useful here in a broader discussion of the Whiteman album to introduce several key illustrative tables and examples that I will reference. With an eye toward illustrating the formal conventions of Modern Metropolitan Music via adaptations of the *Serenade*, table 3.1a outlines several orchestrated versions of *Serenade* that will be discussed. Table 3.2 outlines the structure and expressive passages of the Robbins 1928 piano solo that forms the foundation for other realizations. In addition, examples 3.1a and 3.1b present the A and C thematic strains from the piano solo, respectively, and example 3.2 presents the 1931 Savino-orchestrated version of theme B. The latter is dominant in both song versions as the chorus, as well as in several filmic adaptations. As noted, I will reference these illustrative materials across this chapter.

TABLE 3.1A Formal outlines of four orchestrated versions of Louis Alter's *Manhattan Serenade*

m.	Section	Shilkret 1928 Recording + MGM 1929 Film Short, *Manhattan Serenade*	Savino 1931 Stock	Whiteman 1931 Radio	Whiteman 1940 Recording
1	Introduction C min	0:00/mm. 1–4 Solo bass clarinet, with strings, piano, and celeste at cadence	mm. 1–4 *Assai moderato* Solo cello/bassoon, percussion accents	mm. 1–4 Bass clarinet solo (piano and bass parts copied from stock through REH. H)	0:00/mm. 1–4 *Assai moderato* Solo bass clarinet, with bass-clarinet trio, strings and celeste at cadence
5	*Moderato (lazily)* → *adagio* Strain A^1 C min	0:14/mm. 5–20 Oboe/flute lead with muted low brass, clarinet choir, banjo. Strings/woodwinds on phrase b. Instrumental color expands on a^2b^2 with added flute, tremolo strings, woodblock accents, and gong	mm. 5–20 *Moderato (appena mosso)* Strings and saxes on theme. Muted brass background. Tympani accents	mm. 5–20 REH. A/B. Oboe solo on phrase a theme with muted-brass/strings backing. Strings, clarinet trio, tenor sax on phase b^1. Saxes/strings on phrase b^2	0:13/mm. 5–20 *Moderato (appena mosso)* Oboe lead (Engl. horn repeat) with flute, and with muted low-brass/bass-clarinet-choir responses. More rubato and concert-like. No rhythm. Muted brass on phrase b with string accents. Fills out on with flute and greater strings
21	*Più mosso (molto express. e legato)* Strain B^1 A♭ maj	0:53/mm. 21–39 Full strings on theme with rhythm section and wind-section backing. Phrase b has dance-band muted trumpet and jazzy clarinet solos with sax-section and pizz. strings backing. Piano arpeggiation, varied phrase b^2 with flute and bass clarinet solos, etc.	mm. 21–39 *Mosso* Strings, piano, clarinet, alto saxes on theme. Active rhythm section. Trumpet and clarinet solo responses w/vibraphone and pizz. strings	mm. 21–39 REH. C/D/E. Saxophones/strings on lead; brass background. Trumpet and clarinet solo responses first time; oboe and bass clarinet on second responses, with muted brass backing. Gong accents	mm. 21–39 *Mosso* **CUT** Strain B^1 orch., mm. i–xvi

m.	Section	Shilkret 1928 Recording + MGM 1929 Film Short, *Manhattan Serenade*	Savino 1931 Stock	Whiteman 1931 Radio	Whiteman 1940 Recording
40	*Vivace* Strain B^2 A♭ maj	1:39/mm. 40–51 Piano solo (two pianos) with drum accents. Phrase b trumpet with piano, to slide guitar with piano. Phrase a^4 adds solo violin over piano on theme. 2:21/ **INSERT A, mm. i–viii** Strain A^2 *Moderato* Repeat of Strain A^1 scoring with varied end	mm. 40–55 *Allegro moderato* Trumpet solo (w/piano) on theme, violin countermelody, reed accompaniment. Active rhythm section. Oboe and trumpet responses with solo violin countermelody. INSERT A, mm. i–xvi Strain A^2 *Moderato* Slightly varied repeat of Strain A^1 scoring and music	mm. 40–55 REH. F. 8 bars piano solo with "hot rhythm [section] background." REH. G/H 4 bars vocal soloist (male?) on LYRICS 1 with choir backing (harmony humming); 4 bars choir humming with Jane Fromann on phrase a^3 theme (no lyrics?). Piano/bass (+ drums?) background. **CUT SCORE ORIG. REH. I/J**	0:58/mm. 40–55 *Allegro moderato* Dual piano "exposition." Strings enter at phrase a^2. Phrase b has dance-band muted trumpet and clarinet solos backed by jazzy clarinets, drums, and lush strings with piano arpeggiations. Phrase b^2 in classicized lush strings alone until brass cadence. 1:34/**INSERT A, mm.i–viii** Strain A^1/Cmin Recopied 8 bars from phrases a^1 and b^2 scoring. (**CUT** Leeman's b^1a^2.) Varied transition with both new and Shilkret-related material
56	*Deciso* Interlude 1	2:39/mm. 56–59 Strings and brass with cymbal accents, to solo cello + gong transition	mm. 56–59 *Deciso* Tutti	**"RESCORE"** *Note*: These inserted 71 measures of "Rescore" material are a manuscript insertion. This second manuscript starts with **INSERT A** (see table 3.1b for closer details of the full "Rescore" insertion.)	mm. 56–59 are heard at 1:56 *Deciso* Saxophones/brass unison with lush string backing responses and rhapsodic, full piano
60	cadenza	2:49/m. 60 Varied m.60 piano cadenza **INSERT B, mm. i–iii** Solo piano cadenza extension plus two-bar vamp with brush + snare backing	m. 60 Reeds section or solo piano with percussion accents **INSERT B, mm. i–iii** Exactly as Shilkret: Solo piano cadenza extension. 2 bars "blues" piano vamp with drums		2:04/m. 60 + **INSERT B, mm. i–iii** *Allegro* Varied interlude: 1-bar clarinet quintet overlay (upwards run; piano downwards). 1-bar piano solo; then Shilkret vamp with rhythm

TABLE 3.1A (*continued*)

m.	Section	Shilkret 1928 Recording + MGM 1929 Film Short, *Manhattan Serenade*	Savino 1931 Stock	Whiteman 1931 Radio	Whiteman 1940 Recording
61	*Moderato (blues tempo)* Strain C^1 Fmaj	2:58/mm. 61–76 Big, sweeping strings with brass backing, piano comping and brushed snare, and reeds + brass accents. Alternating rubato piano backed by tremolo strings and reeds	mm. 61–76 *Moderato (Tempo di Blues)* Strings, trumpets, piano on theme. Saxes divide theme and countermelody, with trombone accompaniment. Rhythm section	mm. 61–76 REH. K/L. Big tutti scoring on theme. REH. L. Piano solo response	2:12/mm. 61–75 *Pesante* Big-band brass/strings lead, with saxophones countermelody. Gives way to alternations both with rhapsodizing piano interjections, and a classicized woodwinds/celeste response
77	Strain C^2 Fmaj	3:29/mm. 77–88 Previous scoring with more piano rhapsodizing at end	mm. 77–88 Slightly varied repeat of Strain C^1 scoring and music	mm. 77–88 Slightly varied repeat of REH. K/L	2:46/mm. 77–88 Repeated scoring for 10 bars. Then lush tutti orchestral phrasing with piano rhapsodizing transition
89	*Meno (dreamily)* Interlude 2	3:50/mm. 89 Strings melodic lead; reeds countermelody; light brass backing. **INSERT C, mm. i–ii** Piano interlude/cadenza with ornamental ad lib	mm. 89–92 *Assai meno* Strings melodic lead; reeds countermelody; light brass backing; snare accents. **INSERT C, mm. i–ii** Near piano transcription of Shilkret (without ad lib.), strings, reeds on melodic lead	mm. 89–92 Lead vocal on LYRIC 2 with humming chorus. Rhythm backing and solo piano cadenza	3:09/mm. 89–92 Lush tutti orchestral phrasing w/ piano rhapsodizing response 3:14/**INSERT C, mm. i–ii** Extension of strings and brass with piano solo rhapsodizing

m.	Section	Shilkret 1928 Recording + MGM 1929 Film Short, *Manhattan Serenade*	Savino 1931 Stock	Whiteman 1931 Radio	Whiteman 1940 Recording
93	*Moderato (dreamily).* Strain A² ("recap") Cmin→Cmaj	4:12/mm. 93–98 Slightly varied repeat of Strain A¹ scoring and music. Varied m.98 of tremulous string cadence. (**CUT 99–106**) mm. 107–110 Jazzy muted trumpet leading to lush string finale with percussion accentuation and piano rhapsodizing	mm. 93–110 *A tempo (poco piú mosso di prima)* Slightly varied repeat of Strain A¹ scoring and music	mm. 93–110 Theme A³. "Stock orchestration." Lead vocal on LYRIC 3 with humming chorus. **CUT** final 3 bars orig. ms. **INSERT B** (3 bars final pg. RESCORE)	3:27/mm. 93–110 *A tempo (poco piú mosso di prima)* Recycles Strain A¹ scoring w/ added variations leading to a big Hollywood-style finale of the cadence with jazzy alto sax solo lead

Note: The measure numbers and structural sections are based on the 1928 Robbins piano solo. The Shilkret orchestration relates closely to the 1931 Domenico Savino commercial orchestration (with differences noted). The latter is the foundational reference for the two Whiteman-commissioned orchestrations (with differences noted). Where the scores deviate from the formal and melodic foundations of the Robbins piano solo are indicated by boldface INSERT and CUT in notes. Roman numerals indicate material not in the piano solo. Where newly inserted material is shared across scores is labeled A, B, and C. Insert A is additional Strain A material not included in the Robbins piano solo.

The lyrics referenced in the table for the 1931 Huxley radio arrangement are:

LYRIC 1: Manhattan, you're a weird, mysterious song, your moods enrapture a delirious throng.

LYRIC 2: Singin' and swingin' that Manhattan Serenade.

LYRIC 3: Manhattan, you are like a wonderful strain / a mystic, futuristic, haunting refrain / Just like your town is / Every sound is / printed indelibly in my brain / Manhattan, you're a weird, mysterious song / Your moods enrapture a delirious throng / Searching for thrills all night / You bring both joy and despair.

TABLE 3.1B Formal table of the ten-page "Rescore" insert for the 1931 Huxley radio arrangement of Alter's *Manhattan Serenade*

m.	Length	Key	Expressions and Notes
i	9 mm (extra bar)	C min / E♭ maj	"(announcer)" written on score REH. I. Starts as if Strain A^2 but with an extra bar between phrase a statements. (This is the INSERT A reference on table 3.1a.) Clarinet choir then trumpet solo on leads with strings and muted brass backing.
x	9 mm	G maj	*piu mosso* "Italian" REH. J. Strings lead with sustained reeds and active brass backing. No *Serenade* motives.
xix	8 mm	E maj	REH. K. 3/4 meter. Saxophones lead, strings and rhythm backing. No clear *Serenade* motives.
xxvii	4 mm	D min	"(announcer)" REH. L. 4/4 meter. Strain A, phrase a motives in sequence. Passed strings > muted trumpet > strings in unison with piano.
xxxi	8 mm	B♭ min	*slow* "Jewish" REH. M. Theme B motivic references. Solo clarinet "ad lib." (klezmer evocation?). Sustained sax, brass, strings backings with active vln. 1 and 2 triplet runs.
xxxix	8 mm	E♭ maj	"(announcer)" REH. N. 3/4 meter. Strings on sustained melodic lead with sub-tone bass clarinet and celeste (with arpeggiations) backing. No *Serenade* motives.
xlviii	12 mm		"Irish" REH. O. 4/4 meter. Triplet-based jig-like violin melody (no *Serenade* connection) doubled with celeste/piano, with reed and strings backing. Repeat 1–6 of REH. N (3/4 meter).
lx	12 mm	F maj > F min	"Harlem" REH. P. 4/4 meter. Brass with wah-wah mutes lead, then brass + saxophones in unison. Rhythm section. Strings out. No *Serenade* motives. Transitional but stylistically placed like a hot-style penultimate chorus leading to the big finale.

Note: This "rescore" adds quasi-developmental sections to the initial score. The additional ten-page insertion manuscript outlined in this table includes the first-page note "Copy other [initial] score to [reh.] I then + [add] this ms." The score centrally outlined in table 3.1a (i.e., up through reh. I) is the initial score referenced in this note. On page 9, just after measure 71 of this insertion manuscript, is additional instruction to the copyist(s): "Copy from ([reh] K) (other parts) to 3 bars from finish." This note is in reference to the initial first draft score. After "3 bars to the finish" of the initial first draft, Huxley adds a tenth page marked "Ending" with a final seven bars of cadential music. This tenth-page cadential material is not indicated on table 3.1b.

The first-draft score's Whiteman-library cover, which was likely added later, includes the subtitle "Rescore," to indicate the changes to be added by the "Rescore" insert of this eleven-page manuscript, hence referring to this second manuscript as the "Rescore." Both full-score manuscripts are stamped "1554 1." Despite the aforementioned note regarding this insertion, the materials for this Huxley arrangement do not include a second-draft full score that merges both these initial manuscripts. It is likely that copyists simply made this change for the parts only without this middle full-score step.

TABLE 3.2 Formal outline of the 1928 Robbins Music piano-solo publication of Louis Alter's *Manhattan Serenade*

m.	§ and Length	Key	Expressions + Notes
1	Introduction 4	C min	*Moderato* (dreamily). Primarily a solo melodic line (inspired by *Rhapsody in Blue*?). Sequential
5	Strain A^1 16 $a^1b^1a^2b^2$	C min	*Moderato* (lazily) → *adagio* Modulation in m.19
21	Strain B^1 16+4 $a^1a^2b^1a^3+b^2$	A♭	*Più mosso* (*molto express. e legato*) Chromatic counterpoint + cadential delay
40	Strain B^2 16 $a^1a^2b^1a^4$	A♭	*Vivace*. Variation
56	Interlude 1 4	chromatic	*Deciso*. Chromatic descent of half-dim 7th chords
60	Cadenza	n/a	[*rubato*] Whole tone scale + modulation
61	Strain C^1 16 a^1a^2bc	F	*Moderato* (blues tempo). "Blues tempo" refers to blues *style* not form
77	Strain C^2 10 $a^1a^2b^2$ → interruption	F	*Moderato* (blues tempo)
89	Interlude 2 4	modulation	*Meno* (dreamily). Nods to intro and novelty ragtime
93	Strain A2 ("recap") 16+2	C min	*Moderato* (dreamily). Cadence in C major

Figure 3.1 reproduces the Whiteman album packaging. The album also included an accompanying, six-page liner-note booklet. Despite the Decca label's elevated positioning of this Whiteman "Concert Orchestra" album, a January 1940 issue of *Variety* in its "Dance Band" coverage notably announces the in-progress *Manhattan Album*.[10] *Billboard*'s later "critical analysis" of the album is that it "musically, visually and commercially . . . has a great deal to recommend it."[11] The Whiteman concert orchestra is described as an "augmented ork," or augmented dance-band orchestra, and the five Alter concert work selections are simply said to be "in the *Manhattan Serenade* vein," thereby underscoring the presumed interest and an identifiable signature

EXAMPLE 3.1, A AND B Thematic material as scored in the Robbins piano-solo score to Louis Alter's *Manhattan Serenade*, arranged by Domenico Savino. (A) Strain A excerpt, mm. 5–6 (first half phrase a[1]); (B) end of Interlude 1, Cadenza, and Strain C excerpt (phrase a[1]), mm. 58–61.

(A)

(B)

sound. *Billboard* further describes the three-disc set as "one of the most attractive albums released in sometime," thus calling attention to the album's deluxe packaging.

The album packaging is an intentional collage of sustained high-low cultural juxtapositions. Such sustained high-low juxtaposition is absolutely central to understanding the Whitemanesque MAM aesthetic and will be seen in all the examples discussed in this chapter. Note the prominence of an aerial shot of lower Manhattan—a viewpoint that had also been an important image in the 1929 film short, to be discussed later—on the luxuriant, red-framed album cover. (This is reproduced in the liner-note booklet as well.) The high-leaning "Concert Orchestra" designation is undercut by the mass-appeal reference to Decca's "Personality Series," and the entertainment

EXAMPLE 3.2 Strain B excerpt, mm. 25–29, as scored in the Robbins stock orchestration for Louis Alter's *Manhattan Serenade*, arranged by Domenico Savino.

FIGURE 3.1 1940 Decca-label deluxe Paul Whiteman 78 rpm album, *Album of Manhattan: Metropolitan Impressions by Louis Alter.*

reference to this collection as a "presentation." The inside, back-cover feature of an extended poem, "My City," from noted novelist-essayist Theodore Dreiser, suggests an elevated framing alongside artful touristic snapshots that recall the film-short travelogue. The career-overview notes in the booklet partly elevate Alter as a "composer" but simultaneously describe him as a mongrel product of the conservatory, vaudeville, Broadway, Tin Pan Alley, and Hollywood.

These observations on the album packaging, its promotional-copy positioning of Whiteman, Alter, and the Alter "Manhattan" concert-music repertory, and so forth, illustrate the "sustained" or unresolved nature of these high-low cultural juxtapositions. There is a high-low simultaneity and tension that define this tradition as what is best called the "classy" American entertainment tradition. As noted previously, while there is a common association of much of this classy, glamorous, or aspirational culture to white, well-to-do America, there were a wealth of Black entertainers and public figures (e.g., Duke Ellington) who offered influential Black cultural expressions, adaptations, and adoptions of this classy American entertainment tradition. I have described this tradition previously as "middlebrow-adjacent, *class*-aspirational popular music," with "*class* and *classy* being understood as glamour-based stylistic adjectives [more commonly] relating to aspirational, socioeconomic status, rather than high-culture pretension."[12] This entertainment tradition spans the twentieth century and still influences popular entertainments and constructions of America's self-image. Whiteman's symphonic jazz was one cornerstone upon which this tradition was based in popular music, often via the MAM repertory's promotion across physical recordings, radio, performances, print and advertising, and sheet music. Alter's "Manhattan" compositions, especially *Manhattan Serenade*, are central to this classy musical-entertainment history.

The 1940 first release of the three-disc *Album of Manhattan* consisted of five Alter compositions, with *Manhattan Serenade* as the opening track. This was by far the best-known Alter composition due to its top-selling Robbins piano solo and its history of stage, radio, and film performances. Despite Alter's long career as a songwriter, circa 1940, the popularity of this work also overshadowed public familiarity with his songs, but this likely changed with the 1942 song version of *Manhattan Serenade* with lyrics by Adamson. Beyond Dorsey's hit recording, this song was widely performed and recorded by Harry James, Dinah Shore, and others. Whiteman's *Album* was re-released in 1949 as a high-fidelity ten-inch "microgroove" vinyl release. Though less luxe in packaging, this later release extended the Whiteman brand into the era of hi-fi hype. The new graphic of the 1949 album recalls earlier MAM Robbins covers that glorified New York's skyline profile and its impressive, modernist buildings. Here, in figure 3.2, the image suggests nighttime Manhattan with a glow of skyscraper lighting (an illuminated foggy haze) and brooding building outlines that create a stylized black-and-white Manhattan profile. Alongside its new cover and recycled liner notes by *New Yorker* writer (and music critic) Robert A. Simon, Decca's back-cover catalogue listings firmly place this release within a decidedly middlebrow orchestral pops–marketing framing. (The promotions range from "easy listening" artists to both "symphonic" Broadway musical selections and nineteenth century "classics," each of which is a pops-concert staple.) The top item is Whiteman's premium-priced *George Gershwin Music* album, itself a reissue, with the ensemble's later renditions of the *Rhapsody in Blue* and the *Second Rhapsody*, *An American in Paris*, and *Cuban Overture*. Within this promotional framing, the two Gershwin piano rhapsodies—the first premiered by Whiteman in 1924 and the second with its roots in a Hollywood film—suggest how the Gershwin-Whiteman repertory had moved from its 1920s Broadway-Hollywood, hybrid dance-band roots in Whitemanesque Experiment[s] in Modern Music to middlebrow pops-orchestra symphonizing. This 1940

FIGURE 3.2 1949 Decca-label 33⅓ rpm, 10-inch LP reissue of *Album of Manhattan: Metropolitan Impressions by Louis Alter.*

album is in alignment with Whiteman's career evolution, such as his work as a musical director for the fledgling ABC radio and his tenure on the new medium of television. The former work resonates with this "pops" middle-brow album, while the latter underscores Whiteman's centrality to mainstream popular entertainment.

The *Album*'s five compositions are all Robbins MAM scores. The album begins with the *Manhattan Suite*, which combines the *Serenade* with Alter's 1930 *Manhattan Moonlight* and 1932 *Manhattan Masquerade*. The fourth, the 1935 *Metropolitan Nocturne*, is described as "the most dramatic of the series," adding that "RKO produced it as a two reel featurette without words" that "won a bronze medal at the Venice International Film Festival." The album's arrangement is said to "condens[e] . . . the cinema score." The touristic-minded *Side Street in Gotham* is characterized as the only album orchestration "that has any straight jazz touches." This is perhaps a New Yorker's spin on French flâneur culture, as it depicts the experiences of a Manhattanite traversing a "thoroughfare from river to river."[13] The "Metropolitan Impression" idiom heard in the album holds considerable kinship to the scores of numerous 1930s New York–themed Hollywood film productions, including for example, Alfred Newman's score to the 1931 *Street Scene* (discussed later). This particular score was orchestrated by Ray Heindorf, the protégé of a key symphonic-jazz arranger, Arthur Lange. The proximity of this music to Whitemanesque idiomatic conventions is evidenced in the *Street Scene* film score's reworking for the Robbins MAM catalogue by Savino. These real and implied connections to film music are easily imagined to be heard in the *Album* arrangements that echo many period underscoring conventions for Hollywood depictions of modern urban life and, specifically, New York.

The Williams College Paul Whiteman Collection's various Savino-scored commercial MAM orchestrations offer one area of evidence for Whiteman's interactions with the Robbins publishing circle. Savino was the editor of the MAM score series as well as a cofounder, chief editor and arranger, and musical director of Robbins Music.[14] For example, *Masquerade* was introduced in the early 1930s by Whiteman and Alter at New York's Biltmore Hotel in a Whiteman-commissioned arrangement by Savino.[15] And, among other connections Savino held to Whiteman over the 1920s and 1930s, Savino's MAM orchestrations were, likewise, foundations for customized Whiteman-orchestra arrangements. This can be seen, for instance, in an early 1930s Whiteman-contracted radio arrangement of *Serenade* by Carroll Huxley, discussed later.[16]

The Savino arrangement of *Manhattan Masquerade* in the Whiteman Collection reflects the pre-swing-era instrumentation of the expanded Whiteman orchestra: four saxophone parts (two altos, two tenors) for musicians who could double on other reed instruments; three trumpets, three trombones, and tuba (all masters of contemporary muting effects); drum kit; percussionist (tympani, vibraphone); banjo; and a string section of five violins (with up to three-part divisions), two violas, two cellos, and double bass; and piano. Whiteman's custom arrangements from staff orchestrators typically display close attention to writing for the strengths and specialties of the ensemble's mixed-genre musicians, many of whom were publicly known personalities with diverse backgrounds ranging from both vernacular (dance bands, vaudeville) and cultivated (concert-music, Broadway pit orchestras) music traditions. This Savino arrangement does not include such written name references, a fact that perhaps suggests Savino's "outside" relationship to the organization. Lastly, while the Whiteman orchestra of the 1920s and 1930s did occasionally leave arrangement room for improvising soloists, much of its repertory was performed largely as scored compositions. This is the case, for example, with *Manhattan Masquerade*, where Savino's sophisticated and virtuosic showcase piano score for the arrangement is fully written out in great detail.

The 1940 *Album*'s arrangements were prepared by George Leeman, a dance-band, radio, and television arranger. The manuscript for *Serenade* dates to September 20, 1939. While written on Columbia Broadcasting System paper (indicating Leeman's professional ties), the manuscript's reeds scoring includes Whiteman player names and expectations of considerable doubling, thus revealing this to be an ensemble-specific arrangement. As seen in the final column of table 3.1a, the production process included typical session revisions found within popular music production, including the deletion of a Strain B^1 orchestration. Leeman was not a longtime "inside" Whiteman arranger. This engagement, perhaps, suggests Whiteman's movement toward a freelance "personality" career independent of a regular ensemble. Likewise, the 1939 session's blending of studio musicians and known Whiteman associates suggests an ensemble transition. The *Album* orchestrations are for twenty-two to twenty-six score parts, including various combinations of woodwind players with doublings but centrally clarinets and flutes/piccolos and oboe/English horn rather than saxophones (only *Manhattan Masquerade* has prominent saxophones); five to seven brass (three trumpet, two to three trombone, tuba); five to ten string parts (with violins regularly in three divisions), likely for a studio-orchestra complement of twelve to sixteen players rather than a symphonic contingent; double bass (in orchestral and rhythm-section roles); two pianos; guitar; drum kit; and tympani/percussion.

Robbins and Modern Metropolitan Music

Manhattan Serenade's history with Robbins Music reveals much about the cultural and musical topics attributed to the MAM idiom and its MMM topical subset. For example, in 1930, Robbins Music tried to capitalize on the popularity of the *Manhattan Serenade* piano solo by offering a song rendition. With lyrics by Howard Johnson, this little-circulated publication was a literal song about modern Gotham. It opens, for example, with the line, "Manhattan you are like a wonderful strain a mystic, futuristic haunting refrain," and a chorus observing the metropolis "bring[s] in both joy and despair." The 1942 Adamson lyrics smartly tap into Hollywood's romance with the city, telling us, "That night in Manhattan was the start of it. We lived it and we loved every part of it."[17] Adamson focuses on the "madness" of two lovers sharing a moonlight kiss in Central Park. This lyric evokes widely circulated New York touristic and filmic tropes. A similar framing of *Serenade* is evidenced, for instance, in the 1945 Tom and Jerry animated short *Mouse in Manhattan* (MGM). This film has the mouse, Jerry, leaving the country for big-city adventure à la Aesop's fable "The Town Mouse and the City Mouse." In *Mouse in Manhattan*, *Serenade*'s musical low-high class tensions are mapped onto a narrative of a wide-eyed rural innocent encountering urban sophistication. As shall be discussed, this is exactly the same framing—and includes many of the same images—for the 1929 film short based on *Serenade*.

Neither Paul Whiteman Publications nor the Robbins MAM scores ever defined their "modern idiom" in the promotional copy on their scores. Nonetheless, consumers would have easily mapped stylistic associations onto the series' top-tier popular composers, such as Harold Arlen, Vernon Duke, and Harry Warren, and jazz-world contributors like Ellington and Bix Beiderbecke.[18] Through both graphics and programmatic titles and promotional copy, alongside familiar stylistic associations tied to the music of the series' better-known composers, it is likely that consumers new to the series could accurately anticipate the sound of the Modern American Music idiom. But some consumers likely discovered the series through cross-entertainment promotions of its top titles, including by Whiteman himself, or Whiteman-styled orchestral musical entertainments on stage, radio, or recordings. The MAM repertory's cornerstone composers were arguably Alter and Whiteman's arranger Grofé, the two contributors who had the greatest sales and largest numbers of compositions within the series. Both were central to the series' metropolitan-themed compositions.

While growing out of the earlier Robbins-Richmond and Robbins-Engels companies, Robbins Music was established in 1927 (in near parallel with Paul Whiteman Publications). The young company's dual positioning of *Serenade* as both hit popular music and "concert" music was present from its earliest Robbins promotion. In light of the proximity of the 1928 piano solo and the premiere recording, there was likely some promotional connection between the two. The Victor Records ledger for the Shilkret recording gives a March 1, 1928, recording date for the Shilkret release and an instrumentation list of "4 violins, cello, bass, flute, 4 saxophones, 3 cornets, 2 trombones, tuba, banjo, 2 pianos, accordion, and 2 traps [drum set and percussion?]."[19] This early-spring session predates the Alter live-performance press (late spring and summer 1928) discussed later. It seems likely that the piano solo was published between or after these periods. The Savino-arranged Robbins score may partly transcribe the uncredited Shilkret recording orchestration, work from the Alter original piano manuscript, or both. The recording orchestration may be from Shilkret, Savino, or someone else. That said, the piano solo's dedication to Shilkret suggests close associations among Alter, Shilket, Savino, and Robbins. Table 3.1a shows that the Shilkret and piano-solo realizations include small deviations, but it is reasonable to assume that Shilkret worked from an Alter manuscript. The 1931 Savino stock orchestration seems to lightly update the recording's orchestration. Its largest deviation is an insertion of a full Strain A^2 statement. Commercial "stock" arrangements were intended as adaptable and affordable scores for use by ensembles of various sizes and quality. However, the front and back covers to the *Serenade* orchestration are on high-quality paper in two-tone green and purple print with elaborate Art Deco graphics and script (see fig. 3.3). This emphasizes "class" over affordability but distances itself from staid classical publishing. Nonetheless, prominent reference to the "Robbins Edition of Modern American Music for Orchestra" (later more commonly referred to as the "American Concert Series") underscores the juxtaposition of Tin Pan Alley promotion and elevated concert-music framing. Though undoubtedly many performances widely adapted this score (as evidenced in table 3.1a), the Savino *Serenade* orchestration seems more like a fixed arrangement that requires much of its sixteen-part ensemble scoring (three saxophones; clarinet; flute; two trumpets; trombone; piano; tenor banjo; drums and tympani; and strings). This instrumentation expands the Shilkret orchestration but aligns with the Whiteman Concert Orchestra of the late 1920s as well as top radio and theater popular orchestras.

Tables 3.1a, 3.1b, and 3.2 firstly illustrate how deeply embedded *Serenade* is in popular music arranging. This is apparent even in the piano score, which evidences the novelty-piano three-strain formal design (discussed later). This is not a sacred concert-work text to be faithfully realized; it is a mutable

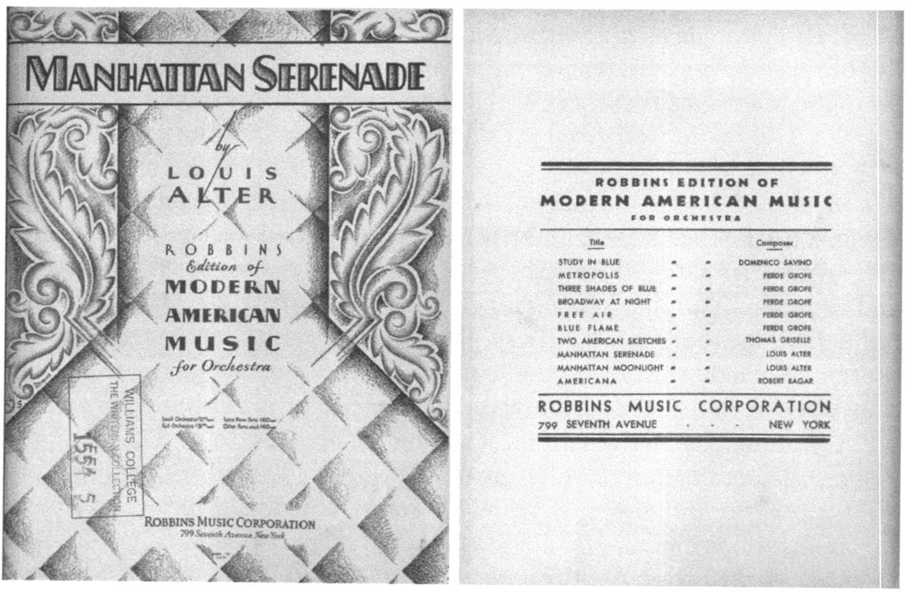

FIGURE 3.3 *Manhattan Serenade* deluxe publication cover and back page, 1931 Robbins stock orchestration.

"script" that is adapted to a range of realizations.[20] This mutability is evident across table 3.1a. Thus, while the album liner notes remark that the "orchestrations were prepared . . . by George Leeman from sketches by the composer," his *Serenade* rendition, nonetheless, references recognizable "script" elements from the Shilkret and Savino orchestrations. And the latter seems the more immediate model for both the 1931 Whiteman radio arrangement and several film adoptions of *Serenade*, though the 1929 MGM film short, *Manhattan Serenade* (discussed in detail later), uses the Shilkret recording outright. In comparing the 1928 Shilkret and 1940 Whiteman orchestrations, one can view a historical shift within the MAM idiom's dance-band-to-concert-music spectrum. While the Shilkret recording suggests 1920s novelty dance-band scores (part of symphonic-jazz repertory) in its use of slide guitar, banjo, woodblocks, and certain reed-and-brass performance practices, the 1940 orchestration reveals an updated "pops" cultural agenda in the privileging of semi-"serious"-sounding radio/television orchestral scoring, although precursors to these semi-"serious" qualities are certainly present within the "light music" framing of Shilkret's Salon Orchestra.

As I discuss elsewhere, novelty compositions (a popular piano solo and orchestra tradition with close ties to three-strain ragtime forms) were a major tributary to the MAM idiom.[21] The chief difference lay in expressive character—that is, where novelty works maintain a steady, dance-oriented tempo, early MAM works add contrasting "concert music" expressivity. This novelty/MAM idiomatic semi-overlap is suggested, for instance, through a comparison of *Manhattan Serenade* and Alter's contemporaneous "novelty" *Dolly Dimples*, published as both a piano solo and in a commercial "concert edition" orchestral arrangement by Paul Whiteman Publications in 1927.[22] *Manhattan Serenade* was likely the first MAM score published after the dissolution of Paul Whiteman Publications. Whiteman recorded an arrangement of *Dolly Dimples* with his regular dance orchestra in January 1928.[23] I have previously compared *Serenade*'s three-strain MAM formal model to both earlier three-strain novelty ragtime piano works and *Dolly Dimples*, as well as to greatly extended MAM symphonic jazz strain–based arrangements.[24] There is a clear shared "production" or show-music arranging tradition that undergirds all these MAM concert works.

From the 1910s these popular-leaning orchestral scores were regularly performed in nonfilm entertainments given by movie palace orchestras. By the mid-1920s, the syncopated orchestral novelty idiom equally found its way into both dance bands and musical theater and Hollywood production-number traditions. Across the late 1920s the MAM scores expanded the novelty formal model to include classicistic musical melodrama, with regularly varied tempi and performance expressions, and contrasting textures derived from dance bands, concert music, and Broadway-Hollywood show music. Many of these hybrid qualities are apparent in tables 3.1a, 3.1b, and 3.2 and examples 3.1 and 3.2. But the dividing line between novelty orchestral music and the MAM scores is thin in the late 1920s. For example, in 1928 Robbins published both *Manhattan Serenade* and *Dolly Dimples* in the Modern American Music series.

Press announcements concerning Alter's *Serenade* appear in the months before the Shilkret recording release. For example, *Billboard* announced that Alter, the "solo pianist of the *Greenwich Village Follies*," "has written a jazz concerto called *Manhattan Serenade*" to "be featured in the revue."[25] Following the recording release, *Variety* called the Shilkret premiere recording "a gem" "in contemporary orchestration" of "the modernistic school."[26] Not long after, Alter had solo piano performances of the *Serenade* over New York radio (alongside *Dolly Dimples*), and the performance was showcased in a film-prologue variety revue and vaudeville.[27] In April 1929 Alter joined the Broadway migration to Hollywood. He followed Jack Robbins and the arranger, Lange, to MGM studios. MGM's interest in capitalizing on the "Modern American" symphonic-jazz idiom is central to the hire of Lange. In addition to his top-tier work for New York publishers, stage shows, and dance bands, Lange's 1926 book, *Arranging for the Modern Dance Orchestra* (whose second edition was printed by Robbins), was the primary manual of this practice.[28] In November 1929 *Variety* announced the MGM "deluxe production" *Serenade* film short. This reportedly cost $40,000 (about $715,000 in 2023). According to Lange—the film's musical director—this short was the studio's first experiment with prerecorded playback synchronization.[29] Robbins trade advertisements continued to prominently feature *Serenade* well into the following decade, and it was at the forefront of the 1942 Robbins innovation of adding lyrics to themes from the MAM scores. As noted, the vocal version of *Manhattan Serenade* became hits for Dorsey's orchestra and for singer Dinah Shore.[30] The score also found its way into prominent 1930s film and radio. This mini history of *Serenade* thus suggests a cross-entertainment transmission map for Modern Metropolitan Music that follows the Broadway-to-Hollywood talent migration.

The contextual history outlined thus far amply illustrates a number of core cultural themes connected to *Manhattan Serenade* and the Modern Metropolitan Music trope it represents. Of the five MAM metropolitan themes—the luxury smart-set lifestyle, the city symphony, the city as theater, the melting-pot city, and Harlem entertainment—the "city symphony" idea is perhaps the most obscure. The city-symphony trope of popular media includes the mythological aspects of the skyscraper and the glorification of the machine, the cultural collisions of modern urban life, and the omnipresent hectic ambiance of the urban milieu.[31] These Modern Metropolitan Music themes hold associative ties to glamorous lifestyle depictions and metropolitan mythology in popular media images of modern urban America. The stylistic traits of the MAM idiom formed widely disseminated musical topics for communicating a lexicon of such "metropolitan" associations when underscoring this popular media.[32] Two of *Serenade*'s early film adaptations offer insights into this interwar Broadway-to-Hollywood cultural lexicon.

Metropolitan Impressions and Early Sound Film

The *Manhattan Serenade* film short amply illustrates all five MAM cultural themes. The short is framed with Central Park dialogue between strangers, where a man describes the glorious culture of New York to the disheartened newcomer, the woman. The opening is filmed in a brownscale, or sepia, print. Alter's *Serenade* is initially employed as the main title cue and initial underscoring. The man's supposed explanation is filmic, rather than oral, resulting in an audiovisual travelogue sequence celebrating New York. The film stock switches to grayscale black-and-white, and an aerial and street-level tour ensues, all set to a full Shilkret recording of *Serenade*. All other *Serenade* borrowings in the film were arrangements by Lange. The uncredited use of the commercial recording for the tour montage likely offered a cost-cutting benefit, and it further allowed Lange to focus on the development of other musical scenes.

The tour opens with a template for a soon-to-emerge visual cliché for establishing-scenes within Hollywood's New York–themed films: beginning with urban-glamour aerial shots of New York harbor, the Statue of Liberty, and the majesty of lower-Manhattan skyscrapers (see fig. 3.4 top, which foreshadows the later Whiteman *Album* cover), the camera descends into the hard "reality" of lower-income life of the Lower East Side. This New York–Hollywood visual trope takes shape in the opening sequences of influential films like the 1931 *Street Scene* (discussed later).[33] Like the latter film, many of these productions employ the MAM idiom as underscoring for such American urban high-low social collisions. The tour in *Manhattan Serenade* takes its time to lay out this trajectory over the melancholy mood of Strain A. Lower Manhattan is then followed by shots above the buildings and traffic above Midtown South. Strain B arrives to underscore aerial shots above lower Fifth Avenue, the Flatiron Building, and Madison Square Park. This is followed by shots high above Lenox Hill and shots of Roosevelt Island and more skyscrapers. A brief arrival at street level in Midtown allows the latter half of the Strain B¹—which shifts between assertively active and rubato reflective phrases—to illustrate both the jostling life of dense New York street and foot

FIGURE 3.4 Screen shots from the 1929 film *Manhattan Serenade*. (*Top*) an aerial shot of lower Manhattan; (*middle*) a superimposition of two shots of traffic at Times Square with the Paramount Theatre in the background; (*bottom*) a still from "Harlem Heaven."

traffic, as well as Lower East Side immigrant life with street vendors, Hassidic Jews, and laundry on fire escapes. The bustling vivace return of Strain B^2 underscores an unusual superimposition (using two images of the same intersection) of Midtown traffic and pedestrians just in front of the Times Square Paramount Theater. This effect heightens the frenzy of urban life (see fig. 3.4 middle). There are then shots under the elevated trains and the East River under the Brooklyn Bridge. The latter is notably set to the Strain B, phrase b, first with solo slide guitar, and then with Shilkret's new, reflective solo violin scoring as well as interpolated Strain A material. The film subsequently arrives again at the bustling Times Square, this time emphasizing the diversity of entertainment signage. Then, following Columbus Circle, there are shots of grazing cattle in Central Park (!) with tall buildings as a backdrop. The tour closes in Times Square at nighttime at the eight-minute mark of this twenty-minute film.

The next extended middle core of the short offers a film prologue revue in brief. Following the recapitulation and final cadence of *Manhattan Serenade*'s Strain A^3, the camera zooms in on the nighttime neon of a *Ziegfeld Follies* sign. This segues to an unusual sequence of two extended Technicolor-film production numbers, the "Owl Number" and "Harlem Heaven" (see fig. 3.4 bottom). The first represents white Broadway, the latter represents Black Broadway and Harlem nightclub entertainment. These are separated by a brief, street-shot transition filmed while driving up Harlem's Seventh Avenue at night. This shows the neon of famous Harlem clubs like Connie's Inn. Each number employs *Serenade* motives as transitional material. The first production number stars the Brox Sisters, who soon appeared in Whiteman's 1930 Technicolor extravaganza, *King of Jazz* (Universal). The Harlem-entertainment number features Nina Mae McKinney, who also starred in the 1929 King Vidor–directed *Hallelujah*, a landmark all-Black film. Both numbers include extended, multithematic arrangements with richly staged sets and a multitude of costumed chorus girls. The conclusion to *Manhattan Serenade* returns to the couple. The woman joyfully proclaims that she finally "understands" New York, just as the pair lean in to embrace, and the *Serenade* theme A swells to a climax.

A more widely circulated and better-integrated underscoring employment of *Serenade* in Hollywood production practice can be seen in *My Man Godfrey*, starring Carole Lombard and William Powell. A *Billboard* review of this "ace entertainment" "with social significance" describes its plot as follows: "Godfrey Parke, once a socialite but now a hobo . . . on a city dump, is taken . . . by Irene Bullock, a Park Avenue brat, as her trophy in a 'scavenger hunt.' . . . [He] . . . is prevailed upon to become Butler by the Bullock family. . . . Godfrey, . . . among the screwiest family, rehabilitates himself[,] . . . save[s] the Bullock family fortune . . . [and] is successfully pursued by amorous Irene."[34]

The cue for the film opening and establishing bridge adapts *Serenade* into an ostentatious, jazzy Broadway-Hollywood variation on the classical Hollywood main title cue. The scoring is in every way bigger, brassier, more lush, more melodramatic, and more rhythmic, beginning with a flashy, rhythmically "straight" opening of blaring trumpets, crashing cymbals, and a busy musical flourish. The screen card announces the title cast via a Broadway-style, rooftop, flashing-neon billboard sign. The camera then continues a long rightward pan of Art Deco–stylized buildings with flashing-neon film-credit signs on the Brooklyn waterfront. After the title card (see fig. 3.5, top), a swinging, brassy statement of Strain B appears as the primary theme. This leads to a swelling sequence of suspense chords before an all-out Broadway-Hollywood, brass-and-saxophone Strain B "swing" scoring. After more rising-suspense chords, a brassy cadence (with cymbal crash) announces the production company. Following a harp sweep, a varied Strain B returns with high-register strings and swinging drum kit. In sync with the Gregory La Cava director card, phrase b provides a contrasting lighter flute-harp-and-sustained-strings scoring. At the second Powell and Lombard credit card, the score returns to full-on swing and brass-section blare. Then a varied phrase ending leads viewers directly from the title sequence down into the homeless slums just as the melancholy Strain A enters as a bridging theme—literally underneath the Brooklyn Bridge (see fig. 3.5 middle). Viewers see an impoverished homeless camp of "forgotten men." The bridge is set against a backdrop of the glamorous Manhattan skyline. This visualizes the chasm of high-low social-class divisions, while the modern metropolitan, sustained high-low topics of the *Serenade* audibly invoke the same tensions.

Like the 1929 short, *Serenade*'s contrasting strains and its hybrid scoring and stylistic gestures support a string of sustained high-low class images and narrative conceits that span most of the aforementioned program-topic areas of modern metropolitan music. Like the narrative of the film, the final impression is a sense of witty cultural commentary calculated for the culturally "middle" tastes of the mass-market every(wo)man despite its outward packaging as classy urban culture. Like the fantasy of Godfrey himself—or the film's Whitemanesque MAM-derived underscoring—such high-low, street-smart classiness is something we all might aspire toward.

The second passage in which *Godfrey* adapts *Serenade* involves a bridge cue two-thirds into the film. The previous scene ends with the now-dapper Godfrey returning to the homeless encampment to discuss business plans. Godfrey—in Powell's famous mid-Atlantic, elevated diction—tells his well-dressed, British associate that he plans to employ these "forgotten men" (homeless) in a new "swanky nightclub." The high-low "class" associations

FIGURE 3.5 Screen shots from the 1936 film *My Man Godfrey*. (*Top*) the film title card; (*middle*) the opening backdrop image for the establishing scene; and (*bottom*) the initial meet-cute, high-low juxtaposition of Godfrey (William Powell) as a "forgotten man" and Irene (Carole Lombard) as a glamorous society love interest.

of *Serenade* provide a suitable underscoring bridge between this scheme for a swanky transformation of low culture and the swanky malaise of the Park Avenue blue bloods. The montage cue first underscores a lady's hands opening an issue of *Gotham Gossip*. This stylized magazine depicts a tuxedoed gentleman, a flapper girlfriend in mink, background skyscrapers, and a quasi-Cubist checkerboard background. The lady's hand lands on the "Park Avenue Chatter" page with a glamour photo of Irene. The trumpet-lead scoring here (with woodwind and string backing) borrows much from the main-title orchestration. Sequenced Strain C motives lead to a busy "city symphony" rhythmic bustle. Several texture shifts (including dance-band saxophones) and Strain-C motive sequences, heighten the anticipation of this Park Avenue chatter. A cymbal crash leads to Strain B motive sequences and the cue's conclusion: a sharp brass chord, a harp sweep, comically "laughing" clarinets, wah-wah brass, sighing saxophones, and a lonely bass clarinet statement of the minor-key Strain A as the viewer lands in the elaborate Park Avenue mansion of the Bullocks.

These two sequences trade on *Serenade*'s New York, Broadway, and modern metropolitan class—or *classy*—programmatic cultural topics. Further, it should be recalled that each of these entertainment contexts are escapist entertainment products of the Depression. Depression-era Hollywood films abound in such glamorized, sustained high-low entertainment juxtapositions. The entire catalogue of Fred Astaire and Ginger Rodgers RKO film musicals comes to mind, with sparkling "modern American" (Whitemanesque) Gershwin and Cole Porter snappy song arrangements and production numbers and narrative tropes of self-made, successful (obviously white) American everymen and-women who rise from the tenements to the penthouse and embodying glamorous, jazz-inclined, aspirational, modern lifestyles with a hint of Broadway/Hollywood glitz. Entertainment that can be enjoyed for the cheap price of a movie ticket. And the free airwaves of radio provide even greater public access to such Depression-era modern American high-low glamour. The Whitemanesque modern American orchestral model dominated this medium across this era. The emergence of this radio orchestra model, though, had much to do with the Whiteman orchestra's late 1920s influence on "class" variety entertainment.

Jazzique and Interwar Classy Popular Music

Whiteman himself articulated the particularities of his entertainment brand in interviews and private business correspondence. For instance, in the late 1930s Whiteman wrote to a professional acquaintance and potential sponsor for a new Whiteman radio program. The letter reminds his acquaintance of the bandleader's many "show business" contributions to the history of radio and the influence of these contributions on popular radio programming.[35]

After noting an earlier, mutual sponsorship discussion with General Motors, Whiteman proposes a new variety entertainment program that he wants to broadcast from a specially built radio theater "on Broadway." This venue would boast the "largest and most attractive showroom" that could attract "more people . . . than go to a World['s] Fair in a day." The hoped-for "automobile sponsor" would have their own clubroom, and the show would offer a "million . . . tie-ups for customers." He even describes this as a "monster musical circus" and "a miniature [musical] world brought to your door."[36] Following the models of his earlier, 1920s and 1930s radio programs, Whiteman suggests a musical-variety format involving hit popular music, guest popular- and concert-music singers and instrumentalists, and various "most played" light—or pops-oriented—concert-music arrangements.[37] He mentions in the same sentence both several recent Whiteman-band-plus-symphony pops events and a sold-out, major-grossing New York Hippodrome Theatre engagement of his orchestra (a fifty-three-hundred-seat venue for large theatrical and vaudeville spectacles, including circuses).[38] Whiteman proposes that the radio program's staging would set "the boys . . . in uniform," sectionally dressed in red, white, and blue on a bandstand "in ultra-modern chromium . . . suitable to [Art Deco–stylized] streamlining, just like the new autos."[39] In contrast to symphonic radio programs that "do not play music as, for or with the general public,"[40] Whiteman describes a "great selling program" with a "titular effect." His show would feature an orchestra that combines the popular appeal of "old Sousa marches, the [jazzy] swing of the ballroom, tricks of the stage, grandeur of the symphony, led by an international name" celebrity (i.e., himself). He characterizes this orchestra as a "streamline age" ensemble that was "not a symphony" of "200" but, rather, the distinct, smaller "grouping of instruments such as I use."[41] By this, he is referring to the Whiteman-modeled interwar studio or stage orchestra. Such an ensemble comprises a jazz-leaning dance-band core (with multi-instrumentalists) merged with a contingent of strings and select orchestral instruments. This ensemble is said to be as "versatile as an automobile trailer." He describes this ensemble model repeatedly as "an *American* institution" and underscores that it is not a symphony, brass band, nor swing band but relies on the top talent from all three, combining each idiom in a more "sparkling, scintillating, brilliant . . . manner than ever played before." And they "can really swing—and how!"[42] He suggests promotional bylines such as "As Modern as This Streamline Age," "For Modern American Music," "As Versatile as the Latest Motor Trailer," "The Last Gasp in Swingcopation," and "Sparkling Modern American Music."[43]

This letter demarcates the "show business" parameters of both Whitemanesque entertainment aesthetics and his conception of Modern American Music. This phrase is exceptionally meaningful to Whiteman. Indeed, many areas of this letter reinforce W. Anthony Sheppard's observation that across the 1930s Whiteman's promotional title ultimately changed from King of Jazz to "the greatest name in modern American music."[44] Despite the requisite application of arranging textures derived from concert music, the Whitemanesque idiom is fundamentally based on the stylistic and formal idioms and conventions of American popular music and jazz. The above-cited letter amply suggests how this Whitemanesque aesthetic engaged period "show business" modes of musical glamour in production, performance, and presentation.

This letter was written to an entertainment executive in Beverly Hills. They became acquainted during Whiteman's early 1930s film work. While the letter's showbiz framing—in language, in aesthetic allusions, and in many other ways—grounds the Whitemanesque musical aesthetic in Hollywood, it also centrally grounds this entertainment mode in New York and Broadway. I argue that this Broadway-Hollywood entertainment framing, and especially the entertainment myths of New York in the popular imagination,[45] are central to understanding Whitemanesque Modern American Music.

These sustained high-low cultural tensions and promotional pretensions were, likewise, central to both the critical disparagement of Whiteman and Whitemanesque MAM in post-1930 jazz historiography. For example, Winthrop Sargeant, a mid-1930s critic, described Whiteman-styled symphonic jazz as a "variety-show type of jazz band" for "musical yokels" who were not able to appreciate a symphony orchestra. The idiom was characterized by its "fusion of the pretentious and commonplace," its "plushy tone," "gilded, exotic, orchestral effects," and excessive "variations, and . . . modulations."[46] Sargeant further contends this "musical vulgarity" reflects the music's "theatrical surroundings," the garish deluxe movie palaces like Grauman's Chinese Theatre and the Roxy Theater. It was precisely this classy cultural context that nurtured the MAM idiom.

A 1927 trade announcement of Paul Whiteman Publications notes both the Paramount film prologue revues (invoking the prestige of this engagement) and the series' inclusion of the three core categories of symphonic jazz: dance-band arrangements, concert works, and "jazzed" classics.[47] From 1927 Modern American Music became the epithet for this repertory. When Robbins took over the publication series in 1928, it was narrowed to solo piano and orchestral arrangements.[48] Robbins's aspirational respectability politics are seen in the pronouncement that "the great significance" of these scores is that they "permit greater seriousness in popular publications."[49] But there was also money to be made in catering to such middlebrow interests.

The context of "class" variety entertainment is central to this milieu. Whiteman's mid-1920s concert-orchestra enlargement was likely motivated both by "symphonic" aspirations and by interest in the theater, vaudeville, and movie-palace orchestra market. Ties to such class variety entertainment are evidenced in their repertory, radio work, the film *King of Jazz,* and many stage and revue engagements. In the latter, MAM compositions played a variety-act role equivalent to production numbers and even in Whiteman's Experiment[s] in Modern Music concerts and concert tours of the 1920s and 1930s, this variety aesthetic governed programming. For example, in reviewing Whiteman's 1928 Third Experiment concert, Olin Downes writes of symphonic-jazz practices "no doubt good for *musical vaudeville*" despite their "pretentiously cut" arranging.[50] Whiteman's orchestra represented the consummate 1920s dance band because of its emphases on showmanship, stylistic diversity, and virtuosic spectacle alongside both artful symphonic and syncopated stylizations. *Variety* often referred to music in this mode as "jazzique," denoting an elevated, jazz-indebted and/or syncopated musical entertainment. For instance, in September 1927, *Variety* announced "Broadway houses' band policy" for film prologue revue shows were going "jazzique."[51] Similar phrasings are seen throughout Whiteman press coverage of the day. The word combines "jazz" plus "classique," meaning classical in a glorified French spelling, but classique likewise invokes notions of "classy" culture.

Whiteman's variety-stage work can be partly illustrated via the orchestra's 1928 film-prologue collaboration with the later director of *King of Jazz,* John Murray Anderson. The class-entertainment spectacle of these coproduced prologue shows was highly touted by the Paramount Publix theater chain:

> The Paramount Theatre is going to top any previous . . . popular entertainment. Not only is Paul Whiteman being brought back with his full orchestra, but . . . the whole act will be surrounded by a stage show that is the last word in Broadway entertainment. Special costumes, scenic designs, special talent, special songs, chorus girls, and all the accompanying elements that go to make up a big Broadway revue will find a place on the Whiteman program.

The band's solo performances in this lavish revue included specialty instrumental numbers, accompanied vocal solos and trios, the occasional concert work, and medleys. In the prologue called *Rainbow Rhapsody,* for instance, was an extended medley, *Shades of Blues,* which was based on "a potpourri of indigo-titled themes including the *Blue Danube Waltz,* a snatch of the *Rhapsody in Blue,* the *Waltz Bluette* with violin quintet interludes, *Wabash Blues, Alice Blue Gown* (saxophone septet arrangement) . . . [and] *St. Louis Blues* climaxed by Mike Pingitore at the banjo."[52] The title of this particular production obviously references the *Rhapsody in Blue*, but it does so in a manner that equates this symphonic-jazz landmark with the colorful variety (the "rainbow") of revue entertainment.

King of Jazz was absolutely framed under the same entertainment aesthetics, as were many sound-transition musical films. Compare, for example, the advertising for *King of Jazz* with a 1929 Paramount Pictures advertisement. In typical entertainment industry Broadway-Hollywood-*Variety* ballyhoo, the Paramount ad (in a manner akin to the Paramount-Publix prologue promotion) touts their 1929–30 sound-and-color film releases as "New and Greater Entertainments of a New Show World" with "talking, singing, dancing. Flashing with Color . . . Stage, motion pictures, radio, and music wedded. All the arts and sciences enriching the screen. Broadway reaching around the world. And Paramount putting your theatre on the Gay White Way to super-profits." *Variety*'s pages in this era are filled with similar "super-show" productions that are "all-talking," "singing and dancing," often in "Technicolor," and can feature spectacular "music score[s] and sound effects."[53] This is seen with the advertising copy for Universal's *King of Jazz*, which is characterized as a "bon bon of musical morsels," a "thrilling . . . pulse-quickener" and a "once in a lifetime show" "glorified by COLOR!" Universal proclaims "they'll all want to see" the lavish production numbers to the *Rhapsody in Blue* "dramatization" and "The Melting Pot," "a tremendous number, remarkable for size, music, color, and scenic effects" with "the music of all nations."[54] Remember, of course, that 1928–29 was also the period of the *Serenade* short and the New York–to-Hollywood talent migration that brought Alter, Lange, Heindorf, Robbins, and others West. Whitemanesque symphonic jazz was *the* Modern American show-music sound.

As argued, the conventions of MAM concert works greatly overlap with the elaborate production-number arranging practices of musical theater and musical revues, contemporary radio programming, and other related popular orchestral entertainments. The NBC arranger, Tom Bennett, noted in 1946 that "the present radio orchestra is an outgrowth of Ferde Grofé's innovation[s]" in the arrangement of "popular and light pieces in a style that is neither dance nor concert music."[55] In Bennett's opinion, the 1920s Whitemanesque arranging models of Grofé and Lange were especially important for the concert-style production-number traditions—what Bennett calls "the big, spectacular arrangements"—of interwar radio programming. In parallel, across the 1920s to mid-1940s period that Bennett discusses, beyond producing such production arrangements, national radio also pursued considerable licensing of Robbins MAM scores for radio themes and underscoring. Such theme licensing included Grofé's "On the Trail" for the Philip Morris program, Grofé's *Metropolis* and Newman's *Street Scene* for

CBS's *This Is New York*, and *Manhattan Serenade* for the comedy *Easy Aces*. Further, Whiteman and his competitors regularly performed such works as production numbers. Whiteman's variety shows in this vein include the 1929–30 *Old Gold Hour* and the 1933–35 *Kraft Music Hall* show. Each regularly featured production-style extended song arrangements as well as MAM concert works in production-number entertainment roles. Whiteman's 1932–33 *Buick Program* even broadcast a notable arrangement of *Manhattan Serenade* that combined both practices.

Spectacular Productions in Whitemanesque Radio Arranging

It is difficult to know the precise entertainment programming context of the aforementioned *Serenade* arrangement by Huxley for the *Buick Program*. However, various press documents provide useful facets and contextual understandings of the program overall. A 1935 internal NBC report indicates that General Motors sponsored several 1920s and 1930s musical-variety programs. Musical entertainments were central to sponsored programming and, thus, a key forum for product advertising. As a product advertised during the Depression, then as now, the automobile industry focused on this big-ticket purchase as a lifestyle and socioeconomic marker for upwards mobility, social and financial success, modernity, and fashion. This GM radio-sponsorship framing for the Whiteman show is instructive.

The first GM program was a Carnegie Hall July 1927 broadcast that featured former John Philip Sousa Band star Arthur Pryor, then fifty-eight years old and still associated with middlebrow "light" concert and wind-band music. In 1931–32, the *Buick Revellers* program featured a "lively program of semi-classical and popular songs [with] an orchestra directed by Frank Black."[56] Black became a major radio musical director across the 1930s and 1940s, including conducting lighter fare of the NBC Symphony Orchestra. Black entered radio in the 1920s after working as a Tin Pan Alley arranging competitor to Lange. Black produced products like a 1924 series of "Rhythmodic Classics," which were "modern" dance-band medleys of pops-concert and/or light-classical staples.[57] Both areas of Black's career were focused on the middlebrow cultural democratization of concert music. This aligns with conductor Arturo Toscanini's role in NBC's middlebrow radio and recording efforts at both the popularization of "nineteenth-century [European] warhorses [that] were recycled to amass a primer for radio-era listeners,"[58] as well as the larger interwar music-appreciation "racket" (Virgil Thomson's characterization). Joseph Horowitz's middlebrow Toscanini characterization suggests a highbrow-downward push in middlebrow culture.[59] By contrast, the NBC report describes the 1932–33 Whiteman program as featuring "semi-popular music"—as opposed to "semi-classical"—a characterization that suggests a populist-mainstream push "upwards."[60] This is more a popular music middlebrowism in terms of cultural promotion and marketing. This perspective is further evident in the journalism around the show.

Whiteman had previous auto radio-sponsorship experience with the 1928 Chrysler-Dodge *Victory Hour* (Whiteman was not the host); the GM-sponsored 1932 *Paul Whiteman's Orchestra* show that promoted Buick, Oldsmobile, and Pontiac cars; and the late 1932 *Whiteman's Pontiac Chieftains*.[61] As a widely popular bandleader with mainstream appeal, particularly to potential customers who could afford automobiles in the Depression, Whiteman's repeat broadcast engagements underscore his investment value to GM. The NBC report documents automotive-industry advertising, noting that by 1934, 9.5 percent of their promotion efforts, totaling $3,772,000, was spent on radio advertising (the rest was print).[62] These numbers represented a nine-fold increase since 1927, "a noteworthy record during the depression years."[63] This report appears a year after the Whiteman program, underscoring the class-culture value—and broad market accessibility—of the Whitemanesque entertainment brand. There is a range of 1932 press on such automotive "exploitation" (advertising) efforts through popular music programming, with Whiteman being the sole "long-term" contract mentioned.[64]

The Whiteman band—and *brand*—clearly benefitted through the cross-entertainment synergy from its multicontext engagements and active recording career. During their radio engagement, the orchestra was featured in at least two deluxe movie-palace engagements, vaudeville theater dates, and a nightclub engagement at the high-class New York Biltmore Hotel.[65] There are, however, suggestions that the Whiteman brand needed to retain at least one foot in popular entertainment. For example, two months into the program, *Billboard* suggests that GM "acknowledged" Whiteman's programming "to be a high-class proposition, [but] a less highbrow form of entertainment is desired and . . . something more lively" might be seen as beneficial.[66] Some of the advertising-friendly qualities of the Whiteman brand are seen in the November 1932 *Billboard* review of the show, which starts:

> Switching from Pontiac to Buick, eliminating hotcha [= hot or swinging jazz?] and injecting . . . concert type arrangements, Paul Whiteman again gives the folks something to talk about. Without being too heavy [i.e., serious minded or highbrow], the program trotted out one of the richest handfuls of modern jazz arrangements ever heard on any half-hour period unless it was one of the maestro's own recent Sunday night concerts.[67]

The programming seems to have given considerable focus to vocalists, which aligns with the post-1930 popularity of crooners. The review notes only one regular Whiteman vocalist, the crooner Jack Fulton, and the addition of a "conservative [soprano-tenor] duo with no frills." The latter were featured in arrangements of numbers from a Rudolf Friml Broadway operetta. The review calls "Whiteman and these singers . . . probably one of the best G.M. radio [shows] period to date." The program included similar quasi-elevated Broadway vocal numbers with "unique arrangement," two romantic "band tunes" from the songs in the 1932 Hollywood Rodgers and Hart film musical, *Love Me Tonight* (Paramount; starring operetta-leaning vocalists Maurice Chevalier and Jeanette MacDonald), and a closing arrangement of the "light" concert staple, *Parade of the Wooden Soldiers*, a number that Whiteman and Grofé had helped to popularize in 1922. The Rodgers and Hart numbers likely functioned as cross-media entertainment promotions (film, sheet music, and radio).[68]

The Whiteman Collection at Williams College contains approximately 115 arrangements by Huxley, the *Serenade* radio-production arranger. He thus had a considerable role in the mid-1930s Whiteman organization. He was, for instance, a contributor to the 1932 and 1933 Whiteman Fourth and Fifth Experiment in American Modern Music concerts. Both events illustrate the class-culture attraction of the MAM brand. The audience for the Fifth is simply described in a review as "Broadway and a sprinkling of the upper-crust," while the coverage for the Fourth describes a "strange mingling of Broadway, Tin Pan Alley, and straight-jacket [highbrow] musicos" that included Serge "Rachmaninoff, a Grofé fan, long-jowled music critics, blues singers, tooters, song pluggers, popular music publishers—they were all there."[69] The latter concert included both Carroll's "five-minute foxtrot" arrangement of Ravel's *Bolero* and his orchestration of Gershwin's *An American in Paris*. While Huxley was contracted for ample popular music arrangements, he is notably a regular contributor to "jazzed classic" arrangements (Johann Strauss's *Blue Danube Waltz* and *Tales from the Vienna Woods*, as well as Debussy's *Golliwog's Cakewalk*). He further wrote extended concert medleys devoted to Broadway shows and scored MAM works like Suesse's *Jazz Nocturne*, Matty Malneck and Frank Signorelli's *Park Avenue Fantasy*, and Rube Bloom's *Song of the Bayou*, among others. This middlebrow concert music points toward his post-Whiteman engagement with Andre Kostelanetz, a celebrity radio-orchestra personality who embraced the middlebrow characterization.[70] A 1935 *Metronome* article mentions Huxley's Kostelanetz *Chesterfield [Cigarette] Hour* work alongside the "brilliant arrangements" of Whiteman's arrangers and then frames this radio idiom as being indebted to mid-1920s Whiteman-Lange-Grofé arranging. The article further connects this practice to Hollywood (via Lange).[71] A 1936 article lists Huxley as Kostelanetz's top "sweet jazz" specialist and notes his "distinct style in deluxe renditions of modern music." *Metronome* characterizes this as "pop music with all the trappings."[72] The latter quip aptly captures a key MAM arranging aesthetic, and such qualities are readily reflected in Huxley's arrangement of *Serenade*.

Tables 3.1a and 3.1b sketch the Huxley arrangement in comparison to other realizations discussed in this chapter. This fascinating production number demonstrates this chapter's cross-entertainment arguments for understanding the MAM concert works as concertized popular music rather than traditional, formal concert music. Huxley first produced a hybrid arrangement that included many of the concert-style piano features seen in the other realizations, but he combined this with vocal solo–plus-choir textures. It is a typically elaborate production number but combines popular-song arrangement with a MAM work. Somewhere in the program-development process (a broadcast transcription has yet to be located), entertainment considerations led to integrating an "announcer" into the performance. Whiteman himself typically acted as a speaking personality in his radio programs. As such, the manuscript "announcer" designations seem to refer to another personality, likely the anonymous announcer who promoted GM/Buick products within the show. It seems likely that this allowed for some promotional copy for the sponsor, Buick. This revision (marked "RESCORE" in tables 3.1a and 3.1b) calls for seventy-one bars to be inserted into the basic formal design seen in other *Serenade* renditions. This quasi-development passage involves a long string of restless subsections (up to twelve bars in length) with regular modulations and frequent motivic references to the A and B strain themes. While the announcer's scripts are lost, the manuscript notes reveal a Manhattan travelogue through many key, meter, and texture changes that guide listeners' imaginations to hear "Italian," "Jewish," "Irish," and "Harlem" neighborhoods. There are narrative announcer interjections, possibly demonstrating Buick's product relevance to all Americans. As seen in the lyrics note after table 3.1a, the lyrics—based on Johnson's song—illustrate numerous Modern American tropes discussed with the MGM short.

Whiteman's peers, likewise, adapted the Whitemanesque entertainment model to radio. This process is readily heard in several 1936 transcriptions of the *Ford V-8 Revue*, directed by Grofé.[73] Again, the automotive industry connected the Whitemanesque musical brand to mid-Depression consumers for automobiles. Each *V8 Revue* program begins and ends with the show's theme music, an excerpt from the "Covered Wagon" movement of Grofé's 1936 Ford-dedicated *Wheels* suite. This theme is a "humble" Americana-style hymn scored for brass choir and strings that underscores an announcer voiceover for the sponsor: "The *Ford V-8 Revue*. A transcribed program presented for your pleasure by your Ford dealer. Music by Grofé. Sweet singing by the noted male octet, the Buccaneers, and Marguerite Howard." This half-hour show regularly consisted of three to four numbers. The first and last numbers were reserved for upbeat, Grofé-Lange–style, popular-song arrangements featuring extended vocal choruses. The first number frequently plugged a recent song published by Robbins. The third slot was a vocal-comedy or novelty number. Following an announcement about Ford's "Renewed and Guaranteed" used-car program, the second number routinely consisted of a movement from one of Grofé's MAM concert suites. This was introduced by a colorful description of the intent of the movement and followed by a second extended advertisement.

The MAM variety-entertainment framing of both show examples is akin to the typical grand production number that closes the first half of a musical revue. In both cases, the function of such a "spectacular" number was to revitalize the audience's interest in the program just before intermission (e.g., advertisements for Ford's V-8 engine rather than intermission). Moreover, in variety-entertainment adoptions of these scores, the MAM works functioned equally well as both production numbers and show themes.

Heading West: Hollywood's Sound Transition and the MAM Idiom

As illustrated, the cultural agenda of the MAM idiom was to "glorify" American popular music by elevating it through "all the [classy] trappings." Early sound film's embrace of the MAM idiom occurred in parallel with radio and relied upon the same talent pool. Visual spectacle became increasingly cinematic in conception, with ever-more elaborate choreography of both staging and camerawork. The Broadway-transplant Busby Berkeley was central to such developments. Martin Rubin argues that an emerging Berkeleyesque aesthetic developed a cinematic "cultural vocabulary" of "showstopping spectacle."[74] Rubin's study frames this within a larger American "Tradition of [Entertainment] Spectacle." Not noted by Rubin is that much of the music of these Berkeley transition films is indebted to Whitemanesque arranging and personnel, and their larger spectacular production numbers frequently show connections between the MAM practices and production-number spectacle.

The history of the 1930 sound-transition film *Whoopee!* (Samuel Goldwyn) exemplifies the interrelation of New York entertainment, the MAM idiom, and Hollywood in this period.[75] In 1928 and 1929, film producer Samuel Goldwyn financed several Broadway musicals by Florenz Ziegfeld in exchange for film rights. This arrangement included Ziegfeld's 1928 hit *Whoopee!* In creating his film, Goldwyn imported to Hollywood virtually the entire original Broadway cast, Ziegfeld as coproducer, and the show's Whiteman-styled orchestra led by bandleader George Olsen. *Whoopee!* was the first film project of dance director Berkeley, and it was the second film of its musical director, Newman. Both were recent Broadway migrants.[76] Whiteman's orchestra had substituted for Olsen's in the Broadway show during a contractual dispute. Connections among MAM, Whitemanesque arranging, and the "spectacular" Broadway-Hollywood production-number traditions are further seen in the grand finale to this film, the "Song of the Setting Sun." The number reveals typical MAM arranging concerns for the musico-dramatic properties of a varied and elastic tempo, frequent modulation, flexible and expressive dynamics, varied performance character (tempo changes, meter changes, etc.), and shifting characteristic and/or style-topic scoring effects. In sum, the routine of this "spectacular" number is solidly grounded in the show-music arranging ideals that typify MAM arranging. *Whoopee!* was marketed as top-class Broadway entertainment for the price of a film.

With regard to the MMM topical interests in these early sound-film developments, Hollywood films of the interwar era continued to foster a strong national interest in New York and its symbolism as the quintessential, modern-American, urban melting pot. In the sound-transition period, this interest was expressed in a host of musical films with Broadway origins (*Whoopee!*, *Sally*, etc.), and through trends like New York–framed backstage musicals (*42nd Street*, *Footlight Parade*, the *Gold Diggers* musicals, etc.). *Manhattan Serenade* was an early sound-synchronization experiment in these trends, and it documents one key node in the New York–to-Hollywood transmission of the MAM idiom.

The off-screen business side of these activities was centrally guided by Jack Robbins, an astute businessman who constantly sought to expand his influence. In 1928 Robbins Music entered a twenty-year agreement allowing MGM, Twentieth-Century Fox, and Universal Studios access to the Robbins music catalogue.[77] Robbins directed the venture and came to Hollywood in 1929 as the publishing chief of MGM just as the studio released such landmark sound films as *The Broadway Melody* and *The Hollywood Revue of 1929*, each with Lange as musical director. Robbins was also behind the *Serenade* short (and RKO's later 1935 short using Alter's *Metropolitan Nocturne*).

Lange was brought west to establish the MGM music department. (Robbins was on the same westward train.)[78] Lange's expertise in the symphonic-jazz idiom of New York's jazzy Broadway musicals, movie palace orchestras, and the nation's top dance bands ideally positioned him for this assignment. As Lange notes, "the transition from the dance field into Hollywood was through the [Broadway] shows, and . . . these symphonic [jazz] arrangers." In Hollywood, Lange imported New York arrangers who became major film-music figures, including Heindorf. The exodus further included future cornerstone composers of classical-era movie music, Newman and Max Steiner, both of whom had been major names in 1920s Broadway musical theater. This bridge between Hollywood and Tin Pan Alley–Broadway is perfectly represented in the MAM catalogue in its broad list of composers who made their names in Hollywood, in compositions from the MAM score series being adapted into films, and in film scores adapted for the series. A sizable number of musical film shorts and movie-musical production numbers in the late 1920s to the 1940s (and beyond) directly employed a "glorified," concert-style, popular music vocabulary that was unmistakably derived from the MAM idiom.

In early sound film, Hollywood had yet to find a musical topic that captured the vibrancy of cosmopolitan modern America. Premigration sound-film depictions of New York entertainment and underscoring for depicting the American city employed the generically neutral sound of contemporary mood-music underscoring (akin more to Broadway melodrama and quasi-operetta than contemporary popular music). These transitional films were developed precisely when the Whitemanesque idiom was at its dance-band peak and widely heard in Jazz Age musical-theater stage productions. Famous early non-MAM film-music depictions of New York are heard, for instance, in the dramatic underscoring of Vitaphone's 1927 *The Jazz Singer* and the 1928 *The Lights of New York* (both Warner Bros.), each of which are set in the milieu of jazzy Broadway. When a popular-idiom underscoring does appear, as in the latter film's shots of Times Square, such films employ outdated songs like the 1904 "Give My Regards to Broadway" or the 1894 "East Side, West Side." The underscoring style has little to do with symphonic jazz–influenced Broadway scores.

Donald Crafton has documented early sound film's shift from class-oriented marketing and productions, with the promotion of high(er) culture (opera, operetta, and classical music) and more-elevated Broadway idioms ("class" Broadway like the *Ziegfeld Follies*), to mass-culture aesthetics. This occurred over 1927 to 1929, when the problems of sound-film technology encouraged what Crafton calls "virtual Broadway," with long, static camera shots and prominent stage-based filming.[79] Contemporary jazzy popular music arrangements—with limited symphonic-jazz trimmings—first emerged in musical-revue showcases such as *The Broadway Melody of 1929* and *The Hollywood Revue of 1929* (both MGM). Each film employed Robbins-exclusive music. Later films, such as the April 1930 *King of Jazz* and the September 1930 *Whoopee!* evidence a growing cinematic visual vocabulary free from traditional stage confines and prominent showcases for symphonic-jazz scoring, instrumentation, and production numbers. In complement, it was the 1931 *Street Scene* (Samuel Goldwyn and United Artists) and *Delicious* that seem to have established the MAM idiom as New York underscoring (building on the 1929 *Manhattan Serenade* MGM experiment).[80]

The Whitemanesque orchestra of the 1920s formed the basis for interwar radio orchestras *and* "lighter," or more popular-idiom, Hollywood film orchestras. As seen, this sort of popular studio orchestra was an expanded dance or stage band of between eighteen and forty-five instruments that consisted of trumpets, trombones, saxophonists that could double on various instruments, a rhythm section, and strings, and possibly a harp, French horn, or tuba. Despite the importance of the symphonic-orchestra model that defines much of Hollywood's underscoring from the early 1930s forward, this secondary hybrid orchestra is heard frequently among Hollywood scores at the beginning of the sound era. Its aural imprint can even be heard in the saxophone colorings of the dramatic cues in Steiner's 1933 score to *King Kong* (RKO). By the mid-1930s, though, the romantic symphonic ideal entrenched itself as the preferred idiom for dramas. However, this hybrid orchestral sound remained central to lighter film genres, like with *Godfrey*, and it informs urban dramas like *Street Scene*.

The 1931 *Street Scene* production featured Newman's first film score, and its Whitemanesque sound owes much to Heindorf, its Lange-protege orchestrator. Like *Manhattan Serenade*, the main title sequence for *Street Scene* offers a remarkable "city symphony" tour that anticipates an interwar Hollywood establishing-scene convention for New York narratives. In the two-and-a-half minute scene, the camera slowly descends from the glamorous modern skyscrapers down into the street-level poverty of the Lower East Side, a convention that again sustains high-low cultural tensions. Nearly the first full minute of the Newman score, though, accompanies film title cards projected over a static painted backdrop of the Lower East Side. The musical bridge to the establishing scene is a rising, jazzy clarinet glissando. This leads to the main-title theme, which is central to both the Robbins-published MAM piano-solo and orchestral scores and its 1933 hit song "Sentimental Rhapsody" with lyrics by Adamson.[81] The bridge and the lush, jazzy brass and strings scoring of the theme together accompany a skyline shot of Lower Manhattan. The camera then slowly pans downward from the gleaming skyscrapers toward the dirty-brick architectural mayhem of the Lower East Side. An "East Side, West Side" quotation effects a transition with children playing in the streets, before a montage of street life for Lower East Side inhabitants in the sweltering summer heat.

The main title cue for this sequence displays jazz-derived ingredients common to Gershwin's *Rhapsody in Blue* and late 1920s Broadway scoring, including flatted seventh-scale degrees, dance-band voiced brass and reed sections, coloristic effects, and a wah-wah muted trumpet, among other things. While there are direct Gershwin allusions, such as the *Rhapsody in Blue*–derived clarinet glissando,[82] the score centrally aligns with MAM conventions. In their film-narrative adoption, such textures capitalize on both the urban and melting-pot programmatic associations of the greater Modern Metropolitan Music topic. This city-symphony conception is suggested in the staging notes of Elmer Rice's original play—in its setting in a "mean quarter of New York," its dilapidated brownstone apartment building on a sweltering summer day, its prominent and diverse ethnic references, and so forth.[83] What is missing from this city symphony are Hollywood's typical juxtapositions of this lower-class New York milieu against the glamour of the city's skyscrapers and smart set. Such conventions are clearly seen in *Godfrey*, for example. The MAM idiom suitably underscores both films, however.

Hollywood's second-earliest underscoring paraphrase from the *Rhapsody in Blue* was by Gershwin himself for the 1931 film *Delicious*, which was his first film score. Fox asked Gershwin to compose an extended "New York Rhapsody" or "Melting Pot" sequence that would depict an immigrant's first experience of New York at night.[84] A prefatory scene describes the inspirations behind the young immigrant composer's "New York Rhapsody" (music later adapted to become Gershwin's *Second Rhapsody*). The character explains that the work "begins like we all see the City first—The great towers, almost in the clouds." He then plays the work's bustling allegro theme and adds "down below, in the long furrows, human seeds trying to grow to the light." Themes are said to represent city noise, "steel riveters," and so forth. These melting-pot, skyscraper, and urban-noise themes are central to Hollywood's typical Modern Metropolitan Music cues, as well as the titles, programs, and graphics of the Robbins MAM scores. They were not just Hollywood or Robbins constructs: these myths emerged from a web of intersecting themes in journalism, myths surrounding Tin Pan Alley and Broadway, and the Robbins MAM scores. Composers like Gershwin would describe their jazzy, modern-American rhapsodies as depicting "our vast melting pot, our metropolitan madness."[85]

Such high-low, melting-pot collisions evoke the gold-digger cliché of this period's MAM-indebted backstage film musicals, which depicted blue bloods slumming with red-blooded chorus girls for lowbrow entertainment. This cliché is famously realized in the 1933 *42nd Street*, which notably includes Berkeley's choreography alongside Heindorf's winning scoring of composer Harry Warren and lyricist Al Dubin's songs. A forty-four-page marketing manual characterizes this Depression-era glamorous film and its music as "a new deal in entertainment" "pulsating with passionate rhythm," and a "super spectacle." The manual further touts the film's bevy of stars and its "beauty-chorus of 200 dazzling girls."[86] In sum, it offered the height of entertainment spectacle. The Whitemanesque MMM idiom is foregrounded in the movie's main title cue, which employs the song "42nd Street" as its first theme. The brassy, near-swing dance-music enhancement of the music points toward the glitzy main-title cue scoring of *Godfrey*. In *42nd Street*, melting-pot collisions of class, place, identity, social power, and even race (white quasi-symphonic textures set against jazzy, swung, big band scoring)—"side by side, they're glorified," as the lyrics state—are entwined in the Whitemanesque scoring. After a brass-heavy fanfare, the cue segues into the high-low juxtaposed swooning strings and blaring, jazzy brass and reeds of the title tune. The unsung lyrics' intermingling of references to elite culture and street life glorify the cultural collisions of glamorous New York. The film's Heindorf-arranged production number for the title song tropes on *Street Scene*: the class collisions of Manhattan life and the tenement melodrama with a lover's murder, all set to song, dance, jazzy orchestration, modulations, and style-topic shifts. A moment after the street murder, the camera pans up to the apartment window of Dick Powell, dressed as a smart-set swell, singing in a faux operatic intonation, with a barman shaking a cocktail shaker behind him. In these mixed elements—in staging, words, music, and scoring—we experience a full high-low, Whitemanesque cultural lexicon of extramusical topical tropes from the Modern Metropolitan Music tradition.

Whiteman, Classy Popular Music, and the High-Low Divide

The lineage and reception threads I have traced illustrate a gradual accumulation of musical practices, entertainment contexts, and cultural associations associated with the Whitemanesque Modern Metropolitan Music idiom between circa 1927 and 1936. On the big screens of gilded movie palaces, celluloid images elevated New York to the level of art and myth. This idealized cinematic vision of New York reached its zenith during the Depression. The Modern Metropolitan film-scoring traditions of this film repertory are considerable. And while the big-band-plus-strings underscoring idiom changes to embrace modern jazz in the postwar era, this sound extends to a long line of Hollywood noir-, procedural-, and criminal-themed films well into the 1970s.

This high-low Modern American entertainment tradition was manifest in multiple, mutually reinforcing levels in these Hollywood productions. For example, the speech conventions for certain dually high-low characters offer additional lessons for understanding the MAM idiom. As observed, a low-confused-with-high cultural collision is central to *Godfrey*. Film critic Katie Walsh has written about the Warner Brothers' reinvention of Powell's masculinity that helped him become the epitome of a debonaire, witty leading man, most notably in his role as the character of Nick Charles in the

Thin Man film series.[87] While his demeanor and look (especially his pencil-thin mustache) were often characterized as the height of masculine suave classiness in the 1930s (Whiteman, of course, cultivated similar facial hair), Walsh documents the centrality of Powell's employment of the cultivated mid-Atlantic accent as being central in this image reinvention. The latter practice offers useful cultural parallels for understanding the implications of the classy cultural associations of the Modern Metropolitan Music idiom, and these connections in turn are embedded in the marketing of the MAM scores.

The Hollywood mid-Atlantic accent and its elevated mannerisms were part of interwar entertainment's invocations of "class" through markers of glamour and elevated social status. Not all such markers invoke highbrow culture. In a recent essay on the Robbins MAM score series, I argue that the class airs of MAM suggest an analogue to such Hollywood class pretensions.[88] As Dan Nosowitz observes, the mid-Atlantic accent—epitomized by actors like Katherine Hepburn—is said to geographically point to "somewhere in the middle of the Atlantic Ocean, halfway between [upper-crust] New England and England."[89] The accent affected "a vaguely British-y speech pattern meant to sound aristocratic, excessively proper, and, weirdly, not regionally specific." The accent invokes popular associations of *classy*, glamorous lifestyles. Nonetheless, Hollywood also embraced the dialects of lower-class everymen like Humphrey Bogart. Interwar Hollywood film practice regularly juxtaposed smart-set glamorous lifestyles against relatable lower- and/or middle-class fantasy. This tension is central to *Godfrey*, and the film also precisely captures the mid-Atlantic *musical-middlebrow* dialect (halfway between pop and concert culture) of the classy, jazz-pop "with all the trappings" MAM scores and their MMM subtopic.

This chapter's opening discussion of Whiteman's 1940 *Album of Manhattan* and the above extended overview on Whitemanesque relations to classy cultural tropes in American entertainment, spectacular entertainment traditions, and so forth amply illustrate a wealth of modes in which the concert-dressed, show-indebted, MAM idiom sought to convey a sustained, market-savvy tension between "airs" of classy culture and popular entertainment. Through the former area, it evokes codes of "distinction," "merit," and attributes that retained considerable American-entertainment market relevance in the interwar years, as seen in *Godfrey*.[90] In many ways the quintessentially American, classy-entertainment cultural framing of Whiteman's *Album of Manhattan*—in packaging, in advertising and liner note text copy, in musical repertory—parallels the intentionally sustained high-low tensions of American classy culture seen in the film short, *Godfrey*, the promotion of the MAM scores, and other examples.

An additional sustained tension is here: between the 1928 composition of *Manhattan Serenade* and the 1940 *Album of Manhattan* is also a sincere hope from Whiteman and Robbins to establish this extensive MAM compositional tradition as a genuine concert music practice with cultural esteem. This is seen in press reports of Robbins Music's promotional efforts with the MAM score series, in Whiteman's mid-1930s donation of materials for a Modern American Music archive at Williams,[91] and in Whiteman's increasing associations from the mid- to late 1930s with the pops configurations of various national orchestras, including the NBC symphony, the Philadelphia Orchestra's Robin Hood Dell Pops performances, the New York Philharmonic's Lewisohn stadiums pops concerts, and others.

Despite Decca's framing of the *Album of Manhattan* via the label's Personality Series and other middlebrow entertainment cultural markers, the unusual 1940 deluxe recording set and its packaging are also evidence of a bid for seriousness. But again, there is a sustained mixed-brow tension that runs wholly through the Whiteman brand with no clear resolution to being one thing. Nor should it resolve these tensions as American Modern Metropolitan Music. In closing, it should be stressed again that Whitemanesque symphonic jazz did not entirely originate with Whiteman, Grofé, Lange, or Alter; these figures were high-profile transmitters of larger musical traditions. A metropolitan-themed MAM work like *Manhattan Serenade* thus underscores the vital nexus of cultural and entertainment history that had coalesced around Whitemanesque music in the late 1920s and early 1930s. It offers a synecdoche (a part representing the difficult-to-grasp whole) of the complicated paths through which Whitemanesque Modern American Music—and its Modern Metropolitan Music topical subset—went from dance bands, to Tin Pan Alley concert works, to the Broadway stage and radio, to Hollywood film.

Notes

1. "Whiteman Quits Music Publishing Alliance." Also see "Paul Whiteman Publications Soon Ready."

2. See appendixes 1–3 in Howland, "Between the Muses and the Masses."

3. There were smaller competing MAM-style score series from publishers like Mills Music, Handy Bros., Harms, and others. See Howland, "Between the Muses," ch. 4.

4. See Howland, "Between the Muses," ch. 4.

5. See Horowitz, *Understanding Toscanini*.

6. Alter, *Manhattan Serenade*, piano solo; *Manhattan Serenade*, ed. Robbins; Shilkret and the Victor Salon Orchestra, *Manhattan Serenade*; *Manhattan Serenade*, dir. Lee; Alter, *Manhattan Serenade*, ed. Savino; *My Man Godfrey*; and Paul

Whiteman and His Concert Orchestra, *Album of Manhattan*, and Whiteman, *Album of Manhattan*.

7. The present chapter expands upon my earlier work on Whiteman-influenced Modern American Music. See Howland, "Paul Whiteman and Glorified," *Hearing Luxe Pop*, *"Ellington Uptown,"* and "Between the Muses."

8. Discussed in Howland, *Hearing Luxe Pop*, chs. 3 and 4.

9. Discussed in Howland, "Between the Muses" and *"Ellington Uptown."*

10. "On the Upbeat: Paul Whiteman."

11. Richman, "On the Record: Paul Whiteman Concert Orchestra."

12. Howland, *Hearing Luxe Pop*, 115, original emphasis.

13. Liner-note booklet to Whiteman, *Album of Manhattan*, 1940. On *Metropolitan Nocturne*, also see "Alter 'Nocturne' Used for Film Pantomime."

14. Additionally, Savino had a significant career as a conductor, composer, and arranger associated with the film industry and CBS radio across the 1920s and 1930s. See Musiker and Musiker, "Savino, Domenico," and Sanjek, *American Popular Music*, 102.

15. Liner-note booklet, Whiteman, *Album of Manhattan*, 1940.

16. *Billboard* and other industry sources place the Buick program arrangement in 1932–33 but the Whiteman Collection folder for the arrangements curiously dates this as 1931.

17. Alter and Adamson, *Manhattan Serenade*.

18. For overviews of the series, see Howland, "Between the Muses" and "Paul Whiteman and Glorified."

19. "Manhattan Serenade / Victor Salon Orchestra."

20. Howland, "Between the Muses," xxv–xxvi.

21. A "strain" within period-song popular-instrumental practice denotes both a theme and formal section. On the relation between novelty piano and MAM compositions, see Howland, "Between the Muses" and "Paul Whiteman and Glorified."

22. Louis Alter, *Dolly Dimples* (New York: Robbins Music, 1927).

23. Paul Whiteman and His Orchestra, *Dolly Dimples*.

24. Howland, *"Ellington Uptown,"* 152–55 passim.

25. "Musical Comedy Notes."

26. Green, "Disk Reviews."

27. "Melody Mart Notes."

28. Lange, *Arranging for the Modern Dance Orchestra*. See also "Tribute to Arthur Lange."

29. "Pictures: $40,000 Short."

30. Tommy Dorsey and His Orchestra, *Manhattan Serenade*.

31. See Jacobs, Kinik, and Hietscher, *City Symphony Phenomenon*.

32. On musical topics, see Hatten, *Interpreting Musical Gestures*.

33. Recent film music scholarship that in part builds on some of my earlier research discussions about Hollywood's employment of the symphonic jazz idiom can be seen in Konstantin Jahn, "Paul Whitemans *Symphonic Jazz*."

34. "*My Man Godfrey*."
35. Paul Whiteman to [G. A. (Dick) Richards], "Whiteman Letter to Sponsor," undated, 1–2, Whiteman Collection.
36. Paul Whiteman to [G. A. (Dick) Richards], "Whiteman Letter to Sponsor," undated, 10, Whiteman Collection.
37. Paul Whiteman to [G. A. (Dick) Richards], "Whiteman Letter to Sponsor," undated, 4–5, Whiteman Collection.
38. Paul Whiteman to [G. A. (Dick) Richards], "Whiteman Letter to Sponsor," undated, 2, Whiteman Collection.
39. Paul Whiteman to [G. A. (Dick) Richards], "Whiteman Letter to Sponsor," undated, 9, Whiteman Collection.
40. Paul Whiteman to [G. A. (Dick) Richards], "Whiteman Letter to Sponsor," undated, 1, Whiteman Collection.
41. Paul Whiteman to [G. A. (Dick) Richards], "Whiteman Letter to Sponsor," undated, 2, Whiteman Collection.
42. Paul Whiteman to [G. A. (Dick) Richards], "Whiteman Letter to Sponsor," undated, 3, Whiteman Collection.
43. Paul Whiteman to [G. A. (Dick) Richards], "Whiteman Letter to Sponsor," undated, 4, Whiteman Collection.
44. See ch. 8, Sheppard, "Integration and Segregation in Whiteman's Music Television, 1948–55," in the current volume.
45. See Sanders, *Celluloid Skyline*.
46. Sargeant, *Jazz*, 231–32.
47. "Paul Whiteman Publications Soon Ready."
48. See Howland, "Between the Muses."
49. "Robbins Reports Folios on Upbeat."
50. Olin Downes, "Whiteman's Jazz," *New York Times*, October 8, 1928.
51. "B'way Houses' Band Policy," 31.
52. "At the Paramount," vol. 6, Scrapbooks and Clippings, 1921–72, Whiteman Collection.
53. "New Show World, 1929–30."
54. "*King of Jazz*."
55. Bennett, "Arranging Music for Radio," 77, 79.
56. *Automotive Industry*, 23.
57. Published by Forster Music. See Howland, "Between the Muses," 201–2.
58. Horowitz, *Understanding Toscanini*, 262.
59. On music and the middlebrow, see Chowrimooto, Guthrie, Howland, Flory, McDonald, Wiebe, and Taruskin, "Colloquy," and Chowrimootoo and Guthrie, *Oxford Handbook of Music and the Middlebrow*.
60. *Automotive Industry*, 24.
61. *Automotive Industry*, 20, 23, 26.
62. *Automotive Industry*, 3.
63. *Automotive Industry*, 5.
64. "GM's New Move May Affect Ads," 17.

65. "Buick Signs Whiteman, 16.
66. Simon, "Chain Chatter."
67. "Program Reviews."
68. "Program Reviews."
69. Kemp, "Paul Whiteman's Fifth Experiment"; Blue, "Fourth Experiment."
70. See Howland, *Hearing Luxe Pop*, 115, 154; Johnston, "Tunesmiths."
71. Hathaway, "Boys Who Arrange the Tunes."
72. "Presenting Pop Music."
73. "Music by Ferde Grofé." Lance Bowling, Cambria Sound Archives, Lomita, California, provided a cassette copy of these transcription discs to the author.
74. Rubin, *Showstoppers*.
75. *Whoopee!* dir. Thornton Freeland, Samuel Goldwyn, prod., 1930.
76. Rubin, *Showstoppers*, passim.
77. Alan Warner, vice president, EMI Music Publishing, to author, email, January 4, 2000, about the merger. Also see Richman, "On the Record," and Green, "Colorful Music Man Jack Robbins." On the New York talent exodus, see Crafton, *Talkies*.
78. "Interview with Arthur Lange and Ernest Klapholz," 146.
79. Crafton, *Talkies*, passim.
80. *Street Scene*, dir. King Vidor, United Artists, 1931, and *Delicious*, dir. David Butler, Fox Films, 1931.
81. Newman and Adamson, *Sentimental Rhapsody*. Also see Newman, *Street Scene*.
82. On Gershwinisms in the *Street Scene* score, see Steiner, *Making of an American Film Composer*.
83. Rice, *Street Scene*.
84. See Pollack, *George Gershwin*, ch. 26.
85. Mordden, *Broadway Babies*, 91.
86. "*42nd Street*," passim.
87. Walsh, "Selling Masculinity at Warner Bros."
88. Howland, "Paul Whiteman and Glorified."
89. Nosowitz, "How a Fake British Accent."
90. See the MAM marketing discussion in Howland, "Paul Whiteman and Glorified."
91. Green, "Inside Stuff."

Select Media Cited

Alter, Louis. *Dolly Dimples*. New York: Robbins Music, 1927.
Alter, Louis. *Manhattan Serenade*. Piano solo. New York: Robbins Music, 1928.
Alter, Louis. *Manhattan Serenade*. Robbins ed. of Modern American Music for Orchestra, edited by Domenico Savino. New York: Robbins Music, 1931.
Alter, Louis, and Harold Adamson. *Manhattan Serenade*. Song. New York: Robbins Music, 1942.

Dorsey, Tommy, and His Orchestra. *Manhattan Serenade*. Victor 27962, 1942. 78 rpm.

Manhattan Serenade. Directed by Sammy Lee. MGM, 1929.

My Man Godfrey. Directed by Gregory La Cava. Universal, 1936.

Newman, Alfred. *Street Scene*. Robbins Edition of Modern American Music for Orchestra, edited by Domenico Savino. New York: Robbins Music, 1933.

Newman, Alfred, and Harold Adamson. *Sentimental Rhapsody*. New York: Robbins Music, 1942.

Shilkret, Nathaniel, and the Victor Salon Orchestra. *Manhattan Serenade*. Victor 35914, 1928. 78 rpm.

Street Scene. Directed by King Vidor. United Artists, 1931.

Whiteman, Paul. *Album of Manhattan: Metropolitan Impressions by Louis Alter*. Decca DL5109, 1949. LP.

Whiteman, Paul. "When Day Is Done" / "Soliloquy." Victor 35828, 1927. 78 rpm.

Whiteman, Paul, and His Concert Orchestra. *Album of Manhattan: Metropolitan Impressions by Louis Alter*. Decca 116, 1940. 78 rpm album.

Whiteman, Paul, and His Concert Orchestra / [Victor] Salon Orchestra. "When the Day Is Done" / "Manhattan Serenade." His Masters Voice C.2823, 1936. 78 rpm.

Whiteman, Paul, and His Orchestra. *Dolly Dimples*. Victor 21301, 1928. 78 rpm.

Whoopee! Directed by Thornton Freeland. Samuel Goldwyn, 1930.

4

Arranging Orientalism for Whiteman

RYAN RAUL BAÑAGALE

Musicologists continue to acknowledge and navigate the ways in which systems and structures of white supremacy and power lay at the foundation of our discipline. As a biracial—white and Filipino—historical musicologist, I reflect often on how my personal and professional lineages continue to influence the ways I understand the world around me. This chapter investigates how music constructs difference and examines in detail arrangements of East Asian–themed songs prepared for performance by the Paul Whiteman ensemble by musicians such as Ferde Grofé and others. My path toward archival and analytical scholarship in this area began many years ago with an investigation into the ways the Tin Pan Alley songs of George Gershwin contributed to the hardening of sonic tropes known as "musical Orientalisms."[1] I see now that this earlier work was but a first attempt to grapple in my scholarship with the casual racism of my lived experience, from childhood taunts on the playground from kids who saw me as Asian to conversations about "minorities" with colleagues who see me as white. Here I return to the powerfully diminishing effects of sonic stereotype with an emphasis on archival methodologies to address a musical trope that never seems to go fully out of style: Orientalism.[2]

More than 170 arrangements could be classified as Orientalist in the Paul Whiteman Collection: songs marked as being about people or places spanning the entire continent of Asia and beyond (see this chapter's appendix). This includes the Indian subcontinent of South Asia, the Middle East, East Asia, and the Southeast Asian mainland and islands. With exoticism being just as indiscriminate as it is discriminatory, these Orientalist works, in their range of representational targets, also stretch into the realm of the Hawaiian Islands, Native Americans, and various immigrant communities in the United States, perhaps most popularly, Chinatowns. Whiteman's performance of such works begins with his 1920 recording of "The Japanese Sandman"—the flip side to his orchestra's first hit record, "Whispering" (Victor 18690). And it extends beyond Whiteman's lifetime when a pickup version of the historic ensemble performed a version of "Limehouse Blues" to mark the sixtieth anniversary in 1984 of Whiteman's landmark first Experiment in Modern Music concert.[3]

This chapter focuses on the early application of Orientalism in the musical arrangements performed by Paul Whiteman's orchestra at the outset of the ensemble's popularity in the 1920s. What I am attempting here is to continue a scholarly discourse about musical semiotics, popular song, and power dynamics that has been ongoing since the 1990s. Since that time, scholars such as Ellie Hisama (1993), Judy Tsou (1997), Charles Hiroshi Garrett (2004), and W. Anthony Sheppard (2019) have drawn out the ways that Tin Pan Alley songs established and maintained a lexicon of Orientalisms inherited from Western classical music: pentatonic scales, parallel fourths, repetitious staccato rhythms, "primitive" bass ostinatos, and gongs.[4] This body of literature has focused lines of inquiry primarily on the rhythmic, melodic, lyrical, and iconographic analysis of published Tin Pan Alley piano-vocal sheet music. Individually, such musical elements may not necessarily signify an "Oriental other," but in combination they are routinely employed to identify and make distinct their targeted East Asian and East Asian American subjects. Such musical means are often deployed directly and succinctly at the outset of a piece of music to establish an Orientalist frame for the song to come. Perhaps the most enduring—if not cliché—combination of these elements is what Sheppard sums up as the "standard musical sign for East Asia" (see example 4.1).[5] Considering the ways such elements come together and are extended through arrangements of Asian-themed songs performed by the Paul Whiteman Orchestra provides an opportunity to explore not only the role of arrangers in Whiteman's organization but also the realm of these so-called musical Orientalisms through the musicological subfield of arrangement studies.

The risk and the reward of the arrangement-studies approach lies in its removal of the boundaries surrounding the object of study (composition versus arrangement). Any discussion of music performed by the Whiteman ensemble combines considerations of the original song and its subsequent

EXAMPLE 4.1 Enduring example of musical Orientalism featuring pentatonicism, parallel fourths, and repeated staccato rhythm.

arrangement. As the ensemble continued to grow in popularity and number of musicians, so did the arrangements performed—even as the songs the arrangements were based upon remained a fixed entity. Given the development of the genre of jazz and popular music more broadly over time—especially in the 1920s—this observation may seem obvious. However, a more detailed examination of how Orientalisms emerged through such music provides an additional sense of the significant effect—for better or worse—that the Whiteman Orchestra had on popular (music) culture from its earliest recordings forward. It also opens space to consider the power dynamics such arrangements established in the second quarter of the twentieth century.

Ultimately, my goal is to model additional ways to understand how sonic stereotypes took shape, were arranged, and circulated during the first half of the twentieth century. The focus will be on three songs first arranged and performed over the course of the 1920s: "Cho-Cho-San," "Orientale," and "The Japanese Sandman." But to contextualize this process, I preface my analysis of these pieces by exploring musical Orientalism in practice and in theory first through a consideration of Whiteman's Experiment in Modern Music—one of the most fabled music events of the 1920s—and then through Arthur Lange's primer *Arranging for the Modern Dance Orchestra* published just a few years after that concert. Through this process we begin to see how East Asian tropes (aka "Chinese"), in particular, separated away from more generalized "Oriental" aesthetics during this decade as well as how such signifiers remained present even as subsequent arranging techniques continued to evolve with the times.

Orientalism and an Experiment in Modern Music

Paul Whiteman's 1924 Experiment in Modern Music concert has long preserved his place in American music history, even if that location remains rather liminal. Ultimately, this concert is remembered for presenting the much-discussed premiere of George Gershwin's *Rhapsody in Blue* with the composer at the piano—an instant success based on contemporary reports with an ongoing critical legacy that continues to ebb and flow even as the work surpasses one hundred years old.[6] As I have documented elsewhere, much of the success of the work emerges from the ways arranger Grofé innovatively played with the timbres at hand.[7] He prepared Gershwin's two-piano short score for the specific talents of musicians in the Whiteman ensemble, which included for that night additional violins and a pair of French horns. In the process Grofé extended techniques located in other contemporary arrangements for the Whiteman ensemble from that time.

One such example from within the *Rhapsody* emerges with Grofé's treatment of the "ritornello" theme: the melody played by the clarinet at the opening of the work and that repeats intermittently throughout the piece—both in fragment and in its full Tin Pan Alley 32-bar AABA form.[8] The third time the listener encounters this theme in its full AABA form (reh. 22), it appears in an Orientalist arrangement, with Mozartian Turkish band-style percussion and with the theme played in octaves by the highest and lowest saxophones—sopranino and baritone, respectively.[9] The sonic signification of such a combination would have been immediately apparent to the audience given the Orientalist milieu of the 1920s. However, when Grofé subsequently rearranged the *Rhapsody* for a more standard symphony orchestra, this section as well as other portions of the work became more "classical" in instrumentation. Such timbral novelties disappeared. Repetitions of the ritornello theme became more monotonous as a result, and this particular iteration is often cut from live and recorded performances of the work.[10] The musical exoticism originally experienced at Whiteman's public experiment grows further distant as a result. But perhaps not as much as with two other works on that same program that also dabbled in musical exoticism.

A Suite of Serenades by Victor Herbert also had its premiere that evening, though it has been lost in the shadows of *Rhapsody in Blue* from the outset. Herbert was, nevertheless, one of the most popular composers in the United States. But as David Schiff notes, the suite was "a new work based on old materials by a composer who was already old-fashioned."[11] In fact, it was the final music that Herbert, known primarily for his operettas, would complete prior to his death later that same year. Nonetheless, as Schiff also notes, the four individual movements "demonstrate how the exoticism of operetta served as a means of absorbing up-to-date classical devices into popular music."[12] It comprises four movements, each with its own cultural or nationalistic title: "Spanish," "Chinese," "Cuban," and "Oriental." Whiteman recorded the full suite on June 11, 1924 (Victor 55226), the day after he first captured the *Rhapsody* on disc. The ensemble recorded Herbert's suite again (Victor 35926, using orthophonic electrical technology) at the outset of March 1928. Like the *Rhapsody*, Herbert's piece employs an expanded violin section as well as two French horns. The two "Asian" movements provide a sonic contrast. In "Chinese," pizzicato strings and a fluttering oboe convey the sound of East Asian instruments. Its two contrasting melodies—the first faster moving and staccato, the second slower and legato—unfold in eight-bar phrases and employ a major pentatonic scale primarily over a pedal-tone tonic. The movement concludes, inevitably, with the hit of a gong. "Oriental," by contrast, employs low brass instruments and woodwinds to present the minor pentatonic melody. As the final movement of the suite, it builds toward a dramatic climax by moving through increasingly elevated key areas and a faster tempo. Its final moments are more vaudeville in style than anything else.

More immediately recorded—and more popular from the outset—is a third example of exoticism on the program that night: "Limehouse Blues" by Douglas Furber and Philip Braham. It appeared under the program section "Recent Compositions with Modern Score." The song had been making the rounds since its West End debut in a review titled *A to Z*. At the time of Whiteman's experiment, "Limehouse Blues" had become a prominent feature in *André Charlot's Revue of 1924*, having opened on Broadway one month earlier on January 9. The song warns of the dangers of "Limehouse," a district in East London known at that time for its settlements of Chinese merchantmen involved in the opium trade. The first verse cuts right to the chase: "In Limehouse / Where yellow chinkies love to play." The racialized language continues in the chorus:

> I've the real Limehouse blues
> Learned from chinkies those sad China blues
> Rings on your fingers and tears for your crown
> That is the story of old China town.[13]

Grofé made the first piano-roll arrangement of the song for the American Piano Company (Ampico) in 1922, which appears to have formed the basis for this arrangement for the Paul Whiteman Orchestra. The two share a similar introduction, and the verses, choruses, and transitions also mirror each other—including ornate trills, countermelodies, and rhythmic accents. In many regards, the inclusion of this piece on the concert makes sense. It was both "in the air," and the ensemble had recorded the arrangement just three weeks earlier on January 22 (Victor 19264), releasing it to the public on March 7, not long after its initial concert performance. Notably missing from Whiteman's performances of this and the many arrangements of "Limehouse Blues" appearing in the Whiteman collection are the original lyrics, which audiences of the 1920s would have heard in their head even when not sung. All of this adds up to an appreciable level of racialized exoticism emerging throughout Whiteman's Experiment in Modern Music—an emphasis bound up as much in the compositional aspects of these works on the program as it is in their sonic arrangement for performance by the Whiteman ensemble.

Dance Band Arrangers and Arranging

Prior to exploring the ways Orientalisms emerge from arrangements of such songs, it will be instructive to summarize the role of arrangers within this era of popular dance-band performance, more generally. As Elijah Wald observes, among many of Paul Whiteman's innovations, he "defined the arranging style that would be used by virtually every later bandleader."[14] Of course, Whiteman did not do this on his own. He had scores of arrangers under his employ over the decades, creating and crafting the way his songs sounded both on recordings and in live performance.

Over the course of his career, Whiteman worked with at least forty individual arrangers to prepare custom charts for his ensemble. Most prominent amongst this list are white arrangers, such as Grofé, Bill Challis, Tom Satterfield, Matty Malneck, and Ken Hopkins, each of whom would go on to have significant careers in the music and entertainment industry—with most of them also helping to shape the early sounds of Hollywood. Several members of Whiteman's ensemble also arranged for the group, including Roy Bargy, Max Farleey, and Joseph Anthony "Fud" Livingston. Additionally, because Whiteman could not place Black musicians alongside white ones on stage, in the later part of the 1920s he began to hire Black arrangers to help "adapt his outfit to this new interest in hot-style music."[15] This included names such as Don Redman and William Grant Still. Some of Whiteman's arrangers provided only a handful of arrangements, while others, such as Grofé, prepared hundreds.

Grofé is credited with more than three hundred arrangements for recordings made by the Paul Whiteman Orchestra prior to the summer of 1926 alone. At that time, the Victor recording label asked the band to begin re-recording their catalog using new electrical microphone technologies that would increase the fidelity. Both an increase in performers in the Whiteman ensemble as well as new musical standards in how these musicians came together in their presentation of well-known melodies and harmonies meant that Grofé prepared new "up to date" arrangements that present a different sonic experience of a given song than those made earlier. And these later recordings contributed greatly to the national reputation of Whiteman as he became known as the King of Jazz. To this end it is helpful to look at the earlier arrangements by Grofé to understand the role that he played in establishing the Whiteman sound in addition to the ways he participated in the development of Orientalist arranging techniques.

In the introduction to his book *Blue Rhythm Fantasy: Big Band Jazz Arranging in the Swing Era*, John Wriggle outlines the wide range of tasks that fall to an arranger: "Assignments might not only call for scoring band orchestrations, but also creating piano lead sheets, setting lyrics, collaborating with stage choreographers, transcribing (notating by ear) other arrangers' work off recordings, editing older orchestrations to fit new combinations of players (most successful big bands grew in size throughout the Swing Era), or serving as a 'copyist' (notating individual musicians' parts from an arranged score)."[16] But these roles only emerged once the practice of notating what would become known as "jazz" was established, which remains perhaps one of Grofé's most significant musical contributions.

Following a classically trained upbringing, pianist Grofé joined one of the first West Coast jazz bands, under the direction of Art Guerin, in 1919. Initially, this group followed the "huddle system" used by most bands wherein they would simply gather in a circle prior to playing a tune and assign individual musicians the melody, harmony, and solos. Such improvisation was used by all jazz ensembles, regardless of how we might categorize their individual style or sound today. It led to surprising and exciting sonic combinations, some of which were captured on recordings by groups such as the Original Dixieland Jazz Band. But Grofé ultimately wanted Guerin's group to be able to replicate these spontaneous creations in subsequent performances, so he began notating these efforts as transcribed arrangements. When the then California-based Whiteman hired Grofé in March 1920, it was for this ability to craft personalized and reperformable arrangements that could help fill up the more than five hours of music required of their nightly gig at the Alexandria Hotel in San Francisco.[17]

Ultimately, as the primary arranger for the Whiteman ensemble throughout the 1920s, Grofé developed the "roadmap" for what dance-band arrangements would become, setting in place a model that would be repeated endless times by countless arrangers. Just as Tin Pan Alley composers conformed to and evaded expectations of the 32-bar AABA popular-song format, jazz band arrangers relied on various techniques to continually surprise and thrill listeners. These emerged over time and eventually codified into a set of standard approaches to arranging not only for dance orchestras of Whiteman's early era but also swing bands in the 1930s.

The first book to set such techniques in place was *Arranging for the Modern Dance Orchestra*, published by Arthur Lange in 1926. It quickly became "the primary manual for symphonic jazz arranging," influencing a generation of musicians and bandleaders including Glenn Miller.[18] Moreover, as Wriggle notes, even as the genre moved into the swing era, Lange's 1926 book "appears to have had a significant influence on subsequent publications that emerged throughout the following decade" and even up through Miller's 1943 *Method for Orchestral Arranging*.[19] Musicologist John Howland details the ways that Lange's text documents the roadmap that he and others, such as Grofé, had established during the initial years of the decade. An accomplished arranger in his own right, Lange trusted that "if the reader will read this book carefully, and make what it contains his own, I believe that he will have at his command the main tools of the orchestra arranger's art."[20] Notably, the word "jazz" appears only once in the entire volume.[21] By the late 1920s, Lange had a popular series of arrangements, "Arthur Lange's Selected Repertoire for Modern Orchestra," published by the Boston Music Company that provide additional models of the techniques introduced in his book. Although stock arrangements such as these were increasingly available from publishing houses, the most successful bands created custom arrangements suited to the needs of their musicians as well as the venues in which they shared their music—both live and on recording.

Howland delineates what he calls the "Grofé/Lange Arranging Idiom of the 1920s" and extends a summary of Lange's publication through the analysis of archival arrangements by Grofé.[22] One standard formal unfolding of an arrangement progresses as follows: introduction, verse, 1st chorus, 2nd chorus, 3rd chorus, final chorus. Each section receives at least one distinct musical setting—often two—utilizing a series of different "effects." The various techniques available to achieve such effects occupy a majority of Lange's manual. Howland describes these as the "governing instrumental and musical character of a given passage of an arrangement. Each so-called effect involves distinct features of melody and accompaniment, a certain palate and distribution of tone colors, and specific types of counterpoint, harmony, and form."[23] In addition to introducing "instrumental effects," "ensemble effects," and "trick effects," Lange establishes a set of "characteristic effects" that suggest specific cultures and nationalities.

Lange's Orientalist Effects

Like the tropes found in the published sheet music of Asian-themed popular song, a common set of sonic applications emerges for each sonic stereotype, be that Oriental, Irish, Indian, Chinese, Italian, Russian, or Jewish. These effects are accomplished by applying one or more scoring choices to a preexisting melody. The origins of the various "characteristic effects" catalogued by Lange emerge from similar anthologies published for accompanying silent film, known collectively as "Moving Picture Music."[24] Accordingly, many of the same effects are applied to different cultural characterizations, emphasizing W. Anthony Sheppard's observation that "aiming for exotic 'authenticity' is an entirely quixotic project, in any case, given that cross-cultural presentation and/or representation ultimately plays out diversely in the minds of individual audience members."[25]

What one can deduce, however, from early 1920s arrangements are the ways that "Oriental" and "Chinese" became distinct from each other. Howland notes that the "characterization 'Oriental' in this era was a category that referenced a wide body of exotic 'eastern' musics. Depending on the author, these references could embody caricatures of Japanese-, Chinese-,

Russian-, Eastern European-, or Arabic-themed music."[26] Of this list, only "Chinese" receives its own treatment by Lange in his arranging book. And, perhaps unsurprising, there remains significant overlap between the musical and rhythmic effects applied to both the "Oriental" and "Chinese" categories. However, by 1926 these two categories—at least, on paper—had distinct differences, and one can see the shift play out in various arrangements performed and recorded by the Whiteman ensemble.

Almost thirty different arrangers contributed to the scores and parts of East Asian–themed works in the Whiteman Collection. In addition to "The Japanese Sandman," this includes other popular tunes, such as "Chinatown, My Chinatown" and "Limehouse Blues." Each of these three pieces was arranged multiple times for performance by the Whiteman ensemble, with "Limehouse Blues" appearing in nine different versions. Additional East Asian–themed songs include such titles as "Broken Idol," "China Boy," "Chinese Lullaby," "Chopsticks," "Glow Worm," "Japanese Mammy," "Japanese Moonlight," "Nagasaki," "Not for All the Rice in China," "Shanghai Lil," and "When Buddha Smiles." Some of these arrangements were never recorded in the studio but were heard regularly in live performance. Whiteman's East Asian Orientalist arrangements are not limited to popular song. The aforementioned *A Suite of Serenades* by Victor Herbert appears in the Whiteman Collection. There are also numerous selections from operettas and operas, such as Gilbert and Sullivan's *Mikado* and Puccini's *Madama Butterfly*. And adding to the multilayered complexity of racial representations during this period, three additional items called "Hot Mikado Medley" capitalize on the "Black Mikado" craze of the late 1930s.[27]

According to Lange, the instruments best suited to an "Oriental effect" are percussion instruments, such as the gong and tom-tom (also associated with "Indian effect"), the oboe, and the trumpet with a wa-wa or kazoo mute, which is "particularly suitable in Oriental effects, as a substitute for Oboe." Ultimately, the success of such effects "depends upon the character of the melody. A slow-moving melody requires a different instrumental treatment than a fast-moving melody. Such color effects as the Muted Trumpet (wa-wa or kazoo mute), Soprano Saxophone or Oboe, if available may be freely employed." Lange also identifies a "concerted unison" as another "Oriental effect," wherein a single melodic pitch of a given passage is spread across three or four different octaves, even within the same instrumental categories. Doublings at each octave are only to occur using an instrument with a different tone color. In addition to parallel octaves, Lange emphasizes that "*fourths* are prevalent. This is a peculiar characteristic, distinctive of Chinese music." Elsewhere in the book he notes—like any Western-trained musician might observe—that "intervals of *perfect fourths, perfect fifths* . . . should only be written when unavoidable, and at such time should not be associated with notes of long duration."[28] By association—although not acknowledged as such in contemporary texts—the prevalence of fourths in "Chinese" music highlights the "incorrectness" of such music, further establishing the power dynamics of Western ideals that emerge from East Asian songs in repertoire of the era.

For Lange, rhythm also plays an important role in drawing out sonic characteristics of a particular nation or culture. To further demonstrate "Oriental" characteristics, Lange shares an example that draws on the "Arabian Dance" movement from Peter Ilich Tchaikovsky's *Nutcracker* (1892). Here, he identifies the application of "rhythmic paraphrase," which Howland summarizes as occurring when "any type of musical genre is playfully combined with, signified upon, or juxtaposed against the rhythmic sensibilities of contemporary dance music."[29] This occurs frequently not only in the 1920s through playful juxtapositions of Western classical works over a fox-trot beat but also in the phenomenon of recasting something familiar from the past over a more modern drumbeat that appears in genres such as rock, disco, and hip-hop as well.

Lange's arrangement of "Arabian Dance" recasts the 3/8 rhythm of Tchaikovsky's original composition, as seen in example 4.2. The rhythm emerges from a steady stream of eighth notes grouped as 1+2+2+1 played by the cellos and violas and alternating between a lower and upper octave that emphasizes the tonic while sounding parallel fifth intervals.[30] In Lange's transposition of this rhythm for dance orchestra, he recasts the basic orientation of Tchaikovsky's model into 4/4 time, to demonstrate what he calls the signature "Oriental Rhythm." The 1+2+2+1 groupings are maintained but with an extension of the duration of the first and last beats. Accordingly, Lange's rhythm unfolds as a quarter note followed by four eighth notes and another quarter note on the final beat of the measure (example 4.3). For instrumentation, Lange notes that his arrangement "employs two Trumpets with wa-wa mute, and two Saxophones, which are scored in quartet form. To this is added an Oriental Rhythm, characteristic of Oriental drums."[31]

EXAMPLE 4.2 Opening figure of "Arabian Dance," Peter Ilich Tchaikovsky's *Nutcracker* (1892).

EXAMPLE 4.3 Oriental effect example, Arthur Lange's *Arranging for the Modern Dance Orchestra* (1926), 182.

Lange's 1926 primer on arranging set the stage for expectations of dance-band arrangements in the years to follow—particularly, for the predominant white bands performing in what has become referred to as the "sweet" tradition.[32] However, it masks the development of such techniques and the ways that these exotic "character effects" functioned in such arrangements prior to their published standardization by Lange. To better understand this early 1920s approach, I now turn to a set of Orientalist arrangements Grofé prepared initially.

"Cho-Cho-San"

Examples of "Oriental" rhythmic paraphrase emerge early in the Whiteman catalogue. During the fall of 1921, while the popularity and reputation of his ensemble were on the rise, Whiteman played nightly engagements at the Palais Royal. In mid-October, the *New York Clipper* noted changes in this house band's repertoire. This included hot takes on well-known tunes from the classical repertory including Pietro Mascagni's intermezzo from *Cavalleria Rusticana* and "an aria from *Madame Butterfly*. . . . Mr. Whiteman proved himself to be no mean showman judging by the way his offerings were arranged."[33] "Cho-Cho-San" is an arrangement of an arrangement. In 1921 Hugo Frey published a fox-trot rendition of melodies from Puccini's opera, including Cho-Cho-San's famous aria "Un bel dì, vedremo" for the song's chorus. The new lyrics, authored by Jesse Winne read:

> Flow'r of old Japan
> I'll return again
> Sweet Orange blossom
> Do not grieve
> For your sailor man
> Dry your tears
> Little Cho-Cho-San.

The manuscript for the arrangement of "Cho-Cho-San" recorded by the Whiteman ensemble bears all the physical and sonic markings of a Grofé arrangement: instrumentalists' names assigned to individual staff lines and parts, the time-saving use of large capital letters to indicate a repetition of corresponding measures, and ample use of "8ve" indications to keep pitches within bar lines.[34] It is scored for three reeds, a cornet, a trombone, drum kit, bass, and piano—the full instrumental extent of the Whiteman ensemble at this time. Commenting on the 1921 recording, Don Rayno notes, "'Cho-Cho-San' is an outstanding example of Whiteman's modern treatment of a classical theme. It is an especially pleasing arrangement, with Byers occupying center stage. His soprano sax work is lovely, particularly in combination with an alto obbligato in the final chorus by Ross Gorman, who, according to the Victor session log, co-arranged this piece with Grofé."[35]

The arrangement largely unfolds in 32-bar phrases that follow the melody and harmony of Frey's published arrangement: verse—chorus 1—interlude—chorus 2—coda. The 16-bar interlude (example 4.4) is not original to Frey's arrangement and represents an addition made by Grofé that is documented only on the 1921 (Victor 18777, acoustic) and 1926 (Victor 20200, orthophonic) recordings. It appears neither in the manuscript score nor the parts

EXAMPLE 4.4 Reduction of Grofé's "Cho-Cho-San" interlude.

(copied sometime in the 1930s) that appear in the Williams archive. In the interlude, Grofé moves from A♭ major to C minor as a return to the original key of the piece. Both this interlude and the brief 8-bar coda that Grofé also added (which does appear in his original manuscript) demonstrate examples of what Lange would later define as a "concerted unison," one of the key effects used to evoke an "Oriental" character.

As recorded in 1921, the arrangement unfolds along similar lines to what might be expected of an early 1920s Whiteman performance of an Orientalist song. After a 4-bar introduction, the 32-bar verse unfolds in two clearly distinct sections. In the first, the alto saxophone (Donald Clark) takes the lead with support from a repetitious three-part harmonic figure played by the remaining woodwinds and cornet. In the second, the melody moves to a unison brass soli with the three-part harmony figure continuing. During the latter part of this second 16-bar phrase, the tune modulates from Ab major to A major for the start of the chorus. Like the verse, each chorus also unfolds in two distinct 16-bar sections—each of which features the soprano saxophone playing the "Un bel dì, vedremo" melody. Each chorus begins with a 16-bar phrase featuring just the soprano saxophone over the steady accompaniment of the rhythm section. As the same melody repeats for the second phrase of each chorus, another solo instrument adds a call-and-response-style obbligato line in answer to the soprano saxophone. The first time this is a high trombone riffing on a quarter-note based echo line (example 4.5). The second time, an alto saxophone (Ross Gorman) plays a highly ornate line that at one point features the "standard musical sign for East Asia" (example 4.6).

Labels attached to recordings released by Whiteman do not typically include a credit line for the arranger. Rather, they prominently display the title of the song, then in smaller font "Paul Whiteman and his Orchestra," and in even smaller font the composer of the song. However, in the case of "Cho-Cho-San," the label specifically designates the recordings "on melodies by G. Puccini arranged by Hugo Frey." However, Frey was not the one who prepared the sonic arrangement heard on these recordings. The presence of his name merely acknowledges his own published arrangement of this fox-trot medley. Rather, the Victor recording logs reveal the arrangers of this arrangement as Grofé and reedman Gorman. Grofé's name makes sense—he was the primary arranger for all of Whiteman's music in the first half of the 1920s. Coarranger credit is rare in general but especially so during this era.

Understanding Gorman's role requires a look at Grofé's original manuscript for this arrangement, specifically the obbligato lines found in each iteration of the chorus (see examples 4.5 and 4.6). It appears that these countermelodies for trombone and alto saxophone were prearranged by Grofé. On the recording, trombonist Sam Lewis follows the scored obbligato line, adding both rubato and slurs to his recorded interpretation. However, saxophonist Gorman takes a significant departure. Just as he would later recast

EXAMPLE 4.5 Transcription of "Cho-Cho-San" melody with trombone obbligato.

EXAMPLE 4.6 Transcription of "Cho-Cho-San" melody with alto saxophone obbligato.

through improvisation the 32-note diatonic scale that opens *Rhapsody in Blue* into the now-iconic and always-imitated clarinet wail, here Gorman takes what he was given and embellishes in a way that ultimately become part and parcel to future performances of "Cho-Cho-San." The top staff of the score documents the alto line originally assigned to him. However, this is wavily crossed out with a pencil. Layered on top of that—also in Grofé's hand—is this improvised-sounding obbligato line in black ink. The awkward spacing of this inked line, including Grofè's second attempt at the final bar of Gorman's improvisatory run, reveals this to be an after-the-fact transcription. One that resonated with Grofé to the extent that it became part of the physical arrangement from this point forward, leading as well toward Gorman's coarranger status on this recording.[36]

Unfortunately, the original parts used for both recordings of "Cho-Cho-San" do not survive. The extant parts located in the Whiteman Collection were produced at some point in the 1930s, and likely because they were copied from Grofé's original score, they include Gorman's subsequently transcribed obbligato line. But they do not include Grofé's "concerted unison" interlude (see example 4.4), which seems odd given that this could have easily been transcribed and re-created from the 1921 recording. One possible explanation for its absence would be that such a dramatic interlude is unsettling to the fox-trot rhythms of the piece. It causes a disruption that would not be easily followed by dancers.

Regardless, this subsequent 1930s arrangement finds other outlets for its exoticized expressions that emerge in part from the expanded instrumentation—with three alto saxes, a tenor, and a baritone; three trumpets, three trombones; first and second violins; a tuba, banjo, and piano. The percussion part calls for the use of "Temple Bells," and the two violins frequently play in parallel fifths and octaves. In the second part of the verse, all six brass players remain in unison. They provide brief harmonized support in the final refrain (aka the shout chorus) but return to a unison coda to end the piece. In this 1930s rearrangement of "Cho-Cho-San," the brass and violin parts reaffirm, if not amplify, the parallel octave musical Orientalism of the original. This is something that achieves a greater impact when heard alongside the temple-bell percussion.

"Orientale"

In "Paraphrasing Classics," a subsection of his book, Lange notes that "the art of transcribing classical works for the modern dance orchestra requires more thought and *technique* in scoring than popular music. Therefore, the arranger must first be proficient in scoring popular dance arrangements before attempting to score classical fox-trot paraphrases."[37] Whereas the "rhythmic paraphrase" occurring in "Cho-Cho-San" suits its original Puccini melody quite smoothly—perhaps, the reason Frey created his initial arrangement in the first place—the recasting of an existing triple-time melody over a duple-time rhythmic paraphrase did not always yield a satisfactory result. But even such examples provide an instructive model for early Asian-themed arrangements. On June 16, 1922, the Paul Whiteman Orchestra recorded a fox-trot version of Cesar Cui's "Orientale," which was released the following November (Victor 18940).[38] They would release an electronically recorded version six years later (Victor 21599). As Rayno observes, something about this arrangement of "Orientale" proved challenging. It "was a difficult piece to record. A total of twenty-two takes spread out over five sessions in 1922, 1926, and 1928 produced two discs."[39] The likely challenge of this arrangement lies in the "rhythmic paraphrase" at hand.

"Orientale" is the ninth movement of a larger work titled *Kaleidoscope* (1893) for piano and violin by Russian composer Cesar Cui (1835–1918). Perhaps the lesser known of the so-called Russian Five, which included contemporaries Modest Mussorgsky and Nikolay Rimsky-Korsakov, Cui composed both large-scale operas and miniatures, such as "Orientale." Like Tchaikovsky's "Arabian Suite" from ten years earlier, "Orientale" is set in triple time—here 6/8—with a repeating string ostinato setting the rhythmic stage before the entrance of the melody (see example 4.7).

Grofé began wrestling with the rhythmic challenges of "Orientale" in the fall of 1921. In the Williams archives, there exists a lead sheet outlining the melody and its instrumental assignment (dated October 13) as well as a piano accompaniment (dated October 21). Sometime thereafter Grofé created a score that outlines the division of the individual parts for just ten musicians: oboe, alto saxophone, tenor saxophone, violin, cornet, trombone, piano, bass, banjo, and percussion. Notably, this score is notated fully in concert pitch, rather than in transposition. No individual parts from this 1921 effort survive. The introduction begins with a brief chromatic big-band entrance—less syncopated but like that heard at the outset of "The Japanese Sandman"—before establishing a fox-trot paraphrase of Cui's original rhythm. Here the syncopation of the original emerges from the alto saxophone (see example 4.8). Shortly thereafter Gorman introduces the melody in the lower register of the oboe that fits squarely—in the negative sense of the word—over the fox-trot rhythm (see example 4.9).

Another sign of the challenges Grofé faced in assembling a cohesive arrangement of "Orientale" emerges from the ways that the initial 1922 recording represents a stitching together of various arranged elements. With the addition of an extra trumpet and the celeste, the recording begins with a slightly extended and revised introduction that quotes from the closing chromatic figure of Cui's original piece. Grofé arranged this change on a separate

EXAMPLE 4.7 Opening bars of "Orientale," Cesar Cui's *Kaleidoscope* (1893).

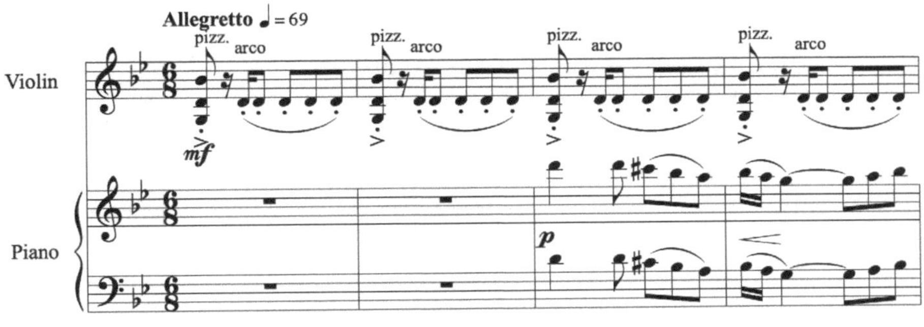

EXAMPLE 4.8 Piano and alto saxophone parts for Grofé's 1921 arrangement of "Orientale" (mm. 1–6).

EXAMPLE 4.9 Piano and oboe parts for Grofé's 1921 arrangement of "Orientale" (mm. 7–13).

sheet of manuscript paper, bearing the title "Orientale (Intro. My Heart at Thy Sweet Voice)." The 1921 score subsequently had rehearsal letters added so that the copyist could piece together this new introduction, the previously prepared arrangement, and then insert a 32-bar chorus of "My Heart at Thy Sweet Voice," an aria from Camille Saint-Sëan's opera *Samson and Delilah*. The recording concludes with a 24-bar outro, standing as an early iteration of what would become known as the "shout chorus," a full ensemble conclusion to any jazz-band arrangement.

This requisite rhythmic manipulation of the melody through rubato also appears in the 1928 re-recording of "Orientale." It uses the same basic arrangement as was captured in 1922, with the only addition being a second violin. The primary difference is that the latter clocks in at nearly 220 beats per minute (bpm), while the former is a more relaxed 122 bpm. Additionally, by contrast to other recordings by the Whiteman ensemble from the late 1920s, the total personnel size is one-third smaller than typically encountered. That Grofé did not take the opportunity to expand his arrangement of "Orientale" for this later recording perhaps demonstrates a lack of interest in continuing to wrestle with this particular song. Regardless, it certainly contrasts significantly from the expanded ensemble experienced in the re-recording of "The Japanese Sandman" also released in 1928 (Victor 21731).

"The Japanese Sandman"

This 1928 arrangement of "The Japanese Sandman" also contrasts with the version of the song that appeared on the flip side to Whiteman's first hit record, "Whispering," from 1920.[40] Such a change makes sense given the changes in arranging techniques and audience expectations over the course of the decade. Howland offers an in-depth assessment that accounts for the ways that Grofé's 1928 effort "closely echoes the model effects suggested by Lange" in his 1926 *Arranging for the Modern Dance Orchestra*.[41] These examples emerge from the choice of instrumentation: "Grofé liberally employs the exotic 'color effects' of muted trumpets, high-registered, often nasal-sounding reed instruments (oboes, soprano saxophone, and clarinet), flute, staccato brass, wood block/temple blocks, string glissandi, various ornamental trills, and so forth. In his use of these color effects, Grofé emphasizes parallel octave and fourth harmonizations of pentatonic melodic material."[42] Howland's condensed transcription of the introduction of this 1928 arrangement provides examples of several of these techniques (see example 4.10). The "standard musical sign for East Asia" emerges in parallel fifths and fourths in the upper woodwinds, reinforced by the temple blocks. Meanwhile, the celeste plays rolled chords to the pizzicato pedal tones of the violins and banjo. The first

EXAMPLE 4.10 Introduction and excerpt from Chorus 1 (mm. 1–16), Grofé's arrangement of "The Japanese Sandman." Prepared by and used with permission from John Howland.

ten seconds of the recording clearly articulate the exotic tone of the song to follow.

Although the 1928 arrangement conforms largely to Lange's ideals, the introduction from the original 1920 arrangement reveals quite a different sonic foundation. No physical score for this early version survives in the Whiteman Collection, but the arrangement captured on the recording closely follows the accompaniment provided in the piano-vocal sheet music published by Jerome H. Remick & Company earlier that same year. The introduction of this arrangement opens with the band playing a unison descending chromatic line, voiced in parallel dominant ninth chords (see example 4.11). The rhythm section (piano, bass, banjo, and drums) then settles into the steady rhythmic pulse of the brass and woodwinds playing a basic fox-trot groove, with two eighth notes appearing on each offbeat of the measure. Over this pulse, the soprano saxophone (performed by Hale "Pee Wee" Byers) plays the 16-bar melody of the verse. The soprano continues into the chorus, with alto (Gus Mueller) playing a lower harmony. Captured on this early-career recording is Paul Whiteman himself, playing an obbligato violin line that fills in the space between melodic phrases. His line continues into the second statement of the chorus, this time played by muted trumpet (Henry Busse) and trombone (T. E. "Buster" Johnson). The final chorus features all the instruments playing the melody, except for the trombone, which takes over the obbligato part. The outro consists of a fragment of the verse melody before arriving at a unison chord, punctuated by cymbal crash.

Accordingly, the 1928 iteration of "The Japanese Sandman" represents a rearrangement of that which appeared on the original 1920 recording. The updates were likely due to the increased size of Whiteman's orchestra, a set of new players, the new electrical recording technologies, and, perhaps most important, the ways that Lange's "character effects" quickly spread throughout the sonic space of late 1920s arrangements following the publication of his book in 1926. In "The Japanese Sandman," for example, there is a clear shift from a 1920 arrangement that sounds more "Oriental" toward a more distinct "Chinese" character in 1928. This sort of separation from one effect to another emerges from other arrangements in the Whiteman Collection, whether they were prepared by Grofé or others.

EXAMPLE 4.11 Piano introduction from "The Japanese Sandman," composed by Richard A. Whiting (1920).

Conclusion

As a way of extending this tradition of rearrangement documented in the Whiteman archives beyond the 1920s, I want to return briefly to "Limehouse Blues"—which, as previously noted, was first performed by the Whiteman ensemble at the Experiment in Modern Music concert in February 1924. Although the score and parts for this original version of "Limehouse Blues" are lost, the Whiteman Collection holds eight additional arrangements.[43] The song was a popular mainstay of his live performances for several decades after it was first incorporated into his repertoire in early 1924. The song's enduring popularity speaks in part to the persistent appeal of Orientalism in the United States throughout the twentieth century, which was surely aided by its continual arrangement and rearrangement over time.

Each of these "Limehouse Blues" arrangements was increasingly "modern," adapting as the years progressed to both the size of the band as well as to audience expectations for what a dance band should sound like. Like other arrangements discussed here, Grofé's original 1924 version relies more on a general "Oriental" approach rather than "Chinese" musical elements as Lange delineated. However, each of the subsequent arrangements—largely through the use of temple blocks and gongs—sets an East Asian tone for this piece. Such updates appear in a version arranged by Challis for performance by the Whiteman ensemble on Whiteman's *Chesterfield Radio Hour*.[44]

A review of a live concert in Hartford, Connecticut, from around the same time as this radio broadcast notes a performance of "Limehouse Blues" that "show[s] us Whiteman knew all about swing before it was christened formally by the jitterbugs."[45] Indeed, as this critic observes, the 1938 arrangement swings much more than the fox-trot original almost twenty years its junior. Arrangements that Whiteman played over time certainly were updated as expectations of arranging continued to expand. The same was true of most bands with an extended career. At the same time, as this critic inadvertently observed, such rearrangements can be deceiving. They provide a sense that the most recent version of something is what audiences have always heard. This phenomenon remained the case until the practice of reissuing music recordings of the past began to emerge in the final quarter of the twentieth century. To this end, arrangements readdress and redress the past in the sounds of the present.

Yet, in the case of sonic stereotypes and musical Orientalism, the clothes draped upon such songs become more pronounced over time. Exploring these works as they survive both within the Whiteman Collection and on recording demonstrates that while arrangements traverse the move from fox trot to swing as they move out of the 1920s and through the 1930s, the exoticizing techniques used become sharper. Much of this appears as the result of the standardization of musical-arrangement approaches professed by Lange's publication and taken up by key arrangers throughout the field. Looking more broadly at arrangements in the Whiteman Collection from the mid-1920s and forward, we hear this in use of Asiatic percussion, such as temple bells and gongs, and more breaks that employ unisons and other parallel intervals, as well as instrumental combinations used to signify the sounds of the so-called Orient. For example, the 1930s arrangement of "Cho-Cho-San" sets in stone the ornate alto saxophone line—complete with its application of the "standard musical sign for East Asia"—now for performance by a high alto saxophone and baritone saxophone pairing. Probably not by coincidence, this same instrumentation was used by Grofé in the original arrangement of *Rhapsody in Blue* during the Orientalist iteration of the ritornello theme as first heard at Whiteman's Experiment in Modern Music concert.

Taking a closer look at such techniques frames the larger assumptions, realities, and power dynamics at play in jazz band arrangements from the 1920s forward. Looking at the physical arrangements themselves—the manuscript scores and parts—can open crucial perspectives, be they on the original creation of a piece such as "Cho-Cho-San" or the sonic development of a work over time such as "Limehouse Blues." As Stephanie Doktor argues in investigating the ways Whiteman's music arranges "whiteness" over time, "bringing Whiteman's arrangements into the fray of jazz historiography helps construct a more nuanced understanding of the relationship between race, sound, and capitalism and demonstrates how bandleaders and their arrangers profoundly shaped jazz's foundation."[46] And such foundations form the structural underpinning of contemporary experiences and expectations of popular song and also set in place systemically embraced expectations of non-white persons in the United States.

Even as the racialized and racist language and imagery of the original songs disappears through an absence of lyrics, the sentiments echo forward. Many of the physical parts for the arrangements under consideration in this essay capture the marginalia of the arrangers and musicians performing these songs. These parts document an additional layer of prejudice and xenophobia that may not have been heard on the stage or on the recordings but was present in the minds of the performers. One of the many examples emerges from an arrangement of "China Seas" prepared by Ken Hopkins, who spent limited time with Whiteman but had an extended career with MGM. This song was the title track for the 1935 film of the same name starring Clark Gable and Jean Harlow. The front page of the full score includes the annotation "Heavily Accented," which might otherwise be a simple reminder to punch up the specified rhythms. However, the fact that the arranger signed his name as "Sing Lee Hopkins"—which Rayno describes as humorous—points to a racist Orientalism mindset.[47] However, both annotations appearing in this manuscript—to say little of the myriad others that accompany sonic representations of the East Asian population in this period—add up to a more pointed "characteristic effect" that further denigrates the nonwhite population. They reveal an otherwise-private visual manifestation of the inherent white supremacist underpinnings also manifested through the public sonic arrangement and performance of these songs. It may be easy to brush away such occurrences as simply a reflection of their time. Yet, as we all know, the inherent power of such references endures even as we continue to arrange and rearrange their legacies.

Appendix: Orientalist Songs in the Whiteman Collection at Williams College

Several songs contain multiple arrangements. This list only includes music appearing as physical arrangements (scores and/or parts) and does not account for dozens of additional Orientalist songs that appear on recordings by Whiteman's ensemble also in the collection.

Piece	Box	Composer(s)	Arranger(s)
Ah Moon of My Delight	3	Lehman	Bargy
Allah's Holiday	8	Friml	Sodestrom
Aloha Oe (2 versions)	8	Liliuokalani	Huxley and Van Eps
Bagdad	20	Ager	Grofé
Ballet Egyptien (2 versions)	20	Luigini	Grofé
Beach Boy (7 versions)	22	Ronell	Deutsch and Wolcott
Bedouin Dance	26	Friml	Majer
Blue Hawaii	35	Schuster and Boer	Grofé and Caesar
Broken Idol	43	Squires	Still
Burning Sands	46	Onivas	Grofé
By the Shalimar	47	Koehler, Magine, and Delbridge	Grofé
By the Waters of Minnetonka (4 versions)	47	Lieurance	Grofé
Caravan (5 versions)	50–51	Ellington	Borgy and Van Cleave
Cherokee (2 versions)	58	Noble	Rains
China Boy (6 versions)	58–59	Winfree and Boutelje	Hayton, Hopkins, Van Cleave, Lang, and Trumbauer

Piece	Box	Composer(s)	Arranger(s)
China Seas	59	Brown	Hopkins
Chinatown Medley	523	Still	—
Chinatown, My Chinatown (4 versions)	59	Schwartz	Christian, Hopkins, and Van Eps
Chinese Dance	60	Kool	—
Chinese Lullaby (2 versions)	60	Bowers	Grofé and Van Eps
Chinese Suite, A	60	Grofé	—
Cho-Cho-San	61	Puccini	Grofé
Chopsticks (2 versions)	62	Allen	Deutsch and Van Eps
Chopsticks Suite	62	Korsakow and Cui	Deutsch and Liadow
Constantinople	77	Carlton	Satterfield
Dance of the Savages	89	Feist	—
Egyptian Barn Dance (2 versions)	120	Scott	Glover
Egyptian Rose	120	Grofé	—
Egyptian Shimmy	120	Grofé and Jackson	—
Eskimo	121	Wolcott	—
Fallen Leaf (An Indian Love Song)	129	Logan	Grofé
Fantasie Orientale	538	Lange	—
From the Land of the Sky Blue Water (3 versions)	139–40	Cadman	Clark, Still, and Boutelje
Glow Worm, The (2 versions)	147	Lincke	Cutter
Hawaiian Medley (2 versions)	539	—	Ranis and Sosnik
Hawaiian Waltz Medley (2 versions)	540	—	Bargy and Fredericks
Hindustan (2 versions)	168	Wallace and Weeks	Clark
Honolulu Eyes	172	Violinsky	Schultz
Honolulu Moon	172	Lawrence	Grofé
Hot Mikado Medley (3 versions)	342–43	Sullivan	Van Cleave
Hymn to the Sun (3 versions)	176	Rimsky-Korsakov	Cutter and Grofé
In a Persian Market	215	Ketelbey	Grofé
Indian Breezes	219	Young	—
Indian Cradle Song	219	Wayne	Grofé
Indian Dawn	219	Zamecnik	Grofé
Indian Love Call (6 versions)	219–20	Friml	Huxley and Paul
Indian Tribal Songs	220	Sosnick	—
Japanese Mammy	232	Donaldson	Grofé
Japanese Moonlight	232	Friml	Lange

Piece	Box	Composer(s)	Arranger(s)
Japanese Sandman (3 versions)	233	Whiting	Szathmary and Grofé
Ka-Lu-A	241	Kern	Szathmary
Kashmiri Song (2 versions)	241	Woodforde-Finden	Grofé and Macomber
Katinka	241	Friml	Deutsch and Archangelski
Limehouse Blues (12 versions)	261–63	Braham	Challis, Chestnut, Gould, Hopkins, Sack, Satterfield, and Stoker
Lo Nah	268	Stept	Grofé
Love Song of Tahiti	278	Kaper and Jurman	Hopkins
Madame Butterfly—One Fine Day	344	Puccini	—
Mandalay	287	Burtnett, Lyman, and Arnheim	Szathmary
March Orientale	291	Sarino	—
My Little Grass Shack in Kealakekua, Hawaii	155	Cogswell, Harrison, and Noble	Sarino
Mystic Moonlight	323	Friml	Majer
Nagasaki (2 versions)	323–24	Warren	Livingston
Not for All the Rice in China	333	Berlin	—
On a Little Street in Singapore	342	De Rose	Unmarked
On the Road to Mandalay (3 versions)	343	Speaks	Deutsch and Huxley
Oriental Yogi	347	—	Van Eps
Orientale (3 versions)	347	Cui	Grofé
Pagan Love Song	349	Brown	Bargy
Pale Moon (An Indian Love Song)	349	Logan	Huxley
Po Ling and Ming Toy (2 versions)	357	Friml	Schmid and Grofé
Poor Butterfly	358	Hubbell	Grofé
Queen of Sheba	363	Gounod	—
Sakuntala (6 versions)	381	Goldmark	Grofé
San (2 versions)	382	McPhail and Michels	Challis and Sharpe
Scheherezade (4 versions)	386	Rimsky-Korsakov	Cutter
Shanghai Dream Man	394	Davis	Grofé
Shanghai Lil	394	Warren	Wolcott
Sheik of Araby, The (2 versions)	395	Snyder	Wolcott and Rains
Sheik's Patrol	395	Friml	Majer

Piece	Box	Composer(s)	Arranger(s)
Sing Song Girl	402	Hanley and McCarthy	Harlin
Sing-Loo	401	Norman	Grofé
Song of India (2 versions)	411	Rimsky-Korsakov	Bargy
Song of the Islands (2 versions)	413	King	Sosnik
South Sea Island Magic	416	Long	Bargy
South Sea Medley (2 versions)	572	—	Huxley
Suite of Serenades, A	540	Herbert	—
There's Nothing Else to Do in Ma-La-Ka-Mo-Ka-Lu	285	Friend and Mitchell	Wolcott
Tropical	462	Gould	—
Ukulele Lady	466	Whiting	Grofé
Wang Wang Blues	475	Mueler	Van Eps
War Dance	475	Joslyn	Joslyn
War Dance for Wooden Indians	475	Scott	Glover
Where My Caravan Has Rested	489	Loehr	Huxley
Wooden Soldier and the China Doll (2 versions)	499	Jones	Gould and Hayton

Notes

I thank former Williams College undergraduate student Max Thierry for his assistance in the Whiteman Collection while the archives remained closed to the public in the spring of 2021. I am also grateful to the anonymous reviewers of this volume, W. Anthony Sheppard, and my Colorado College undergraduate research assistant, Forrest Tucker.

1. Bañagale, "American in Chinatown."
2. For an overview of the musical practices of and musicological approaches to Orientalism, see Ralph P. Locke, "Orientalism," *Grove Music Online*, 2001, https://www.oxfordmusiconline.com/.
3. Rayno, *Paul Whiteman*, 2:306.
4. Hisama, "Postcolonialism on the Make"; Tsou, "Gendering Race"; Garrett, "Chinatown, Whose Chinatown"; Sheppard, *Extreme Exoticism*.
5. Sheppard, *Extreme Exoticism*, 70.
6. See Pollack, *George Gershwin*, 302–4; Schiff, *Gershwin*, 82–86.
7. Bañagale, *Arranging Gershwin*, 14–46.
8. For more on Tin Pan Alley song form and the *Rhapsody*, see Schiff, *Gershwin*, 3–25.
9. In one of the few instrumental indications given in the two-piano short score (from which Grofé prepared his arrangement), Gershwin suggests the

same combination of instruments used in the 1920 recording of "The Japanese Sandman": clarinet, violin, and baritone saxophone. Grofé opted for a different combination at this point in the *Rhapsody*.

10. Bañagale, *Arranging Gershwin*, 41–42.

11. Schiff, *Gershwin*, 51.

12. Schiff, *Gershwin*, 60.

13. Furber and Branham, *Limehouse Blues*.

14. Wald, *How the Beatles Destroyed Rock 'n' Roll*, 3.

15. Howland, "Between the Muses and the Masses," 109.

16. Wriggle, *Blue Rhythm Fantasy*, 3.

17. For more on this early period of Grofé's career and the development of notated arrangements, see Bañagale, *Arranging Gershwin*, 34–38; Howland, "Between the Muses," 113–20.

18. Howland, *Hearing Luxe Pop*, 62. See also Maher and Sultanof, "Pre-swing Era Big Bands," 274.

19. Wriggle, *Blue Rhythm Fantasy*, 68–69.

20. Lange, *Arranging*, x.

21. Lange, *Arranging*, 188. In a passage that describes the acceptable woodwinds for a modern dance orchestra, Lange observes that the clarinet—"long used in jazz bands before the saxophone was introduced"—can be incorporated into a saxophone part but should otherwise be considered an auxiliary instrument.

22. Chapter 2 of Howland's dissertation is titled "The (Symphonic) Jazz Age: The Grofé/Lange Arranging Idiom of the 1920s and the Vaudeville Aesthetic." Howland, "Between the Muses," 90–177.

23. Howland, "Between the Muses," 128.

24. Regarding the development and maintenance of Orientalisms in popular music, an important chain emerges between European opera and operetta, silent-film accompaniment, Tin Pan Alley song composition, and dance-band arrangements.

25. Sheppard, *Extreme Exoticism*, 9–10.

26. Howland, "Between the Muses," 157–58.

27. Here the songs come from a 1939 Broadway production starring Bill "Bojangles" Robinson. Sheppard notes that with such songs, "African Americans engaged in yellowface performance and racial representation proved multilayered . . . [suggesting] that race is an ambiguous concept and that the maintenance of racial difference is crucial." Sheppard, *Extreme Exoticism*, 80.

28. Lange, *Arranging*, 54, 182, 179, 117, original emphases. Paul Whiteman credits trumpeter Herry Busse with the invention of this technique: "Yet it was he who stuck a kazoo in a regular mute one day (he got the kazoo from a ten-cent store across the street) and got an Oriental quality like an oboe that I had been wanting for a long time." Whiteman and McBride, *Jazz*, 240–41.

29. Howland, "Between the Muses," 159.

30. Note that this rhythmic figure is not unique to Tchaikovsky but was a recurring "Oriental" trope in classical music.

31. Lange, *Arranging*, 82.

32. Jeffrey Magee explores the ways that Black musicians—in particular, the arranger Don Redman—began to distinguish themselves from the "sweet" sound of white dance bands during this time period. Magee, *Uncrowned King of Swing*, 39–71.

33. Quoted in Rayno, *Paul Whiteman*, 1:383.

34. "Cho-Cho-San," Whiteman Collection, Box 61.

35. Rayno, 1:459.

36. Rayno, *Paul Whiteman*, 1:458–59.

37. Lange, *Arranging*, 212, original emphasis.

38. The record credits both Whiteman and Grofé for the arrangement. Rayno posits, "Paul either assisted Grofé on it, or had previously made an arrangement of the tune, at least a basic one, from which Grofé worked." Rayno, *Paul Whiteman*, 1:473–74. This observation is backed up by a short score that appears to be in Whiteman's handwriting located in the Williams archives. "Orientale," Whiteman Collection, Box 347.

39. Rayno, *Paul Whiteman*, 1:609.

40. For a broader discussion of this song, see Sheppard, *Extreme Exoticism*, 74–76.

41. Howland, "Between the Muses," 164.

42. Howland, "Between the Muses," 164.

43. The nine total arrangements of "Limehouse Blues" can be found in boxes 261–63, Whiteman Collection. Each of these was prepared by a different arranger in the following years: 1927; 1928; 1935 (2 arrangements); 1938 (2 arrangements); 1939; 1942; 1943.

44. Bill Challis originally arranged for Whiteman between 1927 and 1930 before departing for Hollywood. He rejoined the ensemble in 1938 specifically in support of performances for the *Chesterfield Radio Program*.

45. Rayno, *Paul Whiteman*, 2:192.

46. Doktor, "Arranging Whiteness."

47. Rayno, *Paul Whiteman*, 2:663.

5

Concertized Jazz

The Divergent Motives of Whiteman (1924) and Goodman (1938)

SARAH CAISSIE PROVOST

Paul Whiteman's media-bestowed title, the King of Jazz, was never secure. In 1932 one Frank Greaves of Albany, New York, who referred to himself as King Jazz, sought to prevent Whiteman from using his given moniker.[1] A judge refused to grant Greaves an injunction. There were, however, other ways of stripping Whiteman of his title, a process that music historians and jazz critics initiated during Whiteman's final years. The word "putative" began appearing alongside the nickname in the 1960s, becoming "the putative King of Jazz."[2] Others declared that the title was entirely mistaken, deeming it a "misnomer," as in "Whiteman's 'King of Jazz' misnomer."[3] Similarly, Benny Goodman was crowned the King of Swing in the media, but critics would come to question this moniker as well. Gunther Schuller wondered in 1989, "If Benny was the 'King,' what was Fletcher [Henderson]?"[4] while others would also note that Goodman's nickname was achieved largely through the musical labors of Henderson.[5] The bestowing—and then withdrawing—of royal titles connects Whiteman and Goodman, both of whom were white men holding King nicknames over Black innovators.

To varying degrees, both Whiteman and Goodman utilized their privilege to attract white audiences to jazz. On the surface, though, these two men's careers appear to have had little in common; they rarely performed together, and Goodman retained a more respectable position than did Whiteman as jazz historians later reexamined and restored the contributions of Black musicians from the 1920s and 1930s.[6] The similarity of their monikers, including the irony some hear in both, appears to be their only common ground. However, I suggest that the two also share another commonality:

their use of the classical concert hall to legitimize their music making. Both benefited from convincing their mainly white audiences that jazz could be artistic as well as entertaining. Through Whiteman and Goodman, audiences discovered that jazz could be a moral form of entertainment. The concert hall gave them the platform to demonstrate jazz's possibilities: the King of Jazz and the King of Swing drew on Western classical standards to be crowned. Examining the backgrounds, programs, and reception of their concert events reveals the ways that each invoked philosophical—and often racialized—ideas of jazz's present state and potential future. Whiteman and Goodman utilized and evaded their relationships with Blackness for a skeptical and sometimes fearful audience. Both framed themselves as jazz educators and ambassadors, even if their educational aims were often flawed. Considering Whiteman and Goodman together reveals the ways that both musicians negotiated their musical identities on the stage and positioned themselves as integral to jazz's developing history.

Each bandleader famously presented a concert at a New York City venue then associated with the most conservative musical values. Whiteman presented his concert at Aeolian Hall (a hall that featured primarily classical soloists and ensembles, such as the New York Chamber Music Society) on February 12, 1924, an event most notable for its premiere of Gershwin's *Rhapsody in Blue*. Goodman performed at Carnegie Hall—considered the premiere venue for classical music in the city—on January 16, 1938. Both concerts primarily featured the bandleader's regular groups, and both programs included hefty servings of the bands' hits and typical fare (Goodman's more than Whiteman's). Both bandleaders had close relationships with classical music that influenced their careers and enabled their productive use of concertized jazz performances. And for both, putting jazz on the classical concert stage was a gamble.

Jazz in the Concert Hall

Whiteman and Goodman used the concert stage to lend legitimacy to a musical style that had many detractors. The moral panic around jazz in the 1910s and 1920s was fresh and relevant for both. Much of this moral panic was due to the music's Blackness, with the common complaint that Black musicians were corrupting white youth. Fascinated white youth flocked to jazz despite their previous disinterest in Black music.[7] The racial nature of this backlash was sometimes masked, with community leaders and critics designating syncopation and jazz's association with dancing as the true problems.[8] Thus, leading white musicians, who were inspired by the creative possibilities of the new style and dazzled by its commercial potential, turned to the concert hall as a neutralizing space. The stationary seats and concert-behavior conventions mitigated the dancing problem, and the venues' association with European classical "masters" lent an automatic respectability.

Before jazz appeared in austere concert halls, jazz's venues fell into three distinct classes: the lowest-status clubs and taxi dance halls, the middle-status ballrooms, and the highest-status hotels and restaurants. Taxi dance halls (venues where patrons would use tickets to dance with hired, mostly female, dancers) and cabarets occupied the lower end of jazz venues in the 1920s and 1930s. Leading bandleaders would restrict themselves to the middle- and high-class venues of ballrooms and high society hotels. The ballrooms, which were where many white jazz musicians performed in the 1920s and 1930s, were specifically positioned as an alternate to clubs: Harlem's Savoy Ballroom manager Charles Buchanan noted that one of the reasons for the Savoy's creation was to "accommodate the many thousands who wished to dance in an atmosphere of tasteful refinement, rather than in the small and stuffy halls and the foul smelling, smoke laden cellar nightclubs."[9] The Savoy would become, along with the Roseland, one of the premiere places in New York City for swing performances. And the higher-status venues were even more prized. Goodman, for example, had a lucrative stint from 1936 to 1938 at the Madhattan Room at Hotel Pennsylvania, in addition to his frequent ballroom performances. This series was a turning point for Goodman's mainstream acceptance, particularly for his mixed-race trio (Goodman, white drummer Gene Krupa, and Black pianist Teddy Wilson) and quartet (which added Black vibraphonist Lionel Hampton). Similarly, his Carnegie Hall performance of 1938 would be acknowledged as another landmark, since Black musicians outnumbered white musicians on part of the program. Such high-status venues signaled a growing acceptance of jazz.

Despite both Whiteman's and Goodman's groups being "dance bands," both had associations with nondancing audiences that carried over into their concert performances. Whiteman's band was probably more associated with dancing than Goodman's because of a marked change that occurred in swing audiences in the mid-1930s. In 1935 Goodman's group had culminated a cross-country tour at the Palomar Ballroom in Los Angeles, where their radio popularity preceded them.[10] The audience comprised both dancers and nondancers; the nondancers were there to listen and cheer, an act that was unusual enough for Goodman to note, "to our complete amazement, half of the crowd stopped dancing and came surging around the stand."[11] Although the changeover in audience behavior from jazz-as-dancing to jazz-as-listening would not truly come until well into the bebop era, the Palomar ballroom seemed a landmark performance, if not for jazz itself, at least for Goodman.[12] The audience's appreciation of Goodman's music away from the dance floor allowed Goodman to consider even more-refined nondancing venues, such as Carnegie Hall.

Although jazz itself was rare in the concert hall pre-Whiteman, this did not hold true of all Black music. The 1910s and 1920s saw increasing acceptance of Black music on the concert stage, often utilizing large-scale structures similar to those of classical music. Scott DeVeaux notes that although syncopated music had existed in the concert hall for at least ten years prior (with Will Marion Cook and James Reese Europe), these concerts were presented as overviews of African American folk styles and thus featured varying styles.[13] Later, Duke Ellington and James P. Johnson incorporated large-scale formal models like suites and sacred works into their jazz and popular music–influenced compositions.[14]

White jazz musicians were also interested in large-scale structures; however, instead of working jazz into classical music themselves, they called upon classical composers to write new pieces for them. These pieces evidenced different motivations from those of Ellington and Johnson; instead of showing that classical music could successfully incorporate jazz, white musicians often sought to show that their personal abilities were on par with classical performers. This frequently took the form of bandleaders commissioning works from composers more often associated with classical music; Woody Herman commissioned *Ebony Concerto* from Igor Stravinsky, Tommy Dorsey commissioned Nathaniel Shilkret's trombone concerto, and both Whiteman and Goodman commissioned works from classical composers. Goodman commissioned a work from Béla Bartók (*Contrasts* for clarinet, violin, and piano), concertos by Paul Hindemith and by Aaron Copland, and several other pieces by classical composers, while Whiteman, whose instrument was truly his band, commissioned *Synconata* and *Symphony for Jazz Orchestra* from the prolific Lee Sowerby (among other commissions discussed below).[15] Composers in the 1920s were already using jazz to flavor large-scale classically structured pieces, such as Darius Milhaud's *La Création du monde*, Copland's *Grohg*, and George Antheil's *Jazz Symphony*.[16] Conversely, jazz musicians could make the jump into the classical concert hall as long as they utilized the structures of classical music. Absent those structures, jazz's home was not yet in the concert hall.

Paul Whiteman Experiments with the Future

Paul Whiteman presented his first Experiment in Modern Music concert at Aeolian Hall on February 12, 1924. Joshua Berrett suggests that Whiteman may have been motivated to offer the event in response to a concert-lecture given by rival bandleader Vincent Lopez.[17] Lopez gave a lecture-demonstration on the history of jazz at an art gallery, sponsored by the League of Composers and including an appearance by Harvard professor Edward Burlingame Hill. In the press release for Lopez's event, the author writes, "Mr. Lopez, who does not believe in the term 'jazz,' will center his talk on what he prefers to call 'modern music.'"[18] Whiteman's concert title An Experiment in Modern Music is remarkably close to Lopez's theme and would become the name of the eight-concert series Whiteman presented over the next fourteen years.

The educational intent of the program is another similarity to Whiteman's event. Lopez explicitly labeled his program a "concert-lecture," while Whiteman described his concert as having educational value: the program notes read, "The experiment is to be purely educational. Mr. Whiteman intends to point out . . . the tremendous strides which have been made in popular music from the day of the discordant Jazz . . . to the really melodious music of today, which—for no good reason—is still called Jazz."[19] This indicates that Whiteman felt the need to educate his audiences, assuming that they would not recognize jazz or might not appreciate its possibilities. This is further reflected in Whiteman's program selections. His concert was arranged roughly chronologically and divided into educational sections (see table 5.1).

The concert opened with the "True Form of Jazz," which included "Livery Stable Blues," and finished not with what would become the most well-known and structured offering on the program, *Rhapsody in Blue*, but with a piece known primarily from the classical world, *Pomp and Circumstance* by Edward Elgar. Howland, in his book *Ellington Uptown*, explains that Whiteman's program closely matches the programmatic outline of vaudeville shows, in which the final piece should be easily heard over the noise of people leaving the theater early.[20] However, Whiteman's concert also reflects a progression, beginning with what Whiteman considered jazz's roots (the Original Dixieland Jazz Band), proceeding through his own brand of symphonic jazz, and ending with two pieces in traditional classical structures. Whiteman's concert also mirrors Lopez's recital, which offered an arrangement of *Carmen* as well as a number from *H.M.S. Pinafore* and several current jazzy hits such as 1923's "My Sweetie Went Away" and "Mamma Loves Papa."

Whiteman's concert could be read as a typically 1920s mix of tunes in various popular styles, including what later audiences would call "symphonic" but what audiences of the day would have recognized as one of the many styles that fell under the heading "jazz." This is partially true. What is also true is that Whiteman was attempting to educate the audience, not only on what jazz was but also what it could become.

Whiteman was specifically interested in jazz's development—in the future of jazz and how he could shape it. This is consistent with his overall career.

TABLE 5.1 Program of Whiteman's Aeolian Hall Concert

Section	Selection	Composer
1. True Form of Jazz	a. Ten Years Ago—"Livery Stable Blues"	LaRocca
	b. With Modern Embellishment—"Mama Loves Papa"	Baer
2. Comedy Selections	a. Origin of "Yes, We Have No Bananas"	Silver
	b. Instrumental Comedy—"So This is Venice" (Featuring Ross Gorman) (Adapted from "The Carnival of Venice")	Thomas
3. Contrast—Legitimate Scoring vs. Jazzing	a. Selection in True Form—"Whispering"	Schonberger
	b. Same Selection with Jazz Treatment	
4. Recent Compositions with Modern Score	a. "Limehouse Blues"	Braham
	b. "I Love You"	Archer
	c. "Raggedy Ann"	Kern
5. Zez Confrey (piano)	a. Medley Popular Airs	none listed
	b. "Kitten on the Keys"	Confrey
	c. "Ice Cream and Art"	none listed
	d. "Nickel in the Slot"	Confrey
	Accompanied by the Orchestra	
6. Flavoring a Selection with Borrowed Themes	"Russian Rose" (Based on "The Volga Boat Song")	Grofé
7. Semi-Symphonic Arrangement of Popular Melodies	Consisting of	
	"Alexander's Ragtime Band"	Berlin
	"A Pretty Girl is Like a Melody"	Berlin
	"Orange Blossoms in California"	Berlin
8. A Suite of Serenades	a. Spanish	Herbert
	b. Chinese	
	c. Cuban	
	d. Oriental	
9. Adaptation of Standard Selections to Dance Rhythm	a. "Pale Moon"	Logan
	b. "To a Wild Rose"	McDowell
	c. "Chansonette"	Friml
10. George Gershwin (Piano)	"A Rhapsody in Blue"	Gershwin
	Accompanied by the Orchestra	
11. In the Field of Classics	"Pomp and Circumstance"	Elgar

Note: Sections 1 to 7 are labeled as the "First Half" in the program and sections 8 to 11 as "Second Half."

He has been dismissed by some as a fad follower: Whitney Balliett quips that Whiteman had a "fad-o-meter," presciently shifting his approach in the late 1910s to a jazz-oriented sound.[21] Whiteman was initially a classical violist, and his first job as a musician with the Exposition Orchestra had him performing operatic and symphonic selections, though probably some dance music as well.[22] He also performed with the San Francisco Symphony, but he found his duties there creatively stifling.[23] Jazz, which he initially found difficult (he was fired after his first night playing jazz), provided him with a creative outlet.[24] His "fad-o-meter" was remarkably sensitive, considering the dearth of resources available to him. Although Whiteman did frequent some of the jazz venues in San Francisco in 1917, he otherwise probably only knew instrumental jazz from the Original Dixieland Jazz Band recordings.[25] No Black jazz musicians were recorded until King Oliver's Creole Orchestra's 1923 recordings, and Henderson's jazz group did not officially exist until 1924. Thus, the chance that Whiteman—or many other white musicians in the 1910s and early 1920s—knew much Black jazz at all was slim even after he relocated to New York. But it is also worth noting that the dearth of Black jazz musicians in the early 1920s in the Northeast meant that Whiteman truly was performing something that would have been considered "new," as drawing directly on any Black jazz tradition was not an option. Whiteman was not the only white musician doing so—and would not be the only one whose influence was later dismissed. Irving Berlin, as Jeffrey Magee has shown, fused blues and ragtime with popular song in a way that was clearly heard as jazz in the early 1920s.[26] The repertoire of Berlin, Gershwin, and Whiteman reveals that no specific definition of "jazz" existed in the 1920s, and the term could encompass any number of genres, from theater to popular song to improvised instrumental performance, and could be heard as "jazz" by both Black and white audiences.[27] However, Whiteman was interested in a fusion of jazz and classical styles from the start or at least in creating a version of jazz without "roughness." In his first published words about jazz, Whiteman states, "Modern jazz can be played without so much roughness and made quite attractive."[28] From his earliest days as a bandleader, jazz was Whiteman's aim.

In addition to roughness, ephemerality was a problem for Whiteman to solve. By the mid-1930s audiences, including (and especially) Goodman's, were drawn to the uniqueness of each individual jazz performance and jazz's possibility as an art form that could be divorced from its original context as dance music. For Whiteman, however, the ephemeral nature of jazz was its weakness. A 1955 documentary script from ABC-TV outlines the problem and Whiteman's solution:

> He noticed that hot musicians would play inspired, improvised music one night and the following evening be listless and dispirited. They were unable to remember, they said, what they'd played the previous evening. Paul asked them why they couldn't score the music on the good nights and read it afterwards, thereby duplicating the top performances consistently.
>
> Well, that had never been done. That was highbrow, long-haired technique. With jazz you just played it and it was lost forever unless you played it through the horns that the recording companies used then to make records.

> The fact that it had never been done before made no difference to Paul. . . . He wrote down the good, hot music he heard and after a spell of playing in other people's jazz bands around San Francisco, he travelled down the coast to the Alexandra Hotel in Los Angeles and organized his own band. Playing subdued, scored music, with the melody sweet and the rhythm insistent, Paul Whiteman and his orchestra were an instantaneous hit and were hired to come east to the Ambassador in Atlantic City.[29]

For Whiteman, preserving the best solos and performances was the way to the future. Whiteman's idea that jazz was a futuristic music also inspired him to change his personnel significantly, using his fad-o-meter to discover the potential for new audiences and adapting his music to attract them. When he made his first recordings in 1920, he had a band the size of other orchestras of the day. This included just eight or nine performers: two saxophones, one trumpet, trombone, piano, banjo, bass, drums, and Whiteman himself on violin (sometimes uncredited). Consider the band for the Aeolian Hall concert four years later: twenty-three performers, including seven violins and two French horns. By surrounding himself with the trappings of classical music—but maintaining the insistent rhythmic basis of jazz—Whiteman acted as an intermediary between what we now know as Black forms of jazz and the white traditions of the European concert hall. This provided Whiteman's audience with the perfect enticements to attend his concerts—they were new and slightly transgressive but legitimized by the surroundings, orchestrations, and extended forms made popular by nineteenth-century Romanticism.

Whiteman's fad-o-meter was likely tuned to the draw of the transgressive. Throughout the 1920s, white middle- and upper-class youths engaged in the practice of "slumming": visiting majority-Black areas of large cities, usually for the purposes of drinking and dancing. Chad Heap, in his book on the history of slumming, notes that these white patrons engaged in this type of racial tourism "not only as a means to ground the changing popular conceptualization of race and sexuality in particular urban spaces but also as an opportunity to shore up their own superior standing in the shifting racial and sexual hierarchies by juxtaposing themselves with the women and men they encountered on their slumming excursions."[30] In the 1920s slumming was strongly associated with black-and-tan clubs and jazz music, but as Heap notes, the radio and recording industries made it possible to "recapture some semblance of their slumming experiences within the privacy of their own homes."[31]

Capturing this semblance of transgression while legitimizing jazz sounded like the future to Whiteman. Thus, he utilized features of classical music, which was considered a marker of legitimacy in the early days of radio and the recording industry. David Goodman (not related to Benny) has shown that radio positioned white classical music as a foil to Black jazz during this period, with broadcasters often defending their programming by noting how much airtime they devoted to classical music.[32] Lacking a visual cue for race meant that broadcasters developed aural cues, particularly for Jim Crow–era Southern cities. These racial politics worked in performance spaces, too. Andrew Berish, in his study of the Casino Ballroom's dance-band events in the 1930s, details the way that spaces could carefully construct notions of race using jazz style. He notes that while sweet Black bands existed, they were seldom hired by venues like the Casino Ballroom to avoid "challeng[ing] the illusion of the particular social order being created."[33] Both Whiteman and Goodman upheld this illusion through appropriation of Black styles performed in white spaces. Whiteman also assured his success by taking the whiteness of the concert stage a step further, presenting a version of jazz connected stylistically with the European symphonic tradition.

Legitimization via the concert hall was a domestic as well as an international goal for Whiteman. "My notion is that the chief contribution of the white American to jazz so far has been his recognition of it as legitimate music," he wrote in 1926.[34] Undertaking several European tours, Whiteman constructed his programs to underline the possibilities of the art form, ostensibly avoiding the trendy "jazzing the classics" that many jazz artists pursued while, in fact, engaging in those same practices. He said, "We don't intend to jazz well-known pieces or, as has been done in Germany, execute jazz variations on well-known motifs. Rather, we want to create something new."[35] Two of his earliest recordings were jazzed versions of well-known pieces: 1921's "Song of India," based on a Nikolay Rimsky-Korsakov aria from *Sadko*, and 1922's "Oriental," an arrangement of an aria from Camille Saint-Saëns's *Samson et Dalila*.[36] Still, he considered himself to have a futuristic outlook: "[I] did not come to Europe to create a sensation for the Europeans. I've come to pave the way for the development of futuristic music."[37] Here, jazz is treated as source material; calling jazz "a sensation" indicates the extent to which jazz did not belong on the concert stage.[38]

Audiences recognized the forward-looking possibilities of Whiteman's program, particularly with *Rhapsody in Blue*. W. J. Henderson of the *New York Herald* comments, "If this way lies the path toward the development of American modern music into a high art form, then one can heartily congratulate Mr. Gershwin on his disclosure of some of the possibilities."[39] Olin Downes of the *New York Times* agrees: "Mr. Gershwin's composition shows extraordinary talent, just as it also shows a young composer with the aims that go far beyond those of his ilk. In spite of technical immaturity, he has expressed himself in a significant and on the whole highly original manner.

This is fresh and new and full of promise."[40] These sentiments were not universally shared; Lawrence Gilman of the *New York Tribune* reports, "Recall the most ambitious piece, the Rhapsody, and weep over the lifelessness of its melody and harmony, so derivative, so stale, so inexpressive."[41] And the notion of the *Rhapsody* as modern was also complicated; Richard Crawford describes critic Paul Rosenfeld as treating "Gershwin and the *Rhapsody in Blue* as threats to the position he had staked out in support of a more uncompromising modernism."[42] David Schiff notes that the "fate of the *Rhapsody* in the critical accounts of jazz and modernism says more about the evolving ideologies of music history than about Gershwin's music,"[43] but these contemporary accounts show that these ideologies were being negotiated from the start. Gershwin may have been performing in a classical venue and with the trappings of the classical style, but his composition was still closely associated with popular music for some. The performers, though, were moved to catharsis: both Whiteman and Gershwin reported they were crying at the performance.[44] Whiteman attempted to repeat the formula at other concert events, performing large-scale works like Gershwin's *An American in Paris*, Ferde Grofé's tone poem *Broadway at Night*, and Eastwood Lane's *Three American Pieces*.

Goodman and Jazz's Present

Whiteman's appropriative pivot to jazz and his claim to be offering the music of the future, while ignoring contributions by Black innovators, are two of the primary reasons he fared poorly in jazz literature of the second half of the twentieth century. On the other hand, clarinetist and bandleader Goodman maintained respectability as the narratives of jazz changed from a story of a popular musical style to one defined by its relationship to African American culture and its appropriation by white musicians. Goodman grew up with jazz. Like most musicians, he was "classically" trained as there were no other options at the time. However, at almost twenty years younger than Whiteman, Goodman heard more jazz during his formative years—he describes going to Jazz Nights at Central Park's Theater in Chicago at age twelve, even performing his impression of Ted Lewis there. And his classical clarinet teacher of two years (and his only formal instructor), Frank Schoepp, was known for teaching some of jazz's other great clarinetists, including Jimmy Noone and Buster Bailey.[45] Goodman, with his barrier-breaking performances with Black musicians Wilson and Hampton, as well as his use of Henderson's arrangements in the 1930s, has been viewed as a more legitimate figure in jazz history because of these associations. His major concert event, an appearance at Carnegie Hall on January 16, 1938, was considered the "first" for several reasons.[46] Some consider it the first jazz concert, as unlike Whiteman, Goodman did not rely on classical structures or instrumentation for any segment of his concert. Additionally, Goodman presented an integrated band—though the integration was realized through special guests and subsets of his own big band, as detailed below in this section. Essentially, Goodman's treatment of Black musicians was visible and verifiable. Whiteman's place in jazz history is far more complicated; he did not put Black musicians on stage, and he made only a few comments acknowledging jazz's relationship to Blackness. However, Whiteman, too, broke certain racial barriers; later in his career, he hired William Grant Still and Don Redman as arrangers—the latter being closely tied to the very arrangements that Goodman bought from Henderson in the mid-1930s. And Christi Jay Wells has convincingly shown that Whiteman's reception in the Black press was more favorable than his scholarly reputation may indicate.[47]

Although Goodman also presented his music on the concert stage, he did not intend his Carnegie Hall concert to suggest a future for jazz. Instead, Goodman wanted to show that jazz could exist in a classical space unaltered. He was also not inspired by Whiteman. Scott DeVeaux notes that the major difference between the two events was that Whiteman imposed concert forms on jazz "from above," while 1930s musicians, Goodman included, allowed concert performances to come "from below, as an outgrowth of the ordinary situations in which jazz was performed."[48] However, although Goodman did not use his band to proclaim a future for jazz, he did seek to prove himself as equal to his classical counterparts in other ways. Later in his career, he commissioned and performed new concert works and recorded pieces from the common practice period, including Mozart's Clarinet Quintet in A major, Copland's Clarinet Concerto, and, as previously mentioned, the trio *Contrasts* by Bartók.

Goodman's concert personnel was more diverse than Whiteman's but remained segregated in important ways. Goodman's concert structure allowed spaces for special guest performers, which he used to include Black musicians. His concert featured the selections and groups listed in table 5.2. Goodman's big band was entirely white in January 1938, but he employed Wilson and Hampton in his small groups. Wilson, Krupa, and Goodman himself made up the trio, and Hampton was added for the quartet. Goodman's small groups performed regularly; they were an integral part of the Goodman concert experience no matter the venue, including the important Madhattan Room residency. Additionally, the Carnegie Hall concert featured special guests from the Ellington and Basie big bands during *Twenty Years of Jazz* and the jam session ("Honeysuckle Rose"), playing alongside some of Goodman's own band members.

TABLE 5.2 Program of Goodman's Carnegie Hall concert

Song Title	Performing Group
"Don't Be That Way"	Big Band
"Sometimes I'm Happy"	Big Band
"One O'Clock Jump"	Big Band
"Twenty Years of Jazz"	Various (Goodman, Ellington band members)
"*Life* Goes to a Party"	Big Band
"Honeysuckle Rose" (jam session)	Ellington, Goodman, and Basie band members
"Body and Soul"	Trio
"Avalon"	Quartet
"The Man I Love"	Quartet
"I Got Rhythm"	Quartet
Intermission	
"Blue Skies"	Big Band
"Loch Lomond"	Big Band with vocalist
"Blue Room"	Big Band
"Swingtime in the Rockies"	Big Band
"Bei Mir Bist Du Schoen"	Big Band with vocalist
"China Boy"	Trio
"Stompin' at the Savoy"	Quartet
"Dizzy Spells"	Quartet
"Sing Sing Sing"	Big Band
"If Dreams Come True" (encore)	Big Band
"Big John's Special" (encore)	Big Band

The integration Goodman displayed on the Carnegie stage is regarded as the most historically significant aspect of his concert. William H. Young and Nancy K. Young report that the "Carnegie Hall audience witnessed how, in a segregated society, swing could act as a bridge, bringing blacks and whites together."[49] Dave Oliphant calls the Carnegie concert "more of a symbolic production than it was a begetter of great jazz," going on to describe the jam session as the main event in this racially symbolic occasion.[50] However,

Goodman's attitude toward race was consciously apolitical; he never set out to be a civil rights pioneer, and he vacillated between challenging and maintaining the racial status quo. He insisted that he hired Black musicians because he was committed to creating the best music possible and that the race of the performer did not matter if they assisted with that goal.[51] Furthermore, he enforced a firm policy to protect his Black musicians: when bookers hired the band, they hired every member with no exceptions. When promoters balked, Goodman did not hesitate to discard his contract and walk out.[52] However, Wilson and Hampton usually had to check into a different hotel than the rest of the band, which Wilson excused by saying there was "no need to make a big fuss" because of the work they had already accomplished.[53] Goodman deemed integrating his big band a business risk and thus avoided doing so. This was not clear to Hampton, who thought he had been hired as part of the orchestra until he attended his first rehearsal.[54] This misunderstanding did not dampen Hampton's enthusiasm for Goodman's racial progress; Hampton even credited Goodman with enabling Black people to break through in baseball and other fields.[55] Wilson, too, called the Goodman band "one happy family," noting that it was made up of African, Jewish, Italian, and Irish Americans and even included a descendant of an Old West outlaw, as Harry James claimed to be a descendant of Jesse James.[56]

While Whiteman and Goodman ran their bands according to differing racial and musical norms, in practice, their concert programming was philosophically similar. Both Whiteman's Aeolian Hall concert and Goodman's Carnegie Hall concert presented portions programmed chronologically. Whiteman's concert moved from "the true form of jazz" through his standard tunes to the music of the future with Gershwin. Although most of Goodman's concert was not chronological, he presented "Twenty Years of Jazz," a five-song retrospective set performed in the first half of the concert. It was Irving Kolodin who suggested Goodman include a historical retrospective of jazz on the Carnegie Hall program to evoke "that family feeling" that jazz musicians have for their forerunners.[57] While retrospectively, twenty years of recorded jazz seem scant for a chronology, Whiteman's own idea of jazz as the music of the future shows that jazz musicians were already thinking of themselves as part of a historical progression early in jazz's story.

Goodman, sticking mainly to music his band regularly performed, did not generally deal in definitions of jazz or its future. However, his "Twenty Years of Jazz" does attempt to outline jazz's past (table 5.3). This list includes several jazz performers who would come to be included in jazz historiography once it began developing in the 1950s. None of the pieces were made famous by Goodman or his band members—Goodman did not position himself as integral to jazz's future like Whiteman did. None were

TABLE 5.3 Goodman's Twenty Years of Jazz retrospective

Song	Source Performer	Source Year	Carnegie Soloists
"Sensation Rag"	Original Dixieland Jazz Band	1918	members of Goodman's band
"I'm Coming, Virginia"	Bix Beiderbecke	1927	Bobby Hackett
"When My Baby Smiles at Me"	Ted Lewis	1920	Benny Goodman
"Shine"	Louis Armstrong	1931	Harry James
"Blue Reverie"	Duke Ellington Orchestra	1937	Jonny Hodges, Harry Carney, Cootie Williams

even songs that Goodman performed regularly (with the exception of "When My Baby Smiles at Me," which Goodman played in his youth as a party trick). And Goodman was not interested in making jazz into a concert music. Even when he began to perform nonjazz concert works, he never conflated his jazz performances with his classical ones, calling his performance career a "double life." The difference between the two, he said, was "expression . . . The greatest exponents of jazz are those with the most originality in ideas plus the technique to express them. In classical music . . . the musician must try and see into the composer's mind and play the way he believes the composer meant the piece to be played."[58]

As previously mentioned, Goodman unintentionally performed the first spontaneous jazz concert at the Palomar Ballroom in 1935, and one might assume that a traditional concert venue like Carnegie Hall would not feel much different. However, standing about on an open floor, cheering for your favorite players, and having those same players respond musically and visually to a crowd are dissimilar from sitting in an assigned seat, dressed up, and viewing your favorite performers at a distance with no possibility for dancing, surrounded by the trappings of the European classical tradition. And the venue differences between their usual locations and Carnegie Hall were stark for both attendees (the swing aficionados) and the musicians. Goodman's report about the first number on the Carnegie Hall program, "Don't Be That Way," underlines the problems. Goodman describes that the band felt very stiff until Krupa, the band's effervescent drummer, added some energetic drum breaks. Critics still reported that the band seemed stiff for the entirety of the concert. James succinctly summed up the band's discomfort when he uttered his famous line before taking the Carnegie Hall stage, "I feel like a whore in church."[59]

Despite Goodman's enduring reputation as a barrier breaker, his retrospective set presented a narrow view of jazz. The retrospective's focus was primarily on white performers and white styles. It reveals the ways that Goodman cultivated history to suit his own purposes. Three of the five numbers were originally performed by whites: "Sensation Rag," Original Dixieland Jazz Band; "I'm Coming, Virginia," Bix Beiderbecke, recorded for Frankie Trumbauer; and "When My Baby Smiles at Me," Ted Lewis.

Including a nod to the Original Dixieland Jazz Band (ODJB) in a retrospective was a natural if not a progressive choice. As the first to record music marketed as jazz, the ODJB was a logical point at which to start a presentation of jazz history. Both Whiteman and Goodman began their retrospectives with an ODJB number. Whiteman began with "Livery Stable Blues," which he expected the audience to find humorous. The program notes describe this tune as offering "Jazz in its true, naked form."[60] However, Whiteman was surprised when the audience seemed to genuinely enjoy it.[61] Goodman's choice, "Sensation Rag," lacked the crude animal noises of "Livery Stable Blues." No matter the selection, placing an ODJB number first in a retrospective had the effect of crediting white musicians as jazz's progenitors. The ODJB would suffer an even worse fate than Whiteman when historians reexamined jazz history in search of Black influences. It certainly did not help their future prospects in jazz historiography when Nick LaRocca, cornetist and leader of the ODJB, insisted that jazz was purely a white style. In a 1936 article for *Metronome*, LaRocca completely denied any Black influence in jazz:

> Our music is strictly a white man's music. We patterned our earlier efforts after military marches, which we heard at park concerts in New Orleans in our youth. Many writers have attributed this rhythm that we introduced as something coming from the African jungles, and crediting [*sic*] the Negro race with it. My contention is that the Negros [*sic*] learned to play this rhythm and music from the whites, and I'm sure that you could go all over Africa and never hear anything remotely resembling our music, unless it were from a phonograph recording of some American or foreign band playing American music.[62]

Despite the many special guests on both Whiteman's and Goodman's concert programs, neither invited the Original Dixieland Jazz Band to perform. All of the ODJB band members were alive and residing in New York City during both events. Neither Whiteman nor Goodman address the omission, but both made a telling choice concerning the ODJB.

Even if one could excuse Goodman for his choice of the ODJB piece as a historical gesture, two other numbers in his retrospective set "Twenty Years of Jazz" were also tributes to white musicians. "I'm Coming, Virginia," one of Beiderbecke's most iconic recordings, is presented note-for-note by guest star Bobby Hackett (Beiderbecke, who had performed extensively with Whiteman, died in 1931).[63] While Beiderbecke's tune is an appropriate addition simply for its masterful melodic improvisation and the consensus that he was an important contributor, he remained a white representative of a style in which Black originators continued to suffer from not being recognized. "When My Baby Smiles at Me," originally recorded by Lewis, was likely included only because Goodman was known for performing an uncanny imitation of Lewis.

Looking closely, even the fourth song, "Shine," is filtered through a white lens; while Beiderbecke's "I'm Coming, Virginia" is copied note-for-note, "Shine" is arranged liberally by Goodman's white trumpet star, James. "Shine" was a tribute to Louis Armstrong, who recorded a version in 1931 and featured it in the 1932 short film *Rhapsody in Black and Blue*.[64] "Shine" is a classic example of both Armstrong's vocal and improvisatory style. However, at Carnegie Hall, "Shine" was transformed into a different song altogether, failing to capture the style of the original. James's version of "Shine" is what one might call "killer-dillerized." A "killer-diller" refers to the style of big band arrangement for which Goodman's orchestra was famous: very fast, energetic, thickly textured pieces, the quintessential killer-diller being the well-known Benny Goodman version of "Sing Sing Sing" arranged by Jimmy Mundy. In "Shine," James takes Armstrong's original notes and presents them at an incredible speed, with Krupa providing a powerful backbeat. It is a good example of James's spirited style but lacks the swing and timing of the original and does not represent Armstrong's style.

Transforming the song in this way was, perhaps, a wise choice on James's part, since few people would put him on the same level as Armstrong and inviting strict comparisons between the two would not have worked in James's favor. However, by transforming "Shine" into a killer-diller, the audience heard a Black artist's original through the lens of a white style and performer. And this performance continued Goodman's focus on filtering jazz creation through whiteness—which mirrors Goodman's own history. This filtering was likely unintentional—but that does not negate its impact. Only with the last song on the retrospective—Duke Ellington's 1937 "Blue Reverie," which was played by some of Ellington's own band members (cornetist Cootie Williams, alto saxophonist Johnny Hodges, and baritone saxophonist Harry Carney, along with Goodman, his trombonist Vernon Brown, and Goodman's rhythm section)—were Black musicians truly credited with a role in jazz history. "Blue Reverie" was performed in its entirety instead of excerpted as were the other four songs, and the original arrangements were used. The difference between the first four songs and the fifth is stark, with the Ellington players clearly outshining Goodman's band members (including a beautiful solo by Hodges).[65]

Perhaps the most enduring difference between Whiteman's and Goodman's events is the philosophies of their concert hall use. For Whiteman, the concert hall represented the future of jazz. His performance of *Rhapsody in Blue* was intended to display jazz's potential; thus, when he progresses from "the true form of jazz" to the future, he shows that the future home of jazz is in the concert hall. Whiteman's progression to the concert hall hinges upon jazz developing into a music that utilizes large-scale classical structures. Conversely, Goodman's program intended to show that jazz, unchanged, could exist on the concert stage. He underlined this with a portion of his program presented as a jam session (a performance of "Honeysuckle Rose," played by members of Count Basie's orchestra with some of Goodman's).[66] Jams allowed players to showcase their talents in a relaxed atmosphere and informal space (usually a nightclub), which was an experience players felt was lacking in the big band format. These clubs also became some of the only places at which Black and white performers could interact freely, besides the few isolated instances of mixed-race bands.[67] By attempting to reproduce a jam session, Goodman reversed the process that brought jazz musicians to the concert hall in the first place. If the concert hall was an opportunity to provide a legitimizing force for the future of jazz, reproducing a format associated with nightclubs represents Goodman's championing of the music's present. And with the jam session, Goodman claimed an important "first." The jam session marked the first time in which a mixed-race band with more Blacks than whites performed live in a major venue.[68] Despite this important milestone, Goodman's full band—which played the majority of the numbers on the Carnegie Hall program—remained white only, like Whiteman's 1924 band. These actions underlined the positioning of their music as white, enabled by the concert hall space.

After the Future: Education in Concert Forms

Both Whiteman's and Goodman's concerts were either explicitly or implicitly educational events. Of course, jazz education as we now know it did not exist in the first half of the twentieth century, but jazz musicians recognized that white audiences would be more receptive if jazz was presented in an educational format. Additionally, adhering to the traditional trappings of the concert hall put patrons, especially those who normally attended classical concerts, at ease. Thus, both Whiteman and Goodman utilized program notes to legitimize their presence in the concert hall. In program notes, improvised music could be presented as carefully planned. Whereas a live performance, particularly those at dancing events, would have capitalized on the element of anticipation that would naturally come with the lack of a printed program, the concert performance would appear similar to a classical symphony concert with the listing of each piece in a prescribed order, an implied act of curation. As noted above, Whiteman's Aeolian Hall concert included a printed program with provocative titles, and Whiteman's manager, Hugh Ernst, noted, "The experiment is to be purely educational."[69]

When Whiteman traveled to Europe, he called on local musicologists (such as Hugo Leichtentritt in Berlin) to write notes. What may have seemed like posturing was probably necessary. In Germany, for example, Whiteman's music generated a lot of press, some of which was dedicated to determining whether jazz could ever be art.[70] Whiteman's carefully planned program notes allowed him to communicate values to what could prove a hostile audience. In the United States, Whiteman also presented his Experiment in Modern Music concerts as educational. His Aeolian Hall program was repeated during a six-week tour in May 1924, where Whiteman targeted schools: "There the orchestra will appear in City Auditorium and make every effort to get a full house of pupils from the public schools. City Auditorium will accommodate close to 15,000 people. The Mayor of Cleveland is expected to declare a school holiday that day."[71]

In the 1930s, when Whiteman's star had begun to fade, we see a change in his concert programming—he increasingly moved to a mix of classical and jazz, sometimes favoring the classical and becoming more and more focused on the past than the future. Later Whiteman concerts also rarely exhibited the kind of historical progression he presented in his original Experiment in Modern Music. However, these later Experiments sometimes featured a shorter segment dedicated to an educational or historical aim. Take, for example, the Essays on Waltzes section of Whiteman's concert in Chapin Hall at Williams College on Friday, May 29, 1936, which featured a selection of waltzes in a slightly altered chronological format (see table 5.4). While many of the composers on this program remain familiar, the last five represent lesser-known popular and light classical composers from the early twentieth century. The program also included Liszt's *Liebestraum*, Gershwin's *An American in Paris*, and Grofé's "On the Trail" and "Cloudburst" from his *Grand Canyon Suite*, and like many other Whiteman concerts, it ended with the same arrangement of *Rhapsody in Blue* premiered at the Aeolian concert.

Another increasing presence on Whiteman's Experiment in Modern Music concerts were larger-scale structured pieces often associated with Romanticism. Whiteman included a large-scale orchestrated piece on virtually all of his Experiment programs (see table 5.5). Except for *A Deserted Plantation*, which was a piano solo, all the large-scale pieces have been recorded by

TABLE 5.4 Essay on Waltzes section, arranged by Adolph Deutsch, Whiteman's concert in Chapin Hall, Williams College, May 29, 1936, as waltzes appear in the suite

Nickname	Title	Composer (as listed in the program)
"The Ancestor"	Minuet in G	Beethoven
"Old Vienna"	"The Beautiful Blue Danube"	Johann Straus [*sic*] the Younger
"The Operatic Waltz"	excerpts from the "Kermesse," scene of Faust, act I	Charles Gounod
"The Ballet Waltz"	"Naila"	Leo Delibes
"The Symphonic Waltz"	Second Theme of the First Movement, Fifth Symphony	Peter Tchaikovsky
"The Concert Waltz"	"Minute Waltz"	Frederic Chopin
"The Hurdy-Gurdy Waltz"	"The Good Old Summertime"	George Evans
"The Street-Song Waltz"	"The Sidewalks of New York"	Lawler-Blake
"The Vocal Waltz"	"Three O'Clock in the Morning"	Terriss-Robledo
"Modern Vienna"	"The Merry Widow"	Franz Lehar
"The Operetta Waltz"	"My Hero" from *The Chocolate Soldier*	Oscar Straus

Note: "Mr Deutsch's ingenious suite is a photograph album, so to speak, of the various members, young and old, of the Waltz family, beginning with a daguerreotype of the great-great-grandfather Minuet."
Source: Folder 8, Whiteman Collection.

symphony orchestras, indicating the extent to which Whiteman's programming crossed genres and prefigured later high-low cultural fusions.[72] The seventh experiment was offered jointly by the Whiteman Orchestra and the Philadelphia Orchestra. Gershwin dominates these large-scale offerings, but also included were several by Whiteman's own arranger Grofé as well as by Still. A later concert, also offered with the Philadelphia Orchestra on November 27 and 28, 1936, at the Academy of Music in Philadelphia, included a large-scale Richard Rodgers and Lorenz Hart premiere called *All Points West*. *All Points West* was a melodramatic piece of program music, in which a train announcer details his discontentment with his stagnant life and then is shot by an escaped prisoner. Rodgers underlines that this piece represented a break from the confines of popular music:

> In answer to the inevitable question about why we had written *All Points West*, I told a newspaper interviewer, "We wanted to do something with

more freedom. We wanted to escape the conventions that hedge in the musical-comedy song. For one thing, you're supposed to work in your title in the first eight bars and then to repeat it at the end. If you're bursting with independence, you might add a few bars here or take away a few bars there, but the form is almost inflexible. Also we got pretty tired of writing about nothing but love."[73]

Even as Whiteman began to include more classically oriented pieces compared with his 1924 concert, his view of futuristic music did begin to include Black composers and women performers. His Sixth Experiment in Modern Music, for example, included not only the three-movement suite *A Deserted Plantation* by Still but also three women: pianist and composer Dana Suesse (nicknamed "the girl Gershwin"), dancer Felicia Sorel, and Ramona Davies ("the singing pianist"). So, while Whiteman was creating an identity based on a white version of jazz, he was also perhaps using that platform to suggest that the music's future was diverse, which he was enabled to do by his association with concert music and his separation from the Black-oriented jazz style.

Whiteman expressed his educational beliefs in writing as well, most notably in his 1948 book on record collecting, *Records for the Millions*. Another effort at educating the public, this book takes the form of a history on sound

TABLE 5.5 Experiment in Modern American Music series

Experiment Number	Date	Hall	Large-Scale Piece
1	February 12, 1924	Aeolian	Gershwin, *Rhapsody in Blue*
2	December 29, 1925	Carnegie	Gershwin, *135th Street*
3	October 7, 1928	Carnegie	Gershwin, Concerto in F
4	November 4, 1932	Carnegie	Gershwin, *An American in Paris* and *Second Rhapsody*
5	January 25, 1933	Carnegie	Grofé, *Tabloid Suite: Four Pictures of a Modern Newspaper*
6	December 15, 1933	Metropolitan Opera House	Still, *A Deserted Plantation*
7*	July 29, 1935	Fairmount Park, Philadelphia	Grofé, *Grand Canyon Suite* ("On the Trail" and "Cloudburst")
8	December 25, 1938	Carnegie	Gershwin, *Cuban Overture*

Note: This list was partially compiled by Carl Johnson, Williams College, 1977.
*The seventh Experiment was not numbered but was identified in the program as part of the series.

recording combined with Whiteman's personal experiences with recording and record collecting. He suggests going back to basics: "Let's just look at a few of the fundamentals you need to know about record players in order to get the most out of your disks."[74] And he emphasizes a dual focus on classical and jazz and includes a chapter on classical recordings to own, "Basic Classics for Your Record Library," as well as a chapter "Basic Pops for Your Record Library."[75] His list of "Classics" indicates the extent to which he considered his own performances part of the Western art music tradition; *Rhapsody in Blue* and Grofé's *Grand Canyon Suite* are included alongside Beethoven and Brahms.

The Concerts in Retrospect

A spate of coverage around a 1984 re-creation of the Aeolian concert underlines how Whiteman's legacy changed over sixty years: John S. Wilson of the *New York Times* writes, "Although the concert was, and is to this day, referred to as a 'jazz concert,' it was really an antijazz concert."[76] A review of another re-creation two years later also uses the word "antijazz": "But the 'Rhapsody,' after all, takes less than 20 minutes, and Whiteman was presenting a full evening's entertainment—and instruction; the venture was frankly educational in nature, attempting to make jazz 'respectable'—a goal not regarded especially kindly by some subsequent commentators, many of whom felt the effort was even anti-jazz, although Whiteman was highly regarded for using true jazz instrumentalists in his band."[77] Gunther Schuller, writing in 1986, accepts the nonjazz status of Whiteman as a foregone conclusion: "It was not jazz—of course—or perhaps only intermittently so. Many of the arrangements were overblown technicolor potpourris, eclectic to the point of even quoting snatches of *Petrushka* and *Tristan und Isolde* (in *Nobody's Sweetheart* and *The Man I Love* respectively). But often enough—to make the point worth making—the arrangements were marvels of orchestrational ingenuity. They were designed to make people listen to music, not to dance."[78] Despite Whiteman's elimination from the prevailing jazz historical narrative by the 1980s, Schuller's words indicate that Whiteman had been successful in transforming jazz: his arrangements made people "listen." And Whiteman's activities after the Aeolian Hall concert underline his dedication to both jazz and not-jazz. Johnson notes that Whiteman expanded his repertoire purposely to avoid conflating jazz and classical: "By juxtaposing jazz and classics as separate musical entities, he avoided the rocks and shoals that modernists frequently encounter when they fuse the two idioms into hybrid compositions."[79] About the sixth Experiment concert, performed in Philadelphia in July 1935 to a sold-out crowd, a critic for the *New York Times* commented that without Whiteman, modern writers would "have no other medium of expression."[80]

Goodman, while he continued to advance his classical career, did not mix classical and jazz on the same programs. The Carnegie Hall concert was almost a singular event in his career, with just one partial re-creation at Boston's Symphony Hall on May 1, 1938. This re-creation was modeled after the Carnegie program but diverted in significant ways, even eliminating the jam session completely. Another important distinction between the two concerts is that Goodman's was recorded, while Whiteman's was not. The recording of Goodman's concert was released in 1950—the year following the disbanding of Goodman's group—and while accounts of why the recording was released twelve years after the event differ, the existence of any recording at all makes Goodman's event seemingly more impactful than Whiteman's. As Catherine Tackley notes, "the presentation of the album undoubtedly influenced its reception and in particular encouraged its canonization."[81] The recording, though, is a mixed blessing. While it may seem like a faithful representation of the event, it is in truth an edited artifact. Bill Savory, engineer of the 1950 release, notes, "On some of the tunes, I had to cut out a whole chorus" because of the poor recording quality.[82] Two full songs, "Sometimes I'm Happy" and "If Dreams Come True," were also eliminated. These cuts were restored in the 1999 Phil Schaap CD remaster, but the sound quality suffered. Despite Schaap's seeming "unmediated" remaster, the 1950 issue had the benefit of preserving something more like the original sound.[83] The differences between the two issues highlight the double-edged sword of historical recording.

The tensions among the past, present, and future of jazz evident in these two historic concerts echoes into today. The retrospective approach exemplified by portions of both Goodman's and Whiteman's concerts became commonplace as formalized jazz education dawned in the 1950s and later. While jazz scholars like Marshall Winslow Stearns were doing important work, performers headed many visible educational endeavors. Billy Taylor—who defined jazz as "America's classical music"—began the educational outreach program Jazzmobile in the 1960s, Mary Lou Williams offered chronological lecture-recitals at colleges, and by the late 1980s, Wynton Marsalis had positioned himself as jazz's ambassador, giving workshops and concerts on jazz history to schools. And critics would continue to challenge the philosophical approaches of these retrospectives. When in 1987 Marsalis became the artistic director at a new series, Jazz at Lincoln Center, he cited jazz's connection with classical music as an inspiration: "Wynton has been talking in the media about respecting the classical sensibility of jazz, about recognizing it as a classical music."[84] A bop revivalist who deemphasized the contributions of avant-garde musicians, Marsalis would be accused of presenting a bland version of jazz at Lincoln Center at the end of the century. Peter Applebome would ask about the concert series, "Does it exist mostly to celebrate jazz's past or should it be helping to shape its future as well?"[85] His question might as well have been asked about Whiteman in 1924 or Goodman in 1938. And though the characters have changed, the plot has not; we still wonder how jazz today should relate to its past, whether jazz has a future, and where the jazz of the future should reside.

Notes

1. "Whiteman's Title Upheld."

2. Crawford, *Summertime*, 302; Firestone, *Swing, Swing, Swing*, 155; Melnick, *Right to Sing the Blues*, 19; J. S. Wilson, "Teagarden and His Times," 86–89.

3. J. S. Wilson, "Misunderstood Pioneer," 24.

4. Schuller, *Swing Era*, 323.

5. Magee, *Uncrowned King of Swing*.

6. Goodman auditioned for Whiteman's group in 1931 but did not accept an offer to join. Rayno, *Paul Whiteman*, 2:77. The two bandleaders often employed the same musicians at different times, including saxophonist Art Rollini (who went from Whiteman to Goodman) and guitarist Allan Reuss and arranger Jimmy Mundy (who both went from Goodman to Whiteman).

7. Ogren, *Jazz Revolution* (1992), 11.

8. Hardesty, "Moral Outrage and Musical Corruption."

9. Engelbrecht, "Swinging at the Savoy," 3.

10. Collier in *Benny Goodman* and Firestone in *Swing, Swing, Swing* provide comprehensive descriptions in their books on Goodman. Goodman himself recalls the event in his autobiography, *Kingdom of Swing*, written with Irving Kolodin.

11. Firestone, *Swing, Swing, Swing*, 149.

12. Even the notion of bebop as primarily a listening style is complex; Wells in *Between Beats* details dancing practices associated with bebop music in ch. 4, "'Counter-Bopaganda' and 'Torn Riffs': Bebop as Popular Dance Music."

13. DeVeaux, "Emergence of the Jazz Concert," 7.

14. Howland, *Ellington Uptown*.

15. See Lampert, "Benny Goodman and Bartók's Contrasts"; Shuler, "Commissions and Compositions."

16. Antheil originally intended Whiteman's orchestra to premiere this piece; W. C. Handy was hired instead. Howland, "Jazz Rhapsodies in Black and White."

17. Berrett, *Louis Armstrong & Paul Whiteman*, 58.

18. "Jazz or 'Modern Popular Music,'" 274.

19. Aeolian Hall concert program (copy), February 12, 1924, folder 1, box 762a, Whiteman Collection.

20. Howland, *Ellington Uptown*, 86.

21. Balliett, *Collected Works*, 645.

22. Rayno, *Paul Whiteman,* 1:16–17.
23. Rayno, *Paul Whiteman,* 1:20.
24. Rayno, *Paul Whiteman,* 1:20.
25. Rayno, *Paul Whiteman,* 1:20.
26. Magee, "Everybody Step."
27. See Savran, *Highbrow/Lowdown.* Savran's first chapter, "America's Music," unpacks the term "jazz" and its many uses in the 1920s. The diversity of styles that encompassed jazz continued into the 1940s and 1950s, as Ake discusses in his work on Louis Jordan, *Jazz Cultures.*
28. "Whiteman Declares Jass Music Can Be Made Alluring," 8.
29. "Whiteman in 34th Yr. of Show Business," 1, 7.
30. Heap, *Slumming,* 7.
31. Heap, *Slumming,* 193.
32. Goodman, "Whiteness of Classical Music," 225.
33. Berish, *Lonesome Roads and Streets,* 34.
34. Wipplinger, *Jazz Republic,* 87.
35. Wipplinger, *Jazz Republic,* 92.
36. "Song of India—Fox Trot" (Victor 18777-B), 1921; "Oriental Fox Trot" (Victor 18940-B), 1922. Notably, Goodman also "jazzed the classics," with his recordings of "Bach Goes to Town" (an imitation of a fugue) and "Avalon" (an appropriation of "E lucevan le stelle" from Puccini's *Tosca*).
37. Wipplinger, *Jazz Republic,* 92.
38. On Whiteman's European performance tours, see also Tackley's chapter in the current volume.
39. Whiteman and McBride, *Jazz* (1974), 107. For a thorough analysis of the reception of *Rhapsody in Blue,* see Schiff, *Gershwin.*
40. Downes, "Concert of Jazz," 16.
41. Jablonski, *Gershwin Remembered,* 30.
42. Crawford, *America's Musical Life,* 578.
43. Schiff, *Gershwin,* 83.
44. The *Fort Worth (TX) Press* reports that Whiteman's crying caused him to miss twenty pages of music. Gordon, "Night to Remember at Aeolian Hall." Gershwin was in tears as well; later, Whiteman reports that he only missed eleven pages, Whiteman, "Gershwin I Knew."
45. Goodman and Kolodin, *Kingdom of Swing,* 26.
46. The 1999 remaster is the most complete, though it suffers from a loss of sound quality in places, as discussed here. Goodman, *Famous 1938 Carnegie Hall Jazz Concert.*
47. See Wells, "Ace of His Race," and Wells's chapter in the current volume.
48. DeVeaux, "Emergence of the Jazz Concert," 8.
49. Young and Young, *Music of the Great Depression,* 130.
50. Oliphant, *Early Swing Era,* 106.
51. Hampton and Haskins, *Hamp,* 64.
52. Firestone, *Swing, Swing, Swing,* 183.
53. Firestone, *Swing, Swing, Swing,* 183.

54. Hampton and Haskins, *Hamp*, 57.
55. Firestone, *Swing, Swing, Swing*, 184.
56. Wilson, Lighthart, and Van Loo, *Teddy Wilson Talks Jazz*, 44.
57. Kolodin, "Liner Notes," 12.
58. Goodman, "I Lead a Double Life."
59. Levinson, *Trumpet Blues*, 53.
60. Aeolian Hall concert program (copy), February 12, 1924, folder 1, box 762a, Whiteman Collection.
61. Sudhalter, *Lost Chords*, 24.
62. LaRocca, "Jazz Stems from Whites, Not Blacks," 20.
63. Goodman's Carnegie Hall concert recording was released several times, as detailed later in this work. All "Twenty Years of Jazz" recordings here refer to the Schaap remaster of 1999, released as *Benny Goodman at Carnegie Hall, 1938* (Columbia C2K 65143).
64. Louis Armstrong, "Shine" (Okeh 41486), 1931.
65. Ellington himself was invited to play but declined, perhaps hoping to one day have his own concert at Carnegie Hall. Kolodin, "Liner Notes," 12. He reportedly told his manager, Irving Mills, that he wanted to give a concert at Carnegie Hall, and Mills scoffed at the idea. Lawrence, *Duke Ellington and His World*, 268. Sources differ on whether Ellington attended Goodman's concert. Lawrence states that Ellington did not attend, but Phil Schaap's liner notes (38) clearly indicate that Ellington was in attendance. *Duke Ellington and His World*, 269. It is possible that Lawrence assumed that Ellington did not attend since he did not perform when he may have attended to support the musicians from his orchestra. Ellington later held a series of concerts at Carnegie Hall, beginning in 1943.
66. The performance was not a highlight musically. The session included: from Count Basie's orchestra, Lester Young, tenor saxophone, Buck Clayton, trumpet, Walter Page, bass, and Freddie Green, guitar; from Ellington's orchestra, saxophonists Johnny Hodges and Harry Carney; and from Goodman's orchestra, Krupa, James, and Goodman himself. This was an abnormally large group for a jam, and Goodman displayed some ignorance concerning Green, whom he signaled to solo even though a rhythm guitarist would not normally solo, and Green never soloed for Basie.
67. Lopes, *Rise of a Jazz Art World*, 152.
68. Monson, *Freedom Sounds*, 338n16.
69. Aeolian Hall concert program (copy), February 12, 1924, folder 1, box 762a, Whiteman Collection.
70. Wipplinger, *Jazz Republic*, 97.
71. *Metronome*, June 24, 1924, 53.
72. Gershwin, *135th Street* (recorded as *Blue Monday*), Concordia Orchestra with Marin Alsop, Angel Records (CDC 7 54851 2 7), 1993; *Tabloid Suite*, Metropole Orchestra, Jan Stulen Basta (30–9119–2), 2002; *Cuban Overture*: Chicago Symphony with Daniel Barenboim, Warner Classics (WEA 2564698165), 2009.
73. Rodgers, *Musical Stages*, 180.

74. Whiteman, *Records for the Millions*, 60.
75. Whiteman, *Records for the Millions*, 76–92, and 93–101.
76. J. S. Wilson, "Music,"
77. Gold, "Jazz Concert by Whiteman."
78. Schuller, *Early Jazz*, 192.
79. Carl Johnson, "From This Place, Sights and Sounds 2," TS, folder 41, box 646, Whiteman Collection.
80. T., "Whiteman Offers Sixth Experiment."
81. Tackley, *Benny Goodman's Famous*, 157.
82. Firestone, *Swing, Swing, Swing*, 369.
83. Tackley, *Benny Goodman's Famous*, 188–90.
84. Palmer, "Honoring the Classics of Jazz."
85. Applebome, "High Notes and Low."

6

"Symphonised Syncopation"

Paul Whiteman in the United Kingdom and Europe in the 1920s

CATHERINE TACKLEY

Paul Whiteman's visits to the United Kingdom in 1923 and 1926 (with time also spent in mainland Europe on the latter trip) brought him to widespread public attention across the Atlantic. Although Whiteman was the leader of the most reported and discussed American band in the British press in the 1920s, and these tours had a formative bearing on his vision and musical style, this chapter is the first time that he has been considered in depth from a European perspective and in which are assessed Whiteman's appearances in revue, cabaret, dance clubs, and large-scale concerts in the United Kingdom and his influence in Europe. Rather than comprehensively documenting his activities in Britain (Don Rayno offers excellent summaries of these tours),[1] this chapter explains Whiteman's impact in terms of aesthetics and principles via processes of performance and discourse. Whiteman's concept of "symphonised syncopation"—as it was most frequently termed in Britain—which combined these elements, played a fundamental role in the development of mainstream British popular music, epitomized by the British dance bands (particularly the Savoy Orpheans and Jack Hylton's groups) in the interwar period and, consequently, had a significant impact in Europe. This mediation of influence is vital to understanding Whiteman's importance in Europe despite him only being physically present on the continent for eight months in total. The chapter also brings to the fore the importance of these European tours for Whiteman's artistry and reputation at home. Specifically, I argue that Whiteman's activity in the United Kingdom, which led to him being crowned King of Jazz on his return in 1923, contributed to the formulation of his landmark 1924 Experiment in Modern Music concert.

Context: Early Jazz in Britain

Jazz had already been established in Britain by the time of Whiteman's arrival in 1923, in particular, through the visits of the Original Dixieland Jazz Band (ODJB) and the Southern Syncopated Orchestra (SSO) in 1919.[2] The ODJB, five white men from New Orleans, later incorporating a white British pianist, had a significant role in confirming an already-circulating definition of jazz as noisy, anarchic, fast-paced dance music. These two groups made a strong impression through their residency at the new Hammersmith Palais de Danse in West London for nearly nine months from its opening night; this was the first of a new type of venue that provided more affordable access to social dancing for middle- and working-class people in the capital. The influence of the Southern Syncopated Orchestra was more subtle but just as important. A group of African American musicians under the leadership of composer and conductor Will Marion Cook, the SSO planted the seeds of a critical appreciation of African American music through their programs that included spirituals, ragtime, and jazz (featuring saxophonist Sidney Bechet and drummer Buddy Gilmore) alongside classical music. The SSO's musicians also had an important pedagogic role; members of the orchestra imparted their knowledge to musicians locally as the large and often dysfunctional group of musicians broke up and scattered, reformed to include Black and even some white British and European instrumentalists, and endured periods of strike that allowed time to experiment and learn. The same patterns of influence—discourse and performative interaction—are in evidence when considering Whiteman's impact on music and musicians in 1920s Britain.

The early development of jazz in Britain naturally began with emulation, initially superficial (photographs abound of unrecorded and otherwise undocumented British bands in "crazy" poses inspired by the ODJB), with the almost immediate development of new bands to play syncopated music in hotels, clubs, and restaurants. The banjo had been dominant before and during World War I, especially in visiting American groups, including Ciro's Club Coon Orchestra and the Versatile Three/Four, but the distinctive sound and sight of the saxophone also began to come to prominence. As much as jazz was appealing to many of the British population, for others it provoked fear and opposition.[3] For institutions of the British establishment, initially London's leading hotels and restaurants, and then the British Broadcasting Company (later Corporation) (BBC), the task was to incorporate elements of this new American music to remain up-to-date while offering music for dancing and entertainment that would be considered "suitable" for upper-class patrons and, consequently, the general public, too. The early BBC, under the leadership of John Reith, was committed to providing entertainment that they considered appropriate for the general public. Jazz, given its associations with African American culture and perceived social deviancy, was not easily compatible with this vision. However, under its entertainments director William F. De Mornys, the Savoy Hotel led the way in reflecting and mediating the latest trends in popular music through the Savoy Havana Band under the leadership of American saxophonist Bert Ralton in 1920 and then the Savoy Orpheans in 1923. These bands dominated the dance music output of the early BBC, which broadcast dance music almost exclusively from the Savoy until 1926. This approach had a significant influence on the audience experience of popular music since, in order to be successful and ultimately achieve prestigious broadcasting opportunities that would bring them to national prominence, other bands were required to tone down and/or balance "hot" tendencies, much to the frustration of many musicians and emergent jazz fans. Although live performances by visiting American musicians could be high profile, they often had a fairly limited reach as events in and of themselves. Discourse and rhetoric were often just as, if not more, important to the reception of visitors abroad who were often as impactful in mediated forms as in the flesh.

Whiteman's Early Influence in Britain

In retrospect it is easy to assume or overstate the impact of American musicians outside America in this period with respect to both live performances and recordings. Whiteman's earliest recordings began to be advertised in Britain from December 1920 as being available via the HMV label, but it should be noted that there was scant critical commentary on popular music on record available in the United Kingdom prior to the instigation of specific trade periodicals for popular music, beginning with *Melody Maker* in 1926. Although the *Gramophone*, which focused on classical music but usually included a "dance music" column, advocated Whiteman from the first April 1923 issue, this coincided with his arrival, and he had not been mentioned in such long-standing entertainment periodicals as the *Stage*, the *Era*, and the *Dancing Times* until around this time. Therefore, there is no reason to assume that his early releases would have particularly stood out from the other groups on offer to potential purchasers, as is evident in figure 6.1.

It is easy to assume that the existence of recordings of American jazz meant that the population at large would have been familiar with the sound of jazz. However, in the case of the United Kingdom, at least, this possibility was limited by the simple fact that both gramophones and discs were expensive. The latter were not easy to obtain and often had to be sourced through specialist suppliers, such as Levy's on Whitechapel Road, East London. It is

FIGURE 6.1 "Dance Music for Christmas," His Master's Voice advertisement. *Sunderland (UK) Daily Echo and Shipping Gazette*, December 23, 1920, 7.

no coincidence that many of the earliest British jazz fans (such as the singer George Melly, trumpeter Humphrey Lyttleton, and bass player Spike Hughes, all of whom became active as critics and broadcasters) began to build up their jazz record collections while pupils at fee-paying schools. Meanwhile, the BBC was generally opposed to playing records (particularly, American records) on the air at this point so there was little opportunity for the wider population to encounter jazz that way and to gain familiarity with the music that might influence or assist in their choice of recordings to purchase.

Although recordings of American bands were often relatively difficult to obtain they were, of course, invaluable for British musicians actively seeking to develop their knowledge and understanding of American popular music to disseminate to their audiences. The bandleader Jack Hylton, born and raised in Lancashire, North West England, provides a rare but important example of a more-or-less chance encounter with Whiteman's music on record in Britain prior to his first visit. Hylton's career in entertainment had developed in London and through military service, leading to work as a pianist at the smaller room upstairs at the Queen's Hall in London, known as the Queen's Hall Roof, where he became the bandleader in 1920. Hylton was to become one of the top British interwar bandleaders, known in mainland Europe and the United States. He played a key role in arranging the British visits of American musicians, including Duke Ellington and Coleman Hawkins in the 1930s, and achieved great success as a producer of stage shows after World War II. Hylton took more inspiration from Whiteman than any British bandleader in terms of both the musical and business aspects of his career, and this contributed significantly to his success.

Pete Faint, who has worked extensively on Hylton, relates the impact of Whiteman's early recordings on the aspiring British bandleader. Apparently, the wife of Herbert Henri, who was managing the Queen's Hall in London where Hylton led the band, had encountered Whiteman on a trip to America in 1921 and returned with a gramophone record that she and her husband felt Hylton's band should emulate.[4] The first titles that appear in both Whiteman's and Hylton's discographies are "Mon Homme" and "Wang Wang Blues," two of four titles Hylton recorded in July 1921, the first sides under his own name. As Whiteman's "Mon Homme" was not released until July 1921, the date of Hylton's session, it seems likely that the disc gifted to him by Madame Henri was "Wang Wang Blues." While Hylton's "Wang Wang Blues" is obviously a carbon-copy transcription, it is important to state that Whiteman's influence on Hylton was more than *just* emulation from the very outset, as Hylton recollected in 1952:

> I had to analyse the secret of this new and heady music by the next morning. Through that night I kept the maid at my diggings winding the gramophone

> while I listened raptly and wrote. . . . By the morning, very punch drunk, I had one complete dance tune, as scored by Whiteman. By late afternoon, that Queen's Hall Roof band was playing it reasonably near to the Whiteman way. That evening the Roof guests were ecstatic. . . . Well, the owner of the Roof wanted to get more Whiteman records. I told him it wasn't necessary. I knew how to score thanks to the Exeter organist. You might almost say, in fact, that British jazz was born in Exeter Cathedral.[5]

Here Hylton describes not only the process of transcribing but also analyzing, internalizing, and reproducing Whiteman's style (the reference to Exeter is Hylton's recollection of an early pre–World War I encounter with the organist of Exeter Cathedral who taught him music theory). This side, as other scholars have pointed out, is actually a bit of an anomaly in Whiteman's early output, being more heavily influenced by New Orleans jazz, but we know that Hylton would have had access to a sprightly number "Anytime, Anyway, Anywhere" on the flip side of the disc. Commensurately, the subtle influence of Whiteman's band can be heard in Hylton's orchestration and smoother rhythmic feel in comparison with his earliest recordings. Whiteman was to remain an important influence on Hylton's career, and in turn, as the chapter later shows, Hylton rapidly developed his band and his entertainment business so that he was ideally positioned to capitalize on Whiteman's European success.

Whiteman in *Brighter London*: Aesthetics and Principles

Due to the limited availability of early jazz recordings in Britain and associated critical commentary on American artists, unlike in his home country, Whiteman would have been a largely unknown quantity for the majority of the population when he arrived in Britain in 1923 primarily to perform in the Julian Wylie–Harry Tate revue *Brighter London* at the London Hippodrome. Incidentally, this theater was where the ODJB first performed in the revue *Joybells* in 1919. Although the ODJB's engagement at the Hippodrome lasted for one night only, most likely due to the objections of the revue's principal comedian, George Robey, who was concerned about being overshadowed by this new novelty, this evidences the consistent importance of theatrical networks in bringing American entertainment, including musicians, to the United Kingdom in this period. Whiteman's 1923 visit coincided with the staging of two competing "plantation revues" in London, *The Rainbow* and *From Dover Street to Dixie*, each requiring the importation of an African American cast and band.[6]

The Wylie-Tate partnership behind *Brighter London* was best known for pantomimes, which were presented simultaneously in several UK cities. After

Tate's death in 1922, Wylie continued to work under the Wylie-Tate name, branching out into musical revues using many of the entertainers who regularly performed in the pantomimes.[7] *Brighter London* was no doubt inspired by the contemporaneous Brighter London campaign instigated by the Brighter London Society, founded in 1922. This "sought to create a brasher, more commercial, and more populist London, and to make London more American—not least in an attempt to attract more American tourists to the city" in contrast to the "ordered and conservative modernization" the regular London Society proposed.[8] The Brighter London slogan was frequently seen on Underground Electric Railways Company of London posters in the mid-1920s (e.g., poster designer Harold Sandys Williamson's "Brighter London for Theatreland, Travel by Underground," 1924) and satirized by cartoonists, demonstrating that although the impact of the campaign was minimal, the concept and phrase were in common parlance.

As this review in the theatrical trade paper *Era* explains, Whiteman and his band took part in a Palais de Danse scene as the finale of *Brighter London*:

> In the last scene, the Palais de Danse, Mr. Paul Whiteman and his band play jazz music on a varied selection of instruments with much skill and effect, and to the evident enjoyment of the audience, being loudly applauded. . . . "Brighter London" had a rapturous reception at its London première.[9]

In general Whiteman was well received, remaining part of *Brighter London* for four months. Their "act" consistently featured Zez Confrey's "Kitten on the Keys" as a vehicle for leading man Lupino Lane's comic dancing and "Say It with Dancing" as a duet for Annie Croft and Reginald Sharland. Advertisements from publishers also suggest the inclusion of "Hot Lips," "Yoo Hoo," "Fate," "The Sheik," and "Chicago" although it is not always completely clear which if any of these the Whiteman ensemble performed. The incorporation of Whiteman's band into a revue, as well as those of James P. Johnson and Will Vodery with the "plantation revues" in the same year, helped to establish the "band act," where an instrumental ensemble was featured onstage as part of the aural-visual spectacle. American bands and musicians who visited Britain in the 1920s were usually engaged to perform in exclusive London venues, and Whiteman's presence in a more mainstream, accessible format, which also meant spending some time outside London (as the show opened in Liverpool), would have undoubtedly contributed to his profile in the United Kingdom as well as demonstrating an alternative function for emergent British dance bands.

Whiteman's *Brighter London* engagement exposes two key debates—on aesthetics and principles—that were to have a profound impact on the American influence on popular music in Britain. The parameters of these debates were introduced to the British public from the outset of the announcement of Whiteman's visit, developed through reviews of the show, and responded to by Whiteman himself, demonstrating his keen awareness and desire to intervene in the emerging discourse. In terms of aesthetics, the announcement of Whiteman's engagement introduced him as a purveyor of a new type of specifically non-noisy jazz, which appealed to Wylie and, more important, his audiences, in his search for new "acts" for his Hippodrome revues:

> During a recent visit to America . . . [Wylie] had been struck by the fact that the big thing in the entertainment world out there was jazz music—not the noisy stuff of which they had so much in London, but something artistic and pleasing—and for their next revue they had engaged Paul Whiteman and his band, who were among the best known exponents of jazz in America, and he promised Londoners an introduction to something agreeable and novel.[10]

This theme was picked up strongly in other commentary on Whiteman's *Brighter London* appearances. It was common for significant visiting Americans to be previewed in the UK papers prior to their arrival, with similar phrases replicated between local newspapers showing the influence of strong public-relations tactics. Note how the preview texts emphasize moderation in terms of volume and timbre in these February reviews:

> He is not . . . the sort of conductor who believes in the "big noise."
>
> . . . an orchestra in which syncopation is made subservient to the rules of harmony, and neither drummers nor cymbalists are allowed to run riot.
>
> . . . piquant effects with saxophones, muted cornets, etc.[11]

Reviews of the performances focus on Whiteman's execution, melodiousness, and humor, qualities that fitted well with the aesthetic of British variety theater at this time. It must be remembered that the writers of these reviews in the mainstream national and local press were not music specialists but generally theater critics. It may be a coincidence that (as distinct from the February previews) the March and April reviews that follow specifically mention jazz, but, perhaps, this is indicative of the audience's growing awareness of the rhetoric around redefinition and elevation of the genre in Whiteman's "symphonic" terms:

> . . . play jazz music with the finish of a symphony orchestra, and have a fine idea of musical humour.
>
> They succeed in making "jazz" music almost melodious.
>
> . . . raises jazz to a high art.[12]

The most extensive commentary from Whiteman himself in 1923 is reported in the *Liverpool Echo*. Notably, here the discourse around deleting noise and adding symphonic elements is specifically linked with race:

> My endeavour has been to smooth out jazzy compositions; to give the ordinary public music that they can understand without being unduly noisy and yet bright and melodious but without the profundity of symphonies. After all, jazz music, as originally introduced, was n[——] music with rhythm and movement, and there were certain musical charlatans in America who found it received great response in the lower quarters. Then it gradually developed, and extended into a wider sphere. I always held the theory that some part of the n[——] melodies which were beautiful could be harmonised and orchestrated, and by a deletion of the noise, made into quite delightful harmonies. It is by adopting this system that I have been so successful as a dance conductor. I make a point of getting the rhythms orchestrated in a proper way. Every number we play we score, and make sure harmonies are correct.[13]

The second debate prompted by Whiteman's visit was around principles. Whiteman's memoirs as represented in *Jazz* (written with the journalist Mary Margaret McBride and originally serialized in the American *Saturday Evening Post* in 1926)[14] suggest that he was invited to Britain by Lord and Lady Mountbatten. Although these connections can be evidenced, it was more likely the Hippodrome booking was made by the Wylie-Tate team through Harry Foster's agency and was instrumental in the band making the trip.[15] All foreign musicians and entertainers had to apply for work permits issued by the British Government's Ministry of Labour under the terms of the Aliens Order (1920). Although quite a number of American bands and individual jazz musicians visited Britain during the 1920s, work permits appear to have been issued or denied in a fairly arbitrary manner, with a background of continual and growing opposition from the Musicians' Union (MU) to American visitors. Whiteman's upcoming arrival brought this particularly to the fore: "The Musicians' Union is up in arms that American bands should be imported into this country when there are so many of the home variety waiting for work. The Union declares that its opposition is not levelled against the musicians as musicians, but as potential ousters from employment of members of the Union."[16] In this context, it was easier to justify American bands as a special turn when appearing in revues or variety theater (in *Brighter London* the regular Hippodrome band would be retained in the pit to accompany the other acts). By contrast, as purveyors of dance music, they would be or at least perceived to be directly putting British musicians out of work.

Certainly, the MU was strongly opposed to the visit, responding by ensuring that a question on the subject of importing American bands was raised in the House of Commons on March 21, 1923.[17] Whiteman recalls difficulties upon the band's arrival ("The Ministry of Labor had an idea we had better not land"),[18] as despite applying for permits in advance, apparently resorting to intervention via the Prince of Wales and the British consul,[19] these had still not been issued. MU London Branch Committee meeting minutes reveal concern about the nationality of some of the band members, as some were naturalized German citizens, which required their passports to be checked carefully, and Whiteman was also interviewed by Secretaries of the MU.[20] In contradiction of some other sources, passenger lists show that the band arrived in Plymouth on the south coast and despite giving the London Hippodrome as their address proceeded to Liverpool for out-of-town tryouts for the show (the rest of the cast had already been rehearsing in London).[21] The decision to preview outside London could have been influenced by ongoing tensions and arrangements that management, perhaps, felt would be diffused if the band spent some time out of the capital.

Under the terms of their work permits, influenced by the lobbying from the MU, Whiteman and his orchestra were initially only permitted to play as an "act" on stage as part of *Brighter London*. The story that they had to turn down the offer of an engagement for a private party at the Savoy Hotel was widely reported. Ironically though, while in Liverpool the band performed for a ball at the Adelphi Hotel after the famous Grand National horse race at nearby Aintree Racecourse.[22] They were probably staying at the Adelphi while rehearsing and performing at the Liverpool Olympia Theatre just up the road. The MU became aware of this and raised the issue with the Ministry of Labour to ensure that Whiteman was prohibited from fulfilling the London private engagement.[23] As if to stoke the fires of union opposition, coverage often mentioned Whiteman's vast earnings. Further demonstration of the tensions around Whiteman's visit is shown by the pressure emanating from the MU on the royal establishment to confirm that the band had *not* been engaged to play for King George V.[24] Apparently responding to the union concerns, in an interview on his second day in Britain, Whiteman seems to be at pains to stress his band was a unique act and so not in competition with British bands and that this was a cooperative venture: "We have not come to show off anything, . . . we have a style of our own. . . . My band works on cooperative lines. Every 'boy' gets a share of what we earn; I take one share and they each take one, but I get double. It is this system, I think, that makes us so successful, as the 'boys' know that it is their band."[25] Wylie also responded to criticisms that "there were English musicians equally as good who could have been engaged" and ran a competition for British bands to find Whiteman's replacement at the conclusion of his engagement in *Brighter London*.[26]

Although Whiteman was eventually granted permission to perform at venues other than the Hippodrome, trade papers like the *Stage* reported success in terms of the MU limiting the band's activities:

> The action of the Ministry of Labour in limiting the activities of the Paul Whiteman band in this country is notable. It may be remembered that I pointed out last year to the Musicians' Union that it was up to them to rectify the injustice of allowing large contingents of American musicians to come over to this country in time for our season, scoop up all the best West End fashionable engagements, which always follow snobbishly dynamic London successes in the theatre and music-hall, then when the Fall comes sail back to America with the boodle. They pay no income-tax, and leave the Britisher still crying on the housetops about the slump in the amusement world and the unemployment problem arising therefrom.[27]

The MU was pacified by the Ministry of Labour's insistence that visiting bandleaders should engage the same number of British musicians within their band, or if a band was to undertake engagements "other than for theatrical purposes, a band consisting of British musicians, of the same size as Mr. Whiteman's own band, under his personal training and supervision, should be employed."[28] In practice these principles were applied in a rather lax and inconsistent way to visiting bands for the next few years alongside continuing MU resistance, which was supported and replicated for British bands by their counterparts in the American Federation of Musicians, culminating in what was in effect a "ban" on American bands performing in the United Kingdom from 1935 until 1955.[29]

Whiteman was by no means unique among American visitors in encountering these difficulties in the 1920s. However, it does seem that his connections via the Mountbattens to the Prince of Wales, as well as his own status that allowed him to cable the US Secretary of Labor for assistance, helped him to surpass these with relative ease.[30] For comparison, there was clear discrimination against the bands brought to perform in the "plantation revues" who were unable to perform outside of their revue for the duration of their time in Britain.[31] Bands of African American musicians (such as Dan Kildare's Clef Club Orchestra and the Versatile Three/Four) had visited before and during World War I, and some musicians from the Southern Syncopated Orchestra remained on the scene, but these racially specific and often-derogatory productions were now the main format in which African American bands could perform in Britain. Other American bands had their applications for permits refused completely. Whiteman's white privilege was fundamental in enabling the impact and influence of American popular music in the United Kingdom at this time.

Whiteman in the Grafton Galleries Cabaret

Whiteman received competing offers to appear in cabaret in London from the Midnight Follies at the Hotel Metropole and the Grafton Galleries, accepting the latter when he was permitted to do so by the Ministry. *Variety* reported that Whiteman received £400 (approximately $1,862) per week at Grafton plus a percentage of the cover charge over £400 having "refused an offer of 500 pounds weekly guaranteed by the 'Midnight Follies,' another cabaret, against a percentage proposition."[32] Whiteman started playing for dinner and dancing at Grafton Galleries from April 14, 1923, working around the twice-nightly Hippodrome performances. Whiteman's wife, Vanda Hoff, was featured as a dancer in the Grafton's cabaret show. Whiteman also fulfilled a large number of private engagements for royalty and aristocracy during this time; the known enthusiasm of the Prince of Wales and the continued support of the Mountbattens undoubtedly aided Whiteman's profile and status. The May 1923 issue of the *Dancing Times* included extended assessment of Whiteman, indicating that he was more successful as a dance band than as a stage act:

> I have the feeling that at the Hippodrome Paul Whiteman and his band have not caught the public fancy to the extent which might be expected. If this is so it is because he is an artist rather than a showman, and does not caper about the stage in the fashion set by some conductors of similar kinds of bands. In the ballroom, at the Grafton Dance Club, there are no two questions about his success—it is colossal.[33]

The Grafton Galleries had been established as a dancing venue before World War I and after refurbishment in 1922 reopened as a dance, dinner, and cabaret club. Jack Hylton's band was in residence initially, until he returned to the Queen's Hall Roof to present and perform in "The Cabaret Follies."[34] Cabaret had been established in London at the notorious Cave of the Golden Calf before World War I but, as Derek Scott notes, "only took off when George Grossmith adopted the New York style of cabaret and produced *Midnight Follies* at the Hotel Metropole," precipitating a cabaret "craze."[35] Whiteman's performances at the Grafton Galleries were not only indicative of his practical freedom from Ministry of Labour restrictions, which allowed the band to play for more than just their segment in *Brighter London*, but also his artistic independence. The cabaret setting, blurring the distinction between a "band act" in popular theater and a "dance band" in a dance hall, is significant in this respect. Most radically, Whiteman exploited the possibilities of the cabaret setting with the inclusion of a "straight" Wagner piece in his section of the evening's entertainment, described by James M. Glover in the *Stage* as a "stunt."[36] The *Daily Graphic* explained that the item was introduced by one of the cabaret performers with the injunction, "You are requested not to dance":

> So the midnight mob of revellers sat still. The syncopation had ceased, and Whiteman used the saxophone and the snaky brasses in his orchestra to reproduce music, to hear which people have journeyed to Bayreuth from all over the world. . . . Yes, the dancers sat still and looked; and the room was as quiet as a grave. And then there burst applause, as noisy as Whiteman's band is when it is playing to please the public.[37]

Whiteman took the opportunity to stage a demonstration of the "new jazz" at a lunchtime event at the Grafton Galleries for "pressmen and friends" at which he developed this "stunt" into something more akin to a concert. A description of this event in the *Westminster Gazette* reiterates the disparagement of jazz as "noisy" and positions Whiteman's music as art:

> Mr. Paul Whiteman, whose band is probably the best-known dance orchestra in the world, gave a novel demonstration at the Grafton Galleries yesterday to prove that jazz and music are not necessarily in conflict. Original jazz was largely made up of noise and cacophony, and we had a sample of it yesterday from the fourteen instrumentalists who make up Whiteman's band, but the new jazz, as developed by Paul Whiteman, is nothing more than the application to dance music of modern musical idiom and symphonic instrumentation. Evidence of this came from the playing in the Spanish, Italian and Wagnerian modes of a popular fox-trot like "Dancing Honeymoon." But the band is musicianly enough to play a fully-orchestrated Wagner selection in which the "Ring" motifs are cleverly interwoven, and the Wagnerian crescendi are powerfully worked up.[38]

The Wagner arrangement performed at the Grafton Galleries is most likely to have been *Grand Fantasia*, also referred to as *Wagneriana* arranged by Herman Hand,[39] as this is the only Wagner medley in Whiteman's discography (he recorded it in 1928) and in the scores and parts in the Paul Whiteman Collection at Williams College. Whiteman had begun to introduce a "concert hour" at the Palais Royale, where he was resident in the latter part of 1922, at which point Hand joined the orchestra as a French horn player and contributed arrangements.[40] It is important to note that *Wagneriana* is a "straight" medley rather than an example of "jazzing the classics," a common practice of the time and something for which Whiteman had become known but was distancing himself from by 1926 in *Jazz*:

> Until we went to Atlantic City [in 1920], the only recognition we had won, aside from the approval of those who danced to our music, came from

> persons interested in our trick of jazzing the classics—that is, of applying our peculiar treatment of rhythm and color to well-known masterpieces.... Not that I mean to imply that there was any real musical value in our jazzing the classics. Of course not. It was partly a trick and partly experimental work. We were just fooling around with the nearest material, working out our methods.... The old masters are not the best material we can use. A jazz orchestra is better off when playing scores that have been written expressly for it.[41]

Whiteman's 1926 reflection exposes the performance of Wagner in 1923 as part of the progress of his artistic vision—moving away from "jazzing the classics" to further experiments, albeit still drawing on the "old masters" at this stage but working toward the idea of scores written specifically for a jazz orchestra. This Grafton Galleries event clearly prefigures Whiteman's famous 1924 Experiment in Modern Music concert at the Aeolian Hall in New York City; in *Jazz,* Whiteman confirms, "We began to rehearse for the concert as soon as we came back from England."[42] The strategy in 1923 was the same as the 1924 Experiment concert—to begin with cacophonous jazz (the "True Form of Jazz" in the 1924 program) as a foil to Whiteman's symphonic approach, demonstrated by special arrangements of familiar, popular material, in this case "Dancing Honeymoon" arranged in different national styles (Victor Herbert's "Suite of Serenades" in 1924) but also "In the Shadows" by Herman Finck, composer of *Brighter London* ("Adaptation of Standard Selections to Dance Rhythm" in 1924). Whiteman was encouraged to play a version of the British National Anthem at the Grafton Galleries, which could have influenced the rather incongruous inclusion of Elgar's *Pomp and Circumstance* in 1924, the only preexisting classical work in the concert and, perhaps, a reference to this 1923 trial of the concert in Britain.[43] Following this logic, George Gershwin's newly commissioned *Rhapsody in Blue* takes the place of *Wagneriana*; both do share a rhapsodic aesthetic although the underlying material is obviously very different. John Howland identifies Whiteman's indebtedness to "the era's dominant model of variety entertainment," especially in relation to the 1924 Experiment concert.[44] Further to this, it is clear that Whiteman's stay in the United Kingdom allowed him not only the time, space, and inspiration but also *required* him to experiment to create a concert with such a distinctive mix of repertoire that was to be so influential on the history of American music.

In both 1923 and 1924 Whiteman was keen to invite influential and potentially critical voices from the musical establishment and attempt to win them over. The rhetoric behind the 1924 concert was "to show these sceptical people the advance which had been made in popular music from the day of discordant early jazz to the melodious form of the present ... that it had taken a turn for the better. My task was to reveal the change and try to show that jazz had come to stay and deserved recognition."[45] However, in 1923 the emphasis was on the recognition of the ability of his musicians and arrangers, to which performing works by the "old masters" and "symphonic" versions of popular material, allowing the performances to be valued in "classical" terms, was central.

"Symphonised Syncopation" and Its Influence on the Savoy Orpheans

In April 1923 the *Dancing Times* quoted extensively from "Dance Music Playing," an interview with Whiteman printed in the magazine of the Trianon Ballroom (in Chicago, where Whiteman had played for the opening week in December 1922). This introduced the concept of "symphonised syncopation" under the heading "Paul Whiteman's Ideals": "I have attempted in my playing, for I once played in a symphony, to symphonise syncopation and I believe I have been successful."[46] The term "symphonised syncopation" was not as prominent in the contemporary American press and does not appear in Whiteman and McBride's *Jazz* (even accounting for the UK English spelling) but provided a basis for extensive emulative activity and discourse in Britain after Whiteman's departure in August 1923.

Whiteman was replaced in *Brighter London* by Welsh violinist Emlyn Thomas and the London Band, winners of Wylie's aforementioned competition. However, their success was quite limited, and the clearest manifestation of Whiteman's sustained influence on British dance bands in the 1920s can, instead, be seen at London's Savoy Hotel. De Mornys had organized the dance music at the Savoy Hotel since 1919, and, clearly, Whiteman was on his mind when forming a new group, the Savoy Orpheans, which made its debut in October 1923 a few months after his departure. De Mornys said:

> Jazz is becoming more dignified. Even in America, the nursery of jazz, there is no jazz to be heard any more. It has been replaced by symphonised syncopated music. So I have decided to form a new band featuring sweet music at the Savoy. I am certain that although the British public likes the rhythm, they want to hear the melody and dislike the music too swingy—they want melody and quality of tone.[47]

The Orpheans celebrated their first birthday with a concert Revolution of Syncopated Music from Ragtime to Symphonised Syncopation on September 24, 1924, which was clearly modeled on Whiteman's Experiment in Modern Music concert first staged in New York earlier that year. The accompanying program book explains that the Orpheans' concert provided an opportunity for the audience "to study syncopated music from its birth and origin, through its gradual phases and improvements, finishing with the modern symphonised music of to-day." As in Whiteman's concert, the printed program cited the Original Dixieland Jazz Band, emphasized the importance of arrangements, and highlighted "symphonised syncopation" extensively, in florid prose, as the most highly developed form of syncopated music, disavowing the ready appeal of popular music so that this could be valued in artistic terms:

> The symphonised-syncopated melody of to-day is so subtle that it can be heard many, many times before it can be even partly committed to memory. It can be heard many more times than any other form of "popular" music that has yet been devised—again and again without being tiring. It has the disadvantage that we can spend a full evening of great pleasure and excitement—and then by next morning we can recall no individual tune to mind.

The program featured a few items that had been included in Whiteman's original 1924 concert, such as Edward MacDowell's "To a Wild Rose" and Jerome Kern's "Raggedy Ann." While *Rhapsody in Blue* is a notable omission, the inclusion of *Wagneriana* demonstrates the direct influence of Whiteman's live performances in Britain (noting that he did not record this piece until 1928), particularly, the Grafton Galleries experiments. The program acknowledges Whiteman only briefly, proceeding to assert:

> It is now impossible for symphonised-syncopated orchestras to be only American, and to feature their own national ideas. It is necessary to go further:—
>
> Syncopated-symphonic orchestras must be international. They certainly will get a great many ideas of syncopation and originality from America, but it is necessary to produce sweetness and beauty of tone to the sacrifice of all harsh brass effects. This sweetness and beauty of tone they will get from British players. The resources of the Continent will be called upon to give expression in melody in which the Continental musicians excel.[48]

The Orpheans' claim to ownership of "symphonised syncopation" via the international profile of the band is significant, exposing it as a foundation for the development of a European approach to popular music that strove to surpass American sources, an impulse that grew stronger and became more specifically identified as British later in the decade.

The Orpheans' first birthday concert was not only widely reported, with the concept of symphonised syncopation very much at the forefront, but then immediately was followed up by a newly augmented band (from twelve to nineteen players) in their national broadcasts, offering an accessible musical articulation of this concept.[49] As a result, Whiteman's approach was most pervasively mediated in Britain via the Savoy Orpheans' BBC radio broadcasts in the years between his visits. It is no coincidence that the BBC was heavily reliant on the Savoy for their broadcast dance music in the period 1923 to 1926 and continued to advocate Whiteman specifically as a model for their popular music output as late as 1932, as symphonised syncopation offered a solution where a balance could be struck between the demands of the public for the latest popular music and the BBC values. It offered a practical approach to dance music that kept the threat of "hot" jazz content under control and provided a source of justification for the programming decisions by drawing on familiar values of classical music.

De Mornys was keen to capitalize on the success of the Orpheans by developing the band's profile beyond the hotel (the Savoy's resistance to these external activities was eventually to lead De Mornys to resign in 1927).[50] To this end, the Orpheans gave three successful concerts at the Queen's Hall in early 1925, again broadly following the Whiteman Experiment model (the concerts were sometimes referred to in contemporary reviews, perhaps coincidentally, as "experiments") with a program divided into two parts—"successes of the past" and the "evolution of syncopated music." The concerts were followed by the Orpheans' engagement for Wylie's new revue *Better Days* at the Hippodrome, another obvious parallel with Whiteman. Although this failed to achieve the success of *Brighter London*, the Orpheans were well received, and there was particular fascination in their ability to return to the Savoy after their Hippodrome performance in time for their evening broadcast.[51]

After further Queen's Hall concerts in late 1925, the Savoy Orpheans Augmented Symphonic Orchestra toured to five provincial cities in January 1926, with a new concert program that was now more biased toward popular numbers they had recorded but retaining their by-now famous rendition of Dvorak's "New World" Symphony and including Victor Herbert's *Suite of Serenades* and George Gershwin's *Rhapsody in Blue*, both of which had been included in Whiteman's 1924 concert.[52] *Rhapsody in Blue* had already been brought to widespread attention as a result of the first broadcast performance of the work in Britain by the combined Orpheans and Savoy Havana Band with Gershwin himself at the piano on June 15, 1925. Although the piece was known in Britain to some extent (the first Whiteman-Gershwin recording being advertised and reviewed in the United Kingdom without a lot of enthusiasm from autumn 1924), the broadcast made a significant impression upon British listeners, for whom it represented "the blending of two extremes of music" and a "new era in music."[53] *Rhapsody in Blue* was thus understood in terms of disrupting the tendency to polarize popular and classical music, a distinction that had been reinforced by the BBC where popular music output was overseen by the Variety Department and thus kept separate from the Music Department, which was focused on classical music.

Similarly, symphonised syncopation was presented as a solution both for those who were opposed to jazz and for those who sought to advocate it. The most vociferous objections to jazz in Britain often came from establishment figures, such as the classical conductor Henry Coward. In a widely reported lecture early in 1926, he described jazz as vulgar "with its jerky rhythms, its blatant, muted trumpets, its hooty out-of-tune saxophones, its grotesque howlings, its boisterous banging of the kitchen utensils, its ceaseless commotion, and its constant degrading of artistic taste."[54] Coward proceeded to link this negative criticism unequivocally with race: "Jazz is degrading in that it tends to lower the white races to the level of the 'lesser breeds.'"[55] Ever alert for publicity opportunities, Whiteman sent a highly publicized telegram to Coward inviting him to attend one of his forthcoming 1926 British concerts, aligning symphonic syncopation as an antidote to jazz and its racial threats. Apparently, Coward's attendance at one of Whiteman's performances in Sheffield did not change his opinion—the novelty aspects of the program meant that it was easy enough for him to write the concert off as "Barnumesque," leveling familiar criticisms at the Ferde Grofé and Gershwin works as being "fragmented."[56]

Aside from the most extreme objections, symphonised syncopation was increasingly understood not so much in complete antithesis to jazz but as a way of approaching it both musically and socially that was commensurate with emerging ideas of a British approach to (American) popular music. Taken together, the Savoy Orpheans' appearances in a range of high-profile broadcasts, recordings, concerts, and a revue show established them as the leading purveyors of symphonised syncopated music in Britain, cleverly and precisely capitalizing on the void left by Whiteman's absence between August 1923 and April 1926. The Orpheans not only emulated Whiteman, representing his approach pervasively and in such a way that it quickly became the standard to which other British bands would aspire, but began to take this in distinct directions, too. The Orpheans made advances on Whiteman's achievements in 1923 by demonstrating symphonised syncopation much more explicitly and repeatedly representing his Experiment concert format, seen only in an embryonic form by a very select audience in the United Kingdom in 1923, and then developing this in their own way. As a result, they came close to physically taking their music into mainland Europe, anticipating Whiteman in 1926, through an unusual engagement to play for the Dutch Royal Zoological Society in The Hague and broadcast from Hilversum, plans that were again halted by union objections.[57] De Mornys was even "exploring the possibility of taking the [Orpheans] band to the States, where he is sure they would have cleaned up, introducing sweet music long before it did eventually arrive."[58] This demonstrates the degree to which the Orpheans had assimilated and developed Whiteman's influence toward popular music that was not only relevant for British audiences but also readily exportable—a pattern Jack Hylton was to replicate.

The Reception of Whiteman's British Concerts, 1926

By 1926, the time of Whiteman's second visit to the United Kingdom, the dominance of symphonised syncopation and the Savoy bands specifically had begun to slip as the BBC introduced a greater variety of bands to the schedules responding to the demand for dance music, including making some small concessions to the "hot" variety. In the wake of *Rhapsody in Blue*, symphonised syncopation was debated on BBC radio and within the pages of music journals, such as the *Musical Times* and *Music & Letters*, where the comparisons with classical music that the term naturally provoked tended to find symphonised syncopation wanting.[59] Meanwhile, there was greater awareness of "hot" jazz, and, particularly, improvisation, supported by record reviews and practical advice to players in new publications, such as *Melody Maker*, which was quickly established as Britain's leading music trade periodical. The critic and bass player Spike Hughes, at this time an undergraduate at the University of Cambridge, recalled: "We were at a rebellious age, and while we were all prepared to hire a car and drive to London to hear Paul Whiteman at the Royal Albert Hall, we were naturally proud to know that we appreciated the purely esoteric art of Real Jazz which was above the head of the rabble."[60] Overall, this shift in the British viewpoint left Whiteman on shaky ground conceptually and aesthetically at the time of his return visit in April 1926. He was engaged primarily, initially at least, to perform in concerts (in contrast with the theatrical booking of three years previously). This is indicative both of the increasingly symphonic orientation of Whiteman's orchestra as well as the practicalities of securing work permits. This time his British agent was Powell and Holt, whose business was primarily concerned with representing classical artists, including Clara Butt and Nellie Melba. The concerts were, most notably, two at the Royal Albert Hall and three at Alexandra Palace and extended to a national tour of concert venues (as distinct from variety theaters) in key cities.

The program was quite consistent throughout this series of engagements, usually opening with Grofé's *Mississippi Suite* and inevitably including *Rhapsody in Blue* near the end. Otherwise, Whiteman appeared to aim toward mainstream tastes with light classics (arrangements of Fritz Kreisler's *Caprice*

Viennois and Nikolay Rimsky-Korsakov's "Hymn to the Sun"), foxtrot songs ("Dreaming of a Castle in the Air"), jazz standards ("Tiger Rag"), and novelties, often spotlighting the particular talents of his musicians ("Nadine" as a saxophone solo for Chester Hazlett, "Nola" for the two-piano team of Harry Perella and Ray Turner). Whiteman's program both influenced and reflected popular repertoire; while "Dreaming of a Castle in the Air" was introduced by Whiteman and then picked up by British bands, "Valencia" (unusually in 6/8 time) was already familiar to British audiences. Although "amazing scenes" at Albert Hall were noted, with the venue reportedly packed to its capacity and many turned away, this hyperbole seems to have been exacerbated by the advertisements for Whiteman's regional engagements (for example, see fig. 6.2). Another advertisement reported that a £5,000 (approximately $24,300) prize offered by Whiteman for a member of the audience who could keep their feet still while the band played was divided between "a deaf woman and a man who was paralysed."[61]

Undoubtedly, it was novelty aspects of the concerts that received the most attention in reviews, particularly the act by trombonist Wilbur Hall, described in the *Daily News*: "Among the minor orchestral excitements yesterday were the performances of a 'stunt' musician, who, among other things, played two

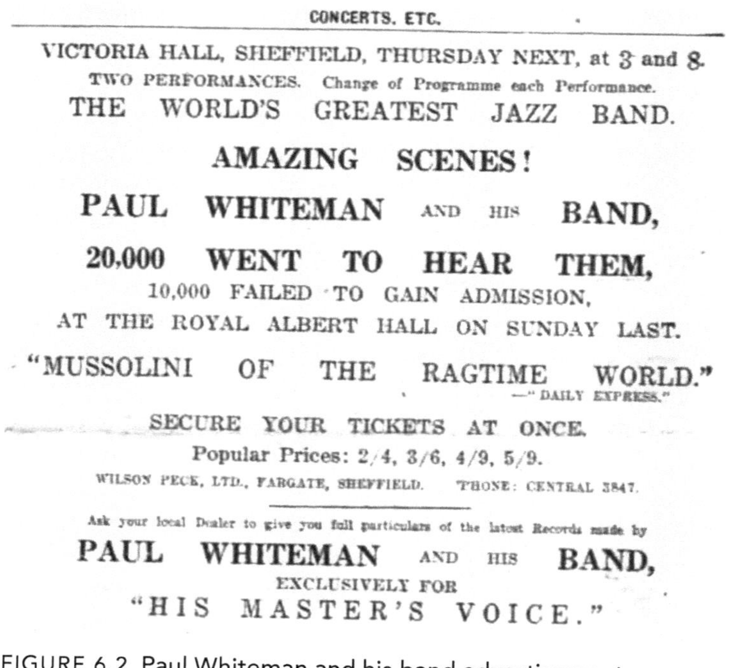

FIGURE 6.2 Paul Whiteman and his band advertisement. *Sheffield (UK) Daily Telegraph*, April 13, 1926, 1.

instruments at the same time, reversed the usual order of violinists by playing the bow with the fiddle, and finally revealed the hitherto unsuspected powers of the bicycle foot-pump as a maker of music."[62] However, for some UK audiences, this went too far. The *Scotsman* even described the performance as "a burlesque—a burlesque even to Jazz," and for the *Acton Gazette*, it was "an excellent afternoon's amusement, but hardly to be described as a musical performance."[63] *Melody Maker* regretted that the "lay press" focused on "the show side and the novelty of the performances" and that "there was not a word of the wonderful balance and control of the renderings, the precision of attack, the technique, and, above all, the tonal quality."[64] Where reviewers did comment on the more serious aspects of the program, it was generally to offer an adverse comparison with "real" symphonic music, a theme that had emerged in the discourse between Whiteman's visits: "An expert observer could detect the growing signs of lassitude in the audience. One of the attendants to whom I spoke said: 'Give me a real symphony orchestra!' and one noticed the relief and enjoyment with which a frankly comic music-hall turn by the trombonist, Wilbur Hall, was received."[65] The greater availability of records resulted in initial hints of what was to become a more significant topic in evaluations of American visitors in the 1930s as expressed in the "Gramophone Review" column in *Melody Maker*: "I must admit I like Paul Whiteman's records better than his actual performances. In the records he seems to realise the seriousness of the job more, and the rendering contain less of the 'rough stuff,' while being more musical."[66]

Whiteman's reception seems to have been rather lukewarm overall, with coverage fueled by the revitalization of old debates rather than close attention to the performances. Reviewing the concerts in "The Lessons of the Whiteman Visit: How to Profit from His Advent," *Melody Maker* reflected that: "The programme appeared to be too clever. As an effort to convert the opponents of jazz from their unreasoning hatred to a sympathetic understanding, the demonstration would have done better to have erred on the side of simplicity . . . through the medium of simpler melodies than through the more extravagant labyrinth of Gershwin's 'Rhapsody in Blue.'"[67] According to those who were there, "Tiger Rag" was the musical high-point of the first Albert Hall concert, due to the hot trumpet solo by Teddy Bartell.[68] This is revealing of the British pleasure in hearing visiting Americans conforming to expectations and playing jazz and, particularly, to hearing a rendering of a number that would take emergent jazz fans back to the beginnings of the music in Britain: the ODJB.

Undoubtedly, Whiteman was still in a period of ascendency in the United States in 1926, especially in the wake of the Experiment concert, which makes his relative lack of impact in Britain all the more surprising at first.

However, the same debates around aesthetics and principles reappear in response to his final UK appearances and increasingly merge. As we have seen, the idea of symphonised syncopation was already well established and by 1926 was becoming outdated and even being surpassed. Whiteman had been held up consistently as a model for bands from the first issue of *Melody Maker* in January 1926, but there was also an increasing sense of national pride in the achievements of British musicians, particularly Hylton, who had emerged as a key figure and continued to align himself with Whiteman. An article by Hylton, "The Prophets of Doom," in the January 1926 issue sketched the development of jazz to symphonic syncopation in very similar terms to Whiteman in *Jazz* that had not yet been published (for example, Hylton uses the metaphor of an orchid growing from an "ugly brown seed," where Whiteman devotes a chapter to an analogy with a mango seed). Hylton compares "symphonic syncopation" to a debutante: "It has developed during ten years from its first blatant beginnings and its crude gaucheries, into a thing of charm and grace, wherein, the skill of musician, composer, and arranger is exercised to the utmost. But, you may reply, a debutante marries, grows old, and passes away. Not, however, before she has given the world children as beautiful as herself." He proceeds to explain that these "children" are likely to be British: "British dance orchestras are becoming some of the finest in the world. We have reached a level equal to that of the American dance bands, which a few years ago were well ahead of us. We have produced a People's Music which satisfies every musical need of those for whom it is intended."[69]

The format of Whiteman's Experiment concert had been extensively replicated and developed in Britain by the Orpheans in the years between his visits, including on a national tour just a few months prior to his arrival. This naturally led to comparisons between the bands, even prior to Whiteman's arrival, especially in the so-called provinces, which even prompted critiques of his vision. "[Whiteman said] 'It has long been my idea that music is most effective when it is co-ordinated with one or several of the arts.' . . . Here again the Orpheans are with him only up to a point. They believe in a little atmosphere, and very cleverly arranged it is too, but they have no high falutin ideas of co-ordinating the arts."[70] The consequent challenge to Whiteman's claim to be "original" added weight to the Musicians' Union opposition to his visit (considered below)—it was increasingly difficult to argue that Whiteman offered something that local bands were unable to provide. Even the inclusion in the concerts of Whiteman's apotheotic work, *Rhapsody in Blue*, had, of course, already been trumped the previous year by the composer's performances with the Orpheans, who, as we have seen, easily took the accompanying roles of Whiteman and his orchestra and then included the work in their 1926 tour. Gershwin was in the audience for Whiteman's first

Albert Hall concert, reportedly dissatisfied with the bandleader's choice of tempi for the *Rhapsody*, almost certainly the result of more than two years of constant performances of the piece.[71] The Orpheans, too, had taken a particular approach to their performances of the *Rhapsody*, apparently with the British public in mind, "introducing all the comic effects we can, especially in 'Rhapsody in Blue.' . . . The novelty, surprise, humour, and efficiency of treatment alone justify such extraordinary compositions as the rhapsody to a representative British public."[72] This suggests that, building on their ownership of symphonised syncopation, the Orpheans were satirizing this now well-known work (we can only assume that they developed these "effects" after their performance of the piece with Gershwin; they did not record the piece until 1935 with the harmonica virtuoso Larry Adler as soloist and main novelty aspect), and in doing so, making this most American of works British.

Whiteman's visit took place against the backdrop of increasing industrial tension leading to the General Strike in May 1926 (see fig. 6.3). The General Strike was called by the Trades Union Congress as a response to the adverse pay and conditions of coal miners and took place over nine days, involving

FIGURE 6.3 Whiteman and some of his orchestra members on bicycles in London during the General Strike in 1926. Paul Whiteman Collection, Williams College Special Collections.

many industrial workers (including in transport, hence, Whiteman's band riding bicycles, albeit as a stunt) with the British Army drafted in to provide some continuity in vital areas. Especially given this context, it is unsurprising that Whiteman's visit again provoked opposition from the MU. The local replication of American bands was undoubtedly a source of criticism that they had little to offer that could not be provided by British musicians: "The success of several American bands last year led to threats of a general invasion. . . . To the casual observer they were all alike, even to the lack of nothing original."[73] *Melody Maker*'s commentary began to address the conflict that was to dog British musicians for the next decade—evaluating the threat that visitors presented to their livelihoods against the importance of the encounters with American musicians for their development: "Although we do not agree with unnecessarily restricting the short visits of bands of other nations from whom we may learn something, we shall certainly at all times throw every ounce of our influence into the scale to protect the British musicians from being deposed in favour of the foreigner."[74] Specifically, the MU opposition to the plan for Whiteman, after his concert tour, to double at the Tivoli cinema (on the Strand in central London) while resident at the Kit-Cat Club had been widely reported even prior to his arrival in the United Kingdom.[75] It was likely that a deal was done to make Whiteman's return to Europe feasible by offsetting the considerable costs for the Kit-Cat Club—the band was "sublet" to the Tivoli, which had opened in 1923 and was known for its advance showings of the latest Metro-Goldwyn-Mayer films supplemented with live entertainment. The common assumption was that the Tivoli's resident band would be laid off (minutes of the London Branch of the MU confirm that the orchestra had been given their "preliminary notice" by the end of March),[76] and the MU successfully petitioned the Ministry of Labour to have Whiteman's permission to play at the Tivoli withdrawn. Although this was apparently reinstated in time for Whiteman's arrival and was even called out as a publicity stunt in the *Stage*, the coverage served to link Whiteman unequivocally with the ongoing threat of visiting Americans.[77]

As in 1923, Whiteman chose his moment to counter the accusations, writing in a letter published in numerous newspapers as well as *Melody Maker* in May 1926: "I should like, as modestly as possible, to contradict the suggestion that I am a kind of malevolent superman whose sport it is to create unemployment amongst honest British musicians," and, instead, claiming that he had played a part in creating the "happy economic state of dance musicians at the present day."[78] Nevertheless, Whiteman's billing as the "Mussolini of the Ragtime World" struck a more sinister tone than his more familiar designation, the King of Jazz.[79] Although this is extreme, it is indicative of perceptions of Whiteman's dominance and control over the dance music industry at this time and explains the resentment of this by British musicians.

Whiteman and Hylton at the Kit-Cat Club

Since making his first Whiteman-inspired recordings early in the decade, Hylton had become one of Britain's leading bandleaders and entrepreneurs. In 1926 he was asked to form a band for the Kit-Cat Club, which had opened in the previous year in the basement of the Capitol Theatre on Haymarket in central London, billed as "the most luxurious Luncheon, Dinner and Dance Club in the world." In addition to an illustrious membership, it attracted a theatrical crowd and alongside cabaret entertainment sought to provide a constant succession of American bands for dancing in addition to the resident orchestra supplied by Hylton under the leadership of American saxophonist Al Starita. As such, the club had already been subject of discussions between the MU and the Ministry of Labour, who seem to have been taken by surprise and admitted in internal memos that their policies on American bands had been inconsistent.[80] The idea of recruiting English musicians to play in the visiting bands, the solution adopted at the time of Whiteman's 1923 visit, had been abandoned as impractical; so, instead, a British band of equal size to that of the visitors had to be engaged. In order to allow Whiteman to play at the Kit-Cat Club for dancing, Hylton enlarged the band under Starita by adding a string quartet, who are also represented in the band's recordings from this date.[81] As such, we can see how practical and aesthetic impact of the circumstances of Whiteman's visit were powerfully intertwined, here pushing Hylton further in the Whiteman "symphonic" direction.

Whiteman's band was well received at both the Tivoli cinema and the Kit-Cat Club. His contemporary repertoire and "act" seemed to work well in a shorter burst in an environment where he did not have to deal with criticisms from either jazz or classical music fans. The *Dancing Times* was again impressed by his provision of music for dancing:

> Paul Whiteman has proved an immense attraction at the Kit-Cat Club, where, although his music is fast, it is so wonderfully rhythmical that it is delightful to dance to even on a crowded floor. His band is an entertainment in itself, as many individual members give songs and play solos on their special instruments—one can even produce a tune from a tyre-pump. There was even a large gathering towards the end of the month to hear him play, by special request, Gershwin's "Rhapsody in Blue" and great regret was felt that a bad cold prevented Miss Vanda Hoff (Mrs. Paul Whiteman) from dancing to it.[82]

Whiteman's presentation was also commensurate with the cabaret aesthetic of the Kit-Cat Club, with Wilbur Hall's pump act again receiving mention. Hall was to reprise this act in *King of Jazz*, a film in musical-revue format released in 1930, showing that as with the 1924 Experiment concert,

Whiteman's British tour encouraged the development of his style of presentation and even the inclusion of particular numbers and acts. It is also notable that while *Rhapsody in Blue* was given a tired reception at the concerts, there was a demand for it at the Kit-Cat, especially as a dance number, in which form it was eventually included in *King of Jazz* (it was presented concurrently as a ballet choreographed by Quentin Tod at the rival Midnight Follies cabaret, distinct from a previous version staged at Ciro's in New York with choreography by Sammy Lee). Despite this success, journalist Hannen Swaffer reported:

> Paul Whiteman is not so happy in London, this time. He misses the Prince of Wales, who is in Biarritz. Besides, the Kit-Cat Club has not provided enough stage room for his band. In the Grafton Galleries, last trip, he was "King Paul." Now, after carting a band of 30 around the meagre hotel accommodation of the English provinces, Paul does not like the arrangements at the Tivoli, where he shows twice a day, or the arrangements at the Kit-Cat, where it plays from 11 p.m. "until unconscious."[83]

Admittedly Swaffer was never shy of stirring up controversy, but Whiteman did leave his engagements at the Kit-Cat and Tivoli earlier than expected at the end of May, probably due to concerns around the continuing impact of the General Strike.

Whiteman and Hylton in Mainland Europe

In June, Whiteman traveled with his band to perform in Berlin, Germany, and Scheveningen and Amsterdam in the Netherlands and spent most of July fulfilling engagements in Paris before returning home.[84] By all accounts, the challenging circumstances of the 1926 tour meant that Whiteman was relieved to be leaving Europe. His reception had been decidedly mixed, particularly among the critics, but he had reestablished an approach to popular music that was to have a significant legacy in Europe. In particular, just as the Savoy Orpheans had addressed the demand created by Whiteman in 1923, so in 1926 Jack Hylton was poised to take his place, especially in mainland Europe, where there was arguably greater demand for a Whiteman replacement.

Whiteman's visit was highly anticipated in Germany; Jonathan O. Wipplinger notes the widespread enthusiasm for the "symphonic jazz" concept from German arrangers and bandleaders by 1925. The concept had been introduced to Germany by Sam Wooding's *Chocolate Kiddies* plantation-style revue show, which included a "jazz concert" that "as becomes clear from the song selection, was in dialogue with Paul Whiteman's earlier 'Experiment in Modern Music' from 1924." However, although "Berliners sold out

[Whiteman's] four concerts and heartily applauded the performances, the response by Berlin's music critics remained rather cool." In Germany, it seems that there was more discourse over Whiteman's relationship with the art music establishment than with jazz, either in terms of the threat that symphonic jazz presented or, more positively, in terms of his potential to create art music of the future. In both respects, the 1926 concerts were a disappointment to the Berlin critics, with a greater focus than in contemporary British reviews on the perceived artistic paucity of the *Mississippi Suite* and *Rhapsody in Blue*.[85]

Whiteman enjoyed a generally more positive reception during his brief time in the Netherlands and a longer residency in Paris. Jeffrey H. Jackson argues that Whiteman's music was welcomed as it was "far less shocking to the ears of many listeners than other jazz of the day."[86] But Whiteman's positive reception in Paris may have also been influenced by the contexts in which he was presented; rather than formal "concerts" in venues such as the Royal Concertgebouw in Amsterdam or the Grosses Schauspielhaus in Berlin, he appeared in Paris at the Café des Ambassadeurs, which had been redesigned as a "théâtre restaurant" earlier that year, doubling at the Théâtre des Champs-Élysées, where his performance took over the second half.[87] At the Ambassadeurs Whiteman's orchestra formed part of the bill for *Blackbirds of 1926*, a revue nègre starring Florence Mills. Andy Fry argues that this English-language show was as much about American modernity than the articulations of primitivism for which such productions are more readily associated.[88] This meant that Whiteman presented an alternative to French culture but in a different way to his African American counterparts and also in a different way than in Berlin. Although his presence was threatening to some, he had great appeal overall.

Fry identifies the importance of Jack Hylton's "re-embodying, then assimilating" Whiteman in a French context but proceeds to note the neglect of the "pivotal role Hylton played in the history of jazz in France," where he was arguably more influential and popular than Whiteman.[89] Hylton had been touring the provincial variety theaters in the United Kingdom since at least 1924 while building up his business so that he could provide bands for several venues concurrently. This allowed him to have a presence in London's exclusive and trend-setting clubs as well as nationally in more accessible theaters. Therefore, at the time of Whiteman's 1926 visit, Hylton was able to present a band opposite Whiteman's at the Kit-Cat and also tour nationally to a much greater extent than Whiteman. This gave Hylton a much more consistent presence and reach than Whiteman, and in fact, as *Variety* noted, this mirrored Whiteman's business model in America: "Hylton's success is due in no small measure to patterning the organization on the lines of

American jazz bands. It is said Hylton was assisted and encouraged in this by Paul Whiteman when Hylton had a relief bunch to Paul at Grafton Galleries. Hylton is continually improving in his stage presentations."[90] As this review in *Variety* suggests, Hylton was attentive to the possibilities of the "band act" that would enable him to easily infiltrate a national network of variety theaters and, from 1927, achieve great success in Europe, as well. Again, some inspiration came from Whiteman, as dance band guitarist Sid Colin explains: "Jack Hylton saw the Whiteman band at the Hippodrome, liked what he saw, and said in effect, that's for me. The following year he was appearing at the Alhambra Theatre in Leicester Square with the band that was to dominate the stages of Britain and those of most of Europe for the next decade."[91] Hylton's "band act" was undoubtedly inspired by Whiteman's success in theater and cabaret, enabling him to make "steady progress toward the central space of Parisian musical life" and to achieve both public and critical acceptance in France in the late 1920s.[92] Similarly, in Germany, countering the criticisms of Whiteman's appearances in concert halls, in 1928 Hylton introduced his band at the Scala, a famous vaudeville hall in Berlin, where a balance of musical styles ensured mainstream appeal, as Michael Kater explains: "With his light touch, sense of humor, and the sheer precision of his style, Hylton was closer to the essence of jazz and thus effectively counteracted the pomposity of both Wooding and Whiteman. Yet he was also inclined to a 'sweet' quality of sound that characterized Whiteman's music as well."[93]

Whiteman undoubtedly provided an important foundation for Hylton and other European bandleaders, in terms of both music and business, but just as in his first responses to Whiteman on record in 1921, Hylton's approach was quite distinct and much more than straightforward emulation. Perhaps the key point here is the frequency with which Hylton is listed in the same breath as Whiteman in Europe after the latter's departure—Whiteman no longer stood out in the same way as earlier in the decade. For example, in *The Appeal of Jazz,* pursuing a then-familiar race-based argument, Mendl goes on to cite the role of white musicians in "improving" early jazz: "In the hands of Whiteman, Hylton, and others, the orchestration of the jazz band was improved and brought to so much higher a level that the modern syncopated dance band can hardly be put on the same footing or appropriately designated even by the same name, as the primitive organisms from which it took its origin."[94]

UK Ministry of Labour restrictions meant that by the end of the decade, it was much more difficult for entire American bands to visit Britain, although it was still possible for individuals to join British bands on a fifty-fifty basis. The development of a distinctively British approach to popular music was informed both by the resultant practice of incorporating American musicians within British bands, and aesthetic priorities as British dance bands often continued to strive for a balance between jazz and symphonic elements, steering a broader stylistic path than the soon-apparent distinction between hot and sweet American ensembles. This was influenced by pro-British and/or anti-American sentiments where out-and-out racism toward African Americans was rarely far away:

> While syncopated music comes from America, the Savoy Orpheans are particularly anxious to add a British touch to it, by introducing some characteristic humour and comedy.
>
> Was it not possible, I [Jack Hylton] wondered, to combine the colour of jazz music with that element of harmony which is so beloved of our race?[95]

Two examples serve to demonstrate the progression from Hylton's emulation of Whiteman in 1921 toward this "British" approach. First, consider Paul Whiteman's May 9, 1927, recording of Grofé's arrangement of "I'll Always Remember You" by Jesse Greer.[96] Grofé uses a full orchestra, resulting in a lush, string-dominated, "symphonic" sound, later reinforced by the brass and complimented by woodwind decoration. Modulations for successive choruses are reasonably involved, incorporating some interesting harmonic substitutions and a small amount of "hot" cymbal. Overall the melody dominates, with a very functional two-beat rhythm section accompaniment to the vocal, and the trombone solo on the middle eight of the final chorus (often the place for "hot" and/or improvised content in arrangements) consists of the melody without elaboration. The cor anglais in the coda offers a final "symphonic" touch. The Savoy Orpheans recorded the same number on May 12, 1927, with a similar instrumentation (albeit fewer players) in an arrangement by Fred Elizalde, who was leading another band at the Savoy at this time.[97] This is the only known British recording, so it is likely that Elizalde introduced them to the number, but it may have been influenced by Don Voorhees's recording featuring Red Nichols. Although the melody is dominant in this version, too, there is no vocal; the recording begins with the verse and then repeats the chorus with more succinct modulations. The tempo is faster, and the feel is lighter, propelled by the bass often picking up on the fourth beat as well as "hot" cymbal and banjo. The predominant sonority is saxophone, but there is more variation in instrumentation within each chorus, and the strings are featured on the second chorus. There is some light decoration of the melody by the tenor saxophone on the third chorus, and the final chorus features the "hot" obligato trumpet of American Frank Guarente, but the legato melody is also clearly present, demonstrating a fine balance of "sweet" and "hot."

A further instructive comparison can be made between Whiteman's and Hylton's versions of the jazz standard "Tiger Rag," frequently the vehicle for showcasing virtuosity in popular music performance in this era. Whiteman apparently only started playing "Tiger Rag" on his 1926 European tour, recording his "New Tiger Rag" with augmented forces much later, in July 1930. Although Hylton would record a version of "Tiger Rag" that was more in the Whiteman "symphonic" mode in 1936, the arrangement by Leo Vauchant (one of several musicians whom Hylton recruited from mainland Europe) recorded in January 1930 develops the idea of stylistic diversity within a single arrangement. Although not short of novelties, notably a "hot" ocarina solo, the arrangement also references the New Orleans jazz origins of the number with extensive florid upper-register clarinet (which the parts in the Jack Hylton archive at the University of Lancaster, United Kingdom, confirm included improvised content), sometimes in polyphony with trumpet, and "tailgate"-style trombone, driven particularly by the string bass. Alongside this are spectacular "hot" choruses, a written trumpet trio, and improvised piano solo and harmonically adventurous transitions and coda in an arrangement that provides constant variety in timbre and texture. Hylton's version even includes a brief quotation from *Rhapsody in Blue*. In comparison Whiteman's arrangement only hints at New Orleans, particularly in the opening chorus. It also showcases an impressive notated "hot" chorus, for saxophone ensemble, and includes novelty percussion effects, but overall this seems rather routine, especially in the predictable antiphonal "chase chorus" section.

Together with his attention to stage presentation, Hylton's musical approach led to his success in Europe. British bandleaders such as Hylton were even in demand in America because they offered something distinctive, but the denial of his own requests for work permits in the United States and the restrictions on importing Americans for the Kit-Cat Club effectively brought the opposition between the British Musicians' Union and the American Federation of Musicians to a head, resulting in the aforementioned "ban" on transatlantic reciprocity when this exchange ought to have been at its peak.

The Impact of Europe on Whiteman

Although it is important to consider the effects of the in-person visits to Europe of bands such as Whiteman's on the development of jazz and popular music outside America, it is clear that these trips often had great importance for the careers of the visitors, too. In Whiteman's case, "Growing Pains," chapter 3 of his book *Jazz*, provides an extensive reflection on his 1923 trip to Europe, establishing this as a vital component of his formative years as a bandleader. Europe had both conceptual and practical importance for

Whiteman. Evoking primitivist mythology, Whiteman defends jazz on the basis of its potential, as-yet-unrealized other than in European concert works such as Darius Milhaud's *La Création du Monde* and Igor Stravinsky's *Ragtime*. Whiteman understands his inability to "jazz it up" as a young musician not in terms of his own inadequacy but that of the material; his solution to the problem being to understand enough about what the other players were doing in terms of "faking" to write this into orchestrations. Interestingly, though, he is critical of the British players whom he was bound to incorporate into his band at the Kit-Cat Club for their inability to "ad lib" and their requests to have something written out for them, claiming a sense of American authenticity while doing so: "Jazz was simply not in their blood. They lacked the spontaneity, the exuberance, the courage—I do not know what. The something, whatever it is we call America, the indefinable something that is jazz."[98]

Whiteman's visit to Europe was motivated by wishing to find an "adequate laboratory for testing my inventions" as he terms it, where he would be taken seriously (i.e., alongside Milhaud and Stravinsky), and we have seen that his 1923 visit was important to the development of his vision. But the trip was also important for him to obtain "a little of the foreign stamp" (comparing himself to singers who achieved legitimacy and profile by studying in Italy or France) to ensure his longer-term success at home beyond being the latest novelty. Whiteman's reception on his return to America, particularly in 1923 but also in 1926, matched if not exceeded his reception during his time in Europe (see fig. 6.4). Most obviously, when he arrived home in 1923, he was literally crowned King of Jazz, and "a gold crown bossed with various musical instruments was placed upon his head" in a publicity stunt organized by Buescher Band Instrument Company.[99] This status was unequivocally linked with the success of his trip to Britain, which was described as 'triumphant' both in terms of Whiteman being "honored by English royalty and the British public" and due to his benevolent influence in "creating work for many thousands of men by the increased demand for syncopated music resulting from his engagement."[100]

In conclusion, Paul Whiteman had an undeniable impact on European audiences and musicians in 1923 and 1926, but this was arguably to come to full fruition only when he was *not* present, in that he created a legacy that was to be developed in the hands of capable musicians who understood their local music markets as well as they did their art. The discourse around Whiteman's appearances was also significant in stirring the fires of European music criticism, not only around jazz but also more broadly around national and European identities and popular music. These visits were also important to Whiteman, who used them as an opportunity not only to make money,

FIGURE 6.4 Serenading musicians in the water as Whiteman, onboard the SS *Leviathan*, returns to the United States, 1923. The sign reads, "Welcome home Paul Whiteman, United Orchestras Submarine Unit." Paul Whiteman Collection, Williams College Special Collections.

achieve success beyond the United States, and to create demand at home due to lack of supply during his time away, but also to develop his reputation and artistic vision that would allow him to remain distinct and aspire to longevity within an ever-crowded marketplace. Specifically, Whiteman's time in Europe had a formative influence on the output most fundamental to his public reputation—the 1924 Experiment in Modern Music concert. Most importantly, while "symphonizing" meant elevation of jazz to the status of art music for Whiteman, in Europe it informed a way forward for popular music at this crucial juncture.

Notes

1. Rayno, *Paul Whiteman*, vol. 1.

2. See Parsonage, *Evolution of Jazz in Britain*.

3. Mendl, *Appeal of Jazz*. These perspectives are neatly represented in Mendl's 1927 book *Appeal of Jazz*, the first on jazz to be published in Britain, which contains a chapter "The Dislike of Jazz."

4. Faint, *Jack Hylton*, 32.

5. "Fame!"

6. See Parsonage, *Evolution of Jazz*, ch. 7.

7. Ellacott, "Impresarios Wylie-Tate."

8. Gilbert, "*London of the Future*," 95.

9. "'Brighter London' at the Hippodrome."

10. "Variety Gossip."

11. "Jazz Expert"; "Plays and Players," *Northern Whig* (Belfast, Northern Ireland), February 24, 1923, 10; "£25,000 a year," *Sunderland (UK) Daily Echo*, February 27, 1923, 2; also in the *Belfast Telegraph* (Northern Ireland).

12. "Brighter London," *London Daily News*, March 29, 1923, 3; "Brighter London," *Birmingham (UK) Daily Gazette*, March 31, 1923, 4; "Good Revue."

13. Quoted in "Conductor's £25,000 a Year."

14. Whiteman and McBride, *Jazz* (1974).

15. "London Gets Whiteman."

16. Editorial, *Encore* (London), March 1, 1923, 3.

17. "Artists and Foreign Bands."

18. Whiteman and McBride, *Jazz* (1974), 71.

19. Rayno, *Whiteman*, 1:64.

20. London Branch Committee Meeting Minutes, April 4, 1923, Musicians' Union Archive, Archives and Special Collections, University of Stirling, MU/4/3/1/3/4.

21. "Variety World."

22. "National Ball." The MU became aware of this and raised the issue with the Ministry of Labour to ensure that Whiteman was prohibited from fulfilling the London private engagement.

23. London Branch Committee Meeting Minutes, March 28, 1923, Musicians' Union Archive, Archives and Special Collections, University of Stirling, MU/4/3/1/3/4.

24. "Musicians' Letter to King." Also see London Branch Committee Meeting Minutes, March 21, 1923, Musicians' Union Archive, Archives and Special Collections, University of Stirling, MU/4/3/1/3/4.

25. "Style of Their Own."

26. "Best Band?" 11.
27. Glover, "Music Box," March 22, 1923.
28. Editorial, *Encore*, March 22, 1923, 1.
29. This is explained in detail in Parsonage, *Evolution*, and Cloonan and Brennan, "Alien Invasions."
30. Whiteman and McBride, *Jazz* (1974), 72.
31. Parsonage, *Evolution*, 180.
32. "Whiteman's Bit."
33. "Sitter Out," 804.
34. Faint, *Jack Hylton*, 37.
35. Scott, "Other Mainstreams," 329.
36. Glover, "Music Box," May 31, 1923.
37. *Daily Graphic*, April 16, 1923, quoted in "The Greatest Success That Ever Came to London," *Variety*, July 4, 1923, 40.
38. "Musical Jazz."
39. This piece is referred to as "Grand Fantasia from Wagneriana" in discographies. This is not the same piece as *Wagneriana* (Kleine Fantasie aus Wagnerschen Opern, op. 38) by Friedrich Eberle (1916).
40. Rayno, *Whiteman*, 1:54.
41. Whiteman and McBride, *Jazz* (1974), 60.
42. Whiteman and McBride, *Jazz* (1974), 87.
43. "Paul Whiteman."
44. Howland, *Ellington Uptown*, 30, 83–87.
45. Whiteman and McBride, *Jazz* (1974), 24.
46. The Sitter-Out, "Whitemanising Our Bands," *Dancing Times*, April 1923, 708.
47. Quoted in Hayes, *Dance Music*, 18. The rejection and reformulating of jazz on the grounds of its associations with African American culture is strongly implied here, as in so many contemporary judgments of the music.
48. *Savoy Orpheans: Revolution*.
49. The augmented band appears on record only for the Orpheans' recording of an arrangement of Dvorak's Symphony in E Minor "From the New World," which often featured in their concerts.
50. Hayes, *Dance Music*, 34.
51. "Savoy-Orpheans."
52. A reproduction of this program is in Hayes, *Dance Music*, 42–47.
53. Brooke, "New Era in Music."
54. "'Vulgarity' of Jazz."
55. "Jazz a Crime."
56. "Farcical Jazz." Whiteman seemed keen to keep his public exchanges going, challenging Coward to a debate before Coward declared the matter closed.
57. "Ways of Officialdom."
58. Hayes, *Dance Music*, 34.

59. For example, Austin, "Jazz." In July 1926 the BBC staged a "Jazz vs Classical" debate between Landon Ronald and Jack Hylton with illustrations from the Wireless Orchestra and Hylton's band in July 1926, which sparked a huge reaction from listeners in the letters pages of the *Radio Times*.

60. Hughes, *Opening Bars*, 309.

61. Advertisement.

62. "Albert Hall Siege."

63. "Paul Whiteman and His Band"; "Jazz in Excelsis."

64. "Lessons of the Whiteman Visit."

65. "Jazz at the Albert Hall."

66. "Gramophone Review."

67. "Lessons of the Whiteman Visit."

68. Rayno, *Whiteman*, 1:130.

69. Hylton, "Prophets of Doom."

70. "Dancing Time on Merseyside."

71. Rayno, *Whiteman*, 1:162.

72. "Dancing Time on Merseyside."

73. "Threatened Orchestral Invasion."

74. "Whiteman and the Tivoli."

75. For example, "Coming of Americans Resented."

76. London Branch Committee Meeting Minutes, March 31, 1926, Musicians' Union Archive, Archives and Special Collections, University of Stirling, MU/4/3/1/3/5.

77. "Mr Paul Whiteman: No British Ban on Orchestra"; "Music Box."

78. "Whiteman and the Tivoli." The April 9, 1926, *Newcastle Daily Chronicle* even printed a photograph of Whiteman and his orchestra studying their income tax forms!

79. See figure 6.2. The nickname Mussolini of the Ragtime World was derived from a review in the *London Daily Express*.

80. Correspondence concerning a Meeting with the Management of the Kit Kat Club and Piccadilly Hotels regarding Non-admission of American Bands, 1925, Employment Department and Employment and Insurance Department, National Archives, United Kingdom, LAB 2/1188/EDAR278/41/1925.

81. Hylton also added a violinist to his own band at this time to create a violin trio.

82. "London Dance Notes."

83. Swaffer, "What London Looks Like."

84. Rayno, *Whiteman*, 1:416–17.

85. Wipplinger, *Jazz Republic*, 88, 66, 89, 89–98.

86. Jackson, *Making Jazz French*, 110.

87. "Welcomes Whiteman," *Variety*, July 7, 1926, 3.

88. Fry, *Paris Blues*, 41.

89. Fry, *Paris Blues*, 18, 86.

90. In this context, "bunch" means "band." "Palladium."

91. Colin, *And the Bands Played On*, 85.

92. Fry, *Paris Blues*, 90. Fry also explains and explores in a French context Hylton's demise in the early 1930s.

93. Kater, *Different Drummers*, 9.

94. Mendl, *Appeal*, 49.

95. "Syncopated Symphony"; "Why I Play Jazz."

96. "I'll Always Remember You/Who Do You Love," Paul Whiteman Orchestra, Victor 20784, 1927.

97. "Little White House at the End of Honeymoon Lane/I'll Always Remember You," Savoy Orpheans. HMV B-5299, 1927.

98. Whiteman and McBride, *Jazz* (1974), 10, 39, 74.

99. "Sensational Welcome Home."

100. "Big Reception Planned."

7

RCA v. Whiteman and the Case for Radio Broadcast Rights

KATHERINE M. LEO

As an early leader of the US music industry, Paul Whiteman's influence extended well beyond the bandstand. He notably contributed to the founding and governance of several music industry organizations, including the American Society of Composers, Authors, and Performers (ASCAP), the National Association of Broadcasters (NAB), and the National Association of Performing Artists (NAPA); he also maintained long-standing relationships with the American Federation of Musicians (AFM). From negotiating contract disputes to lobbying before the US Congress,[1] Whiteman championed the rights of musicians in an industry struggling to adapt to evolving media technologies, aging laws, and mounting government regulations.

Whiteman's advocacy culminated in a landmark federal copyright lawsuit over radio broadcast of recorded music, known to legal specialists as *RCA v. Whiteman*. Litigated between 1937 and 1940, this case involved two main complaints: one against the unauthorized broadcast of Whiteman records by local New York radio station, WNEW, and a second involving contracts between Whiteman and his record manufacturer, RCA Victor, over putative property rights in those records as intellectual property, including the right to control broadcast of them. Although Whiteman ultimately did not prevail in court, the litigation process identified key industry shareholders and their externalized contract negotiations. Perhaps more importantly, the case offers insight into fundamental understandings among bandleaders and recording artists about their music as intellectual property at a critical moment of technological and economic transformation.

Through an interdisciplinary examination of extant archival holdings related to *RCA v. Whiteman*, this chapter locates Whiteman at the epicenter of early commercial radio broadcast and the challenges it posed for musicians.

It begins with a review of the Copyright Act of 1909 and federal regulation of radio broadcast, gaps in which presented opportunities for the commercial exploitation of recorded music. The chapter then traces the responses of Whiteman and other bandleaders to advocate for the rights of recording artists to control and receive compensation for their records broadcast over radio airwaves. Whiteman and his industry colleagues turned first to Congress and then to the federal judiciary for legal clarification, out of which the case of *RCA v. Whiteman* emerged. Although the US District Court validated Whiteman's claim to copyright in his ensemble's records, the US Second Circuit Court of Appeals later decided that right was terminated upon sale of a record. Recording artists, therefore, could not prohibit radio broadcast of lawfully purchased records. Ultimately, this chapter circumscribes the bandleader's advocacy both for recorded music as intellectual property and for his own interests in broadcast rights as a recording artist, public personality, and music industry leader.

Archival Sources

A principal reason for the fragmented state of narratives about Whiteman's professional advocacy work is the limited scope of relevant archival material, which is sparse beyond a few thank-you notes and press clippings. When Whiteman gifted Williams College with a massive collection of "scripts, arrangements, orchestrations, records, and instruments" in 1935,[2] his primary goal was to illustrate "American Music," ostensibly a category to which he believed himself to be an essential contributor. At that time, his goal was not to create a comprehensive repository for his own career and organization. Whiteman's business records, therefore, were retained by his legal team, but those documents were subsequently destroyed in a warehouse fire.[3] As a result, most of Whiteman's professional correspondence with attorneys and other business associates as well as his account books are lost.

The best documentation of the *RCA* litigation still housed in the Whiteman Collection therefore is not letters or contracts related to the lawsuit but, rather, contemporaneous news coverage and analysis of the *RCA* case preserved in press-clipping scrapbooks. These scrapbooks juxtapose Whiteman's industry activities with his performance career, where news of the lawsuit is pasted side by side with advertisements for new records and live appearances. Court documents from the *RCA* dispute are, instead, preserved in the incomplete case record held at the National Archives and Records Administration—Kansas City, Missouri, branch. This archive houses the Southern District of New York record bound for use by the Second Circuit Court of Appeals, including pleadings; some exhibits; testimony from several witnesses, including Whiteman; and presiding Judge Vincent Leibell's July 1939 district court opinion; documents associated with the Second Circuit appeal culminating in Judge Learned Hand's July 1940 majority opinion; and the US Supreme Court's December 1940 denial of certiorari.

Although Whiteman's celebrity pervades the *RCA* lawsuit and popular press about it, his voice appears mostly silent outside of documented trial testimony. Careful efforts to curate Whiteman's professional image, carried out first by Whiteman himself and later his estate, likely motivated limiting public statements about litigation as well as the exclusion of written correspondence with the NAPA, other colleagues, or even friends, from archival collections. Perceptions of Whiteman's failure—in the lawsuit, the NAPA's mission, or in contract negotiations with record labels—likely contributed to gaps in archival documentation and minimized treatment in biographical narratives. What documentation is available places Whiteman as a member of the NAPA, a professional network that relied on his celebrity to advance its cause as much as the elaborate legal strategy traceable to fellow bandleader Fred Waring. On the one hand, Whiteman's leadership of the NAPA and similar organizations implies his commitment to advocating for the rights of musicians; on the other hand, Whiteman's actions, written letters, and verbal testimony cast him as reluctant, at times opaque, and even defensive, typically prioritizing performance engagements above commitments to professional advocacy. Despite any reservations Whiteman may have held, his NAPA activities did much to draw nationwide attention to problems with copyright laws made antiquated by rapidly evolving sound and broadcast technologies. They furthermore reveal Whiteman's sense of duty to the music industry, but his primary loyalty remained with his own organization.

The Problems with Radio Broadcast and Recorded Music

Whiteman signed the first of several lucrative recording agreements soon after the end of World War I, beginning with the Victor Talking Machine Company in 1920. Appearing on 78 rpm records first as "Paul Whiteman and His Ambassador Orchestra," Whiteman and his large instrumental ensembles recorded several tunes over six sessions. By November 1920 the name of the ensemble was changed to the enduring "Paul Whiteman and His Orchestra," when the famous records "Whispering" / "Japanese Sandman" and "Avalon" / "Best Ever Medley" were released. "Whispering" notably sold 2.5 million copies, an extraordinary accomplishment in its time. Whiteman's rapid success with record sales, coupled with an ambitious schedule of live appearances in high-profile urban ballrooms, generated a public reputation that Whiteman directed the top dance band in the United States. His meteoric rise to fame even prompted media speculation that the bandleader annually earned over $1 million.[4]

The Copyright Act of 1909, which was in effect for nearly all of Whiteman's career, notably excluded robust legal provisions for artists whose music—either live or recorded—was broadcast over radio airwaves. The act did introduce a compulsory mechanical license intended to compensate copyright holders when their music was later recorded by ensembles or solo artists.[5] These records were not legally treated as copyable property on their own; instead, because they were not considered "writings," records were classified as performances.[6] As a result, the act remained silent regarding any rights in a record held by its recording artist(s) and the use of those records in public spaces.[7] While several professional organizations, such as ASCAP, soon began to assess fees for live performance and local record airplay related to the mechanical license, these fees only compensated copyright holders for musical compositions. Artists, including Paul Whiteman and His Orchestra, whose interpretations of those compositions were captured on record had no federal statutory claim.

The rise of commercial radio broadcast in the 1920s seemed to capitalize on gaps in legal protection for recorded music. Because they were classified as performances rather than copyright-protectable works, "canned music" favored bottom-line costs for radio stations, especially small, local operations. Recorded music broadcasts were heard nationwide by the early 1930s, chiefly played by approximately six hundred local stations not affiliated with one of three national broadcast networks (ABC, CBS, and NBC).[8] These large networks were able to secure remote broadcasts for live ballroom performances of high-profile acts, including Whiteman and His Orchestra. Because these national broadcasts were sponsored by major advertisers, such as Ford Motors or Kraft Foods, live broadcast program offers were so enticing to bandleaders that they sometimes even agreed to lower wages in balance with the promise of audience exposure.[9]

Whiteman began his bandleading career in this complex industry climate, initially making the majority of his profit from live performances and the growing market for recorded music. Like other bandleaders, Whiteman was suspicious of radio broadcast because it appeared to compete with the recording and live performance revenue streams that primarily supported their large ensembles.[10] As he recalled, "I made records for Victor without receiving any royalties. I was paid so much per recording date—nothing more. I didn't mind at the time, because I knew that records were my best bet for putting my band over. Then along came radio."[11] Broadcast of recorded music over radio airwaves presented an economic conundrum. Radio could increase exposure and, therefore, increase revenue, but radio could also lead to a decrease in record sales as listeners could hear their favorite broadcast for the one-time cost of a radio rather than the cumulating cost of purchasing records as they were released. There was also potential for declining listener interest in attending live performances as more people gathered around radios in their own homes and neighborhoods. Indeed, by the late 1920s, listeners accessed music via radio more than any other audio technology.[12]

No matter how lucrative national live broadcast may have seemed, these programs competed against airplay of the same ensembles' records simultaneously broadcast by smaller local, and typically independent, stations. While bandleaders had at least some control over live broadcast, there was little, if anything, they could do about broadcasts of their records. As Waring complained, bandleaders did not want "our records playing in competition to us, and it was a growing menace to all performers."[13]

In lieu of definitive copyright laws, the problem appeared to warrant Progressive Era administrative regulation. As early as 1922, under the auspices of the Radio Act of 1912, then secretary of commerce Herbert Hoover banned large radio stations from broadcasting records;[14] and the US Department of Commerce that same year granted preferred licensing to radio stations who would pledge not to use recorded music.[15] A 1927 update to the Radio Act introduced more detailed regulations, including a requirement that stations identify recorded music if and when it was aired.[16] Yet, record airplay, often carefully disguised by chatter from announcers until after the record had started or simply not announcing it at all, continued to be problematic.[17]

Bandleaders soon took matters into their own hands. In 1932 Fred Waring and His Pennsylvanians ceased making new records to prevent competition with their own live broadcasts, and dozens of creators followed. The next year, in 1933, bandleaders and recording artists coordinated with the Music Publishers Protective Association (MPPA) to request that Victor, Columbia, and Brunswick include the following warning on newly pressed records: "Not Licensed for Radio Broadcast." Of course, "a flood of mail from concerned members to the [NAB] followed,"[18] as broadcasters nationwide grappled with the economic and legal implications of the printed warning. With little, if any, enforcement from record manufacturers or courts, however, the warning had little effect.

Three years later, in 1935, Philadelphia-based entertainment attorney Maurice Speiser united bandleaders and other recording artists, including Waring and Whiteman, to form the board of directors of the NAPA. The organization swiftly grew to nearly seven hundred artists with the common mission of "providing stronger copyright protection for musicians."[19] To this end, the organization sought to establish a right in records for the artists that created them, ostensibly so that they could control use, especially by radio stations. Members of the organization began by seeking legislative solutions. Two years prior, in 1933, Waring had unsuccessfully applied for copyright of a recording of "Lullaby of Broadway." The Register of Copyrights explained in a rejection letter, "There is not and never has been any provision in the Act for the protection of an artist's personal interpretation or rendition of a musical work not expressible by musical notation in the form of 'legible' copies."[20]

Under the auspices of the NAPA, Waring and others then lobbied for federal legislation granting legal control over the commercial use of sound recordings to be introduced.[21] NAPA members testified before the US House of Representatives Committee on Patents. Whiteman was not present for these hearings, but he signed two letters that were read into the *Congressional Record*.[22] In prose undoubtedly influenced by Speiser, Whiteman's letters enumerated the problems with radio broadcast of records, from difficulty securing sponsors for live broadcast due to overplay to the production and sale of bootleg copies. His letters cast commercial radio broadcast of records as "one of the most flagrant evils in our profession today."[23] In addition to promoting what was called the Daly Bill, named after J. Burrwood Daly, a Pennsylvania Democratic representative, the NAPA called for the provision of a $250 minimum damage for the unauthorized broadcast of recorded music.[24] None of these proposals met with congressional approval.

NAPA Lawsuits Begin

Undeterred by congressional rejection, NAPA bandleaders and other music industry leaders—primarily Waring and Whiteman along with fellow bandleader Don Voorhees, composer Walter O'Keefe, and vocalists Frank Crumit and Lawrence Tibbett—commenced a series of lawsuits across jurisdictions that were designed to force a judicial decision regarding the rights of recording artists, specifically regarding commercial radio broadcast of the records they created.[25] Waring brought the first state-level case, known to legal specialists as *Waring v. WDAS Broadcasting Station*, against Philadelphia radio station WDAS, demanding payment for each one of his records when it was played on air.[26] On January 28, 1936, the *Philadelphia Record* summarized the motivation for Waring's complaint: "The present copyright laws have not been amended since 1909, when the radio and the 'talkies' were unknown and when even silent pictures were regarded as a curiosity. The rapid development in mass entertainment made existing copyright laws archaic."[27] The lawsuit continued Waring's effort to assert legal control over records as separable creative works from the copyright-protected musical compositions they captured due to his ensemble's creative interpretation when performing those compositions. In response, WDAS claimed that it purchased the Pennsylvanians record and paid the ASCAP fee, therefore the record was lawfully its property to use as it wished regardless of any label warning. The legal question for the Pennsylvania state court to answer was, "Does the performer's interpretation of a musical composition constitute a product of such novel and artistic creation as to invest him with a property right therein?"[28] Perhaps surprisingly, the lawsuit was resolved in Waring's favor, with a judicial determination that recording artists could print and enforce radio broadcast restrictions on their records. As the opinion outlined, the language of the label warning "may [lawfully] restrain the commercial use of such records by a radio station."[29]

This favorable outcome for recording artists motivated more NAPA lawsuits.[30] Waring became the most prolific litigant regarding radio broadcast rights;[31] indeed, Waring's unwavering commitment to advocating for the broadcast rights of recording artists caused him to spend thousands of dollars on a decade of litigation while refusing to record so long as the lawsuits were pending.[32] Yet, it was Whiteman's federal lawsuit against radio station WNEW and his record label, RCA, that generated the landmark decision. The NAPA's reasoning for backing Whiteman's lawsuit likely had as much to do with the total quantity of similar complaints filed in courts nationwide as with Whiteman's celebrity. As Waring later explained, "We had planned for Paul Whiteman to be our banner suit [because] he was the most important musical artist of the day."[33]

Indeed, Whiteman's professional reputation during the late 1930s was evolving beyond simply bandleader to also include film actor and broadcast host. By 1936 to 1937, Whiteman ensemble engagements had temporarily declined in quantity due in part to profound changes in personnel, especially among its vocalists, which had mired Whiteman in contract disputes.[34] Yet, a *Chicago Daily Times* review of the Whiteman and His Orchestra's May 1937 performance in the Gold Coast Room seemed to reify Whiteman's presence in public consciousness: "It is no longer possible to dismiss Paul Whiteman as merely a bandleader. . . . passing of the years has made the amply-proportioned baton-waver into a national institution to be compared with Sears-Roebuck, Mickey Mouse, or J. P. Morgan and Co."[35] By the end of 1937 Whiteman began hosting the *Chesterfield Time* radio program on CBS and continued nationwide performance engagements. This expansion of his audience engagement promoted the Whiteman organization and brand, which, in turn, furthered Whiteman's own celebrity. The NAPA strategized its litigation efforts to take advantage of Whiteman's public presence by making his lawsuit the flagship of their efforts. As Waring recalled, "We felt that there was no way we could lose that key battle."[36]

The *RCA v. Whiteman* Litigation

Whiteman's lawsuit began in July 1936 against WBO Broadcasting Company, which at that time owned local New York station WNEW.[37] WBO had purchased nine Paul Whiteman records, some of which bore the label "Only for Non-Commercial Use on Phonographs in Homes," and proceeded to air them on WNEW. As a spokesperson for the station reportedly explained: "We just go ahead and play any record we feel like using, as we have done for years. We will utilize records constantly as a source of program material, and most artists are glad to have us do so. We have no arrangement with Whiteman or any other artist for the use of their recordings."[38] Whiteman, along with the NAPA and his legal team, sought an injunction against playing Whiteman records and bootleg copies of the ensembles' live performances.[39] Even if federal copyright law under the 1909 Act failed to adequately limit this use of recorded music, Whiteman also claimed state-level common law copyright protection on two grounds: first, based on a legal "loophole" that ostensibly granted a common law property right in unnotated or so-called unpublished music—in this case, Whiteman records. This argument relied on and hoped to reinforce precedent set by the *Waring* lawsuit. Second, Whiteman sought to establish that broadcasting records created unfair competition against live broadcasts of his ensembles, rendering him less able to negotiate live performances with other radio stations and, perhaps more importantly, their corporate sponsors.

RCA joined the lawsuit against WNEW but also cross-sued Whiteman. It claimed that Whiteman had contractually granted any common law property rights in those records to Victor and therefore to RCA through business acquisition in 1929. Because RCA believed it controlled the early Whiteman catalog, RCA attorneys argued that the corporation was entitled to any licensing fees for radio airplay ostensibly owed by WNEW and any other station. RCA also argued that if Whiteman could claim the records as creative works, so, too, could the corporation via its employees involved in the recording process. In sum: "If any rights were violated by the broadcasting of these recordings, those rights belonged to RCA rather than Whiteman."[40] The following nine songs are named in the complaint, all of which were released on the Victor label: "San," "Oh So Blue," "Whiteman Stomp," "By the Sycamore Tree," "You Excite Me," "Cuban Love Song," "There's Nothing Else to Do," "Singing a Happy Song," and "A Waltz Was Born in Vienna."[41] The first three compositions were recorded under a 1924 contract, the next four were recorded based on a 1931 agreement, and the last two were completed under a third agreement dated 1934.[42] In a legally offensive gesture, RCA also sent letters to other radio stations warning against airplay of records it had manufactured.[43]

As Waring predicted, print media outlets capitalized on Whiteman's enduring celebrity through wide coverage of the lawsuit. Journalists notably publicized Whiteman's peculiar attempt to withdraw just before trial. On December 8, 1938, *Variety* ran the article with the headline, "Whiteman Disinclined But WNEW Action Forced to Trial by RCA Victor," which alleges Whiteman's reticence to engage in litigation:

> Test case which the National Association of Performing Artists brought against WNEW, N.Y. [on] behalf of Paul Whiteman was on the verge of blowing up last week when the band leader advised Maurice Speiser, NAPA general counsel, that he wanted nothing further to do with the litigation.[44]

The article alleged Whiteman's reason for withdrawing as:

> Even if he got a verdict in his favor restraining WNEW from broadcasting his records, the order would only apply to discs cited in the complaint. There was also the possibility that he would lose much if the award went against him.[45]

In a contemporaneously sent letter written to Waring, however, Whiteman claims:

> My withdrawal . . . was for reasons that had nothing to do with the controversy. I want to assure you of my belief in the purposes for which the Association [the NAPA] stands, to wit, the recognition and protection of the artist to his interpretations.[46]

Whiteman's actual reason is not conclusively documented, but it may have had more to do with what Waring called "the fine print" of Whiteman's contracts with Victor that assigned the corporation all rights to Whiteman records and, therefore, any financial interest he may have had in the case. As Waring recalled, "To our utter dismay, it was learned during the suit that Paul Whiteman had unwittingly signed a contract with his recording company, which, somewhere in the fine print, granted to the recording company all rights."[47] At trial, Whiteman described a fast-paced, informal process for negotiating recording agreements: "Very often we sign a letter when we are on the road, because you negotiate with your man and he would like to have you, and if you know the man you more or less agree and 'You had a contract with us but it would be along this line' and we sign this and it would be okay."[48] It would have been unlikely for Whiteman to then read carefully every clause of the resultant written agreement before signing.

The "fine print" to which Whiteman and Waring metaphorically referred likely appeared in three agreements executed between Victor and Whiteman on behalf of his ensemble. The first agreement was effective May 12, 1924, until May 11, 1928. In this agreement, introduced in litigation as exhibit 4, Whiteman agreed to record 160 mutually determined "musical selections," forty of which were supposed to be recorded within the first year of the contract.[49] Paragraph 3 explicitly assigned any copyright Whiteman held in the manufacture and sale of Victor records to the manufacturer:

> *Mr. Whiteman,* for himself and by authority and on behalf of the Orchestra and each and all of the members thereof, hereby *grants to the Victor Company the right,* at any and all times during the period of this agreement and thereafter, *to manufacture, advertise, and license or sell,* and any and all these rights and powers, in all parts of the world, *records of the performances of the Orchestra* of selections of which approved master records have heretofore made or shall hereafter be made *including the right to produce and reproduce the recorded performances* of the Orchestra *by any and all mechanical, electrical or other means for disseminating or transmitting* the same.[50]

On the one hand, this language could be interpreted as Whiteman assigning his rights to control record use to Victor; on the other, the clause remained unclear as to the status of records produced for home use separate from those that could have been produced for radio broadcast.

According to Whiteman and other NAPA members, these distinctions mattered to the economic viability of their ensembles. In light of the *Waring* decision, control of record use amounted to not only sales profit but also broadcast licensing fees. This newer income stream seemed critical to accommodating the estimated losses bandleaders claimed radio caused by reducing record and live performance revenue. As Judge Leibell summarized during trial: "This is a difference between you having your orchestra at a broadcasting station and broadcasting a number . . . and a record being played in a broadcasting station, a record that you have made and then have the record broadcast."[51] The unclear legal status of records and industry suspicion surrounding radio broadcast widened gaps in contract provisions over control of recorded music, to the perceived detriment of recording artists.

RCA v. Whiteman: Trial and Whiteman's Testimony

Regardless of Whiteman's reason for intending to withdraw, RCA pushed the case forward because "all witnesses were available in the city; that a great deal of money had been spent on preparation of the case and that Victor would proceed to ask for an adjudication of its claim to the exclusive right to license the commercial use of its own records."[52] At the time, Whiteman and His Orchestra had a reduced performance schedule, only appearing on the *Chesterfield* broadcast, in part because of personnel issues and in part because they were rehearsing for the 1938 Experiment in Modern Music performance at Carnegie Hall. With Whiteman's increased availability, the trial was heard over six days from December 12 to 20, 1938, in the District Court of the Southern District of New York, beginning with Whiteman's formal withdrawal and Judge Leibell's dismissal of it.[53] The trial featured testimony from sixteen witnesses, including conductors and artists signed to Victor, such as Boston Pops Orchestra conductor Arthur Fiedler and violinist-conductor Mishel Piastro, as well as fellow bandleaders and NAPA members, notably Whiteman and Waring; AFM representative, Samuel Tabak; and Victor executives, including Fredrick Erdman and Edward King.

Despite his reluctance to be involved, Whiteman was called as a witness on the last day of trial.[54] Most of Whiteman's examination interrogated his recollection of the verbal negotiations that might have clarified the otherwise unclear contract language. His testimony revealed an evolving perspective toward the impact of radio broadcast on recording artists and his own suspicions about it.

Whiteman's responses to questions posed by either attorney or Judge Leibell remain consistent that, prior to 1931, contract negotiations focused on live broadcast without mention of permissions to air recorded music. During this period, Whiteman toured and recorded with ensembles extensively, while appearing infrequently on radio. Whiteman described the 1924 negotiations, which included discussion of radio and Victor executives' suspicion of it:

> Sometimes when the broadcasting grew[,] I was warned by members of the Victor organization that they thought it was very wrong to broadcast because if you did broadcast they felt it would hurt the sale of your records. I know Mr. King and I at different times discussed this and he thought it would be very silly for me to go on the air all the time; that I would eventually undo the thing that was an important part of my work.[55]

Victor executives did not support radio broadcast at this time because it appeared to reduce record sales. Despite these known issues, the Victor-Whiteman contract remained silent as to any broadcast rights.

The examination continued with a second Victor agreement executed on September 8, 1931, after intervening years when Whiteman had split with Victor to record with Columbia. This contract, composed as a letter, included the clause "in accordance with our verbal understanding," leaving unclear the content of that verbal agreement. At trial, Whiteman revealed a shift in Victor's position on broadcasting records over radio, now describing ambiguity in the potential value of the practice:

> LEIBELL, J.: Was there anything said at the time this letter was signed, this letter of September 8, 1931, between you and Mr. Erdman about the

use of any record you made for broadcasting purposes; using them for broadcasting purposes?

WHITEMAN: I am sure there was not; not to get my permission to broadcast.

LEIBELL, J.: Was there anything said about it at all?

WHITEMAN: Well, I guess I have discussed with everybody almost that I contacted in the Victor organization—it was always quite prevalent that—well, *I don't know up to the time I might say that they were friendly to the broadcasting, I think we first thought it was a bad thing to do and then we did not know whether it was a good or bad thing to do.*[56]

Whiteman continued to recount the mixed advice he received from Victor:

> I have been told not to broadcast and then I have been told it is all right and I have been told by the clients that the broadcasting of records absolutely kills my business, and I don't know whether it was at this time, but I was assured [that] Victor gave you no right to broadcast but they could not enforce a "non-broadcast" [label warning].[57]

Here, Whiteman reiterated no assistance from Victor over radio broadcast of Whiteman records: they would neither enforce the label nor add explicit broadcast terms to their contracts.

By Whiteman's recollection, rights to a record and broadcast of it were separate, and the latter should remain with him:

SPEISER: Whenever it was did you have a conversation with Mr. Erdman on that subject?

WHITEMAN: Yes; that I was against broadcasting of records; was there any way to control it?

SPEISER: And what did he say?

WHITEMAN: He said, "You could control it if you got them out." The right to make them and sell them was different and they could not enforce whether they could broadcast them or not. It was up to me.

SPEISER: Was that what he told you[?]

WHITEMAN: Well, that—it was different conversations. I do not know whether it was just at this time because I had always felt that I made the records for one thing, but my broadcasting was a separate thing. I got paid for putting my band on the stage, but broadcasting records were made for an entirely different thing and I maintained that to the length of my contract and still feel it is a dangerous ground and that none of us know whether it paid you to ask somebody to broadcast your records in hope somebody will buy the record or some of your clients say they pay you exclusively and they don't want your records played tomorrow on the air. Other clients say maybe it is a good thing, but I still believe you broadcast for one thing and make records for another.[58]

Here, Whiteman expounded on the complexity of musical intellectual property and his own entrepreneurial separation between live performance, recording, and radio broadcast. Despite the absence of such explicit distinctions in the Victor contracts, Whiteman clarified: "I am sure Fred maintained that the right Victor had was to make the record and sell the record under the agreement that it was made for one purpose, which was the home use, and if somebody broadcasts it, it would have to be up to us fellows to sue and stop it."[59] This explanation succinctly stated Whiteman's case while also voicing the mission of the NAPA. The lack of clarity Whiteman claimed to have received from Victor established the possibility of Whiteman's interpretation to be valid: although he assigned manufacture and sale rights to Victor, he retained the broadcast right because it was not explicitly included in the contract.

By the third Victor contract, executed September 5, 1934, there was clear language about broadcast control, again appearing in paragraph 3 of a form agreement that had been revised since 1924. The clause aligned with Whiteman's explanations throughout a decade of negotiations: "It is understood that the company does not acquire the right to manufacture or sell or otherwise dispose of records for broadcasting."[60] According to this third contract, Whiteman retained a separate broadcast right, ostensibly to be enforced by an organization such as the NAPA.

The King of Jazz Entertains in Court

Journalists, particularly those writing for trade journals, unsurprisingly sensationalized Whiteman's examination. According to *Radio Daily*, Whiteman's testimony "gave the courtroom laughs when he insisted that he would answer questions 'in my own way,' and resented the questions asked" by RCA attorney David Mackay.[61] Extant court transcript did not record these reactions or the "in my own way" statement, however Whiteman's seemingly impatient, yet unflappable demeanor suggested he had greater social control over the proceedings than the prosecuting attorney or even the presiding judge.

Whiteman's responses to Mackay during cross-examination might have been one cause for such amusement. Mackay asked leading questions crafted to elicit simple, yet condemning answers from Whiteman that would support RCA's position. At times, Whiteman appeared unable to provide detailed information, such as dates or terms used in conversation; at others, he appeared impatient with the legal process of confirming seemingly obvious factual details and contract language. In these instances, Whiteman's responses appear to diffuse courtroom tension while undermining Mackay's arguments.

In one instance, Mackay brought up Whiteman's 1928 high-profile move to Columbia Records and the 1930 settlement that led to his return to RCA Victor.[62] The following exchange occurred:

> MACKAY: This is when you were recording for Columbia. Did you perform the Columbia contract in full?
> WHITEMAN: I did not.
> MACKAY: Were all of the records called for by that agreement made?
> WHITEMAN: That is right.
> MACKAY: There was some sort of a settlement, was there not?
> WHITEMAN: There was a little thing like a depression came in there, in between.[63]

Here, Mackay attempted to impugn Whiteman for breach of contract, with the implication that if he would negotiate with Columbia this way, he might have tried similar tactics with Victor. Whiteman's understatement offered a valid economic explanation for breaking the contract with Columbia for reasons beyond contract terms or copyright confusion. Invoking the profound impact of the Great Depression recontextualized the exchange in Whiteman's favor from oppositional to sympathetic. In this light, Whiteman's motivation to break with the contract based on Columbia's alleged pay cuts could not be cast as a matter of financial greed so much as one of economic survival.

Later in cross-examination, Whiteman countered Mackay's questions ostensibly posed to undermine the bandleader's credibility. During one exchange, Mackay brought up Whiteman's satellite orchestra records to establish a limit on Whiteman's creative oversight and, therefore, erode his copyright claim:

> MACKAY: As a matter of fact, Mr. Whiteman, isn't it true that for some of the phonograph records involved in this case you personally did not conduct the orchestra?
> WHITEMAN: As I stated before I supervised my arrangers. I brought them up. The history of every arranger who has left the Whiteman band is he has become a famous arranger; that we did have a style and I claim I can style a band and it would still go as Whiteman style, but I don't think it would be as good as if I were there, but however, I would go in and out and somebody else would take the stick for a time, but as I explained we all tried to help.
> MACKAY: Take this record, "O So Blue" involved in this case: Isn't it a fact, Mr. Whiteman, that you did not conduct the orchestra when that selection was recorded?
> WHITEMAN: Well, let's take "Song of India." I did.[64]

Whiteman's non-sequitur response seems aimed more to undermine Mackay than to provide the court with information. The exchange simultaneously highlighted the practical and creative reach of Whiteman's leadership. Similar to other instances in cross-examination, Whiteman deftly redirected adversarial lines of questioning to reinforce his own character and to destabilize Mackay's strategy. His responses were consistent with his affable public persona, which undoubtedly bolstered the NAPA's strategic reliance on Whiteman's celebrity to influence a favorable trial outcome.

Industry Witnesses Support Whiteman

Whiteman took the stand before other bandleaders and music industry representatives whose testimony served to reinforce Whiteman's statements and to contextualize the economic implications of the lawsuit. Tabak, for example, enumerated the problems of recorded music broadcast for musicians, with the implication that even the entity Whiteman and His Orchestra was not immune from harm. His statements on direct examination enumerated the financial issues for recording artists, beginning with reduced employment for performers and arrangers and continuing with the challenges of commercial sponsorship for ensembles:

> SPEISER: What effect did you find the broadcasting of phonograph records by the station had upon the work of the members of your union?
>
> TABAK: It certainly destroyed employment for hundreds and prevented employment for others.
>
> SPEISER: What effect did it have, if you know, upon the artists whose special talents were used in the arrangement of the music or conducting the orchestra, such as a famous bandleader? . . .
>
> TABAK: The broadcasting industry as we know it today has become to a great extent commercially sponsored. People who wish to exploit their products or the good will of their company have ceased to engage orchestras which they believe are of outstanding merit in order that they may broadcast [on] behalf of that company. Broadcasting has become one of the accepted media of advertising and those whom they engage they hope, as a result of their reputation, will draw the biggest listening audience—in other words, circulation. The difference in the prices paid to those artists is very often a reflection of the comparative popularity that the artists enjoy with the masses.[65]

Tabak went on to explain the consequences of broadcasting records for recording artists and the creative impact that the new broadcast landscape had for ensembles:

> TABAK: The question of the broadcasting of records immediately presents the proposition of destroying the right of the artist to sell his exclusive

> services, because others who are paying him nothing, by the mere purchase of a record, are able to present him in competition with himself and thereby destroy his opportunity for getting high financial pay because of the fact that he can only be heard on the program presented by the particular sponsor who is engaging him. In addition thereto it has hurt him because it does not necessarily present the performer in his present standard as the public knows him. . . .
>
> SPEISER: They can use old records you mean?
>
> TABAK: That is right, and many orchestras have changed their complete style and have changed the type of orchestra.[66]

Tabak asserted that records, as a reflection of a performer's or an ensemble's creative identity—and thus their intellectual property—should remain in the control of the artists who created them. His testimony, considered in light of Whiteman's testimony and that of other witnesses, demonstrated a strategically concerted effort to advocate for recording artists across professional organizations in the music industry. By collectively addressing all musicians, Tabak broadened the reach of the issues in the lawsuit beyond Whiteman and the NAPA.

Waring's testimony was brief and unsurprisingly reinforced both Whiteman's and Tabak's examinations. Waring notably explained his entrepreneurial purpose behind discontinuing the creation of records, which relayed the problems of records broadcast over radio airwaves:

> For a person who wishes to have a progressive business organization it has been brought out in testimony that the revenue possible from recordings has gone down to three-quarters of a cent as against a former earning of $1,275 per selection; also the fact that any person of any common sense would find it very silly to compete with himself in radio. I found it necessary to try to eliminate the possibility of our broadcasting in competition with ourselves in order to secure a good remunerable radio contract. In other words, my ability to show the sponsor that there would be no competitive broadcasts of our material made it possible for us to secure what might be considered a pretty good stipend.[67]

Waring's testimony explicitly documented the adverse financial impact of radio broadcast on record sales and the challenges faced by bandleaders whose ensembles performed for live broadcast. It followed from his testimony that in order to secure the best contracts, bandleaders were unfairly forced to choose between essential revenue streams. Although his commentary specifically addressed the Pennsylvanians, general application of his statements to Whiteman's lawsuit was implied.

Together with Whiteman, the testimony of other industry witnesses contextualized the problems of radio broadcast of recorded music and the impact that the case outcome would have not simply on Whiteman and his organization but the entire music industry. They established an economic need for legally codified broadcast rights in recorded music and enough ambiguity in Whiteman's contracts with Victor to justify a legal interpretation aligned with Whiteman's testimony. In so doing, these witnesses helped cast Whiteman as a reluctant champion of musicians and recording artists by promoting the NAPA's mission.

RCA v. Whiteman: Trial Decision and Appeal

After lengthy delays, on July 14, 1939, the court in the Southern District of New York decided in favor of Whiteman and RCA, granting them an injunction against WNEW for broadcasting Whiteman records.[68] The opinion, which cited the *Waring* decision for persuasive legal authority, held that "because of his unique interpretations of musical selections,"[69] Whiteman had a common law property right in the music captured on record as "unpublished" works. As a result, Whiteman had the right to license or prevent any use by radio stations of records covered under the contracts. This property right ostensibly included Whiteman's ability to assign it to someone else, in this case, to Victor and thus RCA. With regard to RCA's complaint against Whiteman over their contracts and rights to the records, the district court found that Whiteman had assigned all rights to the manufacturer.[70]

Although trial testimony about the technicalities of the recording process had demonstrated that RCA contributed "their research and experience in the production and manufacture of phonograph records, and the skillful use of a highly sensitive mechanism,"[71] the manufacturer could not possess any additional property right in the records. Their technical process was not considered to have made any "intellectual and artistic contribution" to the music recorded by Whiteman ensembles.[72] As Judge Leibell explained in his district court opinion: "The average person could not tell by listening to the finished record which company made the record or which musical director supervised its recording or who manipulated the dials, arranged the microphones or handled the other mechanical devises used in getting the physical recording."[73] As a result, there could be no additional manufacturer's claim to the record as a separable creative product.

The court finally ruled that broadcast of Whiteman's records without authorization constituted unfair competition, both for Whiteman's live broadcasts and RCA's record sales.[74] Judge Leibell applied public policy analysis to the restrictive notice on record labels as well as relevant case law on unfair competition to find that "unfair competition with Whiteman is manifest."[75] While the decision classified radio broadcast of recorded music as unfair competition, its relevance to both Whiteman and RCA failed to retain an exclusive broadcast right in the records at issue.

The promising trial outcome for recording artists regarding broadcast rights garnered fairly immediate response from the music industry: "Victor instituted a fee scale on phonograph record broadcasting, and Decca ordered WNEW to stop using its discs."[76] By August 19, 1939, the NAB had negotiated licenses with Victor, Decca, and Columbia to broadcast records only if they were introduced by the record labels in addition to music covered by their ASCAP licenses.[77] Presumably with Whiteman's acquiescence, the NAPA sought to use the district court outcome as a means to "educate the performing artist so that he reserves his property rights in contracts made with recording companies."[78] At this time, the organization began to establish "a fund whereby musicians would benefit from license fees paid by broadcasters playing their discs."[79] It would seem that the music industry had begun to accept that broadcast rights were retained by recording artists.

The Second Circuit Appeal: "Key Battle" Lost

Although the district court opinion was mostly favorable to the NAPA's mission, by October 20, 1939, Whiteman's legal team had swiftly appealed the decision to the Second Circuit Court of Appeals. They specifically sought a reversal that Whiteman had contractually assigned all rights based on the terms of the record contracts at issue in the case. RCA cross-appealed, hoping to reverse the decision about a common-law property right in the recording process.[80]

In a devastating reversal handed down July 25, 1940, inimitable Judge Learned Hand determined that neither Whiteman nor RCA could claim a right to license records for broadcast, because any common-law property right in a record ended with its public sale. Referring to well-established property law for precedent, writing Judge Hand, with Judges Charles Clark and Robert Patterson concurring, opined:

> Copyright in any form, whether statutory or at common-law, is a monopoly; it consists only in the power to prevent others from reproducing the copyrighted work. WBO Broadcasting Corporation has never invaded any such right of Whiteman; they have never copied his performances at all; they have merely used those copies which he and the RCA Manufacturing Company, Inc., made and distributed. The putatively protested performances were themselves intended for that purpose and that alone.[81]

Although Whiteman could claim a common-law property right in the record, those rights ended with lawful sale. Because broadcasting a record over radio was believed to use, not reproduce, the copyrighted musical work, the court reasoned that no copyright provision could have been violated by airplay.[82]

The three-judge panel reversed the district court judgment, and the complaints were dismissed. "In effect, property rights [in music on record] ended with the sale of a record. Broadcasters could no longer be constrained from using music recorded 'for home use only.'"[83] The appellate decision appears to have resulted from contemporaneous jurisprudence regarding recorded sound and contract law rather than the Second Circuit seizing the opportunity created by the NAPA to reinterpret increasingly outdated federal copyright law. In keeping with the Copyright Act of 1909 and precedent set by earlier US Supreme Court decisions, Hand, Clark, and Pattinson classified records as performances and reified notation, rather than sound recordings, as capturing the essence of music as intellectual property. Arguments about the creativity involved in making a record and Whiteman's celebrity status fell short.

After the Supreme Court declined to grant certiorari, the *RCA v. Whiteman* decision made an immediate and lasting impact on the music industry. The decision appeared catastrophic for the NAPA by overturning both the 1939 district court opinion and countering the decision in the *Waring* suit. The *RCA* appellate decision threw "a knockout blow" to the NAPA, effectively neutralizing its efforts to establish a licensing system for radio broadcast of records.[84] It appeared that Waring, Whiteman, and the NAPA had lost their "key battle."

After the Lawsuit

Through the *RCA* litigation, Whiteman became an early figure to grapple with antiquated copyright laws and to advocate for legal and industry reform. By its conclusion, Whiteman had retreated to his ranch in Fort Worth, Texas, for six months, seeking distance from the music industry altogether and superficially declaring his retirement.[85] Within two years of the Second Circuit decision, legal scholars had begun to review the case and suggested that Hand's opinion left Congress with an opportunity to legislate rights pertaining to commercial broadcast use of records.[86] A total of five NAPA lawsuits reached trial courts by the time the organization folded during World War II, but the *RCA v. Whiteman* decision would remain valid law until the 1955 case of *Capitol Records v. Mercury Records Corp.*, which found that record sale did not relinquish the right to reproduce a record.[87] Judge Hand, perhaps unsurprising, drafted the dissenting opinion in this later case, in which he repeated reasoning from *RCA v. Whiteman* about records as outside the purview of federal copyright.[88]

Whiteman published only minimal reflection on the *RCA* case, at least publicly appearing to maintain his distance from it. In his 1948 monograph, *Records for the Millions*, Whiteman summarized the suit in a manner that seemed to redouble his stance on records and radio broadcast of them as separate, yet equally valuable, professional and creative activities:

> Fifteen years ago I brought suit to try to establish the rights of an artist to the use of his records. You may have noticed that the labels on your records say that the platter is licensed for home use only. Victor, for whom I was then recording, agreed to a clause in my contract limiting the use of my records to the home, but they found it impossible to enforce the rule effectively.[89]

Whiteman's commentary is diplomatic and opaque, restating the main issue in the lawsuit without scathing critique. Yet, the final clause hints at Whiteman's frustration with the outcome.

In the wake of the *RCA* lawsuit—not to mention World War II and the AFM recording strike that devastated the economy for large ensembles—by 1943 Whiteman had redirected his career toward serving as a broadcast media personality. Although for years Whiteman had hosted live music programs, such as *Stairway to the Stars* and *Forever Tops*, that featured live musical performances, he eventually acceded to broadcasting recorded music over radio (see fig. 7.1). In 1947 Whiteman agreed to host *The Paul Whiteman Club* on ABC, a Monday-through-Friday show that interspersed popular songs with interviews featuring "show business" celebrities and commercial advertisements read by Whiteman himself. Following the popular 1930s adage, "If you can't beat 'em, join 'em,"[90] *The Paul Whiteman Club* became the first national network radio program to feature a disc jockey. The unique feature of Whiteman's program compared to local stations that had already been airing recorded music was his interviews with entertainment industry professionals.[91] The national scope of *The Paul Whiteman Club*, nevertheless, appears to mark a profound shift in radio broadcast practice from the 1920s to 1950—known to many scholars and listeners alike as the Golden Age of Radio—signaled by industry acceptance of broadcasting recorded, rather than live, music over radio airwaves. Whiteman's publication of *Records for the Millions* the following year seemed to polish this newly honed facet of his public persona. The professional pivot away from his earlier advocacy work proved to sustain Whiteman's career and performances of Whiteman ensembles nationwide, albeit at the expense of the now defunct NAPA's mission.

FIGURE 7.1 Whiteman spins a record in a publicity still for ABC to announce *The Paul Whiteman Club*, 1947. Paul Whiteman Collection, Williams College Special Collections.

Conclusion

Paul Whiteman's career away from the podium established an essential role for him in shaping US music industry policy and intellectual property law. His landmark *RCA v. Whiteman* lawsuit reveals the legal and economic problems of broadcast media for performing and recording artists at a critical moment in music industry history. Bandleaders, record manufacturers, radio stations, and courts confronted antiquated copyright laws that failed to accommodate new media technologies, both the 1909 Act and common law judicial opinions that excluded records as separable intellectual property from notated compositions. For Whiteman and the NAPA, the case brought to a forefront these issues and the limits of even Whiteman's celebrity.

Fragmented archival documentation and Whiteman's explicit desire to distance himself publicly from the *RCA* lawsuit suggests an uneasiness about the negative effects of litigation on his professional reputation. Extant records, nevertheless, reveal Whiteman's clear stance on recorded music as intellectual property, the putative rights of recording artists, and his own approach to balancing live performance, recording, and radio broadcast as revenue streams. Although Whiteman's work with the NAPA did much to draw nationwide attention to incongruences between copyright laws and radio broadcast to the benefit of the music industry, his role on *The Paul Whiteman Club* radio show suggests that his loyalty remained with his own professional success and the longevity of his organization.

The rise of commercial radio broadcast concurrent with the height of Whiteman's popularity complicated the economic viability of large ensembles and launched him as an apparent advocate for the rights of musicians as recording artists. Whiteman's contributions to the NAPA highlighted the ways that he and fellow bandleaders, chiefly Waring, negotiated this balance at the moment their ensembles seemed threatened by broadcast technology and opportunistic disc jockeys. Although the *RCA v. Whiteman* case was ultimately unsuccessful, Whiteman made a lasting impact on the US music industry both as bandleader and advocate.

Notes

A previous version of this research was featured on the Williams College Library Blog, funded by the Paul Whiteman Fellowship. See Katherine Leo, "Paul Whiteman: Radio Performance Rights Advocate," *Williams College Library Blog,* April 2018 https://library.williams.edu/2019/03/25/paul-whiteman-radio-performance-rights-advocate/.

1. Rayno, *Paul Whiteman,* 2:112 (supporting Louis Armstrong in a 1931 contract dispute).
2. "Paul Whiteman Treasures to Enrich Williams," 56.
3. Sylvia Brown, Williams College archivist, to author, email, September 13, 2022.
4. Rayno, *Paul Whiteman,* 1:app. 3, 46, 60, 57. Rayno explains that such estimates were exaggerated.
5. Pub. L. 60–349, Copyright Act of 1909 §1(e) (superseded 1976). For a legal history on licensing recorded music, see Leo, "Legal Legacy of the Player Piano."
6. See White-Smith Publishing Co. v. Apollo Co., 209 U.S. 1, 18 (1908); *White-Smith,* 209 U.S. at 19–20 (Holmes, J., concurring).
7. See Herbert v. Shanley, 242 U.S. 591 (1917). For a history of ASCAP and the lawsuit, see, e.g., Shavers, *Little Book of Music Law,* 41–49.
8. Rapid growth of the radio industry led to the formation of the Federal Communications Commission (FCC) in 1934. The FCC is responsible for much of music radio broadcast regulation even into the present day, including the infamous prohibition of payola in 1960. For a history of music radio broadcast, see, for example, J. Cox, *Music Radio*; Sanjek, *Pennies from Heaven.*

9. Wald, *How the Beatles Destroyed Rock 'n' Roll*, 94.
10. Wald, *How the Beatles Destroyed Rock 'n' Roll*, 93.
11. Whiteman, *Records for the Millions*, 51–52.
12. Wald, *How the Beatles Destroyed Rock 'n' Roll*, 93.
13. V. Waring, *Fred Waring and the Pennsylvanians*, 144–48, quoted in Epperson, "From the Statute of Anne to Z. Z. Top," 16. See also Rosen, "Common Law Copyright," 1088.
14. Federal Communications Commission, "Radio Service Bulletin of 1922," (Oct. 2, 1922), 8.
15. Passman, "When Deejays Were Forbidden," 51.
16. J. Cox, *Music Radio*, 172.
17. Passman, "When Deejays Were Forbidden," 51.
18. Sanjek, *Pennies from Heaven*, 121.
19. V. Waring, *Fred Waring and the Pennsylvanians*, 139; Rosen, "Common Law Copyright," 1086.
20. Waring v. WDAS Broadcasting Station, 194 A. 631, 633n2 (Penn. 1937), quoted in Epperson, "From the Statute of Anne to Z. Z. Top," 16.
21. HR 10632 in 1936; HR 5265, HR 304, HR 7420 in 1937; HR 4871, HR 6160 (reintroduction after sponsor's death) in 1939; HR 9703 in 1940; HR 3997 in 1942; HR 1570 in 1943; HR 3190 in 1945; and HR 1269 and 1270 in 1947. Rosen, "Fred Waring and the Pennsylvanian Litigation."
22. See *Revision of Copyright Laws*, 679
23. *Revision of Copyright Laws*, 679.
24. HR 10632. See *Revision of Copyright Laws*, 680.
25. See DeLong, *Pops*, 210; Rayno, *Paul Whiteman*, 2:197–98.
26. Waring v. WDAS Broadcasting Station, 327 Pa. 433 (1936).
27. "Harmony (Musical) May Grace Hearing: Radio and Stage Players to Perform Arguments at 'Piracy' Quiz," *Philadelphia Record*, January 28, 1936, Whiteman Collection.
28. Waring v. WDAS Broadcasting Station, 194 A. 631, 633 (Penn. 1937).
29. Waring v. WDAS Broadcasting Station, 327 Pa. 433, 435–56 (1936).
30. See Rosen, "Common Law Copyright," 1088–90.
31. See Rosen, "Fred Waring and the Pennsylvanian Litigation."
32. Waring, *Fred Waring and His Pennsylvanians*, 142.
33. Rayno, *Paul Whiteman*, 2:198.
34. See Rayno, *Paul Whiteman*, 2:160–75.
35. Rayno, *Paul Whiteman*, 2:175.
36. Rayno, *Paul Whiteman*, 2:198.
37. Refrigerator manufacturer Elin Incorporated, which advertised on WNEW, is also named as a defendant.
38. DeLong, *Pops*, 210–11.
39. See also Rayno, *Paul Whiteman*, 2:197–98.
40. Rosen, "Common Law Copyright," 1091.
41. RCA v. Whiteman, joint appendix, 9–10.
42. RCA v. Whiteman, 28 F. Supp. 787, 791 (S.D.N.Y. 1939).

43. Passman, "When Deejays Were Forbidden," 52.

44. "Whiteman Disinclined but WNEW Action Forced to Trial by RCA Victor," *Variety* December 7, 1938, Whiteman Collection. Rayno clarifies that Whiteman spoke to his personal attorney, Julian T. Abeles, to withdraw, who then communicated to Speiser. See Rayno, *Paul Whiteman*, 2:197.

45. Rayno, *Paul Whiteman*, 2:197–98.

46. Rayno, *Paul Whiteman*, 2:198.

47. See RCA v. Whiteman, joint appendix, exhibit 4, 338, ID K000–05–0060–6417, Record Group 21, and Equity Case Files 1876–1907, box #4277, Circuit Court Southern District of New York, both in National Archives and Records Administration Kansas City, Missouri. See also Waring quoted in Rayno, *Paul Whiteman*, 2:198.

48. RCA v. Whiteman, joint appendix, 246 (Whiteman).

49. See RCA v. Whiteman, joint appendix, 338, exhibit 4.

50. RCA v. Whiteman, joint appendix, 339, exhibit 4, emphasis added.

51. RCA v. Whiteman, joint appendix, 246 (Whiteman).

52. Rayno, *Paul Whiteman*, 2:198.

53. Rayno, *Paul Whiteman*, 2:198.

54. RCA v. Whiteman, joint appendix, 222–65.

55. RCA v. Whiteman, joint appendix, 235 (Whiteman).

56. RCA v. Whiteman, joint appendix, 244 (Whiteman), emphasis added.

57. RCA v. Whiteman, joint appendix, 246 (Whiteman).

58. RCA v. Whiteman, joint appendix, 247 (Whiteman).

59. RCA v. Whiteman, joint appendix, 247–48 (Whiteman).

60. See RCA v. Whiteman, joint appendix, 338 (Exhibit 6).

61. See Rayno, *Paul Whiteman*, 2:198; see also RCA v. Whiteman, joint appendix, 249–65 (Whiteman).

62. Rayno, *Paul Whiteman*, 1:197–98.

63. RCA v. Whiteman, joint appendix, 263 (Whiteman). See also Rayno, *Paul Whiteman*, 2:xv.

64. RCA v. Whiteman, joint appendix, 263 (Whiteman).

65. RCA v. Whiteman, joint appendix, 303–5 (Tabak), emphasis added.

66. RCA v. Whiteman, joint appendix, 315 (Waring).

67. RCA v. Whiteman, joint appendix, 315 (Waring).

68. See, for example, "Delay Whiteman Decision," *Billboard*, July 1, 1939, Whiteman Collection.

69. RCA v. Whiteman, 28 F. Supp. 787, 791 (S.D.N.Y. 1939).

70. RCA v. Whiteman, 28 F. Supp. 787, 799 (S.D.N.Y. 1939).

71. RCA v. Whiteman, 28 F. Supp. 787, 792 (S.D.N.Y. 1939).

72. RCA v. Whiteman, 28 F. Supp. 787, 791 (S.D.N.Y. 1939).

73. RCA v. Whiteman, 28 F. Supp. 787, 792 (S.D.N.Y. 1939). The Music Modernization Act would update these provisions. See Orrin G. Hatch—Bob Goodlatte Music Modernization Act Title III: Allocation for Music Producers Act (AMP), 132 Stat. 3676 (2018).

74. RCA v. Whiteman, 28 F. Supp. 787, 791 (S.D.N.Y. 1939).

75. RCA v. Whiteman, 28 F. Supp. 787, 794 (S.D.N.Y. 1939); Sanjek, *Pennies from Heaven*, 143–44.

76. Passman, "When Deejays Were Forbidden," 52.

77. "NAB Seeks License to Use Recordings," *Billboard*, August 19, 1939, Whiteman Collection. See also Passman, "When Deejays Were Forbidden," 53; Sanjek, *Pennies from Heaven*, 144.

78. "NAPA Findings May Mean Class between Acts, Recording Firms," *Billboard*, July 29, 1939, Whiteman Collection.

79. Rayno, *Paul Whiteman*, 2:222.

80. RCA v. Whiteman, 114 F.3d 86, 87 (2d Cir. 1940).

81. RCA v. Whiteman, 114 F.3d 86, 88 (2d Cir. 1940).

82. See also Cummings, *Democracy of Sound*, 45–48; Rosen, "Common Law Copyright," 1091.

83. Sanjek, *Pennies from Heaven*, 146; Rosen, "Common Law Copyright," 1092.

84. Rayno, *Paul Whiteman*, 2:222.

85. Rayno, *Paul Whiteman*, 2:221.

86. See, for example, "Protection of the Performing Artists 'Interpretative Rendition,'" 245; Baer, "Performer's Right to Enjoin," 211.

87. Capitol Records v. Mercury Records Corp., 221 F.2d 657, 663 (2d Cir. 1955).

88. Capitol Records v. Mercury Records Corp., 221 F.2d 657, 664 (2d Cir. 1955) (Hand, J., dissenting). See also Norton, "Turtle Power," 764.

89. Whiteman, *Records for the Millions*, 50.

90. Rayno, *Paul Whiteman*, 2:264–65. By 1947 approximately twenty-three hundred disc-jockey programs were across nine hundred local radio stations nationwide.

91. Rayno, *Paul Whiteman*, 2:265.

8

Integration and Segregation in Whiteman's Music Television, 1948–55

W. ANTHONY SHEPPARD

Paul Whiteman was an early promoter of the possibilities of television for the music industry and television was central to his late career. He held the position of vice president and music director at ABC from 1948 to 1955 and hosted four musical shows on that network: *TV Teen Club* (1949–54), *The Paul Whiteman Goodyear Revue* (1949–52), *On the Boardwalk with Paul Whiteman* (1954), and *America's Greatest Bands* (summer 1955). In 1948 ABC launched several of its first television stations by broadcasting Whiteman conducting his signature piece, George Gershwin's *Rhapsody in Blue*.[1] Throughout the 1950s and into the 1960s, Whiteman made cameo appearances on multiple musical variety shows, most often as a conductor or as a special guest reminiscing about the American musical past.[2] Whiteman's own television shows encompassed popular music from ragtime and Tin Pan Alley to jump blues and the advent of rock 'n' roll. *TV Teen Club*, an amateur competition variety show, reveals the full range of midcentury American youth musical experience, and it shaped subsequent music television, most directly *American Bandstand*. *Goodyear Revue*, in contrast, almost exclusively featured professional adult performers in a deluxe presentation of white middlebrow musical culture, one that persisted in such programs as *The Lawrence Welk Show*.

As Ron Rodman has noted, "[i]n the late 1940s Whiteman became one of the first musical celebrity spokesmen for television."[3] In a 1949 article in *Etude*, Whiteman enthused about the potential of television, in general, and for music, specifically, predicting that music lessons would be given on TV and noting that television allowed him to bring his teen-club concept to a national audience.[4] ABC clearly valued Whiteman's endorsement of the new medium of television and his enduring star persona. This is evident in a

March 1950 full-page advertisement that appeared in *Look* magazine. Whiteman's *Goodyear Revue* received top billing in this ad with a large photograph of Whiteman himself accompanied by other photographs related to the show and smaller photographs announcing a few other ABC offerings. The ad encouraged readers who did not yet own one to purchase a television set so that they, too, could "[i]nvite the one and only Paul Whiteman into your living room this Sunday night." Though he consistently proved uncomfortable and awkward reading cue cards and staring into a camera, Whiteman's enthusiasm for producing music on television was clearly genuine as is evident in episodes of his longer-running shows *TV Teen Club* and *Goodyear Revue*, which are the focus of this chapter. After these shows were discontinued, *On the Boardwalk* briefly extended the youth musical competition format of *TV Teen Club*, and *America's Greatest Bands* allowed him, again briefly, to continue to promote high-level professional musical performance on television and to host big-name guests as had been the aim of *Goodyear Revue*. *TV Teen Club* and *Goodyear Revue* diverged most strikingly at the intersection of music and race.

Prior to his work in television, Whiteman had almost never performed with Black musicians. As Elijah Wald notes, "The one black performer Whiteman featured onstage in the 1920s was a 'pickaninny' dancer and banjo player, ten-year-old Edwin 'Snowball' Harris." Wald also remarks that "though [Whiteman] occasionally appeared with black musicians in later years and made a record with Billie Holiday, he maintained an all-white band even after a lot of other bandleaders had integrated."[5] Whiteman did record with Paul Robeson and Billie Holiday, hired a few prominent Black arrangers (William Grant Still and Don Redman), featured the music of Reginald Foresythe, and commissioned two pieces from Duke Ellington.[6] Don Rayno has argued that Whiteman's relationships with Black band leaders were cordial and were based on sincere mutual respect.[7] Christi Jay Wells, in a study of Whiteman's reception in the Black press, offers a particularly insightful assessment of the divergent critical views on Whiteman's relationship with Black music and musicians.[8] It is striking that Whiteman's work in the visual medium of television would, in part, represent a step toward integration given that his prior appearances on the silver screen may serve as the most egregious evidence of his outsized role (however indirect it may have been) in whitewashing jazz history.

The 1930 technicolor spectacular musical revue, *The King of Jazz*, typically serves as "exhibit A" in these discussions. As Krin Gabbard put it nearly two decades ago, "A more elaborate, more thorough denial of the African American role in jazz is difficult to imagine."[9] Though the film's initial cartoon sequence depicting Whiteman on safari in Africa and Whiteman's own spoken introduction preparing us for the *Rhapsody in Blue* sequence—"the most primitive and the most modern musical elements are combined in this rhapsody, for jazz was born in the African jungle, to the beating of the voodoo drum"—indirectly suggest Black contributions to "modern American music," the film otherwise presents an entirely white version of American music. Though some viewers then, and more recently, assumed that the performer dancing on a drum as an introduction to Gershwin's piece was a Black man, the white dancer Jacques Cartier performed this "voodoo" dance in full body black paint.[10] The only Black performer to appear in the film was a young girl referred to (in racist comic fashion) as "Snowdrop," who appears in a visual gag sitting on Whiteman's knee, in comic contrast to the white heterosexual adult couples otherwise depicted in the scene (see fig. 8.1). As Michael Rogin notes, the comedy here relies on both racial and age differences: "Repeating the paternalist racial relation established in the opening cartoon, the interracial couple is safely set off, as white father and black child, from the adult, dancing partners."[11] The total exclusion of Black music in the film is most blatant in the climactic concluding number, "The Melting Pot of Music," in which musicians from virtually every European nationality or ethnic group are presented as having contributed to American music.[12] The sequence commences with the film's narrator proclaiming, "America is a melting pot of music wherein the melodies of all nations are fused into one great new rhythm, Jazz!" At the end we see Whiteman magically stirring the pot into

FIGURE 8.1 Whiteman and "Snowdrop" in the *King of Jazz* (1927). Screenshot.

which all the groups of white performers have rather bizarrely descended.[13] Though his later television shows would, in contrast to the *King of Jazz*, include Black musicians or at least Black music, other elements of this early sound film may be traced in Whiteman's versions of musical television. The variety structure and diversity of acts presented in this film not only draw on Whiteman's staged performances of the 1920s but also prefigure the format of *TV Teen Club*. Even the famous Whiteman potato-head image appearing on the band members' jackets in *King of Jazz* reappeared on the sweaters of the teenage chorus members in *TV Teen Club*. Furthermore, the lavish production numbers in the film were clearly emulated in episodes of *Goodyear Revue* two decades later, as will be discussed below.

Nationally broadcast in the early civil rights era, both *TV Teen Club* and *Goodyear Revue* were shaped by racial politics. For its time, *TV Teen Club* was a remarkably integrated show, and its filming, scripts, and promotional materials indicate that integration was a conscious goal. Multiple episodes included Black contestants, occasionally performing in integrated groups, and some of these children became adult stars (Leslie Uggams, Diahann Carroll, Annette Swinson). The chorus included approximately 10 percent Black teenagers, and the live audience of several thousand young people, which stayed each week for a dance party, was integrated as well. Though the show was not without aspects of racial prejudice, as detailed below, its progressive efforts were recognized at the time and resulted in Whiteman receiving several awards, including from the Black press. In contrast, *Goodyear Revue* was rigorously segregated, avoiding Black performers almost entirely. This avoidance shaped particular episodes in peculiar ways, as we shall see.

Whiteman held significant artistic control over these shows and helped determine who would appear. By simultaneously embracing integration (on *TV Teen Club*, *On the Boardwalk*, and *America's Greatest Bands*) and maintaining segregation (on *Goodyear Revue*), Whiteman furthered his mixed legacy with regards to acknowledging the contributions of Black musicians to "modern American music." This chapter focuses first on Whiteman's embrace of teen culture and aspirations for integration in *TV Teen Club*. I then detail the more middlebrow aesthetics and evident segregation of *Goodyear Revue* before concluding with a consideration of Whiteman's lasting impact on American music television.

TV Teen Club: "Bringing You Teen Stars of Tomorrow"

In creating *TV Teen Club*, Whiteman was inspired by two goals: combating juvenile delinquency and continuing his career-long quest to discover new musical talent. As retold by Whiteman in several interviews and in the 1949

Paramount Studios documentary *The Lambertville Story*, he worked with local civic leaders in Lambertville, New Jersey, in 1947 to hold weekly dances on Saturday nights to dissuade teens from engaging in more problematic activities.[14] In this film, Whiteman provides voice-over as we see reenactments related to the founding of the dances along with footage that indicates the dances were racially integrated. During a sequence depicting delinquent behavior, we hear, perhaps inevitably during this period of American cinema, nondiegetic jazz played on muted trumpet. Teenage delinquency arose as a national concern in the late 1940s, and afterschool "teen canteens" and television itself were viewed as potent weapons against this set of problems.[15] The film also emphasized that the dances helped to bridge the generational divide that was said to have emerged after the war. Whiteman repeatedly boasted of the several thousand youths who attended his dances each week and the creation of similar teen clubs and dances throughout the country based on his model. Throughout the show's run, Whiteman consistently emphasized its goals of social uplift alongside his never-ending quest to discover the "stars of tomorrow," as the opening voice-over announcer promised in the 1952 season.[16]

Whiteman had held amateur teen talent competitions on radio and in conjunction with his concert touring since the early 1930s, such as his Youth of America Contest, which was launched in January 1932 and held in each city of his tour with winners appearing in his radio broadcast the following week.[17] These talent-contest winners included such major figures as Johnny Mercer and, in a rare example of integration, the legendary Black tap dancer Teddy Hale, who, at age ten, was featured on a June 21, 1936, Whiteman broadcast—the presentation of tap via radio is itself an interesting topic to consider. Whiteman's contests even inspired a feature film starring Mickey Rooney and Judy Garland. This 1940 movie, *Strike Up the Band!* is centered on a group of teenage musicians who aim to participate in a Whiteman contest, and the film features Whiteman, as himself, delivering words of advice to Jimmy, the young would-be band leader played by Rooney, emphasizing the importance of leadership and the role of rhythm in society. In full Whitemanesque spirit, Jimmy dreams of making America great through music—a vision that results in a rather surreal stop-motion sequence in which pieces of fruit are transformed into an orchestra. Whiteman remained committed to his idealistic view of the potential for music in shaping the lives of young people. With *TV Teen Club* he continued to play a role in selecting the finalists who would appear each week, following an initial vetting process led by the producer of the first four seasons, children's musical television veteran Edmund "Skipper" Dawes (see fig. 8.2).

TV Teen Club was broadcast each week from the 103rd Engineer's Armory in Philadelphia (later from Town Hall and then from the large WFIL studio

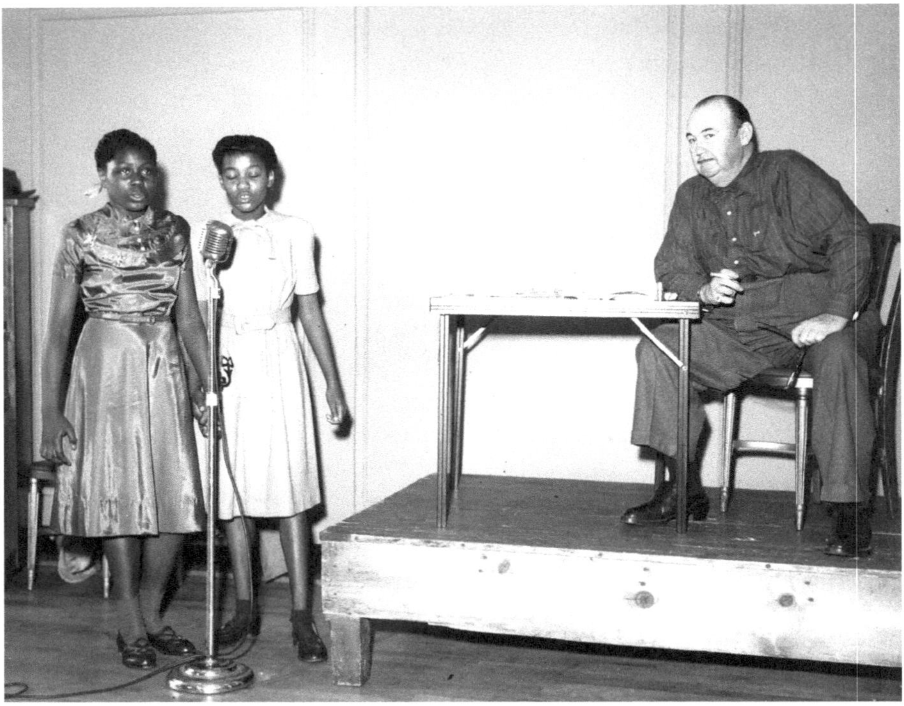

FIGURE 8.2 Whiteman auditioning two Black teenage girls. Publicity still, Howard and Zausner Photography, Paul Whiteman Collection, Williams College Special Collections.

B) by ABC in the Northeast and Midwest as a sixty-minute talent competition, later reduced to thirty minutes. Each live broadcast was then immediately followed by the Whiteman-sponsored weekly dance attended by a couple thousand, which was not broadcast. Kinescope recordings were sent to stations in the West and South for broadcasting the following week. The show premiered on April 2, 1949, and the final episode aired on March 28, 1954, Whiteman's sixty-fourth birthday. In its first several seasons the show was produced through the summers as well, and it was one of the first programs selected for national broadcast by ABC in 1951 when that became possible. Rayno's detailed chronology of Whiteman's career indicates that there was a total of 243 *TV Teen Club* episodes. I have been able to locate extant recordings for only 18 episodes, of which I have studied 16, or 6.6 percent of the total (see table 8.1). However, I have also derived much valuable information about numerous other episodes through scripts, published announcements, reviews, memoirs, and so forth, which allows me to offer more general remarks on the show's evolving format and style.[18]

TABLE 8.1 Extant *TV Teen Club* episodes and location of video recordings

Date	Location
March 18, 1950	University of Georgia Brown Media Archive and Peabody Award Collections
March 25, 1950	University of Georgia Brown Media Archive and Peabody Award Collections
April 1, 1950	University of Georgia Brown Media Archive and Peabody Award Collections
April 8, 1950	University of Georgia Brown Media Archive and Peabody Award Collections
April 15, 1950	University of Georgia Brown Media Archive and Peabody Award Collections
April 22, 1950	University of Georgia Brown Media Archive and Peabody Award Collections
April 29, 1950	University of Georgia Brown Media Archive and Peabody Award Collections
May 20, 1950	University of Georgia Brown Media Archive and Peabody Award Collections
June 3, 1950	University of Georgia Brown Media Archive and Peabody Award Collections
June 17, 1950	University of Georgia Brown Media Archive and Peabody Award Collections
October 14, 1950	University of Georgia Brown Media Archive and Peabody Award Collections
November [?], 1951	Library of Congress J. Fred and Leslie W. MacDonald Collection
January 12, 1952	UCLA Film and Television Archive
February 9, 1952	Library of Congress J. Fred and Leslie W. MacDonald Collection and on YouTube
March 28, 1953	The Paley Center for Media Archive
May 9, 1953	The Paley Center for Media Archive
October 3, 1953	University of Georgia Brown Media Archive and Peabody Award Collections
February 6, 1954	The Paley Center for Media Archive

Whiteman was fully engaged in this program: participating in rehearsals for the production numbers, staying each Saturday night for the dance, and hosting members of the chorus at his farm for cookouts, pool parties, and hayrides. Onscreen, Whiteman projected a kindly paternalistic image, though his frequent on-air comments regarding the attractiveness of adolescent girl contestants strike us now as in questionable taste and behavior. In addition to providing a socially acceptable activity for teenagers, several episodes indicate that the show was also shaped by Cold War political concerns. Multiple episodes emphasized patriotic themes, and Whiteman launched a One World Talent Project, which aimed to feature selected teenage performers from various United Nation member countries. This project was announced in 1952 by the US Information Service and was sponsored by Royal Dutch Airlines and the American Association for the United Nations.[19] During the May 9, 1953, *TV Teen Club* episode, Whiteman was presented with an award from the Freedoms Foundation of Valley Forge—a nonprofit devoted to instilling civic responsibility in American students—and the citation was clearly couched in Cold War patriotic terms. In bestowing the organization's national award, the president of Freedoms Foundation praised Whiteman for having brought out a "wholesome love of God and country" and commended the teens present for helping "tell the American story" during these "critical times with communism swaggering around the world." Ninety boys and girls from Freedoms Foundation from thirty-three states were in the studio for this episode, and Whiteman notes, "The foundation brings them in once a year."[20]

The show's format altered somewhat with each season, but typically each episode consisted of contestants performing in alternation with the *TV Teen Club* chorus (a hundred-member ensemble by my count), solo vocalist regulars who were former contestants (such as Sonny Graham and Junie Keegan), a production number or skit, a dance by the Teenettes or song by the Three Sharps, and spoken commercial plugs for the sponsor. Episodes culminated with voting by the audience, measured by an applause meter, and declaration of the winning performer who would then be invited to return to compete again the following week. Whiteman and his teenage cohost, initially his daughter Margo, exchanged light banter and briefly introduced each act. Whiteman occasionally engaged directly with the young performers, marching in with a group of tappers and spotting a seven-year-old toe dancer on March 20, 1950, or appearing in skits with the select chorus group. The studio band accompanying most of the contestants and the production numbers was almost never visible onscreen and was made up of professional musicians. The camera frequently cut to the teen chorus, which served as an onscreen audience, though in some recordings the presence of a larger offscreen audience can be heard, murmuring in particular during the ads. The chorus and audience consistently responded most enthusiastically to heartthrob crooners, performances of contemporary popular music, and erotically charged dancing, but they also cheered on the cute young contestants as well.

Fully in the old variety show tradition, the range of acts included tumblers, jazz combos, classical pianists, accordionists, many tap dancers, ballerinas, jugglers, gymnasts, puppeteers, and banjo players, among others. The competitions rather oddly pitted very young children against contestants in their late teens, a solo pianist against a baton twirler, "muscle men" acrobats versus very young girl tappers, a classical violinist versus a yodeling cowgirl. Exotic dances were particularly common. For example, the April 1, 1950, episode featured different groups of white children performing a Mexican hat dance, a Spanish dance, and a Hawaiian dance, prompting Whiteman's teenage cohost Nancy Lewis to exclaim that they were "going international tonight." Reflecting a general 1950s interest in Hawaii, hula-style dances appeared on multiple episodes. A somewhat risqué "jungle dance" performed in silhouette by two older teenagers to exotica-style music on the October 14, 1950, episode prompted Whiteman to declare "we're going really arty." The production style was decidedly low budget until later in the show's five-year run. The contestants on both the TV and radio versions of the show were largely from the Philadelphia–New York City corridor and included an astonishing number of musicians who went on to become rock 'n' roll, country, jazz, or pop stars or Hollywood, Broadway, and television actors, such as Frankie Avalon, Diahann Carroll, Dion DiMucci, Timmy Everett, Joey Foreman, Charlie Gracie, Patsy Grady, Bobby Gregg, Keith Jarrett, Junie Keegan, Nancy Lewis, Bobby Lord, Mike Mainieri, Peter Nero, Bernie Rich, Bobby Rydell, Annette Swinson, and Leslie Uggams.[21] Dick Clark joined the show as a regular announcer for Tootsie Roll in 1952.

Whiteman repeatedly emphasized that the show was run by and for the teenagers. However, in the only other scholarly study to date of *TV Teen Club*, Jeff Martin has argued that the show was not actually aimed at teenagers but at their parents.[22] Martin bases his claim on two observations: that much of the music performed by the children dated from ten to fifteen years prior and that the show's sponsors, Nash and Kelvinator, produced cars and appliances that the teens competed for but that only their parents would fully appreciate. Martin bases his discussion of the show on only eight episodes and, therefore, failed to note that Tootsie Roll, with Clark as the young on-air announcer, was a sponsor in later seasons and that during the period of Griffin Shoe Polish's sponsorship, the live commercials emphasized the importance of shiny shoes for teenage dating. Furthermore, American children have historically and continue to perform and consume older popular music, and contestants selected and rehearsed their music and dances themselves prior to their *TV Teen Club* auditions. For example, teenagers belting out "Y.M.C.A." at social events today are performing a song now nearly half a century old, and children continue to select both older *and* more contemporary songs for talent shows and parties and to accompany their skating competitions and dance performances. In several episodes we can even faintly hear the audience singing along to old ragtime songs that accompanied dancing contestants. On April 1, 1950, a fourteen-year-old boy performed Irving Berlin's 1911 "Alexander's Ragtime Band" on saxophone, and the young audience enthusiastically sang along. It has been a fundamental fact of American musical life over the past two hundred years that "out of date" hit songs never really vanish but, instead, are reworked decade after decade.

Martin also fails to note the multiple performances of contemporary jump blues and honky-tonk songs on the show (I discuss some of these performances of contemporary popular music below, but note here Charlie Gracie's 1952 rendition of "Rock the Joint" as but one example). In addition, just as Whiteman had "jazzed" the classics with his orchestra, several contestants performed up-tempo boogie-woogie versions of classical works, such as Aram Khachaturian's "Sabre Dance." Though the offscreen audience and the visible chorus did respond positively to older music, they consistently reacted most enthusiastically to contemporary styles. For example, when the adult performer Jimmy Blaine substituted for the ailing Whiteman as cohost on the March 25, 1950, episode, he opened the show by singing the first verse of the 1949 hit "Chattanoogie Shoe Shine Boy," and the audience went wild. Martin's claim that *TV Teen Club* ultimately reveals anxieties about teens rather than presenting actual teen culture circa 1950 also ignores the rather open acknowledgment of the sex appeal of some of the performers as evidenced by the audience reactions and by comments (such as "wow, wow, wow, wow!") from Whiteman himself.

How successful was *TV Teen Club* in achieving Whiteman's stated goals and as a form of televised entertainment? Given its five-year run, numerous positive notices in the press and awards, featured advertising, a string of corporate sponsorships, and selection for national broadcasting, it seems clear that ABC felt the show was successful in commercial terms. Gauging the response of the live studio audience suggests that at least those teenagers enjoyed attending the show and the dances on Saturday nights. As noted above, numerous future stars did appear as children on the show, and, in some cases, their appearance on *TV Teen Club* directly helped to launch or further their budding careers. It is more difficult to measure the success of the show in living rooms across the country. However, one study provides some limited information. In 1950 and 1951 Paul Witty, a professor of education at Northwestern University, ran surveys in Evanston, Illinois, to assess opinion on the impact of television on children. His report was published by the National Council of Teachers of English.[23] He surveyed twenty-one hundred elementary school pupils in 1950 and fourteen hundred in 1951 and queried teachers and parents. In 1951 students in grades 1 to 3 (six to eight years old) listed the *Paul Whiteman Revue* (*Goodyear Revue*) as the fourteenth-most-popular show, and students in grades 4 to 6 listed it in second place and *TV Teen Club* in eighteenth place. This result among younger children at first appears surprising; however, these children likely had less control over the TV dial. In addition, *Goodyear Revue* was broadcast from 7:00 to 7:30 p.m. on Sundays and *TV Teen Club* from 8:00 to 9:00 p.m. (initially from 9:00 to 10:00 p.m.) on Saturdays—perhaps, the earlier time slot allowed them to watch *Goodyear Revue* with their parents. Students in grades 7 and 8 did not list either show in their top 10. Unfortunately, Witty did not survey high school students—*TV Teen Club*'s prime target audience. Parents ranked *TV Teen Club* as the seventh "most desirable" show for their children to view, but they did not list either show in the top 10 that they enjoyed viewing themselves. Teachers did not list either show as being most desirable for children. This limited study proves ambiguous in gauging the viewership for both of Whiteman's shows during the early 1950s, though all other forms of evidence indicate success for both shows.

As Martin rightly notes, the production style of *TV Teen Club* changed rather dramatically in the show's final season, perhaps signaling a change in its target audience.[24] Dawes left the program after May 1953, and a more formal format with celebrity adult judges and talent agents opining on the performances was adopted for the final season. This new style is evident in the October 3, 1953, episode, which was framed as a "graduation" for three teenage performers, including Nancy Lewis and the drummer Bobby Gregg. The episode began, as did all of the *Goodyear Revue* episodes and at least some *TV Teen Club* episodes starting in 1952, with Whiteman conducting a large professional ensemble in an excerpt from *Rhapsody in Blue*. The entire piece was also led by Whiteman on this episode with a teenage solo pianist. After each performance, agents phoned in to offer contracts on air to the three performers. Whiteman, apparently, was not comfortable with how the show had changed and felt the fancy production style was not in line with the intended spirit of the show and that the teenagers had lost control.[25] However, Whiteman did enthusiastically lead a four-week live show in Las Vegas and then in Reno in June 1953 featuring *TV Teen Club* regulars. Furthermore, a gradual increase in production values is evident when comparing episodes from 1950 and 1952—by 1952 the show began with a carefully crafted montage of performance footage, some performances were supported with simple sets and props, and the filming was more elaborate with multiple camera angles and closeups.[26] In the 1952 season the studio set was more elaborate than in earlier seasons, with teenagers seated at tables as though to suggest a nightclub setting. By its final year, *TV Teen Club* had become somewhat similar in style to Whiteman's other major show, which ran concurrently, *The Paul Whiteman Goodyear Revue*.

TV Teen Club and Race

TV Teen Club's degree of racial integration is perhaps the clearest indication that the show was aimed at a teenage viewership, rather than at the more conservative adult national audience targeted by *Goodyear Revue*.[27] Integration was an explicit goal of the program. In an article, "Teen-Agers Are My Favorite People," Whiteman stated that the aim of *TV Teen Club* was "to provide eager and talented teen-agers with a place and a show to demonstrate their natural gifts of talent and to help build a sound social life" and to bring "together teen-agers of different racial, religious, and national backgrounds. This, I feel, is very important. They can work, play and sing together."[28] WFIL-TV Philadelphia (the ABC affiliate that produced *TV Teen Club*) in a submission to the general awards program of Freedoms Foundation listed four goals for the program: "Talent Development," "Wholesome Recreation," "General Welfare," and "Citizenship Training." The application highlights the show's inclusion of patriotic numbers and expressions of Americana—including a June 30, 1951, script for an Independence Day production number—and emphasizes that the club was "self-governing" and democratic. The application also proclaims that "membership in the chorus is open to all teenagers, regardless of color, training, or background."[29] This aim shaped multiple aspects of the production, as is evident in medium shots of the large chorus, which appear deliberately and consistently to include Black members in the frame, and in the inclusion of Black teenagers in the select choral group, which was often featured in production numbers in the first seasons and initially functioned as the judging panel. In some episodes, Whiteman appears alongside Black children. The June 3, 1950, episode includes a mock high-school-graduation production number for Griffin Shoe Polish, with Whiteman serving as the "principal" awarding certificates of merit. In this skit two of the nine "graduates" are Black teenage boys, and Whiteman awards the first of three certificates to one of the Black teenagers.[30] Whiteman scats as the group sings a graduation hymn. In an episode from later in the program's run, a Black chorus member in costume as a delivery man—a rather subservient position—delivers one of the youngest white performers to the stage (see fig. 8.3). The brief montage that opens each episode (at least in 1952) deliberately included footage of a tall Black male teenager tap dancing, and shots of the postshow dances present Black couples dancing right next to white couples and longer-range shots reveal a thoroughly integrated crowd.[31] One wonders whether the governor of Georgia, Herman Talmadge, had *TV Teen Club* in mind in 1952 when he objected to broadcasts showing Black and white children dancing together and threatened to lead a boycott of products sold by the sponsors of such programs.[32] In several seasons we never see the studio band on screen, and evidence suggests the group included one adult Black musician at least in the 1952 season.[33]

Black musical presence in *TV Teen Club* played out along a continuum. Even in episodes that did not include Black contestants, Black music was frequently present. Several white groups performed jazz and R&B numbers, such as Nat King Cole's "Straighten Up and Fly Right," performed by a white male trio on the April 8, 1950, episode, and Louis Jordan's jump blues hit "Choo Choo Ch'Boogie" by a seven-piece white male band on the April 29, 1950, episode. In a few cases, *TV Teen Club* included integrated groups as

FIGURE 8.3 *TV Teen Club* special-delivery skit. Publicity still, Otto C. Prinz, photographer, Paul Whiteman Collection, Williams College Special Collections.

contestants.[34] A trio of fourteen- to sixteen-year-old boys from Philadelphia appeared on the March 18, 1950, episode. The tall Black banjo player, white accordionist, and white guitarist dubbed themselves Two Dots and a Dash, a phrase of contemporary slang referring to an order of two fried eggs and a strip of bacon but with an obvious and rather clever racial significance for this group. As they begin, the camera cuts directly from the cohosts to a closeup of the Black banjoist's hand. The three boys in matching Western-style shirts sing with a slight country twang (fig. 8.4). The song they perform, "Just Because," was written and first recorded in 1929 and would become a hit for Elvis Presley in 1954. Whiteman declared their performance "mighty solid, very, very solid," and they came in a close second on that episode. Whiteman shook each of their hands at the end. (Vincent Van Dyke, a Black thirteen-year-old from Eddington, Pennsylvania, also performed "Just Because" on the show the very next week.)

Most notable was the show's inclusion of Black contestants. Half of the episodes I have viewed include at least one Black contestant, and newspaper announcements—particularly, in the Black press—and other sources indicate that, at minimum, twenty-four episodes had at least one Black contestant. Though this number included a female classical pianist and a group of

FIGURE 8.4 Two Dots and a Dash on *TV Teen Club*, March 18, 1950. Screenshot.

tumblers, most of the Black contestants performed contemporary songs.[35] When Errol Smith, an eight-year-old male tap dancer, won the grand prize in January 1952, E. B. Rea reported in the *Afro-American*, "Paul Whiteman's TV Teen Club demonstrated Christmas Week that it is truly democratic when eight-year-old Errol Smith of Gary, Ind., walked off with the top prize."[36] The major actress and vocalist Diahann Carroll was also a winner when she appeared on the show in her teens. She was later joined in the 1954 all-Black-cast film *Carmen Jones* by another *TV Teen Club* alum who went on in the entertainment business, Michael St. John (aka Sandy Lewis).[37] Alfred Prettyman, who would first work as a professional opera singer before becoming a publisher, academic philosopher, and cofounder of the Society for the Study of Africana Philosophy, competed on the show in 1950.[38] It is not possible to identify each of the Black children who appeared on *TV Teen Club*. For instance, in the May 9, 1953, episode, cohost Lewis sings a number about mothers. The camera then immediately cuts to a Black boy singing "Mom, I love her" in a full crooner voice and then to a younger white boy, who, resembling an Irish tenor, also sings about his mother.

Three performances by Black contestants are particularly significant. The April 8, 1950, episode included Mildred Iris (later known as Mildred Blyden Davis), a fourteen-year-old Black contestant from Bermuda, whose travel had been sponsored by Colonial Airlines and who sang the 1949 boogie-woogie novelty song "Ragg Mopp" with the audience clapping along with her on the backbeat. Following her enthusiastic reception, Whiteman exclaims, "Oh ho! Looks to be like they know that bop down there." The rating of the audience's energetic applause at the end of this episode seems rather flawed to me, and Mildred officially came in second instead of first. However, she returned to a "hero's welcome" in Bermuda, with parties held in her honor, and she was known for years as "Mrs. Ragg Mopp."[39]

The most notable Black contestant to have appeared on *TV Teen Club* was eight-year-old Leslie Uggams, who came in first place on multiple episodes in February 1952 and in the 1960s was the featured star on the *Sing Along with Mitch* show. In her first appearance on *TV Teen Club*, Uggams performed the jump blues song "Rock-a-Bye Baby," as she held a white doll in a setting depicting a baby's room, with large alphabet blocks and suitable decorations on the backdrop (see fig. 8.5). She was accompanied by a full band, which remained offscreen. The enthusiastic audience response is evident throughout as we can hear them clapping to the beat. Uggams won a refrigerator on this episode, and Whiteman refers to her as "a mighty cute little girl" (see fig. 8.6). It is notable that Whiteman was presented on this episode with an award from the National Conference of Christians and Jews for "bringing together young people of all backgrounds" and "helping to build

FIGURE 8.5 Leslie Uggams on *TV Teen Club*, February 1952. Screenshot.

FIGURE 8.6 Leslie Uggams with Nancy Lewis and Whiteman announcing her win, February 1952. Screenshot.

a prejudice-free America." Uggams's success on the show was celebrated in the Black press.[40] However, later in life Uggams related that due to her race she had not been allowed to win the grand prize on her final appearance. Apparently, a member of the production team informed her that given Smith's grand-prize win a month earlier, the show could not allow another Black child to win so soon, and so the applause meter was rigged against her at the end of her final episode.[41] Uggams's experience is not the only indication of racist strains appearing in *TV Teen Club.*

Running counter to the show's professed progressive aims, elements of racism appeared on multiple episodes. For example, a March 31, 1951, article in the Baltimore *Afro-American* notes that Whiteman had received an award for his service to youth of all races in a recent episode but that this justified recognition was tarnished by the fact that a "mammy" singer "wearing burnt cork and white lips" appeared next on the show. The critic, E. B. Rea, invited his readers to write directly to their local station, to ABC, and to Whiteman himself to ask whether that performance was an example of "Americanism or slurism."[42] In a similar vein, six young white girls from the Dorothy Palmer dance studio in Newark, New Jersey, performed as guests on April 22, 1950, wearing bonnets and executing some cakewalk moves and cabaret-style high kicks. They then turn away from the audience, revealing blackface on the back of their bonnets as they dance (see fig. 8.7). (This choreography and the costumes might have been inspired by the cakewalk scene in the 1943 film *Stormy Weather.*) The camera zooms in and pans down the line to emphasize their blackface performance. After each girl spins back around to reveal their actual white faces, the audience yells, "Yay!" A brief shot of the applauding chorus with one Black girl member decidedly not clapping follows the performance. Whiteman then declares, "They're lovely guests," Nancy Lewis responds "Kinda cute, huh?" and Whiteman concludes: "Ah,

FIGURE 8.7 Girls with blackface costumes on *TV Teen Club*, April 22, 1950. Screenshot.

that was a hunk of nice little guests." Whiteman seems ever so slightly discomfited by their performance as he emphasized that they were guests, not contestants.

One of the final episodes of *TV Teen Club* that was broadcast on February 6, 1954, offers a particularly clear example of the politically progressive and the regressive, of the contemporary and the nostalgic nature of this show and of Whiteman himself. In line with the show's civic goals, Whiteman notes that it is the forty-fourth anniversary of the Boy Scouts of America. He introduces an eleven-year-old Black contestant by stating that "this little sprout" has a voice that plenty of professional singers would be proud of. His serious and sincere tone and demeanor sets the stage for her powerful performance of "I Believe (for Every Drop of Rain That Falls)," a song first broadcast on television and recorded by Jane Froman (a *Goodyear Revue* regular guest) just over a year prior. The performance of this song on *TV Teen Club* took place during a charged period in the civil rights era—the US Supreme Court's *Brown v. Board of Education* decision would be announced that May—and this context must have shaped both the song's production and reception. The young vocalist was Annette Swinson (aka Annette Smith), who had a subsequent career as a member of the Veneers and then the Chantels. The filming accords her great dignity as she performs in front of a stained-glass-window set piece as though in church, with Whiteman leading the orchestra onscreen. She wears a formal blouse and skirt, pearl necklace, and two ribbons in her hair, and the power of her strong alto voice is emphasized by camera closeups of her intensely emotive expression and body movements. The camera pulls back for her final musical climax.

As noted, in its later seasons *TV Teen Club* had become much more formal and professionalized and was filmed with higher production values. Whiteman appears on this episode in formal attire and, as with all broadcasts of *Goodyear Revue*, conducts the professional ensemble in an excerpt from *Rhapsody in Blue* to conclude the show. The three professional judges call in their comments, an element of distanciation that serves to heighten their authority.[43] Whiteman mentions that several auditions were held in preparation for this episode of *TV Teen Club*, and he seems to push for the teenage female pianist who performed Liszt's *Hungarian Rhapsody* and who was followed by a flaming baton twirler. (The pianist won, and Swinson was accorded second place by the professional judges.) The range of contestants is not surprising for this show, but an extended Tootsie Roll ad performed by a group of adult performers and set in a tavern in Elizabethan England, complete with a drinking song, comes as a shock, as though a production number from a *Goodyear Revue* broadcast had been mistakenly inserted into an episode of *TV Teen Club*.

Middlebrow Glamour and Exoticism on *Goodyear Revue*

The Paul Whiteman Goodyear Revue is a prime example of what John Howland has dubbed middlebrow "luxe pop."[44] This show, broadcast live "without pause or applause" from ABC's mammoth studio B in New York City starting November 6, 1949, and with a final broadcast on March 30, 1952, exhibited fairly high production values with extensive sets and active and innovative camera work, though occasional mishaps (a briefly visible boom mic or an inaudible soloist) attest to the perils of live television. The show's structure consisted of multiple production numbers, performed by the chorus and dancers, that flowed fairly seamlessly one to the next interrupted by performances of an often-clever Goodyear jingle number and more extended infomercials for the sponsor ("the greatest name in rubber"). Whiteman, "the greatest name in modern American music," began and ended each episode conducting an excerpt from *Rhapsody in Blue* and most of the music featured on the show was drawn from Broadway and Tin Pan Alley numbers of the 1920s to 1940s along with some operetta arias and classical orchestral pieces. The orchestra consisted of a full dance band plus strings, with a larger ensemble and more extended screen time for episodes culminating with performances of light classical pieces. (I note that a woman served as first violinist throughout much of the show's run, which, of course, was unusual for this period.) Two vocalists, the romantic "versatile" baritone Earl Wrightson and the "vivacious" and "pert" comic soprano Maureen Cannon ("our Goodyear Girl"), appeared as regular soloists along with frequent guest appearances by teenager Keegan (in the initial season), Mimi Benzell, and Froman.[45] Some of the most famous guest performers included Peggy Lee, Rosemary Clooney, Mel Tormé, and Hoagy Carmichael. The choreography, blending elements of midcentury modern dance and Broadway, was particularly distinctive. The celebrated choreographer Valerie Bettis created the show's dance sequences in its first months, followed by Frank Westbrook as choreographer from February 1950 to the end of the series in March 1952.[46] The show received positive reviews with particular focus on its staging and choreography. For instance, *Billboard* cited *Goodyear Revue* as "one of the best-produced in video. For sheer smoothness, integration, and movement, it is hard to match"—"integration" referring here to the combination of art forms, not to race—and Arthur Todd opined, "The program 'moves' with a notable animation and there also appears to be a greater synthesis of dialogue, music, song and dance." He stated that the show's success was in part due to the fact that Westbrook was responsible for both staging and choreography.[47]

Episodes of *The Goodyear Revue* were structured by announced themes, ranging from holidays (July 4th, Halloween, Thanksgiving, Christmas), historical periods (the Gay Nineties, ancient Rome, the time of Louis XIV), "hall of fame" tributes to specific composers (Victor Herbert, George Gershwin, Irving Berlin, Cole Porter), places (New York City at night, New Orleans, Swiss Alps), to more eccentric thematic ideas (farm life, water, superstitions, an air force salute). Of the approximately one-hundred episodes, I have viewed twenty-nine and have seen or heard excerpts from several others in addition to gaining information about additional episodes through reviews and announcements.[48] Table 8.2 is a list of the known surviving episodes.[49]

Whiteman was in his early sixties during the run of *Goodyear Revue*, and many of the episodes, particularly the "hall of fame" tributes to American

TABLE 8.2 Extant *Goodyear Revue* episodes with episode theme and location of video recordings

Date	Episode Theme	Location
March 5, 1950	Spanish	Paley Center for Media Archive
March 19, 1950	Vienna	Paley Center for Media Archive
December 10, 1950	George Gershwin	State Historical Society of Missouri; Library of Congress J. Fred and Leslie W. MacDonald Collection
February 11, 1951	Jerome Kern	Paley Center for Media Archive
September 2, 1951	the city at night*	University of Georgia Brown Media Archive and Peabody Award Collections
September 9, 1951	Gershwin, *Rhapsody in Blue*	Paley Center for Media Archive; Whiteman Collection
September 16, 1951	romance and rhythm; Ravel's *Bolero*	Whiteman Collection
September 23, 1951	the South; Grieg's Piano Concerto	Whiteman Collection; Library of Congress J. Fred and Leslie W. MacDonald Collection
September 30, 1951	Gus Kahn	Whiteman Collection
October 7, 1951	Spain; Rimsky-Korsakov, *Capriccio Espagnol*	Whiteman Collection
October 14, 1951	country style	Whiteman Collection
October 21, 1951	Blues	Whiteman Collection
October 28, 1951	Lorenz Hart	Whiteman Collection
November 4, 1951	far-away places	Whiteman Collection

Date	Episode Theme	Location
November 11, 1951	an artist's life	Whiteman Collection
November 18, 1951	seafaring/waterfronts of America	Paley Center for Media Archive; Whiteman Collection; State Historical Society of Missouri
November 25, 1951	Harold Arlen	Whiteman Collection
December 2, 1951	moods of the orchestra	Whiteman Collection; Library of Congress J. Fred and Leslie W. MacDonald Collection
December 9, 1951	fashion salon	Whiteman Collection (audio only); Library of Congress J. Fred and Leslie W. MacDonald Collection
December 16, 1951	astrology/zodiac	Whiteman Collection
January 6, 1952	100th telecast celebration	Whiteman Collection
January 13, 1952	Fairytales	Whiteman Collection; UCLA Film & Television Archive
January 27, 1952	Harry Warren	Whiteman Collection
February 3, 1952	newspaper headlines	Whiteman Collection
February 10, 1952	winter/Alpine	Whiteman Collection
February 17, 1952	Paris	Whiteman Collection
March 2, 1952	Arthur Schwartz	Whiteman Collection
March 9, 1952	Hollywood	Whiteman Collection
March 16, 1952	Gay Nineties	Whiteman Collection

Note: The Paley Center for Media Archive is located in New York City, the State Historical Society of Missouri in Columbia, Missouri, and the Whiteman Collection is held at Williams College, Williamstown, Massachusetts.
* This is a summertime-revue episode without Whiteman.

songwriters, express nostalgia and a decidedly middlebrow aesthetic. Some episodes aimed at a higher rung on the cultural ladder as Whiteman led the orchestra in classical works such as Edvard Grieg's Piano Concerto and Maurice Ravel's *Bolero*. The elevated production style and high-quality musical and choreographed performances are impressive given the tight weekly production schedule. Nostalgia and middlebrow aesthetics are particularly evident in two *Goodyear Revue* episodes celebrating Gershwin and, specifically, Whiteman's association with Gershwin. In a 1949 article on the potential of television for music, Whiteman was credited with "discovering" Gershwin and celebrated for "his adaptation of his skill and knowledge of serious music to music of a lighter type, simpler music, which won him the title of 'The King of Jazz.'"[50]

The December 10, 1950, *Goodyear Revue* episode—airing more than a dozen years after the composer's death—highlighted Whiteman's role in Gershwin's career in a rather didactic manner. Whiteman is joined in this episode by twenty-five-year-old actor Jack Lemmon for brief scripted discussions of Gershwin's career that serve as transitions between numbers. It is evident that Lemmon was brought in as an interlocutor for this one episode to motivate, somewhat artificially, Whiteman's discussion of Gershwin. Whiteman educates Lemmon and, thus, the audience at home about Gershwin's early career, and Froman sings "Embraceable You." Froman then quips to Lemmon, "I'll bet when Paul Whiteman first played it, the arrangement was very different," and the camera pans to Whiteman in front of a small dance band with the famous Whiteman "potato head" logos on their stands. Whiteman winds them up with "Boys, a bubba, a bubba" and leads an up-tempo 1920s-style version of "Embraceable You," as he executes a few dance steps and hams it up with his violin. The show is deliberately framed here as a music-history lesson.[51] Later in the episode, Whiteman and Lemmon stand positioned behind a bust of Gershwin, and Lemmon expresses surprise that Gershwin managed to compose both popular music and the *Rhapsody*, concluding "I guess he had more range and scope than any contemporary composer in America." Setting up "Summertime" as the episode's concluding number, Whiteman explains that *Porgy and Bess* was successful at its 1935 premiere but was not a real rave and, thus, disappointed Gershwin. Whiteman notes that the opera had been preceded by such a "hullabaloo" that even Beethoven would have had a tough time living up to it. Lemmon states that the opera "grows in stature every year, it is becoming a great contribution to American music," and Whiteman agrees, predicting that "years from now it will still be bigger." Displacing Gershwin's intended Black cast, Froman and Wrightson, as soloists, are joined by the chorus and dancers, with Westbrook's choreography, in a grand performance of "Summertime" to conclude this tribute to Gershwin.

The first episode of the third and final season (September 9, 1951) was also devoted to Gershwin's music in an even more glamorous production. Whiteman introduces the episode by announcing that he will lead the orchestra and Earl Wild in a full performance of *Rhapsody in Blue* but that they will first start with "Gershwin in a lighter vein."[52] The all-white chorus in formal dress, with the women in black elbow-length gloves, sings "Clap Yo' Hands"—a minstrel-style number from *Oh, Kay!* (1926)—while executing some choreographed body percussion and offering a stylized imitation of a Black gospel choir. Wrightson then struts in to deliver "Ain't Necessarily So" from *Porgy and Bess*. The episode's tribute to popular Gershwin numbers is rounded out with Frances Langford singing "The Man I Love" and Maureen Cannon solidly belting out "I Got Rhythm." Then the big moment has arrived as the camera offers a closeup of Whiteman's finger on the *Rhapsody in Blue* score and baton held at the ready. This performance of the *Rhapsody* was clearly intended as an apotheosis for the piece, aiming to outdo the lavish production number in the film *King of Jazz* from two decades prior. Whereas the Paul Whiteman ensemble emerged from within an enormous grand piano in that former sequence, here the elaborate sets suggest the innards of a piano. Westbrook's choreography is quite impressive and varied, with rather wild and erotically charged sequences involving lots of shimmying, can-can style passages, and more balletic sections. Four male dancers holding clarinets allude directly to Jacques Cartier's opening clarinet solo choreography from the *King of Jazz* performance. When not presenting the dancers, the television cameras offer dynamic shots of the piano soloist and of Whiteman conducting, including a dramatic long closeup of Whiteman during the piece's extended slow section. Finally, to achieve a full musical glamorization of the piece, grandiose choral, chordal "ahs" were added to the score, particularly at its conclusion.[53]

Goodyear Revue's middlebrow aesthetics are also clearly evident in its engagement with 1950s American popular exoticism in multiple episodes. At the conclusion of the October 28, 1951, episode, Whiteman announces that next week they will "unroll our magic carpet for a trip to the East." The following November 4, 1951, episode duly offered an exotic spectacle set in India in "far-away places." The June 11, 1950, episode had "South Sea Islands" as its theme, the show went "down Mexico way" with the virtuoso Spanish-born guitarist Andre Segovia on February 18, 1951, and a white couple danced the tango in a Gus Kahn number on September 30, 1951. Whiteman's performance of Ravel's *Bolero* (September 16, 1951) was framed as a fantasy ballet set in Spain, performed in a Spanish-tinged modern dance style. In all cases, these productions drew primarily on common exotic stereotypes. In multiple episodes, Whiteman wore outlandish exotic costumes (see fig. 8.8). The most lavish exotic presentations were created for two episodes entirely devoted to Spain.

The special guests on the March 5, 1950, broadcast include performers from "New York's most authentic Spanish nightclub, El Chico," and Whiteman announces "with a lineup like this, things took a slightly Spanish turn and we thought 'Lady of Spain' might be the thing to put you in the mood." The sets, costumes, and flirtatious miming all stereotypically signal Spain. Whiteman appears in a toreador costume as he introduces Rosita Rias, who

FIGURE 8.8 Whiteman as a pasha on *Goodyear Revue*. Publicity still, Paul Whiteman Collection, Williams College Special Collections.

then sings “Granada” in Spanish. Whiteman sets up Wrightson’s first Spanish number by referring to the baritone as a chameleon who always looks the part and saying that he was sure “you wouldn’t mistake him for an Eskimo.” Still in costume, Whiteman later states that “those of us in show business are always sure of authentic Spanish talent when we hear the act comes from El Chico here in New York City. The artists are imported direct from Spain and are sometimes never seen or heard elsewhere in this country.” Thus, *Goodyear Revue* makes a claim to present exotic authenticity while reproducing standard stereotypes. Whiteman then introduces the flamenco-style dance of Pepita Marco by saying she “doesn’t speak a word of English, but when she dances, ha! who cares?” In an effective comic stunt, Johnny Bradford and Tony Romano perform "South Granada Shoe Shine Boy" in Spanish and Spanglish, a comic translation of their hit number "Chattanooga Shoe Shine Boy," and Whiteman gets in on the act by adopting a fake Spanish accent and dropping in a few Spanish words. Leaping from a contemporary hit song to nineteenth-century opera, Irra Petina then sings the "Habanera" from *Carmen*, which morphs into a medley of numbers from the opera, with Wrightson singing as Don Jose and then as the toreador. As in every episode, the show concludes with Whiteman in tuxedo conducting an excerpt from *Rhapsody in Blue*.

In the opening of the October 7, 1951, episode Whiteman declares, "Spain is one of the most fascinating places in the world," and invites us to "visit this land of history and sunshine." Wrightson sings the 1931 popular song "Lady of Spain" and the "Toreador" number from *Carmen* and Cannon performs a clever Spanish-themed song celebrating Goodyear and the 1935 popular Cuban song "Say 'Si Si,'" as sung in English by the Andrews Sisters in 1940. Throughout the episode, Spain is represented musically primarily with works by composers of other European nationalities. With ten minutes remaining in the thirty-minute program, a male voice-over formally announces the performance of Nikolay Rimsky-Korsakov's *Capriccio Espagnol*, and the camera focuses on Whiteman with his score and baton, zooming back to reveal the full orchestra, "Spanish" set, and dancers. At several points the camera cuts back to focus on Whiteman conducting or to solo instruments, as though we are witnessing a telecast of an orchestral concert. Thus, *Goodyear Revue* hit multiple middlebrow aesthetic targets in this episode by presenting popular songs and light classical pieces in a glamorous production and indulging in exotic representation.

Goodyear Revue and Race

In contrast with some other high-profile variety shows circa 1950, such as Ed Sullivan's, *Goodyear Revue* stuck closely to a policy of segregation and of displacing Black musicians with white performers.[54] Of the roughly 105 special guests over the three seasons, Black performers appeared only once when the Hampton Institute Choir performed on the April 8, 1951, episode, which was devoted to the songs of Stephen Foster.[55] The special guest soloist on this episode was Froman, and she sang Foster's "Beautiful Dreamer" and "My Old Kentucky Home," substituting the line "the darkies are gay" with "the people are gay." Those numbers were followed immediately with Wrightson singing "Some Folks." The Hampton choir apparently sang two spirituals as part of the program: "Sit Down Servant" and "Steal Away."[56] The choir also accompanied Froman and Wrightson in the show's finale, a Foster medley. The medley began with Froman singing the line "Gone are the days when my heart was young and gay" from Foster's "Old Black Joe." The strings and wordless choir then delivered the melody from "Jeanie with the Light Brown Hair" followed by an up-tempo orchestral transition at which point the surviving audio recording skips to the medley's inevitable conclusion: Foster's "Old Folks at Home (Swanee)." Wrightson delivered the first verse, and Froman followed with the second, including the original lyrics "still longing for the old plantation." The Hampton choir accompanied Froman with harmonies on "ooh." However, the choir did sing the final lyrics, "Oh brother how my heart grows weary, far from the old folk at home"—notably substituting "Oh brother" for the original "Oh darkeys"—to conclude the number in grandiose fashion along with an orchestral apotheosis. Some evidence exists that suggests the Black student members of this choir initially objected to performing songs by Foster on this episode, given the presence of racial slurs in his lyrics. In fact, the choir appears to have limited its participation in this tribute to Foster to the final medley, and it is possible that the changes to Foster's lyrics noted above stemmed from their objections.[57]

Two other performers of color, the Latina "Puerto Rican Pepperpot" Olga San Juan and Mildred Bailey (whose mother was Native American), appeared once each as guests, but Bailey was considered white by the public at this time. Lina Romay was in three episodes on *Goodyear Revue*. She is often referred to as a Mexican American, given her father's nationality, and was frequently cast in films as an exotic Latina, even though her father was of white European descent and selected "white" in the 1940 census. Perhaps not surprising, and in stark contrast to coverage of *TV Teen Club*, a search in the Black press results in only one reference to *The Goodyear Revue*, a brief announcement of the Hampton Institute Choir's upcoming appearance. However, one other Black performer performed on the show in the November 18, 1951, episode devoted to seafaring tunes and American waterfronts. This episode, with guest soloist Froman, is structured as a historical tour, starting in 1700 New England. In the New Orleans sequence set in 1800, Froman sings the 1933 standard "I Cover the Waterfront." As she concludes, she gives a boy, whose face is hidden by his straw hat, a coin. He suddenly leaps up with an open-mouth grin and starts dancing to "Sweet Georgia Brown" (see fig. 8.9). This uncredited young dancer is Black, and he remains silent, taking a bow and exiting after his impressive solo jazz dance. The boy returns to the screen, sitting next to Wrightson as the baritone sings "They Call the Wind Maria," a hit from *Paint Your Wagon*, which had just opened on Broadway. Wrightson puts his hand on the boy's shoulder as he sings, they hold hands, and at the song's ending the boy walks Wrightson over to a woman whom Wrightson embraces. The boy then turns to the camera with a smile, walks

FIGURE 8.9 Dancing Black boy on *Goodyear Revue*, November 18, 1951. Screenshot.

right up to the camera and then off screen. The historical and geographical setting appears to have pushed the *Goodyear Revue* to break its all-white casting policy, though I note that—as with *TV Teen Club*—the show included this Black child performer rather than any Black adults, as though integration involving a child was deemed lower stakes.

Instead of including Black performers, *Goodyear Revue* repeatedly represented Black musical culture with white performers. No specific theme was announced for the September 23, 1951, episode. Instead, Whiteman starts the show by announcing that the Grieg Piano Concerto will be featured later in the program and then says, "But first, in a little lighter vein, let's travel south with the Goodyear chorus for an old-fashioned cakewalk. Shall we go?" The chorus adopts a light faux-Southern accent and engages in some of the stereotypical hand-waving and high stepping associated with the dance as they perform in front of a set representing a Southern mansion (see fig. 8.10). Histories of racial representation are densely layered in this televised performance. The cakewalk, with roots in blackface minstrelsy and originating earlier in the nineteenth century with enslaved people's mocking performances of whiteness, had become a popular social dance for whites in Europe and the United States in the early twentieth century, though it was certainly outdated as a social dance by 1951. However, the song that they sing

FIGURE 8.10 The Goodyear Chorus performing a cakewalk on *Goodyear Revue*, September 23, 1951. Screenshot.

and dance to, "Cakewalk Your Lady," had a more proximate origin and its own racial ambiguities, as it was a hit number in the Black-cast 1946 musical *St. Louis Woman* created by the white composer and lyricist team of Harold Arlen and Johnny Mercer and based on a book by the Black writers Arna Bontemps and Countee Cullen. Thus, the 1951 *Goodyear Revue* cakewalk performance by an all-white dancing chorus represented another instance of displacement of the Black performers and characters of the 1946 musical. I note that Pearl Bailey, who had been in the original cast of *St. Louis Woman*, would later perform "Cakewalk Your Lady" on *The Ed Sullivan Show* on July 30, 1961, accompanied by a white chorus.

The unstated phantom theme of this *Goodyear Revue* episode could have been announced aptly by Whiteman as follows: "And tonight we explore the Negro musical soul as only Harold Arlen, Vernon Duke, and George Gershwin can score it and white musicians can embody it. We will then leap to the snow-white realm of Scandinavian legend with Edvard Grieg." The cakewalk performance is followed by Wrightson, positioned outside the fence of the mansion and in less-formal dress, singing the Black character Porgy's "I Got Plenty of Nothin'" from Gershwin's *Porgy and Bess*. Following this number, the camera pans down from a high angle to Cannon, who sits with two other ladies posed with fans and fancy dresses, as she sings, "We are sweet

Southern belles," the start of a brief, sung Goodyear ad. After a subsequent Goodyear-filmed commercial about how the company tests its tires and after Cannon's performance of the Goodyear jingle, Whiteman sets up the next number: "In 1940 a show appeared on Broadway that was an instant success." The musical he refers to here is the Black-cast show *Cabin in the Sky*. Special guest Doretta Morrow, a white singer who was known for representing other races as she had just played Tuptim in *The King and I* (1951) and would later take the role of Marsinah in *Kismet* in 1953, then sings Harold Arlen and Yip Harburg's "Happiness Is Just a Thing Called Joe." Ethel Waters had performed the song both in the Broadway production and 1943 film musical. Morrow's performance—positioned in front of the mansion set, with her Italianate-trained voice accompanied by a lush orchestral arrangement—is in stark contrast to Waters's. This serious number is followed by Cannon sitting in a tree in front of the mansion and accompanied by four deadpan white gentlemen, framed rather comically by the camera, as she sings the 1902 "coon song" "Bill Bailey" (see fig. 8.11). Cannon employs her standard growl timbre at several moments, especially as she belts out the line, "Well, ain't that a shame."[58] Finally, Wrightson and Morrow join forces in singing "Cabin in the Sky," by Vernon Duke and John La Touche. Though the number is set in a cabin and they appear to relish the vision of being able to "eat fried chicken every day" in heaven, their musical performance could hardly be further from Black vocal styles (see fig. 8.12).[59]

FIGURE 8.11 Maureen Cannon belting "Bill Bailey" on *Goodyear Revue*, September 23, 1951. Screenshot.

FIGURE 8.12 Earl Wrightson and Doretta Morrow performing "Cabin in the Sky," on *Goodyear Revue*, September 23, 1951. Screenshot.

In summary, this episode featured multiple numbers representing Black characters and Black musical styles penned by white songwriters, in most cases intended for and originally performed by Black performers but performed on *Goodyear Revue* by white performers. In the final sequence of the episode, every aspect of this televised production changes as Whiteman stares seriously at the camera, and the male voice-over announces with great solemnity, "Ladies and gentlemen, Edvard Grieg's Concerto in A Minor." The camera first focuses on Wild's hands at the piano and Whiteman leading the orchestra but then moves on to a fantasy ballet depicting ultimate Nordic whiteness. The dancers first appear dancing underneath a fabric, perhaps in a nod to Martha Graham. Once they emerge, they are soon joined by men wearing horned helmets and holding spears. In typical *Goodyear Revue* fashion, this classical piece is further glamorized by a wordless chorus, though in this case they also sing some text, "Oh land of the midnight sun." Following a rather romantic balletic section, in the final section the dancers appear in Nordic-inspired costumes in a mountainous landscape and dance in a folk-informed style. With this production of Grieg's concerto, *Goodyear Revue* offered a blunt representation of whiteness to conclude an episode otherwise devoted to Black representation. Thus, this episode proved to be Black and white in more than one sense.

Black music and Black-inspired music by white composers were performed on numerous *Goodyear Revue* episodes by white performers. In the December 2, 1951, episode, otherwise devoted to celebrating the instruments of the orchestra, the harp is seized as an opportunity for Peggy Lee to sing the Black spiritual "Little David Play on Your Harp" with the Goodyear chorus. Lee appears as a preacher figure in this faux gospel production number.[60] Even more surprising is the Goodyear chorus's performance, in gowns and tuxes, of the spiritual "Ezekiel Saw the Wheel" on the January 6, 1952, episode in an incredibly overproduced production number as part of the celebration of the show's one-hundredth telecast. Froman sings both "Basin St. Blues" and "Birth of the Blues" on the November 26, 1950, episode. The October 21, 1950, episode is devoted specifically to the blues. The Goodyear chorus opens with "Birth of the Blues," first recorded by Whiteman in 1926, and then Connie Russell—the white "sultry" singer and actress billed by Whiteman at the conclusion of the previous week's episode as "that wonderful interpreter of the blues"—sings "I Gotta Right to Sing the Blues," in a style reminiscent of Billie Holiday. The climax of the show arrives as Whiteman introduces "St. Louis Blues" by stating that W. C. Handy is the most important composer in the history of the genre: "Of all the men who contributed to the development of the blues, there is one person who stands head and shoulders above all the rest whenever blues is mentioned." This acknowledgment of a Black source for the blues comes rather late in the episode. Russell starts the song, but it is then transformed into a deluxe instrumental-and-dance production number. Russell first appears on a very shadowy set resembling a front porch, and her dark hair and the shadows perhaps momentarily suggest she is Black. In any case, Russell is clearly performing Blackness in details of her vocal style. Wearing a simple dress, she is seen in sharp contrast to a solo female dancer appearing in a fancy dress and feathered hat and dancing erotically in the background—the infamous "St. Louis woman" of the song. The music and dance slip into a Latin-style rhythm, and Russell begins to dance as well, with women wearing all black and moving in a Martha Graham–influenced style. The simple, rustic set pulls away to reveal a fantasy rococo dance hall, and the music moves to an elaborate big band arrangement of the tune. The blues have been glamorized in front of our eyes and ears in this performance, and as throughout most of Whiteman's career, Black musicians have been displaced.

Whiteman, Integration, and the Future of American Music Television

To what extent may we view Whiteman's late career in music television as progressive, both in terms of racial inclusion and musical style? As the media-designated King of Jazz in the 1920s and 1930s, Whiteman had avoided hiring Black musicians. However, several Black musicians—including Steve

Gibson and the Red Caps, the Treniers, Duke Ellington, Count Basie, and Louis Armstrong—appeared in episodes of *America's Greatest Bands*, which Whiteman hosted in summer 1955.[61] Though *Goodyear Revue* remained rigorously segregated and repeatedly whitewashed Black musical culture, and both shows perpetuated racist stereotypes on multiple episodes, we have seen that the contemporaneous *TV Teen Club* (debuting in 1949) was surprisingly integrated, given the time period. In her study of the numerous teen dance television shows that aired from 1952 to 1959, Julie Malnig details the standard 1950s onscreen segregation policies, which included "Black only" and "white only" days, though, as she argues, Black and white teens watched each other dance, with Blacks frequently present in the offscreen audience on white-only days.[62] Matthew F. Delmont has shown that the most famous teen dance show of them all, *American Bandstand*, was, unlike *TV Teen Club*, only briefly integrated before Dick Clark became host after which it remained all white until the show moved to Hollywood in 1964.[63] Taking a rather more optimistic position on the social role of music television in the 1950s, one that we might be tempted to apply to a critical evaluation of *TV Teen Club*, Alexandra Harlig writes:

> The media facilitated the embodiment and consumption of movement and meaning of music, steps, and bodies across racial and social lines. Through these cycles of dissemination, development, and mediation, geographically and socio-economically disparate groups became connected through embodied practice and the ritual of watching—both themselves and others—thereby forming a consumer-based youth culture centered on music and dance.[64]

In Whiteman's ventures in music television, onscreen integration was primarily limited to young performers and the emerging youth culture.

Whiteman received considerable praise for the progressive approach of *TV Teen Club*. As we have seen, the show was honored by such conservative-leaning groups as the American Veterans of World War II and the Freedoms Foundation for its service to youth of all races, faiths, and nations. However, the most substantial recognition came from the Black press. The *Chicago Defender* selected Whiteman and daughter Margo, the show's original cohost, as two of sixteen public figures—along with Jackie Robinson, Illinois Governor Adlai Stevenson II, and Arthur Godfrey—for its 1949 honor roll, citing their "devotion to the democratic principle; for their efforts to translate that principle into reality for all, regardless of race, color, or creed."[65] This is particularly striking given that the honor came during the show's first season and that the article in the national edition listed the Whitemans second and accorded them separate images, with Margo appearing in a particularly large photograph. A January 1952 article "Widening Horizons" in the *Chicago Defender* and referring indirectly to *TV Teen Club*, notes, "Racially ignorant Southern whites are learning through the Godfrey, Sullivan, Whiteman, Fadiman, and Sid Cesar shows, to name a few, that they've been swallowing a bill of goods all of these years about Negroes whom TV are showing to be as literate, as attractive and as talented as they."[66] The Baltimore *Afro-American* selected Whiteman as one of only eight white inductees to its May 1950 honor roll list of twenty-nine men and four women. The citation reads: "Paul Whiteman, well-known musician who has always been in the forefront of putting democracy in action—particularly for his TV Teen Club program aired weekly over NBC-TV [*sic*] which gives an opportunity to young people of all races to display their talent and which includes in its regular personnel youngsters of all colors." Whiteman's photo and blurb appear in the paper right next to Thurgood Marshall's.[67]

Considered together, *TV Teen Club* and the *Goodyear Revue* occupy a rather Janus-faced position in the history of American music television. With its retrospective musical styles and loosely connected production numbers, *Goodyear Revue* resembled Broadway and Follies shows of the 1920s and 1930s, but it also offered a model for the later *Lawrence Welk Show*, which ran from 1955 to 1982 and which received a cameo appearance by Whiteman on January 12, 1963. We can certainly hear the stylistic lineage from Whiteman's "sweet band" to Welk's "champagne music," as Bradley Rogers has noted.[68] *TV Teen Club* was based on even older models of variety and vaudeville theater, but it prefigured televised amateur musical competitions such as *American Idol*.[69] *TV Teen Club* led more directly to *American Bandstand*, which began airing from the same ABC Philadelphia station in 1952 and thus overlapped with Whiteman's show. Whiteman even donated his record-shop set from *TV Teen Club* for use on *American Bandstand*, and Dick Clark began hosting the new show in 1956 following his stint as announcer on Whiteman's show. As Rayno has revealed, there was considerable overlap between the production team of *TV Teen Club* and *American Bandstand*, including cameramen and the scenic designer.[70]

Yet another ABC show aimed at young audiences seemed to pick up where *TV Teen Club* left off—*The Mickey Mouse Club*, which premiered in 1955, the following season after Whiteman's show ended. During the period of sponsorship by Griffin Shoe Polish, the chorus began each *TV Teen Club* episode singing "G-R-I-F, F-I-N" (to a modified version of the second half of Big Ben's full-hour chimes), prefiguring the spelling out in song of "Mickey Mouse" in that show's opening number. Whiteman was proud to note the proliferation of "teen club" dances across the nation based on his model, and in the 1952 season of *TV Teen Club* a male voice-over emphasizes at the start of each episode that it was "a real club" and calls out to the teenage audience, "Are you ready kids?" to which they answer, "OK, let's go!" When Whiteman enters the stage, he calls "Hi, gang!" which is answered with an enthusiastic "Hi, Pops!" This call-and-response was also a feature of *Mickey Mouse Club*, which also encouraged children to imagine themselves as members of the club that was "made for you and me." Furthermore, Fridays on the *Mickey Mouse Club* were Talent Roundup Day and even though the regular Mouseketeers were uniformly white—and, therefore, were less integrated than the *TV Teen Club* chorus and select chorus—multiple winners of this weekly competition were children of color. (For example, Cheryl Weinberg's winning performance with Ronnie and Riley Wilson on October 11, 1957, brings to mind Leslie Uggams's victories on *TV Teen Club* five years prior, though these three young Black singers and dancers receive a more elaborate staging than was possible on Whiteman's show.)[71] Finally, just as Whiteman served as a jocular, kindly adult on a show "run by teenagers," the middle-aged Roy Williams (as "Big Mouseketeer") served a similar role on *Mickey Mouse Club*.

In his late-career television work, Whiteman fully embodied his expansive position in American popular music history, continuing to serve as a bridge between musical styles. Both shows, to differing degrees, engaged in musical nostalgia as well as inclusion of up-to-the-minute popular hits. For example, the February 3, 1952, episode of *Goodyear Revue*, with the theme of newspaper headlines, includes a sequence kicked off with the headline "1922 Whiteman Writes Hit Tune," which prompts Whiteman to lead Wrightson in a performance of the Whiteman-Grofé hit "Wonderful One." However, the same episode includes a performance by Mary Mayo of "Cry (If Your Sweetheart Sends a Letter)," which had been a huge hit record for Johnny Ray in just the previous year and which Sonny Graham performed on *TV Teen Club*.[72] *Goodyear Revue* and *TV Teen Club* both featured music dating from Whiteman's birth in 1890 onward, and *TV Teen Club* included performances representing the earliest forms of rock 'n' roll in the early 1950s. In fact, *TV Teen Club* was connected to the emergence of rock 'n' roll in several ways. The show's music director, pianist, and conductor, Bernie Lowe, continued his association with Dick Clark and, with Cameo Records, was crucial to the careers of Charlie Gracie and Chubby Checker, as well as being the cowriter of "Teddy Bear," which became a hit for Elvis. The bassist on *TV Teen Club*, Arthur Singer, was a vocal coach for several early rock 'n' roll musicians.[73] Most notable, a young Charlie Gracie performed "Rock the Joint" on *TV Teen Club* in 1952. Concerned that the studio drummer would not know how to rock, Gracie decided to use slap technique on his guitar to provide the backbeat himself.[74]

Having emerged with ragtime and Tin Pan Alley, peaked with "symphonic jazz," and been declared "the greatest name in modern American music each week on the *Goodyear Revue*, Whiteman even seemed poised to embrace rock 'n' roll at this late stage in his career or at least as performed by white musicians. In July 1956 he emceed a Bill Haley concert and planned to host more rock 'n' roll concerts at auto parks across the country. As reported in the press, "the man who jilted his symphonic viola to become 'Jazz King' in the Twenties will lend his prestige to a stepchild in the music family—rock 'n' roll."[75] In 1957, at age sixty-six, he met Elvis and told the press that he "wouldn't write off this Elvis Presley too fast either. That guy is a symbol to a lot of kids with troubles—but he's got something above his neck, too, and it comes out."[76] In 1956 he predicted that Elvis would enjoy a long career, possibly becoming a superstar like Frank Sinatra and Judy Garland, and he asserted, "The voice was there before the wiggle."[77] Whiteman even claimed to have talked a reluctant Ed Sullivan into having the Beatles appear on his show in 1964 and in 1966, the year before his death, Whiteman was delighted to serve as a judge at an event dubbed the "World Rock 'n' Roll Championship" in Lambertville.[78] With *TV Teen Club* and *The Goodyear Revue*, the new medium of music television enabled Whiteman to remain connected, however tenuously, to the latest trends in popular music while continuing to promote his polished 1920s and 1930s dance band idiom from the period when he had reigned as the most prominent arbiter of American musical taste.

Notes

My research was primarily carried out in the Williams College Paul Whiteman Collection, the Paley Center for Media Archive in New York City, and the New York Public Library for the Performing Arts. For providing access to video recordings of Whiteman's television shows, I am particularly grateful to Ruta Abolins and Margaret A. Compton at the University of Georgia Brown Media Archives and Peabody Awards Collection, to Sylvia Brown at Williams College, and to Laura R. Jolley at the State Historical Society of Missouri. I also thank Zoran Sinobad at the Library of Congress Moving Image Research Center for responding thoroughly to my queries and Ethan Sheppard for his research assistance. Finally, I thank Ryan Raul Bañagale and Catherine Tackley for their comments on an earlier draft of this chapter.

1. Whiteman's appearances on television are detailed chronologically in Rayno, *Paul Whiteman*, 2:563–77. Rayno reports that Whiteman's first television appearance was in 1938 with the songwriter Peter DeRose and notes that ABC turned to Whiteman not only to launch its first three television stations in 1948 (New York City, Chicago, and Detroit) but also to appear as one of the featured stars on its first Thanksgiving Day special that year. See Rayno, *Paul Whiteman*, 2:268–69.

Goodyear Revue was also known as *The Paul Whiteman Revue* and has been occasionally referred to mistakenly with the word *Review* in the title.

2. These appearances included: leading a 1920s dance medley on *Max Liebman Presents: The Follies of Suzy* with the dancer Zizi Jeanmarie (October 23, 1954), a brief cameo on *Stars of Jazz* as a surprise guest reminiscing with Jack Teargarden, a birthday salute to W. C. Handy on *Art Ford's Greenwich Village Party* (November 15, 1957), conducting on *Voice of Firestone* (January 19, 1959), appearing on *The Revlon Revue* for his own seventieth-birthday tribute (March 24, 1960), conducting *Rhapsody in Blue*—surprisingly without one of his trademark overly long batons—with Jorge Bolet as soloist on *The Bell Telephone Hour* (February 3, 1961), narrating a broadcast of *Music of the Thirties* (November 5, 1961), and being interviewed with Dave Brubeck on *Orbit* (February 12, 1962).

3. Rodman, *Tuning In*, 9–10. Rodman discusses the history of musical variety television shows in ch. 6, 170–200.

4. Cooke and Whiteman, "New World of Television."

5. Wald, *How the Beatles Destroyed Rock 'n' Roll*, 81. Edwin Harris's career with Whiteman was short-lived for Whiteman was charged with illegally employing a minor and was ordered to send Harris and his father back to St. Louis. Whiteman apparently informed the judge that he was unaware of Harris's true age. See "Whiteman Exonerated in Court" and "Make Boy, 10, Give Up $100." Black newspapers clearly sided with Whiteman and suggested that it was a shame he had to let the boy go. See also "Boy, 10, Earning $100 Weekly."

6. On Foresythe, see Nicholson, *Jazz and Culture in a Global Age*, 225–28. On Ellington and Whiteman, see Cox, "Duke Ellington as Composer."

7. See Rayno, *Paul Whiteman*, 2:111–14. On Whiteman's relationship with William Grant Still, see Rayno, *Paul Whiteman*, 1:223–24.

8. See Wells, "Ace of His Race," 78–82, and Wells's chapter in the current volume.

9. Gabbard, *Jammin' at the Margins*, 10.

10. On this primitivist sequence and on the origins and impact of Cartier's "Kongo Voodoo" dance see my "Compelled by the Primitive in Cinematic Dance."

11. Rogin, *Blackface, White Noise*, 140. I note that in a memo to Carl Laemmle Jr., September 21, 1929, the film's director, Murray Anderson, offers a progress report on the film and lists composers and performers who might be included. In this memo Anderson listed Bill Robinson, referring to him as "Coloured Dancer." *King of Jazz*, folder 14, box 647, Whiteman Collection.

12. On the exclusion of Black music from "The Melting Pot of Music" number, also see Layton and Pierce, *King of Jazz*, 126. Layton and Pierce intriguingly suggest that the opening of a performance sequence by the Rhythm Boys appearing in deep shadow momentarily suggests that they are Black performers or are performing in blackface. *King of Jazz*, 147.

13. Other films present a strikingly different mythic view of Whiteman's role in cooking up American music vis-à-vis Black musical ingredients. For example, the 1945 Warner Bros. Gershwin biopic *Rhapsody in Blue* suggests that Whiteman

proved instrumental in supporting Gershwin's interest in Black music. Whiteman, playing himself, first appears when Gershwin's *Blue Monday* (later retitled *135th Street*) is almost rejected for performance, and he immediately supports it and agrees to give the score a run-through. The piece is not well received by the white audience at its premiere in a subsequent scene, but the camera conspicuously reveals that two Black ushers have been moved to tears, and Whiteman declares that the "number was really wonderful" and that they just have to work to make the public more "blues conscious"—blues serving as an undeciphered code word for "Black music." Gershwin makes it clear that he would like to draw further on the blues, which immediately gives Whiteman the idea to commission a work for an Aeolian Hall performance to "make a lady out of jazz" and gives Gershwin the idea for the "Rhapsody in Blue" title.

14. On the origins of Whiteman's dances and his teen-club project, also see DeLong, *Pops*, 283–85; Rayno, *Paul Whiteman*, 1:271.

15. On general attempts to harness television as a weapon against delinquency and the rise of "teen canteens," see Martin, "*TV Teen Club*," 27–30. Martin appears to set out to debunk what he refers to as the "creation myth" of *TV Teen Club*, but he does not offer any evidence suggesting an alternative account of the relationship between the Lambertville dances and the show. "*TV Teen Club*," 31. Also see Forman, *One Night on TV*, 160–61. Forman somewhat overemphasizes the "talent search" aspect of *TV Teen Club*. *One Night on TV*, 75.

16. This duel aim is reported, for example, in Wolters, "Whiteman at 60." This article states that the show also helped to elevate economically disadvantaged youth, such as Junie Keegan, who became a child star on the program. However, the goal of "bringing you stars of tomorrow" and Whiteman's role as a "star-maker" were emphasized primarily in the later seasons. The early seasons were presented more in the spirit of a low-stakes amateur competition variety show.

17. Rayno, *Paul Whiteman*, 1:57.

18. Whiteman also hosted a radio version of the show from 1947 to 1952 under the same title, with the early rock 'n' roll star Dion DiMucci appearing as one of the contestants, and this has led to some subsequent confusion.

19. Rayno, *Paul Whiteman*, 2:287. Celebrating the show's role in instilling civic virtue and patriotism, American Veterans of World War II presented Whiteman with an award on March 24, 1951.

20. Rayno's chronology incorrectly states that Whiteman received this award on the February 23, 1952, episode (*Paul Whiteman*, 2:570). However, I have confirmed with the Freedoms Foundation that Whiteman's 1952 award was officially presented in February 1953 at the organization's annual ceremony and that the presentation was made again publicly on the May 9, 1953, episode. I thank Carolyn E. Santangelo at the foundation for her assistance.

21. Given the nature of the show and the scarcity of surviving recordings, it is quite difficult to determine who actually performed on *TV Teen Club* during its five-year run. Some published commentary listing contestants includes famous names without evidence. For instance, DeLong lists Pat Boone and Wayne

Newton as appearing on the show, but this seems to be inaccurate. DeLong, *Pops*, 291.

22. Martin, "*TV Teen Club*." Martin assumes that 150 episodes of the show had been broadcast, but we are in agreement that 18 episodes seem to survive in recorded format. Martin also claims that Whiteman kept his distance from the young performers on the show, but this is not accurate. "*TV Teen Club*," 33. He stood close to his teenage female co-hosts, typically put his arm around contestants as they awaited their scores, performed in skits with the select chorus members, and, as noted above, socialized with the chorus at his home and stayed to participate in the postshow dances most weeks.

23. Witty, "Two Studies of Children's Interest in TV."

24. Martin, "*TV Teen Club*," 38.

25. Rayno, *Paul Whiteman*, 2:290.

26. An application by station WFIL-TV Philadelphia to the general awards program of Freedoms Foundation (found in *TV Teen Club*, folder 7, box 760, Whiteman Collection) includes scripts that indicate the use of more-elaborate sets in some production numbers and solo performances, as with a "Taj Mahal" set for the August 25, 1951, episode.

27. Martin states that "the show's approach to racial issues is interestingly benign" and that Blacks were "treated no differently than white performers," but he otherwise does not discuss racial aspects of *TV Teen Club*, nor does he provide examples to illustrate his brief statement. "*TV Teen Club*," 33.

28. Whiteman, "Teen-Agers Are My Favorite People," 108, television, folder 4, box 760, Whiteman Collection.

29. *TV Teen Club*, folder 7, box 760, Whiteman Collection.

30. The second award goes to a chunky white boy, and Whiteman says, "His name outta be Benny Blubber I think . . . or is that calling the kettle kettle, huh?" Here Whiteman appears to deliberately avoid the word "black." Whiteman's bulk is a source of humor in multiple episodes of *TV Teen Club*.

31. Brief 35 mm films held in the Whiteman Collection reveal that each bit of performance footage seen in the opening montage was staged and filmed specifically for the montage rather than being taken from an actual episode.

32. MacDonald, *Blacks and White TV*, 8–9.

33. Nile Rodgers Jr. (funk and disco musician, cofounder of the band Chic, and a major record producer) has repeatedly stated that his father, the percussionist Nile Rodgers Sr., performed in the *TV Teen Club* studio band and was even performing on the show the day his son was born in September 1952. (I am not able to determine with certainty the race of the drummer visible in the few long shots of the full ensemble in episodes from 1952 and 1953.) In a 2011 autobiographical article, Rodgers Jr. stated that landing a gig with Whiteman was a big break for his father but that "Paul's orchestra was, true to his name, all white," and thus, "Unfortunately, Paul couldn't hire him full time, and Dad had to supplement his income with a day job in the garment district." Rodgers, "Mr. Rodgers's Neighborhood."

34. Some evidence exists to suggest that integrated groups competed on the show even more frequently than I have suggested here. For example, MacDonald states that Phil Taylor and Bill Grant were an integrated song-and-dance duo who appeared on the show in 1951. *Blacks and White TV*, 15. A less-clear reference to the possibility of integrated performance on Whiteman's show appears in a 1953 article that refers to how "interracial acts" in a competition sponsored by a local YMCA could get the chance to audition for Whiteman's TV show. "Melody Kings."

35. On the fifteen-year-old pianist Viviane Young's appearance, see "Winner," and "Talented Youngster Appears on T.V. Show." On the tumblers, see "Nesbit Tumblers On Television Sunday."

36. Rea, "Encores and Echoes," January 12, 1952. Also see an announcement of his win in the *Chicago Defender*, February 23, 1952, 23. Errol Smith also appeared on March 1, 1952, on the NBC *All Star Revue*.

37. "B'Way Actor Sandy Lewis."

38. "Alfred Prettyman to Be Heard."

39. Hardy, "See Mildred Shine."

40. For example, see "Headliners."

41. Uggams made these claims in multiple published and recorded interviews at several points in her adult life. For example, see Amory, "Leslie Uggams." Esther M. Morgan-Ellis has detailed the impact of Uggams's race and of audience racism during her high-profile early 1960s run on the *Sing Along with Mitch* TV show. Morgan-Ellis, "Leslie Uggams." The show received complaint letters from white audience members revealing that they persisted in receiving her performances through the lens of minstrelsy and that they expected her to stay within "her own category" by performing only jazz and rock 'n' roll music. Morgan-Ellis, "Leslie Uggams," 47, 65.

42. Rea, "Encores and Echoes," March 31, 1951.

43. The practice of having professional judges was continued in Whiteman's subsequent and short-lived *On the Boardwalk* show, which premiered on May 30, 1954, broadcast live from Atlantic City. *On the Boardwalk* was produced by veterans of the *TV Teen Club* production team and featured *TV Teen Club* regulars in its first episode. Rayno, *Paul Whiteman*, 2:292, 422. On a July 1954 episode (held at the Paley Center) celebrating Atlantic City's one hundredth jubilee and airing without Whiteman, who was conducting a Gershwin memorial concert at the Hollywood Bowl, a competing jazz band included one Black musician. The substitute host explains that in the previous week's episode two sisters had performed together and their brother had performed separately. The professional judges decided that these three Black teenagers should return and perform together on the show. The brother first sings "I Cried for You" at the piano and is then joined by his two sisters whom he accompanies as they sing "Goodnight Sweetheart, Goodnight" in an early Motown style. The trio placed first in this episode.

44. Howland, *Hearing Luxe Pop*.

45. *TV Teen Club* veterans Margo Whiteman and Sonny Graham also each appeared once on *The Goodyear Revue*, serving, along with Junie Keegan, as the only other links between Whiteman's two shows.

46. Westbrook's contract letters for *Goodyear Revue* are held in folder 1, box 3, Frank Westbrook Collection, New York Public Library for the Performing Arts. A letter dated February 3, 1950, from ABC offered him the position as choreographer and to serve, along with Whiteman, as a member of the weekly planning board for the show, with a weekly salary of $300. A February 21, 1952, letter informed him that the final broadcast of the show would be on March 30, 1952. Don Rayno mistakenly credits Bettis as the choreographer throughout the show's run. See Rayno, *Paul Whiteman*, 2:278, 426.

47. Review, *Billboard*, June 16, 1951, quoted in Rayno, *Paul Whiteman*, 2:568; Todd, "Dolly in On Television Dance," folder 1, box 1, Frank Westbrook Collection, New York Public Library for the Performing Arts. Documentary materials in this collection indicate that much of Westbrook's choreography beyond *Goodyear Revue* was focused on primitivism and exoticism and that several of his works were performed by racially integrated groups. See ballet scenarios in folder 2, clippings in folder 3, and images in folder 4, Westbrook Collection. A video recording held in the Paley Center Archive, New York City (Dance Segment F3090; ID B16845) consists of excerpts from multiple *Goodyear Revue* episodes featuring only the choreographed numbers.

Other early reviews of the show also noted its strong choreography. See Gould, "Television in Review"; Crosby, "Whiteman TV Show Held Handsome Job"; Stein, "Radio Miss Lee."

48. IMDB.com lists ninety-nine episodes, but Rayno lists 101 broadcasts in his vol. 2 chronology. Whiteman confusingly refers to the January 6, 1952, episode (the "100th telecast") as the show's "diamond jubilee."

49. Based on my extensive searches, either thirty-one or thirty-two different episodes exist in recorded form; I have viewed twenty-nine of these. The J. Fred and Leslie W. MacDonald Collection at the Library of Congress holds two recordings that I have not viewed: the March 30, 1952, episode and one of an undetermined date, which might be a copy of an episode I have viewed elsewhere. The UCLA Film & Television Archive holds an episode identified only as "1950 episode with Eddie Albert, Alan McClaine," but this is most likely a recording of the first episode of the show, broadcast on November 6, 1949.

50. Cooke and Whiteman, "New World of Television."

51. Whiteman offers a similar music history lesson on the September 16, 1951, episode when he announces that he would play the same song Earl Wrightson just performed but in 1920s style. He again leads a smaller Dixieland-size dance band with his violin. Similarly, in the November 18, 1951, episode structured as a historic tour of American waterfronts, Whiteman appears with flapper-style dancers at a dock in a coonskin coat in the 1920s sequence. He signs autographs and while playing the violin conducts a small dance band, thus portraying his 1920s self in this 1951 television episode.

52. The full performance of Gershwin's *Rhapsody* was noted and announced in the press. See, for example, "Blue Rhapsody Will Be Given by Whiteman."

53. Not all critics welcomed this episode's bid to glamorize the middlebrow on the small screen. For example, one critic declares, "The Paul Whiteman Revue, which occasionally shows flashes of becoming one of TV's better musical programs, inevitably relapses into a second grade version of its potentialities" and concludes that this all-Gershwin episode "came a cropper because of its pretentiousness." Morse, "Paul Whiteman Revue."

54. For example, Ed Sullivan hosted the Ink Spots, Bill Robinson, Lena Horne, Cab Calloway, Count Basie, Sarah Vaughan, and Louis Jordan in his first season. On the inclusion of Black performers on Sullivan's show, see Nadel, *Television in Black-and-White America*, 7, and MacDonald, *Blacks and White TV*, 13.

55. Unfortunately, no video recording appears to have survived from this broadcast, but an audio recording of numbers featuring Jane Froman is held in the Jane Froman Collection at the State Historical Society of Missouri. The Black press took note of this performance by the Hampton choir. See, for example, "Hampton Choir Sets Debut with Whiteman."

56. "TV Program Highlights."

57. In 1985 Vernon L. Smith interviewed a former Hampton Institute choir member, Willia E. Daughtry of the class of 1952. (Daughtry herself became a professor of music at Hampton University and published a biography of the nineteenth-century Black soprano Sissieretta Jones.) In this interview Daughtry claimed that the choir refused to perform the Foster songs and that in the finale medley the camera focused on the choir "when to the humiliation of the director, the choir simply stood there silently in defiance." The audio recording suggests instead that the issue must have been addressed during rehearsals as the choir clearly sings in the medley and delivers the final line, with the noted alteration to Foster's lyrics. See Smith, "Hampton Institute Choir, 1873–1973," 143. It is possible that the Goodyear Choir performed instead during the final medley, but the choir in the audio recording sounds larger and stylistically different from the standard Goodyear group, leading me to suspect it is the Hampton ensemble. Three days before its appearance with Whiteman, the choir was also invited to perform on the *Kate Smith Hour* television show on April 5.

58. On the December 16, 1951, show Maureen throws in some of her vocal growls as she goes on a trip to the South with "Down Yonder" and sings, "My mammy land, you're simply grand."

59. A similar point could be made about Mimi Benzel and Earl Wrightson's performance of the song "Stormy Weather" on the November 25, 1951, tribute to Harold Arlen.

60. For a more detailed discussion of Lee's performance on this episode, see McGee, *Some Liked It Hot*, 230–31.

61. Notices in the Black press praised Whiteman for working with Black musicians in the mid-1950s. See "Harmonizing Four Sign Record Pact." The Harmonizing Four was a Black gospel quartet. I have been unable to determine which

TV or radio show of Whiteman's they had appeared on. Also see Bolden, "Black and White Keys." Enthused by Whiteman's steps toward integration, Bolden exclaimed, "Real cool Dad, real cool!"

62. Malnig, "Just Kids," 171–72. Malnig surveys the numerous teen dance shows in this period (159–160) and incorrectly implies that *TV Teen Club* was a dance show (164). Also see her more recent survey of dance shows in her monograph *Dancing Black, Dancing White*.

63. Delmont, *Nicest Kids in Town*, 157–79. Delmont notes that Clark claimed to have integrated *American Bandstand* when he became host, but Delmont argues this is false (1–6). He finds that Black teenagers were not allowed on the show until it moved production to Hollywood in 1964 (7) even though it had been briefly integrated early on before admission policies were changed to favor audience members from the Philadelphia suburbs (43–44). *Nicest Kids in Town*, 1–6, 7, 43–44. In "'They'll Be Rockin' on Bandstand," Delmont states that Black teenagers were "denied admission to the show" and discusses Georgie Woods's *Rock 'n' Roll Show* radio program for Black teens in Philadelphia and notes that Woods started concerts for Black teens in 1955. 468, 458–59, 471. Delmont does not mention *TV Teen Club*, but it is certainly possible that Woods was inspired by Whiteman. On *Bandstand*'s lack of integration, also see John A. Jackson, *American Bandstand*, 140–42, and Malnig, *Dancing Black, Dancing White*, 45–49.

64. Harlig, "Communities of Practice," 57.

65. "Defender's Who's Who."

66. "Widening Horizons."

67. "4 Women, 29 Men Listed." Whiteman had been honored by the Black community in the past. On January 19, 1935, he was presented with a silver trophy by W. C. Handy on behalf of "Negro musicians of New York." The trophy engraving reads: "Paul Whiteman in sincere appreciation of your giving world-wide recognition to our negro music presented by the Colored Musicians at the Savoy Ballroom January 19th 1935." Identifier 8, AR 141, box 789, Whiteman Collection. On this event see "News of the Stage," which announces that "Negro musicians of New York will honor Paul Whiteman for his services to jazz." Rayno notes that this event took place at the Savoy on January 20 in the wee hours of the morning and that Whiteman's band played with two thousand dancers attending. *Paul Whiteman*, 2:111. I note that the program at the Savoy Ballroom included a performance of a dance from Austin Dafora Horton's 1934 opera *Kykunkor*. Horton was a Black dancer, drummer, and composer from Sierra Leone. See "BARBARIC DANCE Drives Harlem into Ecstasy."

68. Rogers, "Lawrence Welk," 159.

69. *American Idol* premiered in 2002 and became a global phenomenon. It was but the most prominent of a wave of televised amateur musical talent competitions in the first decades of this century. On this show see Meizel, *Idolized*. On early TV amateur contest shows, see Austen, *TV-a-Go-Go*, 4, 227; he also lists pre-*Bandstand* televised dance shows, 27–28.

70. Rayno, *Paul Whiteman*, 2:423–24.

71. A video recording of their performance is currently available at "Mickey Mouse Club S3—Cheryl Weinberg with Ronnie and Riley Wilson," https://www.youtube.com/watch?v=rs5PLySCxL4.

72. Though I have emphasized the differences in style and repertoire featured on *TV Teen Club* and *Goodyear Revue*, there was some significant musical overlap, and Whiteman himself seems not to have approached the shows as though they were separated by repertoire. This is evident for instance in a January 16, 1951, letter Whiteman wrote in response to his good friend Amon Carter's attempt to plug a song. Whiteman indicates that he could certainly have it performed on *TV Teen Club* but that it would be more difficult to have it appear on *Goodyear Revue*, not due to any aesthetic differences between the shows but because the *Goodyear Revue* programs are decided in detail by a committee. Whiteman concludes, "If it meets with the approval of this gang," there would be a remote chance of performing it on *Goodyear Revue*. Amon G. Carter Sr. Collection, Texas Christian University digital repository, https://repository.tcu.edu/handle/116099117/52633. I have been unable to determine the title of this song.

73. See Rayno, *Paul Whiteman*, 2:424.

74. See Gracie and Jackson, *Rock & Roll's Hidden Giant*, 38–39. Gracie recollected that his competition on the episode was "a black lad who sang and a girl who sang while she played the piano. Both were impressive." He noted that the record executive Graham Prince happened to catch the show broadcast on the radio and signed him up with Cadillac Records and that one of his prizes was a bunch of records that included Fats Waller recordings, 39, 41–43.

75. See "'King of Jazz' on New Beat," Baltimore (MD) *Sun*, n.d., 8, folder 13, Rock and Roll box 650, Whiteman Collection. This report notes that if the Baltimore and New Jersey auto park events are successful, "he'll set up a nation-wide tour with himself as M.C."

76. Whiteman quoted in *San Bernardino County (CA) Sun*, January 17, 1957.

77. Allen, "Rock 'n' Roll."

78. Rayno, *Paul Whiteman*, 2:314–15, 1:316.

Afterword

ELIJAH WALD

As this book demonstrates in numerous ways, Paul Whiteman was far more than a musician, bandleader, or entertainer. He was a central figure in shaping the modern concept of "popular culture," the idea that the art and culture of ordinary people are worthy of the attention previously reserved for art of the aristocracy and the wealthy.

Before Whiteman, there was the high culture of the elite and "folk culture," valued because it preserved the ancient seeds of high culture, maintaining traditional customs and standards that were disappearing as Enlightenment ideas and the industrial revolution erased old agrarian ways. In that formulation, the urban working class had no culture or none worth mentioning; they had lost the fine old ways and were ignorant of the fine new ways. When James Reese Europe produced two groundbreaking concerts at Carnegie Hall in 1912 and 1913, leading Black ensembles playing "symphonic" arrangements of African American styles, his featured musicians played banjos—an African instrument associated with Southern plantations—and he defended the value of ragtime and jazz with the claim that "the music of our race springs from the soil."[1]

Whiteman, by contrast, advertised his groundbreaking 1924 concert at Aeolian Hall as An Experiment in Modern Music and proclaimed the value of showcasing the "thousands of young men writing music today who are not influenced by any school, but are composing in the spirit of the times."[2] It was a revolutionary claim: that, rather than being valuable as ancient heritage and raw material for high art, working-class culture might be pointing the way to the future and releasing high art from the gilded cage of the past. That idea went along with a shift in the balance of global power: imperial Europe had proved its decadence and obsolescence in the carnage of the Great War, and the United States was stepping up to lead the world with its young, fresh, democratic spirit.

Whiteman's legacy reaches into every aspect of popular music and more broadly into a shift in the concept of culture but is rarely or barely noted in most histories. One reason for this omission is that many—likely most—histories of music and art are written from a critical viewpoint. Rather than exploring what happened in the past and how it influenced what happened later, they start, for better or worse, with modern value judgments, exploring the art of the past that still speaks to us today and asking how art of the past influenced and nurtured later movements and artists we care about.

That formulation begs the question of who "we" are. Music scholarship is largely written by people who do not consider themselves typical pop music fans and have at best mixed feelings about the most popular trends and artists of their own time, so they have a tendency to root for the brilliant underdogs, past and present. Most histories of jazz trace the evolution of the vital, brilliantly improvisatory, and largely African American style carried forward from Louis Armstrong to Charlie Parker to Miles Davis and gloss over or decry the success of figures like Whiteman and Stan Kenton, not to mention Henry Mancini or Kenny G, who have generally been far more popular in their moments but made music the historians consider mediocre, dated, or deny is jazz at all.

It is easy to argue that Whiteman should never have been called the King of Jazz, but he was undeniably the most popular bandleader of the 1920s and one of the most influential figures in twentieth-century popular music. His blending of jazz with formal concert music led directly to the mainstream of film soundtracks, mood music, the innovations of the Beatles, and every pop star who ever blended their style with a symphonic string section. More specifically, the big band era began with him, and every important bandleader of the next two decades was directly influenced by his innovations. The first advertisement for Duke Ellington's Washingtonians appeared less than two weeks after Whiteman's Aeolian Hall concert and put itself directly in his camp, claiming a "Combination of Symphonic Jazz Plus Versatility." Ellington regularly named Whiteman's orchestra as his favorite band and decades later was still singling him out as "one of the truly great musicians of the jazz era" and even defending his erstwhile title: "Paul Whiteman was known as the King of Jazz, and no one as yet has come near carrying that title with more certainty and dignity."[3]

Even those of us who are fascinated by Whiteman may be puzzled by Ellington's praise of his musicianship, since, influential as Whiteman may have been, we tend to regard his musical skills as secondary, if we note them at all. Even if we credit him with all the music made by his various orchestras, one of the striking things about this book is how many of its chapters could have been written without listening to his music. A volume of writing about any other major musician would tend to include multiple discussions of compositions, arrangements, and recordings, but it makes perfect sense to compile a volume of intelligent and insightful pieces about Whiteman's career and contributions that largely ignore all of that.

It is easy to understand why most modern listeners have little interest in Whiteman's music. Although he was the most acclaimed and best-selling bandleader of the 1920s—an era still recalled as the Jazz Age—by the 1940s he was already being routinely dismissed as a facile popularizer who played little or no real jazz, didn't swing, and whose large, meticulously organized orchestra clipped the wings of the jazz musicians who worked in it, most famously the young, dead, white legend Bix Beiderbecke. Playing a minor-league trumpeter in the 1940 film *Second Chorus,* Fred Astaire boasted that he'd turned down a job with Whiteman: "Too big a band for me. If I'd've stayed with him, I'd've lost my individuality. Same thing happened to Bix."

Whiteman's reputation sank further in the next fifty years, as jazz was increasingly framed as an African American form, grounded in intricate polyrhythms and carried forward by brilliant improvisers. It didn't help that he had been known as the King of Jazz—and accepted and promoted that title himself—or that his name marked him as a racial standard-bearer. In 1924 Gilbert Seldes wrote an encomium that captures both the praise lavished at the time and one of the reasons it has aged so poorly:

> Nowhere is the failure of the negro to exploit his gifts more obvious than in the use he has made of the jazz orchestra, for although nearly every negro jazz band is better than nearly every white band, no negro band has yet come up to the level of the best white ones, and the leader of the best of all, by a little joke, is called Whiteman.[4]

A century later King Oliver's 1923 recordings with Louis Armstrong still sound brilliantly fresh and inventive, and Whiteman's music has all but disappeared. Even those of us who still listen to him have to do a lot of cherry-picking to find records we like. His innovations changed the course of jazz and popular music—not only in the United States but around the world—in multiple ways, but the only work that remains in any way familiar is *Rhapsody in Blue,* which continues to be featured and recorded by classical orchestras but is generally credited to George Gershwin, with Whiteman, perhaps, mentioned in the program notes.

In its first incarnation, everyone associated *Rhapsody in Blue* with Whiteman, who conceived and commissioned it specifically for his orchestra. He had the idea of giving a symphonic concert that would show how the rowdy new music called jazz could be mined and expanded into serious, long-form concert compositions; hired Gershwin to write such a composition; and assigned his staff arranger, Ferde Grofé, to produce an orchestral arrangement from Gershwin's piano score, tailored to the specific skills of Whiteman's soloists, who refined it further in rehearsals—the clarinet glissando that memorably opens the piece was written as an ascending scale and altered at the suggestion of the clarinetist, Ross Gorman. There is no reason to think Gershwin would have written any concert music if Whiteman had not provided the impulse and forum; Whiteman also made the first recording, with Gershwin playing an improvised piano cadenza, and that performance sounds very different from the versions played by later orchestras.

And yet, it is fair to ask whether Whiteman was a significant musician. He started out as a classical violist and violinist but rarely played with his orchestra, nor did he typically write the arrangements, and there are credible claims that even his conducting was a show for the audience and generally ignored by his players. Bill Challis, who wrote many of the orchestra's most jazz-oriented arrangements, recalled Whiteman making a guest appearance to conduct a couple of numbers by the Jean Goldkette band, which at that time included Challis, Beiderbecke, and other future Whitemanites, and generating a level of excitement and applause that they had never previously experienced, but his recollection doesn't suggest the difference was musical: "With Whiteman there's so much presence there, that 'These are my boys'—that sort of thing. You didn't get that with the other guys."[5]

Whiteman was a master showman, a superlative judge and nurturer of talent, and a brilliantly adaptable promoter who started out leading a small dance band, became the most popular bandleader and recording artist of the 1920s, and went on to pioneer new approaches to the presentation of music on radio and television. When the success of "Rhapsody" shifted his focus from dance accompaniments to concert tours, he hired the first female singer to front a major jazz-oriented orchestra, Mildred Bailey, and shortly a group of male singers, the Rhythm Boys, which included Bailey's brother Al Rinker and Bing Crosby. Whiteman originally presented the Rhythm Boys as a stand-alone unit, performing a short trio set between band numbers, and his recordings with Bailey and Crosby forever reshaped the role of vocalists in popular music. My favorite Whiteman record, 1928's "From Monday On," begins with a male quartet led by a flowery falsetto soloist performing in a style that had been popular since the nineteenth century, only to be interrupted by a burst of exuberant scatting from Crosby, who would be the dominant male pop singer for the next thirty years.

Granting Whiteman's importance and granting that it was musical, was the importance in the music itself? I love that record, but it is one of the few

Whiteman recordings that excites me, and few of my friends or colleagues would even go that far. Most of his music now sounds stodgy and dated, in part because tastes have changed but also because we hear it in a vacuum, without the associations it had for its original audience. All we hear on records is the music itself—and that goes to the heart of one of the most fundamental problems of popular music history: recordings have become central to our understanding of what was played and heard in the past but were a quite minor part of the music business until the 1950s and are not at all reliable as guides to what dancers, concertgoers, or radio listeners experienced.

Whiteman devoted relatively little time or attention to making records, and they preserve only a small fraction of his repertoire. For example, in the late 1920s William Grant Still wrote close to a hundred arrangements for the Whiteman band, which were heard by millions of radio listeners, but only two were recorded. Nor do the pieces that were recorded necessarily give us a good sense of what we would have heard on radio, the medium by which he most effectively reached a mass audience, since they were limited to three minutes and took the music out of the broader context of his programs. They give still less sense of what we would have experienced in his live concerts, which, as John Howland and Catherine Tackley note in their chapters, were full-scale variety shows.

We can try to get a sense of those shows from watching Whiteman's 1930 movie, *King of Jazz*. Typical of his innovations, it was the first major musical to use a synchronized soundtrack because he was not happy with the live sound, and it ranges from an abbreviated version of the "Rhapsody" to a medley showcasing various bandmembers, a stand-alone appearance by the Rhythm Boys, a vignette of novelty violin juggling by trombonist Wilbur Hall—along with Hall's specialty of playing "The Stars and Stripes Forever" on a bicycle pump—and guest spots featuring a wide and at times absurd variety of dancers and singers. For many modern viewers, the novelty vaudeville acts are more interesting than the music, much of which is at best dull and sometimes dreadful—though string jazz fans appreciate the brief glimpse of bandmembers Joe Venuti and Eddie Lang playing a hot duet.

A bigger problem with *King of Jazz*, which for many modern viewers overshadows the music, dancing, and comedy, is the way it portrays—and fails to portray—Black music, culture, and people. It opens with a cartoon segment in which Whiteman discovers jazz while hunting big game in "darkest Africa," featuring an assemblage of dancing animals and loinclothed tribesmen. Later bits include the Rhythm Boys singing "When the darkies beat their feet on the Mississippi mud" and a tableau of loving couples in which Whiteman is comically paired with a grinning little Black girl—a reminder that the only Black performer featured in his stage shows was Edwin "Snowball" Harris, a ten-year-old "pickaninny" banjo player. Finally, in an apotheosis of erasure, the film builds to a grand ensemble demonstrating that "America is a melting pot of music wherein the melodies of all nations are fused into one great new rhythm—jazz!" English huntsmen, Italian accordionists, Scottish bagpipers, Viennese waltzers, Irish harpers, Spanish guitarists, Russian balalaikists, and French military drummers march across the screen, and Whiteman stirs them in a cauldron, which pours forth a bevy of jazz-dancing white chorines in cowgirl outfits as the orchestra revisits *Rhapsody in Blue*, and the credits roll.

That scene has often been noted for its racial erasure, but those cowboy outfits are worth a moment's additional attention. The movie's previous scene was an operatic "Song of the Dawn," likewise with cowboy costuming, and both are a reminder that jazz, as Whiteman conceived it, was at times hailed as an expression not of Black or even urban culture but of America's young, democratic, pioneer spirit. Whiteman began recording in New York, and his work has often been framed as a form of Manhattan modernism, but he was born and got his early musical training in Denver and teamed up with Grofé in San Francisco. California had been a key region for the dissemination of jazz since 1913, when the Original Creole Orchestra came west from New Orleans, and the Bay Area had previously produced the first national ragtime hit, "Bully of the Town," and had been the training ground for Al Jolson, the most innovative pop vocalist in the generation before Crosby. There, again, the focus on recording has served to obscure rather than preserve: since very little music was recorded on the West Coast, it is easy to forget that the region was regarded by many people as a cradle of jazz and Whiteman as bringing a California style east. Nor was that simply a quirk of the teens and twenties. An oft-repeated story from the mid-1930s tells how Benny Goodman's hot swing band was barely noticed in New York and flopped across the country but found a wildly enthusiastic audience when it arrived in Los Angeles.

Myths shift with time. The California of Whiteman's day was associated with the rowdy red light district of San Francisco's Barbary Coast, which was still recalled as a haunt of rough gold miners, and hundreds of Hollywood westerns were filmed on ranches that are now part of urban Los Angeles. Today, "urban" is often used as a synonym for Black, the coasts are associated with urban centers, and it is easy to forget that Los Angeles was then the whitest city in the United States, and most white people still associated Black culture with the rural South. It is also easy to forget how many Black people and Black musicians of the jazz and swing era were living in the prairie and mountain states. Whiteman's father was the director of musical education for Denver's racially integrated school system and taught the future Black bandleaders Jimmie Lunceford and Andy Kirk. The first great electric guitar soloists in blues and jazz, T-Bone Walker and Charlie Christian, came out of Texas. As for white players, despite the New Orleans–to–New York focus of many jazz histories, it is striking how many of the early white devotees of "hot" music came from the West and Midwest.

The cowboy costumes in *King of Jazz* are reminders of a mythology in which the United States was leading a global revolution by combining the free spirit of the western prairies with the industrial modernism of the new metropoles—and the extent to which both, at the time, were exemplified by young white men. By now it is standard for cultural historians to emphasize the extent to which modern America and especially American music were shaped by Black culture and Black innovators, but through the 1980s it was still common to read variations of Seldes's old statement framing Black culture as "the roots" and Black artists as progenitors of styles that reached more developed, mature, serious, and generally higher levels when refined and reshaped by white artists.

I have elsewhere compared Whiteman and the *Rhapsody in Blue* to the Beatles and *Sgt. Pepper's Lonely Hearts Club Band* and suggested it is inconsistent for Whiteman to be reviled for his attempt to "make a lady of jazz" in the era of King Oliver by elevating it to a mature, serious art by European classical standards, while the Beatles are hailed for similarly elevating rock to a mature, serious art form in the era of James Brown.[6] That analogy has obvious limitations, but the inconsistency is striking, and if my title *How the Beatles Destroyed Rock 'n' Roll* suggests I was calling for a reassessment of the Beatles, I am at least as interested in seeing further reassessments of Whiteman and his peers.

The recentering of jazz as essentially Black music was necessary and remains vital and important as a critical and sociological position, but in historical terms we cannot understand the evolution of the music, its reception, and its audiences without studying Whiteman and the diametrically opposite ways he was seen in his time and in later eras. If we want to understand the warping effects of racism, we have to study not only the victims but also the perpetrators; not only the losers but also the winners—as well as how those roles have sometimes shifted. When a new generation of (mostly) white critics reviled Whiteman and placed his erstwhile crown on Ellington and Armstrong while ignoring Ellington's appreciation of Whiteman and Armstrong's love of Guy Lombardo, was that simply redressing an old wrong, or was it a new layer of obfuscation? In a society in which white tastes remain dominant, can we (white scholars, in particular) study Black music and culture without interrogating the role of white tastes, including our own?

Artists like Armstrong and Ellington are often framed as playing an authentic jazz that was diluted and repackaged for white consumption by people like

Whiteman—but Armstrong and Ellington were playing in places called the Plantation Club and the Cotton Club and for segregated white audiences, and the people who frame Armstrong and Ellington as "authentic" and Whiteman as "fake" are arguably maintaining the mythology that presented Black artists under those rubrics and ignoring the ways they embraced and adapted the innovations of people like Whiteman, Lombardo, Grofé, and Challis, not to mention the work of Black composers and arrangers like Still and Will Vodery. If I were to argue that Whiteman's music was in some ways more authentic, in that it was more representative of the mass, majority-white audience of his time, that would not necessarily be a compliment. On the contrary, it could be a call to reassess our standards of authenticity and to question why we choose to frame some people and cultures as "authentic" while rewarding other people and cultures with the fruits of stardom—as well as book contracts, PhDs, and tenure.

Whiteman's Aeolian Hall concert is often decried as an attempt to separate jazz from its authentic roots, though few writers take the next step and decry him for pioneering the idea of jazz as a "classical" style, which continues to have some critical currency. That analogy maintains the old idea that classical music—the music of the court, the wealthy, and the intelligentsia—is a more mature and elevated form than pop music and ignores the reality that classical music has been barely surviving on a life-support system of foundation grants and government funding for decades and has to play centuries-old repertoire to draw an audience, while popular styles have led every significant musical innovation of the last century. Classical music was Whiteman's personally authentic style, the music of his family and culture, which he had been playing since childhood, and if he was praised in his time for elevating jazz by blending it with classical instrumentation and pretentions, in hindsight his innovations probably steered more people in the other direction: *Rhapsody in Blue* undoubtedly attracted some classical listeners to jazz-inflected styles in 1924, but over the years it has surely attracted far more pop and jazz listeners to symphonic concerts.

To me, this volume is part of a broader wake-up call to reassess the major musical stars and trends of the past in a historical rather than a critical framework, exploring their context, evolutions, and influence rather than asking whether we enjoy them. In political history, we all understand the importance of studying figures who changed the world in unfortunate or even horrific ways, as well as figures we admire. I am fascinated by Whiteman, and the fact that I enjoy some of his music is largely irrelevant to that fascination—indeed, I would say the recordings I prefer were tangential to his importance, and his most important contributions steered jazz and popular music in directions that are less to my taste. Recentering Whiteman as a significant figure in popular culture, and specifically in white culture, does not mean simply repeating old charges of appropriation and adulteration; it means interrogating his role in forming popular culture and white culture and in issues of appropriation and adulteration and globalization and law and body image. I hope this book is the beginning of a long-overdue reassessment not only of Whiteman but also of the many mainstream musical figures who shaped what we hear today, all around the world, like them or not. Not necessarily celebrations, not necessarily attacks, but reassessments from different and new points of view, broadening our understanding of the past—without which we cannot hope to understand our present or shape our future.

Notes

1. Europe, "Negro Explains Jazz," 240.
2. Rayno, *Paul Whiteman*, 1:80.
3. D. Ellington, "Royal View of Jazz," 84 (Whiteman is the only white artist mentioned); E. K. Ellington, *Music Is My Mistress*, 103.
4. Seldes, *Seven Lively Arts*, 99.
5. Rayno, *Paul Whiteman*, 1:170.
6. Wald, *How the Beatles Destroyed Rock 'n' Roll.*

Works Cited

Advertisement for Whiteman's His Master's Voice records. *Sheffield Daily Telegraph*, April 14, 1926, 5.

Ake, David. *Jazz* Cultures. Berkeley: University of California Press, 2002.

"Albert Hall Siege." *Daily News*, April 12, 1926, 8.

"Alfred Prettyman to Be Heard on Whiteman Show." *Afro-American* (Baltimore, MD), October 7, 1950, 8.

Allen, Wayne. "Rock 'n' Roll, Presley All Right, with Whiteman." *Illinois State Journal* (Springfield), August 10, 1956, 5.

Alter, Louis. *Dolly Dimples*. New York: Robbins Music, 1927.

Alter, Louis, and Harold Adamson. *Manhattan Serenade* [song]. New York: Robbins Music, 1942.

"Alter 'Nocturne' Used for Film Pantomime." *Tempo*, June 1935, 3.

"American College of Music: A Generous Proposition." *New York Times*, February 13, 1875, 8.

Amory, Cleveland. "Leslie Uggams Had Problems, Too." *Philadelphia Inquirer*, April 20, 1976, 19C.

Anderson, John Murray, dir. 1930. *King of Jazz*. Universal Pictures. 99 minutes.

Applebome, Peter. "High Notes and Low: A Special Report; A Jazz Success Story with a Tinge of the Blues: At Lincoln Center, Defining the Canon Draws Fire." *New York Times*, September 22, 1998. http://www.nytimes.com/.

Armstrong, Lucille, and Louis Armstrong. "Lose Weight the 'Satchmo' Way." *Ebony*, April 1, 1956, 35–37.

"Artists and Foreign Bands Volume 161: Debated on Wednesday 21 March 1923." *Hansard*. https://hansard.parliament.uk/Commons/1923-03-21/debates/9e19a3c8-bfb3–4130-acb2–383744417289/ArtistsAndForeignBands.

"At the Paramount." *Journal* (Jersey City, NJ), March 30, 1928.

Austen, Jake. *TV-a-Go-Go: Rock on TV from American Bandstand to American Idol*. Chicago: Chicago Review, 2005.

Austin, Cecil. "Jazz." *Music & Letters* 6, no. 3 (1925): 256–68.

Automotive Industry and Network Broadcast Advertising. August 1935. National Broadcast Company. *World Radio History*. https://worldradiohistory.com/.

Baer, Herbert. "Performer's Right to Enjoin Unlicensed Broadcasts of Recorded Renditions." *North Carolina Law Review* 19, no. 2 (1941): 202–11.

Baguez, Salvador. "The Jazz King—An Impression." *Los Angeles Times* 48, June 16, 1929, C11.

Baldwin, Davarian. *Chicago's New Negroes: Modernity, the Great Migration, and Black Urban Life*. Chapel Hill: University of North Carolina Press, 2007.

Balliett, Whitney. *Collected Works: A Journal of Jazz, 1954–2001*. New York: Macmillan, 2002.

Bañagale, Ryan Raul. "An American in Chinatown: Asian Representation in the Music of George Gershwin." Master's thesis, University of Washington, 2004.

Bañagale, Ryan Raul. *Arranging Gershwin:* Rhapsody in Blue *and the Creation of an American Icon*. New York: Oxford University Press, 2014.

"Barbaric Dance Drives Harlem into Ecstasy and 'Steals' Big Jazz Show Civilized Veneer Slips Off in Magic." *Pittsburgh (PA) Post-Gazette*, January 21, 1935.

Bassler, Samantha. "Madness and Music as (Dis)ability in Early Modern England." In *Oxford Handbook of Music and Disability Studies*, edited by Blake Howe, Stephanie Jensen-Moulton, Neil Lerner, and Joseph Straus, 529–38. New York: Oxford University Press, 2016.

Bederman, Gail. *Manliness and Civilization: A Cultural History of Gender and Race in the United States, 1880–1917*. Chicago: University of Chicago, 1995.

Bennett, Tom. "Arranging Music for Radio." In *Music in Radio Broadcasting*, edited by Gilbert Chase, 76–90. New York: McGraw-Hill, 1946.

Berish, Andrew S. *Lonesome Roads and Streets of Dreams: Place, Mobility, and Race in Jazz of the 1930s and '40s*. Chicago: University of Chicago Press, 2012.

Berrett, Joshua. *Louis Armstrong & Paul Whiteman: Two Kings of Jazz*. New Haven, CT: Yale University Press, 2004.

"Best Band, The?" *Stage* (London), July 5, 1923, 11.

Bigelow, Edith. "The Sorrows of the Fat." *Harper's Bazaar* 30, no. 14, April 3, 1892, 278.

"Big Benefits Planned." *Chicago Defender*, June 19, 1926, 7.

"Big Reception Planned for Whiteman's Return." *Variety*, August 11, 1923, 12.

Blue, Gill. "The Fourth Experiment in Modern American Music." *Metronome*, December 1932, 17.

"Blue Rhapsody Will Be Given by Whiteman." *Chicago Daily Tribune*, September 9, 1951, SW12.

Bolden, Frank E. "Black and White Keys Make Harmony for My Melody." *Pittsburgh (PA) Courier*, October 8, 1955, 19.

"Boy, 10, Earning $100 Weekly, Goes Back to Mo." *New York Amsterdam News*, April 13, 1927, 9.

"Brighter London." *Birmingham (UK) Daily Gazette*, March 31, 1923, 4.

"Brighter London." *London Daily News*, March 29, 1923, 3.

"'Brighter London' at the Hippodrome." *Era* (London), April 4, 1923, 11.
Brooke, R. W. "A New Era in Music." *Radio Times*, July 3, 1925, 55.
Bruce, W. Cabell. *The Negro Problem*. Baltimore, MD: Murphy, 1891.
"Buick Signs Whiteman; Band Has 2 Loew Dates." *Billboard*, October 15, 1932, 16.
"B'way Actor Sandy Lewis Now Writing in H'ywood." *Philadelphia Tribune*, April 29, 1967, 16.
"B'way Houses' Band Policy Convinces Capitol It's Thing." *Variety*, September 7, 1927, 31.
Capitol Records v. Mercury Records Corp. 221 F.2d 657, 2d Cir. (1955).
"Chicago Theatrical News." *Chicago Defender*, January 14, 1928, 7.
Chowrimootoo, Christopher. *Middlebrow Modernism: Britten's Operas and the Great Divide*. Berkeley: University of California Press, 2018.
Chowrimootoo, Christopher, and Kate Guthrie. Introduction to "Colloquy: Musicology and the Middlebrow." *Journal of the American Musicological Society* 73, no. 2 (2020): 327–34.
Chowrimootoo, Christopher, and Kate Guthrie, eds. *Oxford Handbook of Music and the Middlebrow*. Oxford: Oxford University Press, 2023.
Chowrimooto, Christopher, Kate Guthrie, John Howland, Andrew Flory, Chris McDonald, Heather Wiebe, and Richard Taruskin. "Colloquy: Musicology and the Middlebrow." *Journal of the American Musicological Society* 73, no. 2 (2020): 327–95.
Cloonan, Martin, and Matt Brennan. "Alien Invasions: The British Musicians' Union and Foreign Musicians." *Popular Music* 32, no. 2 (2013): 277–95.
Cockrell, Dale. *Everybody's Doin' It: Sex, Music, and Dance in New York, 1840–1917*. New York: Norton, 2019.
Colin, Sid. *And the Bands Played On: An Informal History of British Dance Bands*. London: Elm Tree, 1977.
Collier, James Lincoln. *Benny Goodman and the Swing Era*. New York: Oxford University Press, 1989.
Collier, James Lincoln. *Louis Armstrong: An American Genius*. New York: Oxford University Press, 1983.
"Coming of Americans Resented." *Yorkshire (UK) Evening Post*, March 30, 1926, 10.
"A Conductor's £25,000 a Year: Syncopation and Smoothing Jazz Compositions." *Liverpool (UK) Echo*, March 17, 1923, 6.
Cooke, James Francis, and Paul Whiteman. "The New World of Television." *Etude* 67 (1949): 341–42.
Cooper, Charlotte. "Can a Fat Woman Call Herself Disabled." *Disability & Society* 12, no. 1 (1997): 31–42.
Copyright Act of 1909, Pub. L. 60–349. Superseded 1976.
Cox, Felix. "Duke Ellington as Composer: Two Pieces for Paul Whiteman." *Jazz Perspectives* 6, nos. 1–2 (2012): 57–74.
Cox, Jim. *Music Radio: The Great Performers and Programs of the 1920s through Early 1960s*. Jefferson, NC: McFarland, 2005.

Crafton, Donald. *The Talkies: American Cinema's Transition to Sound, 1926–1931*. Berkeley: University of California Press, 1999.
Crawford, Richard. *America's Musical Life*. New York: Norton, 2001.
Crawford, Richard. *Summertime: George Gershwin's Life in Music*. New York: Norton, 2019.
Crosby, John. "Whiteman TV Show Held Handsome Job." *Detroit (MI) Free Press*, December 14, 1949, 34.
Cummings, Alex Sayf. *Democracy of Sound: Music Piracy and the Remaking of American Copyright in the Twentieth Century*. Oxford: Oxford University Press, 2013.
Curran, Andrew S. *The Anatomy of Blackness: Science and Slavery in an Age of Enlightenment*. Baltimore: John Hopkins University Press, 2011.
"Dancing Time on Merseyside." *Liverpool (UK) Echo*, January 11, 1926, 11.
"Dave Peyton on 2 Weeks Trip East." *Chicago Defender*, July 27, 1929, 7.
Davis, Angela. *Blues Legacies and Black Feminism*. New York: Vintage, 1998.
"Defender's Who's Who of Honor Roll for 1949." *Chicago Defender*, December 31, 1949, 1.
"Delay Whiteman Decision." *Billboard*, July 1, 1939.
Delmont, Matthew F. *The Nicest Kids in Town:* American Bandstand, *Rock 'n' Roll, and the Struggle for Civil Rights in 1950s Philadelphia*. Berkeley: University of California Press, 2012.
Delmont, Matthew F. "'They'll Be Rockin' on Bandstand, in Philadelphia, PA': Dick Clark, Georgie Woods, and the Value of Rock 'n' Roll." *Journal of Popular Music Studies* 24, no. 4 (2012): 457–85.
DeLong, Thomas A. *Pops: Paul Whiteman, King of Jazz*. Piscataway, NJ: New Century, 1983.
DeVeaux, Scott. "The Emergence of the Jazz Concert, 1935–1945." *American Music* 7, no. 1 (1989): 6–29.
"Dietary Discoveries Better Human Health." *New York Times*, March 10, 1929, 158.
Doktor, Stephanie. "Arranging Whiteness: The Gendered and Racialized Sounds of Early Jazz." In *The Oxford Handbook of Arrangement Studies*, edited by Ryan Raul Bañagale. New York: Oxford University Press, 2023.
Doktor, Stephanie. "The Jazz Problem: How US Composers Grappled with the Sounds of Blackness, 1917–1925." PhD diss., University of Virginia, 2016.
Dolan, Mark K. "Cathartic Uplift: A Cultural History of Blues and Jazz in the *Chicago Defender*, 1920–1929." PhD diss., University of South Carolina, 2004.
Dolmage, Jay. "Disabled upon Arrival: The Rhetorical Construction of Disability and Race at Ellis Island." In *The Disability Studies Reader*, edited by Lennard J. Davis, 43–70. 5th ed. New York: Routledge, 2017.
Door, Gregory Michael. "Assuring America's Place in the Sun: Ivey Foreman Lewis and the Teaching of Eugenics at the University of Virginia, 1915–1953." *Journal of Southern History* 66, no. 2 (May 2000): 257–96.
Douglas, Susan J. *Listening In: Radio and the American Imagination*. Minneapolis: University of Minnesota Press, 2004.

Downes, Olin. "A Concert of Jazz." *New York Times*, February 13, 1924, 6.
Downes, Olin. "Whiteman's Jazz." *New York Times*, October 8, 1928.
Dunkel, Mario. *The Stories of Jazz: Narrating a Musical Tradition*. Vienna: Hollitzer Verlag, 2021.
Dunkel, Mario. "W. C. Handy, Abbe Niles, and (Auto)biographical Positioning in the Whiteman Era." *Popular Music and Society* 38, no. 2 (2015): 122–39.
Dyer, Richard. *White: Essays on Race and Culture*. New York: Routledge, 1997.
Ellacott, Nigel. "The Impresarios Wylie-Tate." *The Magic of Pantomime*, 2015. https://www.its behind-you.com/wylietate.html.
Ellington, Duke. "A Royal View of Jazz." *Jazz: A Quarterly of American Music* 2 (Spring 1959): 84.
Ellington, Edward Kennedy (Duke). *Music Is My Mistress*. Garden City, NY: Doubleday, 1973.
"Editorial." *Encore* (London, UK), March 1, 1923, 3.
"Editorial." *Encore* (London, UK), March 22, 1923, 1.
Engelbrecht, Barbara. "Swinging at the Savoy." *Dance Research Journal* 15, no. 2 (1983): 3–10.
Epperson, Bruce D. "From the Statute of Anne to Z. Z. Top: The Strange World of American Sound Recordings, How It Came About, and Why It Will Never Go Away." *John Marshall Review of Intellectual Property Law* 15 (2015): 1–62.
Erenberg, Lewis A. *Steppin' Out: New York Nightlife and the Transformation of American Culture, 1890–1930*. Chicago: University of Chicago Press, 1981.
Europe, James Reese. "A Negro Explains Jazz." *Literary Digest*, April 26, 1919, 28–29. Reprinted in *Readings in Black American Music*, edited by Eileen Southern. New York: Norton, 1983.
Evans, Nicholas M. *Writing Jazz: Race, Nationalism, and Modern Culture in the 1920s*. New York: Garland, 2000.
Faint, Pete. *Jack Hylton*. Self-published, lulu.com, 2014.
"Fame!—and What Feverish Fun We Had." *Daily Herald*, December 24, 1952, 3.
"Famous Bunch, A." *Chicago Defender*, December 15, 1923, 7.
"Farcical Jazz." *Sheffield (UK) Daily Telegraph*, April 16, 1926, 7.
Farrell, Amy Erdman. *Fat Shame: Stigma and the Fat Body in American Culture*. New York: New York University Press, 2011.
"Feature Picture at the Grand; Beulah Benbow Co. at Monogram." *Chicago Defender*, May 5, 1923, 6.
Federal Communications Commission. "Radio Service Bulletin." 66. October 2, 1922. Bureau of Navigation, *US Department of Commerce*. https://docs.fcc.gov/public/attachments/DOC-338241A1.pdf.
Finck, Henry T. *Girth Control, for Womanly Beauty, Manly Strength, Health, and a Long Life for Everybody*. New York: Harper, 1923.
Firestone, Ross. *Swing, Swing, Swing: The Life & Times of Benny Goodman*. New York: Norton, 1993.
Forman, Murray. *One Night on TV Is Worth Weeks at the Paramount: Popular Music on Early Television*. Durham, NC: Duke University Press, 2012.

"*42nd Street*: Merchandising Plan." Merchandising plan. Warner Bros., 1933. *Internet Archive*. https://archive.org/.
"4 Women, 29 Men Listed on Afro's 1950 Honor Roll." *Afro-American* (Baltimore), May 6, 1950, 1.
Furber, Douglas, and Philip Branham. *Limehouse Blues*. New York: Harms, 1922.
Fürnkranz, Magdalena. "Queer Aesthetics and the Performing Subject in Jazz in the 1920s." In *The Routledge Companion to Jazz and Gender*, edited by James Reddan, Monika Herzig, and Michael Kahr, 43–53. New York: Routledge, 2022.
Fry, Andy. *Paris Blues: African American Music and French Popular Culture, 1920–1960*. Chicago: University of Chicago Press, 2014.
Gabbard, Krin. *Jammin' at the Margins: Jazz and the American Cinema*. Chicago: University of Chicago Press, 1996.
Garrett, Charles Hiroshi. "Chinatown, Whose Chinatown? Defining America's Borders with Musical Orientalism." *Journal of the American Musicological Society* 57, no. 1 (2004): 119–73.
Giddins, Gary, and Scott DeVeaux. *Jazz*. New York: Norton, 2009.
Gilbert, David. "Clef Club Inc.: James Reese Europe and New York's Musical Marketplace." *Journal of Popular Music Studies* 24, no. 4 (2012): 430–56.
Gilbert, David. "*London of the Future*: The Metropolis Reimagined after the Great War." *Journal of British Studies* 43, no. 1 (2004): 91–119.
Gilman, Sander L. *Fat Boys: A Slim Book*. Lincoln: University of Nebraska Press, 2004.
Glover, James M. "Music Box." *The Stage*, March 22, 1923, 17.
Glover, James M. "Music Box." *The Stage*, May 31, 1923, 15.
"GM's New Move May Affect Ads." *Billboard*, April 2, 1932, 17.
Gold, Gerald. "Jazz Concert by Whiteman 60 Years Ago to Live Again." *New York Times*, February 10, 1984.
Goldmark, Daniel. "Audio Commentaries: Daniel Goldmark on *Porky at the Crocadero*." Disc 4, *Looney Tunes Golden Collection, Vol. 5*, dir. by Frank Tashlin. 1938, Burbank. Warner Bros. Home Entertainment, 2007.
Goldmark, Daniel. *Tunes for 'Toons: Music and the Hollywood Cartoon*. Berkeley: University of California Press, 2005.
Goodman, Benny. "I Lead a Double Life." *House and Garden*, April 1951, 181.
Goodman, Benny, and Irving Kolodin. *The Kingdom of Swing*. New York: Ungar, 1961.
Goodman, David. "The Whiteness of Classical Music." *Historicising Whiteness: Transnational Perspectives on the Construction of an Identity*. Melbourne, Australia: RMIT, 2007.
"Good Revue, A." *Sunday Illustrated* (London), April 1, 1923, 8.
Gordon, Bonnie. *Monteverdi's Unruly Women: The Power of Song in Early Modern Italy*. Cambridge: Cambridge University Press, 2009.
Gordon, Jack. "A Night to Remember at Aeolian Hall." *Fort Worth (TX) Press*, February 23, 1961.

Gould, Jack. "Television in Review: Kay Kyser's New Program—Whiteman's Show." *New York Times*, December 11, 1949, X11.

Gracie, Charlie, and John Jackson, *Rock & Roll's Hidden Giant: The Story of Rock Pioneer Charlie Gracie*. Los Angeles: Alfred Music, 2014.

"Gramophone Review." *Melody Maker*, May 1926, 47.

Grant, Madison. *The Passing of the Great Race; or The Racial Basis of European History*. New York: Scribner's Sons, 1916.

"Greatest Success That Ever Came to London, The." *Variety*, July 4, 1923, 40.

Green, Abel. "Colorful Music Man Jack Robbins Victim of a Heart Attack at 65." *Variety*, December 23, 1959, 43, 46.

Green, Abel. "Disk Reviews: Victor Salon Orchestra." *Variety*, May 23, 1928, 60.

Green, Abel. "Inside Stuff: Music." *Variety*, June 17, 1936, 49.

Hall, Gladys. "A Great Big Family Man." *Motion Picture* 39, no. 5, 1930, 32–33, 112–13.

Hampton, Lionel, and James Haskins. *Hamp: An Autobiography*. New York: Warner, 1989.

"Hampton Choir Sets Debut with Whiteman." *Courier* (Pittsburgh, PA), March 31, 1951, 18.

Hansen, Chadwick. "Social Influences on Jazz Style in Chicago, 1920–30." *American Quarterly* 12, no. 4 (1960): 493–507.

Hardesty, Jacob. "Moral Outrage and Musical Corruption: White Educators' Responses to the 'Jazz Problem.'" *History of Education Quarterly* 56, no. 4 (2016): 590–617.

Hardy, Jessie Moniz. "See Mildred Shine on Early TV." *Royal Gazette* (Hamilton, Bermuda), March 17, 2020.

Harlig, Alexandra. "Communities of Practice: Active and Affective Viewing of Early Social Dance on the Popular Screen." In *The Oxford Handbook of Dance and the Popular Screen*, edited by Melissa Blanco Borelli, 57–67. Oxford: Oxford University Press, 2014.

"Harmonizing Four Sign Record Pact." *Chicago Defender*, March 9, 1957, 8.

"Harmony (Musical) May Grace Hearing: Radio and Stage Players to Perform Arguments at 'Piracy' Quiz." *Philadelphia Record*, January 28, 1936.

Hathaway, Charles. "The Boys Who Arrange the Tunes You Hear and Play." *Metronome*, September 1935, 43.

Hatten, Robert. *Interpreting Musical Gestures, Topics, and Tropes: Mozart, Beethoven, Schubert*. Bloomington: Indiana University Press, 2004.

Hayes, Chris. *Dance Music at the Savoy Hotel 1920–1927*. Isle of Wight: Self-published, 1988.

"Headliners." *New York Amsterdam News*, February 16, 1952, 12.

Heap, Chad. *Slumming: Sexual and Racial Encounters in American Nightlife, 1885–1940*. Chicago: University of Chicago Press, 2008.

Hector, Louis J. "Whiteman Concert Draws Capacity House; Nets $1250." *Williams Record*, June 2, 1936, 3.

Herbert v. Shanley, 242 U.S. 591 (1917).
Herndon, April. "Disparate but Disabled: Fat Embodiment and Disability Studies." *NWSA Journal* 14, no. 3 (2002): 120–37.
Hisama, Ellie. "Postcolonialism on the Make: The Music of John Mellencamp, David Bowie, and John Zorn." *Popular Music* 12, no. 2 (1993): 91–104.
Horowitz, Joseph. *Understanding Toscanini: How He Became an American Culture-God and Helped Create a New Audience for Old Music*. New York: Knopf, 1987.
Howland, John. "Between the Muses and the Masses: Symphonic Jazz, 'Glorified' Entertainment, and the Rise of the American Musical Middlebrow, 1920–1944." PhD diss., Stanford University, 2002.
Howland, John. *"Ellington Uptown": Duke Ellington, James P. Johnson, and the Birth of Concert Jazz*. Ann Arbor: University of Michigan Press, 2009.
Howland, John. *Hearing Luxe Pop: Glorification, Glamour, and the Middlebrow in American Popular Music*. Berkeley: University of California Press, 2021.
Howland, John. "Jazz Rhapsodies in Black and White: James P. Johnson's 'Yamekraw.'" *American Music* 24, no. 4 (2006): 445–509.
Howland, John. "Jazz with Strings: Between Jazz and the Great American Songbook." In *Jazz/Not Jazz: The Music and Its Boundaries*, edited by David Ake, Charles Hiroshi Garrett, and Daniel Goldmark, 111–47. Berkeley: University of California Press, 2012.
Howland, John. "Paul Whiteman and Glorified 'Modern American Music,' 1927–1934." In *Oxford Handbook of Music and the Middlebrow*, edited by Christopher Chowrimootoo and Kate Guthrie. New York: Oxford University Press, 2024.
Hubbard, William Lines, ed. *The American History and Encyclopedia of Music*. Vol. 1. New York: Squire, 1908.
Hughes, Patrick [Spike]. *Opening Bars: Beginning an Autobiography*. London: Pilot, 1946.
Hunter, Tera W. *To 'Joy My Freedom: Southern Black Women's Lives and Labors after the Civil War*. Cambridge, MA: Harvard University Press, 1997.
Hylton, Jack. "The Prophets of Doom." *Melody Maker*, January 1926, 14.
"Interview with Arthur Lange and Ernest Klapholz discussing Their Early Days in Hollywood." *Cue Sheet: The Journal of the Society for the Preservation of Film Music* 7 (1990): 158–59.
"In the Loop." *Chicago Defender*, March 20, 1920, 6.
Jablonski, Edward. *Gershwin Remembered*. Portland, OR: Amadeus, 1992.
Jackson, Jeffrey H. *Making Jazz French: Music and Modern Life in Interwar Paris*. Durham, NC: Duke University Press, 2003.
Jackson, John A. American Bandstand: *Dick Clark and the Making of a Rock 'n' Roll Empire*. New York: Oxford University Press, 1997.
Jacobs, Steven, Anthony Kinik, and Eva Hietscher, eds. *The City Symphony Phenomenon: Cinema, Art, and Urban Modernity between the Wars*. New York: Routledge, 2019.

Jahn, Konstantin. "Paul Whitemans *Symphonic Jazz* und seine Spuren im Hollywoodmusical—exemplifiziert anhand der Filme *King of Jazz* und *42nd Street*." *Kieler Beiträge zur Filmmusikforschung* 8 (2012): 186–99. Doi:10.59056/kbzf.2012.8.p186–199.

"Jazz a Crime." *London Daily News*, March 9, 1926, 5.

"Jazz at the Albert Hall." *London Truth*, April 14, 1926, 23.

"Jazz Boys." Advertisement. *Chicago Defender*, March 11, 1922, 7.

"Jazz Expert, A." *Leeds (UK) Mercury*, February 22, 1923, 6.

"Jazz in Excelsis." *Acton Gazette*, April 16, 1926, 8.

"Jazz or 'Modern Popular Music' to Be Heard and Discussed at Composers' League Lecture." *Musical Courier*, February 7, 1924. Reprinted in *Jazz in Print (1859–1929): An Anthology of Selected Early Readings in Jazz History*, edited by Karl Koenig. Hillsdale, NY: Pendragon, 2002.

Johnson, Russell L. "'Disease Is Unrhythmical': Jazz, Health, and Disability in 1920s America." *Health and History* 13, no. 2 (2011): 13–42.

Johnston, Gene. "Tunesmiths." *Tempo*, January 1935, 7–8.

Jou, Chin. "The Progressive Era Body Project: Calorie-Counting and 'Disciplining the Stomach' in 1920s America." *Journal of the Gilded Age and Progressive Era* 18, no. 4 (2019): 422–40. Doi:10.1017/S1537781418000348.

Kater, Michael. *Different Drummers: Jazz in the Culture of Nazi Germany*. New York: Oxford University Press, 1992.

Kemp, Steve. "Paul Whiteman's Fifth Experiment." *Metronome*, February 1933, 12.

Kernfeld, Barry. "Peyton, Dave." *American National Biography Online*, 2000. http://www.anb.org/. https://doi.org/10.1093/anb/9780198606697.article.1802875.

King, Noel. "What Systemic Racism Means and the Way It Harms Communities (interview with Ijeoma Oluo)." *Morning Edition, NPR*, July 1, 2020. https://www.npr.org/.

"*King of Jazz*." *Variety*, May 1930, 38.

"'King of Jazz' Speculates on Weight, Fame: Whiteman Holds 162-Pounds." *Hartford (CT) Courant*, March 25, 1932, 7.

Koenig, Karl, ed. *Jazz in Print (1856–1929): An Anthology of Selected Early Readings in Jazz History*. Hillsdale, NY: Pendragon, 2002.

Kolodin, Irving. "Liner Notes." *The Famous 1938 Carnegie Hall Jazz Concert*. Directed by Benny Goodman. Columbia/Legacy, 1999. CD.

Lampert, Vera. "Benny Goodman and Bartók's Contrasts: An Extraordinary Collaboration." *Musical Quarterly* 101, no. 1 (2018): 6–34.

Lange, Arthur. *Arranging for the Modern Dance Orchestra*. New York: Arthur Lange, 1926. Reprinted in *Arranging for the Modern Dance Orchestra*. New York: Robbins Music, 1927.

Langston, Tony. "Theatrical Review." *Chicago Defender*, March 13, 1915, 6.

LaRocca, Nick. "Jazz Stems from Whites, Not Blacks." *Metronome* 52 (1936): 20, 51, 53.

Lawrence, Austin Harry. *Duke Ellington and His World*. New York: Routledge, 2004.

Layton, James, and David Pierce. *King of Jazz: Paul Whiteman's Technicolor Revue*. Severn, MD: Media History, 2016.

Lemke, Sieglinde. *Primitivist Modernism: Black Culture and the Origins of Transatlantic Modernism*. New York: Oxford University Press, 1998.

Leo, Katherine M. "The Legal Legacy of the Player Piano and the Origins of the Compulsory Mechanical License." In *Player Pianos in Early 20th-Century Life*, edited by Catherine Hennessy Wolter. Champaign: University of Illinois Press, forthcoming.

Leo, Katherine M. "Paul Whiteman: Radio Performance Rights Advocate." *Williams College*, April 2018. https://library.williams.edu/.

Leonard, Neil. *Jazz and the White Americans: The Acceptance of a New Art Form*. Chicago: University of Chicago Press, 1962.

"Lessons of the Whiteman Visit: How to Profit from His Advent, The." *Melody Maker*, May 1926, 1.

Levinson, Peter J. *Trumpet Blues: The Life of Harry James*. New York: Oxford University Press, 1999.

Lewis, Carey B. "The Symphony Concert." *Chicago Defender*, November 21, 1914, 6.

Lieb, Sandra R. *Mother of the Blues: A Study of Ma Rainey*. Amherst: University of Massachusetts Press, 1981.

"London Dance Notes." *Dancing Times*, June 1926, 326–27.

"London Gets Whiteman." *Variety*, February 15, 1923, 2.

Lopes, Paul. *The Rise of a Jazz Art World*. Cambridge: Cambridge University Press, 2002.

MacDonald, J. Fred. *Blacks and White TV: Afro-Americans in Television since 1948*. Chicago: Nelson-Hall, 1983.

Magee, Jeffrey. "Before Louis: When Fletcher Henderson Was the 'Paul Whiteman of the Race.'" *American Music* 18, no. 4 (2000): 391–425.

Magee, Jeffrey. "'Everybody Step'": Irving Berlin, Jazz, and Broadway in the 1920s." *Journal of the American Musicological Society* 59, no. 3 (2006): 697–732.

Magee, Jeffrey. *The Uncrowned King of Swing: Fletcher Henderson and Big Band Jazz*. New York: Oxford University Press, 2005.

Maher, James T., and Jeffrey Sultanof. "Pre-swing Era Big Bands and Jazz Composing and Arranging." In *The Oxford Companion to Jazz*, edited by Bill Kirchner, 264–76. New York: Oxford University Press, 2000.

"Make Boy, 10, Give Up $100 a Week Job." *Chicago Defender*, April 16, 1927, 3.

Malnig, Julie. *Dancing Black, Dancing White: Rock 'n' Roll, Race, and Youth Culture of the 1950s and Early 1960s*. New York: Oxford University Press, 2023.

Malnig, Julie. "'Just Kids': Youth, Community, and Race in Televised Teen Dance Programs of the 1950s." In *Perspectives on American Dance: The Twentieth Century*, edited by Jennifer Atkins, Sally R. Sommer, and Tricia Henry Young, 159–78. Gainesville: University Press of Florida, 2018.

"Manhattan Serenade / Victor Salon Orchestra." By Victor Alter. Victor Matrix CVE-43303. *Discography of American Historical Recordings, UC Santa Barbara Library, 2005–2024*. https://adp.library.ucsb.edu.

Martin, Jeff. "*TV Teen Club*: Teen TV as Safe Harbor." In *Teen Television: Essays on Programming and Fandom*, edited by Sharon Marie Ross and Louise Ellen Stein, 27–42. Jefferson, NC: McFarland, 2008.

McGee, Kristin A. *Some Liked It Hot: Jazz Women in Film and Television, 1928–1959*. Middleton, CT: Wesleyan University Press, 2009.

Meizel, Katherine. *Idolized: Music, Media, and Identity in American Idol*. Bloomington: Indiana University Press, 2011.

Melnick, Jeffrey Paul. *A Right to Sing the Blues: African Americans, Jews, and American Popular Song*. Cambridge, MA: Harvard University Press, 1999.

"Melody Kings Walk Away with Rittenhouse Show." *Philadelphia Tribune*, May 19, 1953, 12.

"Melody Mart Notes." *Billboard*, December 8, 1928, 57.

Mendl, R. W. S. *The Appeal of Jazz*. Glasgow, UK: Maclehose, 1927.

Merriam, Alan P., and Fradley H. Garner. "Jazz—The Word." *Ethnomusicology* 12, no. 3 (1968): 373–96.

Metronome, June 24, 1924, 53.

Mitchell, David T., and Sharon L. Snyder. *Narrative Prosthesis: Disability and the Dependencies of Discourse*. Ann Arbor: University of Michigan Press, 2000.

Mobley, Jennifer-Scott. *Female Bodies on the American Stage: Enter Fat Actress*. New York: Palgrave Macmillan, 2014.

Mollow, Anna. "Unvictimizable: Toward a Fat Black Disability Studies." *African American Review* 50, no. 2 (2017): 105–21.

Monson, Craig A. "Putting Bolognese Nun Musicians in Their Place." In *Women's Voices across Musical Worlds*, edited by Jane Bernstein, 118–41. Lebanon, NH: Northeastern University Press, 2003.

Monson, Ingrid. *Freedom Sounds: Civil Rights Call Out to Jazz and Africa*. New York: Oxford University Press, 2007.

Moran, Rachel Louise. *Governing Bodies: American Politics and the Shaping of the Modern Physique*. Philadelphia: University of Pennsylvania Press, 2018.

Mordden, Ethan. *Broadway Babies: The People Who Made the American Musical*. New York: Oxford University Press, 1983.

"More Emphasis on Music." *Williams Record*, November 5, 1935, 2.

Morgan-Ellis, Esther M. "Leslie Uggams, *Sing Along with Mitch* (1961–64), and the Reverberations of Minstrelsy." *Journal of the Society for American Music* 16, no. 1 (2022): 47–68.

Morrison, Matthew D. "Race, Blacksound, and the (Re)Making of Musicological Discourse." *Journal of the American Musicological Society* 72, no. 3 (2019): 781–823.

Morse, Leon. "Paul Whiteman Revue." *Billboard*, September 22, 1951, 8.

"Mr Paul Whiteman: No British Ban on Orchestra." *Westminster Gazette* (London, UK), April 7, 1926, 7.

Muhammad, Khalil Gibran. *The Condemnation of Blackness: Race, Crime, and the Making of Modern Urban America.* 2nd ed. Cambridge, MA: Harvard University Press, 2019.

Murray, Sean. "That 'Weird and Wonderful Posture': Jump 'Jim Crow' and the Performance of Disability." In *Oxford Handbook of Music and Disability Studies*, edited by Blake Howe, Stephanie Jensen-Moulton, Neil Lerner, and Joseph Straus, 357–70. New York: Oxford University Press, 2016.

"Musical and Dramatic." *Chicago Defender*, April 26, 1913, 6.

"Musical and Dramatic." *Chicago Defender*, June 14, 1913, 8.

"Musical and Dramatic." *Chicago Defender*, November 14, 1914, 6.

"Musical Comedy Notes." *Billboard*, July 21, 1928, 13.

"Musical Jazz: Foxtrots and the 'Ring.'" *Westminster Gazette*, May 26, 1923, 7.

"Music Box." *Stage*, April 8, 1926, 15.

"Musicians' Letter to King." *London Daily News*, March 20, 1923, 1.

Musiker, Reuben, and Naomi Musiker. "Savino, Domenico." In *Conductors and Composers of Popular Orchestral Music: A Biographical and Discographical Sourcebook*, edited by Naomi Musiker and Reuben Musiker, 240–41. Westport, CT: Routledge, 1998.

"*My Man Godfrey*." *Billboard*, September 19, 1936, 22.

"NAB Seeks License to Use Recordings." *Billboard*, August 19, 1939.

Nadel, Alan. *Television in Black-and-White America: Race and National Identity*. Lawrence: University Press of Kansas, 2005.

"National Ball, The." *Liverpool (UK) Echo*, March 23, 1923, 7.

"Nesbit Tumblers on Television Sunday." *Afro-American* (Baltimore, MD), April 26, 1952, 6.

"New Show World, 1929–30, The." *Variety*, June 19, 1929, 40–41.

"News of the Stage: 'Little Shot' Joins the List of Shows Departing." *New York Times*, January 19, 1935, 9.

Nicholson, Stuart. *Jazz and Culture in a Global Age*. Boston: Northeastern University Press, 2014.

"1933 Thompson Concert Committee High-Hatted Whiteman, Charged Lack of Chapin Hall Dignity." *Williams Record*, May 26, 1936, 1, 7.

Nome, Robert. "Dave Peyton." *Musical Enterprise*. Reprinted in *Chicago Defender*, January 29, 1916, 5.

Norton, Christopher J. "Turtle Power: The Case for Common Law Protection for Pre-1972 Sound Recordings." *Berkeley Technology Law Journal* 31 (2016): 759–84.

Norton, Woodward B. "Course in Commercial Music, New Laboratory, Are Paul Whiteman's Plans for Williams College." *Williams Record*, June 2, 1936, 1, 3.

Nosowitz, Dan. "How a Fake British Accent Took Old Hollywood by Storm: The Story behind the Strange Way Katharine Hepburn (and Others) Spoke." *Atlas Obscura*, October 27, 2016. https://www.atlasobscura.com/.

Nye, Russell B. "A Word about Whiteman." *Popular Music & Society* 1, no. 4 (1972): 231–41.

Ogren, Kathy J. *The Jazz Revolution: Twenties America and the Meaning of Jazz*. New York: Oxford University Press, 1989.

Oja, Carol J. *Making Music Modern: New York in the 1920s*. New York: Oxford University Press, 2000.

Oliphant, Dave. *The Early Swing Era, 1930 to 1941*. Westport, CT: Greenwood, 2002.

"On the Upbeat: Paul Whiteman." *Variety*, January 10, 1940, 38.

Orrin G. Hatch—Bob Goodlatte Music Modernization Act Title III: Allocation for Music Producers Act (AMP), 132 Stat. 3676 (2018).

"Palladium, The." *Variety*, June 15, 1927, 26–27.

Palmer, Robert. "Honoring the Classics of Jazz." *New York Times*, August 3, 1987.

Parsonage, Catherine. *The Evolution of Jazz in Britain: c. 1880–1935*. Aldershot, UK: Ashgate, 2005.

Passman, Arnold. "When Deejays Were Forbidden." *Popular Music and Society* 16, no. 4 (1992): 51–53.

"Paul Whiteman." *The Stage* (London), May 31, 1923, 13.

"Paul Whiteman and His Band." *Scotsman* (Edinburgh, UK), April 10, 1926, 9.

"Paul Whiteman and His Band, Now at the R.K.O. St. Louis Theatre!" *St. Louis Post-Dispatch*, January 11, 1932, 3C.

"Paul Whiteman, Jazz King, Loses 85 Pounds in Fast." *Washington Post*, January 6, 1929, M2.

"Paul Whiteman Publications Soon Ready: All Given Test by Famous Orchestra Leader." *Music Trades*, June 11, 1927, 144.

"Paul Whiteman Treasures to Enrich Williams." *Williams Alumni Review* 28, no. 2, November 1935, 56–57.

Peyton, Dave. "The Musical Bunch." *Chicago Defender*, 1925–29, 5–6.

"Peyton, the Music Wonder, Moves to the Loop District." *Chicago Defender*, February 13, 1915, 6.

"Pictures: $40,000 Short." *Variety*, November 6, 1929, 8.

"Plays and Players." *Northern Whig* (Belfast, Northern Ireland), February 24, 1923, 10.

Plotz, Barbara. "*Paul Blart* and the Decline of White Working-Class Masculinities." *Fat Studies* 2, no. 2 (2013): 173–82.

Pollack, Howard. *George Gershwin: His Life and Work*. Berkeley: University of California Press, 2006.

"Presenting Pop Music with All the Trappings." *Metronome*, May 1936, 31.

"Primitive Savage Animalism, Preacher's Analysis of Jazz." *New York Times*, March 3, 1922, 13.

"Program Reviews: Paul Whiteman." *Billboard*, November 5, 1932, 15.

"Protection of the Performing Artists 'Interpretative Rendition' through the Arranger's Copyright." *Illinois Law Review* 37 (1942–43): 647–65.

Radano, Ronald. *Lying Up a Nation: Race and Black Music*. Chicago: University of Chicago Press, 2003.

"'Syncopated Symphony: The Savoy Bands' New Experiment." *Radio Times*, March 19, 1926, 580.
Rayno, Don. *Paul Whiteman: Pioneer in American Music Volume I: 1890–1930*. Lanham, MD: Scarecrow, 2003.
Rayno, Don. *Paul Whiteman: Pioneer in American Music Volume II: 1930–1967*. Lanham, MD: Scarecrow, 2013.
RCA v. Whiteman, 28 F. Supp. 787 (S.D.N.Y. 1939), rev'd RCA v. Whiteman, 114 F.3d 86 (2d Cir. 1940).
Rea, E. B. "Encores and Echoes." *Afro-American* (Baltimore, MD), March 31, 1951, 8.
Rea, E. B. "Encores and Echoes." *Afro-American* (Baltimore, MD), January 12, 1952, 6.
Revision of Copyright Laws: Hearings before the Committee on Patents, House of Representatives. 74th Congress, 2nd Session (February–April 1936).
Rhame, Laurel. "Whiteman's Burden." News and Exhibits. *Williams College Library*. https://library.williams.edu/2018/02/19/whitemans-burden/.
Rice, Elmer. *Street Scene: A Play in Three* Acts. New York: Samuel French, 1929.
Richman, Daniel. "On the Record: Paul Whiteman Concert Orchestra, *Album of Manhattan*." *Billboard*, July 6, 1940, 12.
Rieger, Jon H., and Brian Rublein. "Whiteman as the Don Quixote of Jazz." *Popular Music & Society* 3, no. 1 (1974): 3–23.
Roach, Max. "What 'Jazz' Means to Me." *Black Scholar* 3, no. 10 (1972): 2–6.
"Robbins Reports Folios on Upbeat." *Metronome*, May 1941, 46.
Rodgers, Nile, Jr. "Mr. Rodgers's Neighborhood." *New York Times*, September 11, 2011, SS2–84. https://archive.nytimes.com/.
Rodgers, Richard. *Musical Stages: An Autobiography*. New York: Random, 1975.
Rodman, Ron. *Tuning In: American Narrative Television Music*. Oxford: Oxford University Press, 2010.
Rogers, Bradley. "Lawrence Welk: Champagne Music, Ovaltine Politics." *Journal of Popular Music Studies* 34, no. 1 (2022): 141–66.
Rogin, Michael. *Blackface, White Noise: Jewish Immigrants in the Hollywood Melting Pot*. Berkeley: University of California Press, 1996.
Rosen, Zvi. "Common Law Copyright." *University of Cincinnati Law Review* 85 (2018): 1055–133.
Rosen, Zvi. "Fred Waring and the Pennsylvanian Litigation." (Mostly) IP Blog, January 12, 2018. *Mostly IP History by Zvi Rosen*, 2016–20. http://zvirosen.com/2018/01/12/fred-waring-and-the-pennsylvanian-litigation/#fn-319-5.
Rubin, Martin. *Showstoppers: Busby Berkeley and the Tradition of Spectacle*. New York: Columbia University Press, 1993.
Sammond, Nicholas. *Birth of an Industry: Blackface Minstrelsy and the Rise of American Animation*. Durham, NC: Duke University Press, 2015.
Sanders, James. *Celluloid Skyline: New York and the Movies*. New York: Knopf, 2003.

Sanjek, Russell. *American Popular Music and Its Business: The First 400 Years, 3: From 1900 to 1984*. New York: Oxford University Press, 1988.
Sanjek, Russell. *Pennies from Heaven: The American Popular Music Business in the Twentieth Century*. New York: Da Capo, 1996.
Sargeant, Winthrop. *Jazz: Hot and Hybrid*. New York: Dutton, 1946.
Savoy Orpheans: Revolution of Syncopated Music from Ragtime to Symphonised Syncopation, The. London: Savoy, 1924. Program.
"Savoy-Orpheans, The." *Buckingham Advertiser and Free Press* (Aylesbury, UK), April 18, 1925, 2.
Savran, David. *Highbrow/Lowdown: Theater, Jazz, and the Making of the New Middle Class*. Ann Arbor: University of Michigan, 2010.
Schenbeck, Lawrence. "Music, Gender, and 'Uplift' in the 'Chicago Defender,' 1927–1937." *Musical Quarterly* 81, no. 3 (1997): 344–70.
Schiff, David. *Gershwin:* Rhapsody in Blue. New York: Cambridge University Press, 1997.
Schuller, Gunther. *Early Jazz: Its Roots and Musical Development*. New York: Oxford University Press, 1968.
Schuller, Gunther. *The Swing Era: The Development of Jazz, 1930–1945*. New York: Oxford University Press, 1989.
Scott, Derek. "Other Mainstreams: Light Music and Easy Listening, 1920–70." In *The Cambridge History of Twentieth-Century Music*, edited by Nicholas Cook and Anthony People, 307–35. Cambridge: Cambridge University Press, 2004.
Scott, Michelle R. "'To Help Enlighten Our People': 'Theater Folk' and Stage Advice Columns in the 1920s *Chicago Defender*." *American Studies* 59, no. 3 (2020): 55–76.
Seldes, Gilbert. *The Seven Lively Arts*. New York: Harper, 1924.
"Sensational Welcome Home for Whiteman." *Variety*, August 18, 1923, 12.
Shainman, Irwin. "Notes." *Music Library Association* 14, no. 2 (1957): 189–91.
Shavers, Amber Nicole. *The Little Book of Music Law*. Chicago: American Bar Association, 2013.
Shaw, Elizabeth. *The Embodiment of Disobedience: Fat Black Women's Unruly Political Bodies*. New York: Lexington, 2006.
Sheppard, W. Anthony. "Compelled by the Primitive in Cinematic Dance." In *Elsewhere from a US Perspective: Transnational Appeals, Exoticism, and Enduring Stereotype in Film*, forthcoming.
Sheppard, W. Anthony. *Extreme Exoticism: Japan in the American Musical Imagination*. New York: Oxford University Press, 2019.
Shipton, Alyn. *A New History of Jazz*. Rev. and updated ed. New York: Continuum, 2007.
Shuler, Pamela. "The Commissions and Compositions of Works for Benny Goodman and Chamber Ensemble: History, Style and Clarinet Writing." PhD diss., University of Illinois at Urbana-Champaign, 2017.
Simon, Arthur. "Chain Chatter." *Metronome*, March 1933, 15.
"Sitter Out, The." *Dancing Times*, May 1923, 804.

Sitter-Out, The. "Whitemanising Our Bands." *Dancing Times*, April 1923, 708.
Smith, Vernon L. "The Hampton Institute Choir, 1873–1973." PhD diss., Florida State University, 1985.
Stearns, Peter N. *Fat History: Bodies and Beauty in the Modern West*. New York: New York University Press, 1997.
Stein, Sonia. "The Radio Miss Lee Is Really No Gypsy: 'Pops' Won't Look—He's Missing a Show." *Washington Post*, January 29, 1950, L1.
Steiner, Fred. *The Making of an American Film Composer: A Study of Alfred Newman's Music in the First Decade of the Sound Era*. PhD diss., University of Southern California, 1981.
Strings, Sabrina. *Fearing the Black Body: The Racial Origins of Fat Phobia*. New York: New York University Press, 2019.
Strings, Sabrina. "Obese Black Women as 'Social Dead Weight': Reinventing the 'Diseased Black Woman.'" *Signs: Journal of Women in Culture and Society* 41, no. 1 (2015): 107–30.
"Style of Their Own." *Western Morning News* (Plymouth, UK), March 12, 1923, 5.
Sudhalter, Richard M. *Lost Chords: White Musicians and Their Contribution to Jazz, 1915–1945*. New York: Oxford University Press, 1999.
Swaffer, Hannen. "What London Looks Like." *Variety*, May 12, 1926, 2.
T., H. "Whiteman Offers Sixth Experiment." *New York Times*, December 16, 1933, L13.
Tackley, Catherine. *Benny Goodman's Famous 1938 Carnegie Hall Jazz Concert*. Oxford Studies in Recorded Jazz. Oxford: Oxford University Press, 2012.
"Talented Youngster Appears on T.V. Show." *Philadelphia Tribune*, November 13, 1951, 6.
"Tempo Club Show." *Chicago Defender*, May 17, 1924, 6.
"Threatened Orchestral Invasion." *Stage*, March 4, 1926, 15.
Tipton, Carrie Allen. "Who's Afraid of the Jazz Monsters? For Many Americans, Jazz Was the Music of Demons, Devils, and Things That Go Bump in the Night." *History Today* 69, no. 10 (2019). https://www.historytoday.com/.
Todd, Arthur. "Dolly In on Television Dance." *Theatre Arts*, September 1951.
"Tribute to Arthur Lange (1889–1956): Composer, Arranger, and Conductor." *Cue Sheet: The Journal of the Society for the Preservation of Film Music* 7 (1990): full issue.
Tsou, Judy. "Gendering Race: Stereotypes of Chinese Americans in Popular Sheet Music." *repercussions* 6, no. 2 (1997): 25–62.
"TV Program Highlights." *Hartford (CT) Courant*, April 8, 1951, SM16.
"£25,000 a year." *Sunderland (UK) Daily Echo*, February 27, 1923, 2.
Ulaby, Neda. "Roscoe Arbuckle and the Scandal of Fatness." In *Bodies Out of Bounds: Fatness and Transgression*, edited by Jana Evans Braziel and Kathleen LeBesco, 153–65. Berkeley: University of California Press, 2001.
"Variety Gossip: Concerning the Hippodrome." *Stage* (London), February 15, 1923, 12.
"Variety World, The." *Era* (London), March 1, 1923, 14.

Vogel, Dorothy. "Are You Only an Applauder? American Music Correspondence Schools in the Early Twentieth Century." *Journal of Research in Music Education* 62, no. 4 (2014): 446–61.
"'Vulgarity' of Jazz." *London Daily Herald*, February 1, 1926, 5.
Wald, Elijah. *How the Beatles Destroyed Rock 'n' Roll: An Alternative History of American Popular Music*. New York: Oxford University Press, 2009.
Walsh, Katie. "Selling Masculinity at Warner Bros.: William Powell, a Case Study." *Spectator*, Spring 2013, 45–53.
Waring, Virginia. *Fred Waring and the Pennsylvanians*. Champaign: University of Illinois Press, 2007.
Waring v. WDAS Broadcasting Station, Inc. 27 Pa. D. & C. 297 (1936).
"Ways of Officialdom, The." *Leicester (UK) Evening Mail*, July 29, 1925, 6.
"Welcomes Whiteman." *Variety*, July 7, 1926, 3.
Wells, Christi Jay (fka Christopher J. Wells). "'The Ace of His Race': Paul Whiteman's Early Critical Reception in the Black Press." *Jazz and Culture* 1 (2018): 77–103.
Wells, Christi Jay (fka Christopher J. Wells). *Between Beats: The Jazz Tradition and Black Vernacular Dance*. New York: Oxford University Press, 2021.
"Where the Etude Stands on Jazz." *Etude* 42, no. 8 (1924): 515.
Whiteman, Margaret Livingston, and Isabel Leighton. *Whiteman's Burden*. New York: Viking, 1933.
Whiteman, Paul. "The Gershwin I Knew." *Music Journal*, April 1955.
Whiteman, Paul. *Records for the Millions*. Edited by David A. Stein. New York: Hermitage, 1948.
Whiteman, Paul. "What Is Jazz Doing to American Music?" *Etude* 42, no. 8 (1924): 523–24.
Whiteman, Paul, and Mary Margaret McBride. *Jazz*. New York: Sears, 1926.
Whiteman, Paul, and Mary Margaret McBride. *Jazz*. New York: Sears, 1926. Rev. ed. New York: Arno, 1974.
"Whiteman and the Tivoli." *Melody Maker*, May 1926, 12.
"Whiteman Declares Jass Music Can Be Made Alluring." *Morning Press* (Santa Barbara, CA), March 16, 1919, 8.
"Whiteman Disinclined but WNEW Action Forced to Trial by RCA Victor." *Variety*, December 7, 1938.
"Whiteman Exonerated in Court." *New York Times*, April 8, 1927, 25.
"Whiteman in 34th Yr. of Show Business." "Television Magazine." *Monday Morning Mail* (Loves Park, IL), 4, no. 41, June 24, 1955, 1, 7.
"Whiteman Quits Music Publishing Alliance." *Variety*, February 29, 1928, 53.
"Whiteman's Bit." *Variety*, April 19, 1923, 55.
"Whiteman's Title Upheld: Kingston Judge Rules He Can Call Himself 'King of Jazz.'" *New York Times*, December 28, 1932, 6.
White-Smith Music Publishing Co. v. Apollo Co., 209 U.S. 1 (1908).
"Why I Play Jazz." *Radio Times*, November 27, 1925, 438.
"Widening Horizons." *Chicago Defender*, January 19, 1952, 10.

Wilson, John S. "Misunderstood Pioneer: Whiteman's 'King of Jazz' Misnomer Obscured His Genuine Contributions." *New York Times*, December 30, 1967.

Wilson, John S. "Music: Tribute Recalls '24 Whiteman Program." *New York Times*, February 15, 1984.

Wilson, John S. "Teagarden and His Times—the Early Days Documented." *High Fidelity*, June 1963, 86–89.

Wilson, Teddy, Arie Lighthart, and Humphrey Van Loo. *Teddy Wilson Talks Jazz: The Autobiography of Teddy Wilson*. London: A & C Black, 2001.

"Winner, A." *Philadelphia Tribune*, November 17, 1951, 6.

Wipplinger, Jonathan O. *The Jazz Republic: Music, Race, and American Culture in Weimar Germany*. Ann Arbor: University of Michigan Press, 2017.

Witty, Paul. "Two Studies of Children's Interest in TV." *Elementary English* 29, no. 5 (1952): 251–57.

Woldu, Gail Hilson. "Do These Sequins Make My Butt Look Fat? Wardrobe, Image, and the Challenge of Identity in the Music of Black American Women." *Musical Quarterly* 96, no. 1 (2013): 100–136.

Wolters, Larry. "Whiteman at 60 Is Having Time of Life with TV: Still Seeking and Finding Youthful Talent." *Chicago Daily Tribune*, November 19, 1950, NW14.

Wonham, Henry B. *Playing the Races: Ethnic Caricature and American Literary Realism*. New York: Oxford University Press, 2004.

Wriggle, John. *Blue Rhythm Fantasy: Big Band Jazz Arranging in the Swing Era*. Urbana: University of Illinois Press, 2016.

Yancey-Bragg, N'dea. "What Is Systemic Racism? Here's What It Means and How You Can Help Dismantle It." *USA Today*, January 29, 2021. https://www.usatoday.com/.

Young, William H., and Nancy K. Young. *Music of the Great Depression*. Westport, CT: Greenwood, 2005.

Youngren, William H. "Giving Whiteman His Due." *Atlantic Monthly* 254, no. 1, July 1984, 103–6.

Contributors

RYAN RAUL BAÑAGALE is an associate professor and chair of the Music Department at Colorado College. He has published widely on the music of George Gershwin, including his book *Arranging Gershwin:* Rhapsody in Blue *and the Creation of an American Icon* (2014). He is coeditor of *"We Didn't Start the Fire": Billy Joel and Popular Music Studies* (2020) and is currently compiling the *Oxford Handbook of Arrangement Studies.* His scholarship also appears in the *Journal of the Society for American Music, Jazz Perspectives,* and the *Cambridge Companion to Gershwin.* Ryan is a board member of the Society for American Music and serves as digital and multimedia editor for the *Journal of the American Musicological Society.*

STEPHANIE DOKTOR is an assistant professor of music theory at Temple University. Her research and teaching ask, "How can we hear inequality?" Her award-winning scholarship has been published in the *Journal of the Society for American Music, Jazz & Culture, American Music,* and the *Journal of the American Musicological Society.* Her current book project, *Reconstructing Whiteness: Race in the Early Jazz Marketplace,* evaluates the role of white supremacy in the unprecedented success of 1920s Black dance music. She is associate editor of the *Journal of Jazz Studies.*

JOHN HOWLAND is a professor of musicology at the Norwegian University of Science and Technology. He divides life between work in Trondheim, Norway, and home in Lund, Sweden. His research examines the interrelations among class-hierarchy discourse and arranging, production, and entertainment aesthetics in popular music and jazz-related orchestral idioms. Howland is author of the books *Ellington Uptown: Duke Ellington, James P. Johnson, and the Birth of Concert Jazz* (2009); *Duke Ellington Studies* (2017);

and *Hearing Luxe Pop: Glorification, Glamour, and the Middlebrow in American Popular Music* (2021), among other writings and editorial work. He is cofounder and former editor of the Routledge Press journal *Jazz Perspectives*. He is formerly an associate professor of music and jazz studies at Rutgers University–Newark. Howland's latest book project, *Disco Gold! Dance-Pop Crossover and Mainstream Discomania, 1973–1980*, extends the themes of *Hearing Luxe Pop* through a study of the mainstream, international disco craze across the 1970s.

KATHERINE M. LEO is an associate professor of music at Millikin University. Her research investigates US music and legal histories, with emphases on matters of authorship and originality as well as musical style and similarity in federal copyright law. This research is most notably featured in her monograph *Forensic Musicology and the Blurred Lines of Federal Copyright History* (2021). As a music industry historian and specialist in early twentieth-century commercial popular music, Leo writes and presents on legal issues surrounding mechanical sound technologies and early jazz, including the US piano roll industry, Duke Ellington, the Original Dixieland Jazz Band, and Paul Whiteman. She further serves as a forensic musicologist in copyright infringement matters.

SARAH CAISSIE PROVOST is an assistant professor in the Hartt School of Music at the University of Hartford and was formerly on the faculty at the University of North Florida. Her scholarship is primarily in the areas of early jazz and its intersections with gender, historiography, and creativity. She has published work on Ziggy Elman's Jewish-influenced swing in *Jazz and Culture*, the filmic uses of Benny Goodman's "Sing Sing Sing" in *Music and the Moving Image*, gendered creativity in *Jazz Perspectives*, and a recent piece "Accessing Jazz's Gendered Places and Spaces" in the *Routledge Handbook of Jazz and Gender* (2022). Her research interests also include prison-reform advocacy and acoustic ecology. She has recently served as the president of the Southern chapter of the American Musicological Society.

W. ANTHONY SHEPPARD is Marylin and Arthur Levitt Professor of Music at Williams College, where he teaches courses in twentieth-century music, opera, popular music, and Asian music. His first book, *Revealing Masks: Exotic Influences and Ritualized Performance in Modernist Music Theater* (2001), received the Kurt Weill Prize. His article on *Madama Butterfly* and film earned the ASCAP Deems Taylor Award, an article on World War II film music was honored with the Alfred Einstein Award by the American Musicological Society, and "Puccini and the Music Boxes" received the AMS H. Colin Slim Award. *Extreme Exoticism: Japan in the American Musical*

Imagination (2019) received the AMS Music in American Culture Award and the Society for American Music Irving Lowens Book Award. His edited volume *Sondheim in Our Time and His* appeared in 2022. Sheppard's research has been supported by the National Endowment for the Humanities, the American Philosophical Society, the American Council of Learned Societies, and the Institute for Advanced Study, Princeton, New Jersey. He has served as editor in chief of the *Journal of the American Musicological Society* and as series editor of *AMS Studies in Music*. In recognition of excellence in teaching, Williams College named Sheppard the John Hyde Teaching Fellow for 2020–23.

CATHERINE TACKLEY is Professor of Music at the University of Liverpool, where she was head of the Department of Music from 2016–22, having previously held posts at Leeds College of Music and the Open University. She has written two books, *The Evolution of Jazz in Britain: c. 1880–1935* (2005) and *Benny Goodman's Famous 1938 Carnegie Hall Jazz Concert* (2012); coedited *Black British Jazz: Routes, Ownership, and Performance* (2014); and was a cofounder of the *Jazz Research Journal*. In 2022 she was awarded a Leverhulme Major Research Fellowship for a project on British dance bands. Tackley has curated numerous events in partnership with museums and institutions, most notably, *Rhythm and Reaction: The Age of Jazz in Britain*, an acclaimed exhibition at Two Temple Place in London in 2018 based on her research. She has been interviewed for BBC television documentaries and is heard regularly on BBC Radio 3 and 4. She is an accredited lecturer of the Arts Society and a regular speaker at concert halls and the UK's preeminent jazz festivals. She is a trustee of the National Jazz Archive (UK), the Light Music Society (UK), and musical director of Dr Jazz and the Cheshire Cats Big Band.

ELIJAH WALD is a musician, writer, and historian. He studied guitar with Dave Van Ronk and spent fifteen years traveling and performing in North America, Europe, Asia, and Africa; recorded an LP (best forgotten) and a CD (much better); studied with the Congolese guitar masters Jean-Bosco Mwenda and Edouard Masengo; and toured for five years with the African American string-band master Howard Armstrong. Wald began writing for the *Boston Globe* in 1981 and covered "world" and "roots" music there through the 1990s. His dozen books include *How the Beatles Destroyed Rock 'n' Roll: An Alternative History of American Popular Music* (2009), which foregrounds Paul Whiteman as (for better and worse) the most influential musical figure of the 1920s; *Jelly Roll Blues* (2024), exploring the censored world of early blues and jazz through the songs and stories of Jelly Roll Morton; *Escaping the Delta: Robert Johnson and the Invention of the Blues* (2004); Dave Van

Ronk's memoir, *The Mayor of MacDougal Street* (2005), which inspired the Coen Brothers' *Inside Llewyn Davis*; *Narcocorrido* (2001), about the Mexican ballads of drug smuggling and political corruption; and *Dylan Goes Electric!* (2015). Wald won a 2002 GRAMMY for album notes to *The Arhoolie Records 40th Anniversary Box*, an ASCAP–Deems Taylor award, and an honorable mention for the American Musicological Society's Otto Kinkeldey award. He has taught at University of California Los Angeles, Boston College, and Temple University.

CHRISTI JAY WELLS (they/them, she/her) is an associate professor of musicology in Arizona State University's Herberger Institute School of Music, Dance, and Theatre and a Race, Arts, and Democracy Fellow with ASU's Center for the Study of Race and Democracy. Wells is an interdisciplinary scholar whose research traverses the fields of jazz history; popular music studies; dance studies; music, race, and gender; and arts and cultural policy. A social jazz and blues dancer for the past twenty years, her first book, *Between Beats: The Jazz Tradition and Black Vernacular Dance* (2021), explores the complex intersections among jazz music, social and popular dance, race, power, and discourse from the nineteenth through the twenty-first centuries. They are currently working on a second book, a study of the Smithsonian Institution's substantial history of jazz programming and patronage in the context of Washington DC's broader jazz community.

Index

The University of Illinois Press
is a founding member of the
Association of University Presses.

University of Illinois Press
1325 South Oak Street
Champaign, IL 61820-6903
www.press.uillinois.edu